MASS
COMMUNICATION
THEORY

MASS COMMUNICATION THEORY

An Introduction

Third Edition

DENIS McQUAIL

SAGE Publications
London · Thousand Oaks · New Delhi

© Denis McQuail 1983, 1987, 1994

This edition published 1994

First edition 1983
Second edition 1987

SAGE Publications Ltd
6 Bonhill Street
London EC2A 4PU

SAGE Publications Inc
2455 Teller Road
Thousand Oaks, California 91320

SAGE Publications India Pvt Ltd
32, M-Block Market
Greater Kailash – I
New Delhi 110 048

British Library Cataloguing in Publication data

A catalogue record for this book is available
from the British Library.

Library of Congress catalog card number 94–65489

Typeset by Photoprint, Torquay, Devon
Printed in Great Britain by The Cromwell Press Ltd,
Broughton Gifford, Melksham, Wiltshire

CONTENTS

PREFACE TO THE THIRD EDITION

This revision has, in general, been guided by the same aims as its predecessor — primarily to update the text and take account of more recent theory and research. This has meant a certain amount of deletion as well as significant extension and has also led to a thorough reorganization of the contents. The opportunity has again been taken to improve presentation and increase the clarity of expression. One particular purpose of the substantive changes has been to give more recognition to the contribution of the cultural studies tradition to mass communication theory. Another aim has been to deal more adequately with questions of media structure, policy and economics which, until recently, have been relatively neglected in media theory, except from very limited perspectives. This particular innovation is no more than a beginning.

The book has been revised with an awareness of the great changes that continue to occur in the global media landscape, especially as a result of technologies which provide alternatives to traditional *mass* communication and which have accelerated the internationalization of the media. Nevertheless, it still seems that we are no nearer a condition where mass media are withering away. The reasons why we have mass communication in the way we have it are related more to how society is organized (nationally and globally) than to technology. There seems no less need now than in the past to develop and deploy a body of theory that is specifically relevant to this branch of the wider field of communication science.

The problem of acknowledging debts, intellectual and personal, grows ever larger. In the continuing process of rethinking mass communication theory, the single largest stimulus has probably come from colleagues and students at the University of Amsterdam, where the interval between editions of this book has been marked by a continuous process of renewal and growth in the field of communication studies. I have benefited from this and I hope it shows in the new version of this book. I have also benefited from collegial tolerance of absences during the period — in particular to spend time at the then Gannett Center for Media Studies at Columbia University, New York and at Seijo University, Tokyo. My family has been equally tolerant of mental absences. Lastly, I would like to thank those at Sage, especially Stephen Barr, who have given every support and encouragement to this continuing enterprise, even more than I wanted at the beginning. I think now that it has been worth the effort.

D.M.
Schoorl, N.H., January 1994

To the memory of
my nephew, Stephen McQuail,
who died in 1993

1

INTRODUCTION: THE RISE OF MEDIA OF MASS COMMUNICATION

The significance of mass media

It is a basic assumption of this book that the mass media (newspapers, television and radio especially) are of considerable, and still growing, importance in modern societies. This view of the media is widely shared, and the reasons seem to lie in the fact that the media are:

- a **power resource** — a potential means of influence, control and innovation in society; the primary means of transmission and source of information essential to the working of most social institutions;
- the **location** (or arena) where many affairs of public life are played out, both nationally and internationally;
- a major **source** of definitions and images of social reality; thus also the place where the changing culture and the values of societies and groups are constructed, stored and most visibly expressed;
- the primary key to **fame** and celebrity status as well as to effective performance in the public arena;
- the source of an ordered and public meaning system which provides a benchmark for what is **normal**, empirically and evaluatively; deviations are signalled and comparisons made in terms of this public version of normality.

In addition, the media are the single largest focus of leisure-time activity and means of entertainment. They also help organize and interrelate the rest of leisure. As a result, they are a major and expanding industry, providing employment and a wide range of potential economic benefits.

If these claims are accepted, it is not difficult to understand the great interest which the mass media have attracted since their early days, nor why they have been subject to so much public scrutiny and regulation as well as theorizing. The conduct of democratic (or undemocratic) politics, nationally and internationally, depends more and more on mass media, and there are few significant social issues which are addressed without some consideration of the role of the mass media, whether for good or ill. As will appear, the most fundamental questions of society — those concerning the distribution and exercise of power, the management of problems and the processes of integration and change — all turn on communication, especially the messages carried by the public means of communication, whether in the form of information, opinion, stories or entertainment.

Media and society relationships

This book is about theories of mass communication, but it is hard to draw a line between ideas concerning mass media and wider theories of society. Yet one can at least try to recognize some of the fundamental underlying assumptions about the relation between media and society. Most basic is a view of the mass media as an established social institution, with its own distinctive set of norms and practices but with the scope of its activities subject to definition and limitation by the wider society. This implies that the media are essentially dependent on 'society', especially on the institutions of political and economic power, although there is scope for influence in return, and the media institution may be gaining in autonomy, simply as a result of the extending volume and scope of media activities. Even so, the forces historically at work in societies and the wider world are more potent than the media or the immediate influence which these might exert.

The nature of the relation between media and society depends on circumstances of time and place. This book largely deals with mass media and mass communication in modern, 'developed' nation states, mainly elective democracies with free-market (or mixed) economies which are integrated into a wider international set of economic and political relations of exchange, competition and also domination or conflict. The author's view is that the theory and related research discussed in this book relate generally to social contexts characterized by structured differences in economic welfare and political power between social and economic classes.

Despite apparent stability in these social contexts, deep latent conflicts and tensions exist nationally and internationally, which find expression in conflicts of ideology, competing claims for resources and, occasionally, social crisis. The media are deeply involved in these matters as producers, disseminators and stores of meaning about events and contexts of public social life. It follows that the study of mass communication cannot avoid dealing in questions of values or easily achieve neutrality and scientific objectivity. .

This particular problem arises in another form when it comes to questions of interpreting the meaning of what the media carry or the meanings which are perceived by the 'receivers'. Again the possibility of objective knowledge is at issue and, therefore, also the possibility of formulating or testing theory. This problem is familiar enough in the social sciences, though it may be posed in an unusually sharp form in respect of communication, since values and meanings are at the heart of the matter.

Basic differences of approach

The field of media theory is characterized by widely divergent perspectives. In addition to a fundamental difference between the left and right of the political spectrum — between progressive and conservative, or critical and applied purpose — which plays a major part in structuring theory, there are two main differences of perspective in relation to mass media and society.

One of these separates 'media-centric' from 'society-centric' (or 'social-centric') approaches. The former approach attributes much more autonomy and influence to communication and concentrates on the media's own sphere of activity; the latter takes a view of the media as so much a reflection of political and economic forces that theory for the media can be little more than a special application of broader social theory (Golding and Murdock, 1978). Media-centric theory sees mass media as a primary mover in social change and often themselves driven forward by irresistible developments of communication technology. Whether or not society is driven by the media, it is certainly true that mass communication theory itself is so driven, tending to respond to each major shift of media technology and structure.

The second main dividing line is between those theorists whose interest (and conviction) lies in the realm of culture and ideas and those who emphasize material forces and factors. This divide corresponds approximately with certain other dimensions: humanistic versus scientific; qualitative versus quantitative; and subjective versus objective. While these differences may reflect only the necessity for some division of labour in a wide territory, they often involve competing and contradictory claims about how to pose questions, conduct research and provide explanations. These two alternatives are independent of each other, so that in fact several different perspectives on media and society can be identified (Figure 1.1).

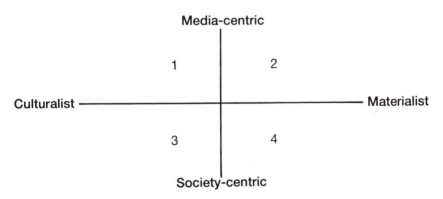

Figure 1.1 *Dimensions and types of media theory: four main approaches can be identified according to two dimensions — media-centric versus society-centric; and culturalist versus materialist*

The four types of perspective can be briefly described as follows:

1   A media-culturalist perspective involves giving primary attention to
    content and to the reception of media messages as influenced by the
    immediate personal environment.
2   A media-materialist approach involves the political-economic and the
    technological aspects of the media themselves receiving the most
    emphasis.
3   A social-culturalist perspective emphasizes the influence of social factors
    on media production and reception and the functions of the media in
    social life.
4   A social-materialist perspective sees media mainly as a reflection of
    economic and material conditions of the society rather than as first
    cause.

Each of these perspectives can be cross-cut by a more radical or more
conservative point of view. However, there has been a tendency for the
critical perspective to be more associated with either a society-centric or a
culturalist perspective (or both).

Different kinds of theory

If theory is understood not only as a system of law-like propositions, but as
any set of ideas which can help make sense of a phenomenon, guide action
or predict a consequence, then one can distinguish at least four kinds of
theory which are relevant to mass communication: social scientific,
normative, operational and everyday theory. The most obvious kind to be
expected in a text like this consists of **social scientific** theory — general
statements about the nature, working and effects of mass communication,
based on systematic and objective observation of media and other relevant
sources.

The body of such theory is now large, although it is loosely organized and
not very clearly formulated or even very consistent. It also covers a very
wide spectrum, from broad questions of society to detailed aspects of
individual information sending and receiving. Some 'scientific' theory is
concerned with understanding what is going on, some with developing a
critique and some with practical applications in processes of public
information or persuasion (see Windahl and Signitzer, 1992).

A second kind of theory can be described as **normative**, since it is
concerned with examining or prescribing how media *ought* to operate if
certain social values are to be observed or attained. Such theory usually
stems from the broader social philosophy or ideology of a given society. This
kind of theory is important because it plays a part in shaping and legitimating
media institutions and has considerable influence on the expectations which
are placed on the media by other social agencies and even by the media's

own audiences. A good deal of research into mass media has been the result of attempts to apply norms of social and cultural performance. A society's normative theories concerning its own media are usually to be found in laws, regulations, media policies, codes of ethics and the substance of public debate. While normative media theory is not in itself 'objective', it can be studied by the 'objective' methods of the social sciences (McQuail, 1992).

A third kind of knowledge about the media can best be described as **operational** theory, since it refers to the practical ideas assembled and applied by media practitioners in the conduct of their own media work. Similar bodies of accumulated practical wisdom are to be found in most organizational and professional settings. In the case of the media it helps to organize experience on many questions such as how to select news, please audiences, design effective advertising, keep within the limits of what society permits, and relate effectively to sources and audiences. At some points it may overlap with normative theory — for instance, in matters of journalistic ethics.

Such knowledge merits the name of theory because it is usually patterned and persistent, even if never codified, and is influential in respect of behaviour. It comes to light in the study of communicators and their organizations (for example, Elliott, 1972; Tuchman, 1978). Katz (1977) compared the role of the researcher in relation to media production to that of the theorist of music or philosopher of science who can see regularities which a musician or scientist cannot be, or does not even need to be, aware of (though usually also without theorists themselves being able to make music or do science).

Finally, there is **everyday** or common-sense theory of media use, referring to the knowledge we all have from our own long experience with media, which enables us to understand what is going on, how a medium might fit into our daily lives, how its content is intended to be 'read', as well as how we like to read it, what the differences are between different media, different media genres and examples of content, and much more. On the basis of such theory is grounded the ability to make consistent choices, form tastes and make judgements. This ability, in turn, shapes what the media actually offer to their audiences and sets both directions and limits to media influence (for instance, by enabling us to distinguish between reality and fiction, to 'read between the lines' or to see through the persuasive aims and techniques of advertising and other kinds of propaganda). The working of common-sense theory can be seen in the norms for use of media which many people recognize and follow (see Chapter 12), and it can play a significant part in the outcome of public debate about the media, whether or not supported by scientific evidence.

This book is most directly concerned with the first and second kinds of theory, but the other two are also important. For instance, a legitimate answer to the question 'What is mass communication?', in place of a formal and abstract definition, would simply be 'What people think it is' — leading to very different perceptions drawn from media communicators, their

---

Four types of media theory

- Social scientific theory
- Normative theory
- Operational theory
- Everyday theory

---

sources and clients and from the many different audiences. The social definitions which mass media acquire are not given by media theorists or legislators but are established in real-life practice and experience. The emergence of definitions (really perceptions) of media, and their uses for individuals and society, is a complex and lengthy process. The results are often variable and hazy, as will be seen when we try to pin them down.

Communication science and the study of mass communication

The study of mass communication is one topic among many for the social sciences and only one part of a wider field of enquiry into human communication. Under the name 'communication science' the field has been defined by Berger and Chaffee (1987, p. 17) as a science which 'seeks to understand the production, processing and effects of symbol and signal systems by developing testable theories, containing lawful generalizations, that explain phenomena associated with production, processing and effects'. While this was presented as a 'mainstream' definition to apply to most communication research, in fact it is very much biased towards one model of enquiry — the quantitative study of communicative behaviour and its causes.

It is especially inadequate to deal with the nature of 'symbol systems' and signification, the process by which meaning is given and taken in varied social contexts. It is unlikely that any single definition of the field can adequately cover the diversity of perspectives and of problems which arise. It is also unlikely that any 'science of communication' can ever be independent and self-sufficient, given the origins of the study in many disciplines and the wide-ranging nature of communication problems.

Levels of communication

A less problematic way of locating the topic of mass communication in a wider field of communication enquiry is according to different *levels* of social organization at which communication takes place. Mass communication can then be seen as one of several society-wide communication processes, at the

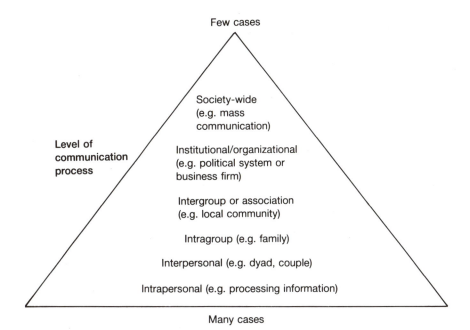

Few cases

Level of
communication
process

Society-wide
(e.g. mass
communication)

Institutional/organizational
(e.g. political system or
business firm)

Intergroup or association
(e.g. local community)

Intragroup (e.g. family)

Interpersonal (e.g. dyad, couple)

Intrapersonal (e.g. processing information)

Many cases

Figure 1.2 *The pyramid of communication: mass communication is one of a few society-wide processes*

apex of a pyramidal distribution of other communication processes according to this criterion (Figure 1.2).

At each descending level of the pyramid indicated there are more separate cases to be found, and each level presents its own particular set of problems for research and theorizing. In an integrated modern society there will often be one large public communication network, usually depending on the mass media, which can reach and involve all citizens to varying degrees, although the media system is also usually fragmented according to regional and other social or demographic factors. Alternative society-wide and public networks are now rare, but at one time these might have been provided by the church or by a political organization, based on shared beliefs and involving a hierarchical but also personalized network of contacts. Such alternatives may still develop, especially informally, under conditions of restricted access to mass media channels.

Different networks

To qualify as a communication network, in the sense intended, there has to be both a means of delivery and exchange and an active flow of messsages in which most or all actively participate. Alternative (non-mass-media) technologies for supporting a society-wide network do exist (especially the network of physical transportation, the telecommunications infrastructure and the postal system), but these usually lack the society-wide social elements and public roles which mass communication has.

At a level below that of the whole society, there are several different kinds of communication network. One type duplicates the larger society at the level of region, city or town and may have a parallel media structure. Another is represented by the firm or work organization, which may not have a single location but is usually very integrated within its own organizational boundaries, within which much communication flow takes place. A third variety is that represented by the 'institution' — for instance, that of government, or education, or justice, or religion, or social security. The activities of a social institution are always diverse and also require correlation and much communication, following patterned routes and forms. Organizations and social institutions are distinguished from society-wide networks by being specific in their tasks. They are also bounded and relatively closed, although communication does flow across the boundaries (for example, when a bureaucracy or firm communicates with its clients, and vice versa).

Below this level, there are even more and more varied types of communication network, based on some shared feature of daily life: an environment (such as a neighbourhood), an interest (such as music), a need (such as the care of small children) or an activity (such as sport). At this level, the key questions concern attachment and identity, co-operation and norm formation. At the **intragroup** (for instance, family) and **interpersonal** levels, attention has usually been given to forms of conversation and patterns of interaction, influence, affiliation (degrees of attachment) and normative control. At the **intrapersonal** level, communication research concentrates on the processing of information (for instance, attention, perception, comprehension, recall and learning) and possible effects (on knowledge, opinion and attitude).

This seemingly neat pattern has been complicated by the growing 'globalization' of social life, in which mass communication has played some part. There is a yet higher 'level' of communication and exchange to consider — that crossing and even ignoring national frontiers, in relation to an increasing range of activities (economic, political, sport, entertainment, etc.). Organizations and institutions are less confined within national frontiers, and individuals can also satisfy communication needs outside their own society and their immediate social environments. The once strong correspondence between patterns of personal social interaction in shared space and time, on the one hand, and systems of communication, on the other, has been much weakened, and our cultural and informational choices have become greatly widened.

Despite the diversity of the phenomena, each level indicates a range of similar questions for communication theory and research.

Concerns of communication theory and research

- Who communicates to whom? (Sources and receivers)
- Why communicate? (Functions and purposes)
- How does communication take place? (Channels, languages, codes)
- What about? (Content, references, types of information)
- What are the consequences of communication? (Intended or unintended)

Alternative traditions of analysis: structural, behavioural and cultural

While the questions raised at different levels are similar in this abstract form, in practice very different concepts are involved, and the reality of communication differs greatly from level to level. (For instance, a conversation between two family members takes place according to different 'rules' from those governing a news broadcast to a large audience, a television quiz show or a chain of command in a work organization.) It is easy to appreciate from this why any 'communication science' has, necessarily, to be constructed from several different bodies of theory and evidence, drawn from several of the traditional 'disciplines' (especially sociology and psychology in the earlier days, but now also economics, history and literary and film studies). In this respect, the deepest and most enduring divisions separate interpersonal from mass communication, cultural from behavioural concerns, and institutional and historical perspectives from those which are cultural *or* behavioural. Putting the matter simply, there are essentially three main alternative approaches: the structural, the behavioural and the cultural.

The **structural** approach derives mainly from sociology but includes perspectives from history, law and economics. Its starting point is 'society-centric' rather than 'media-centric', and its primary object of attention is likely to be media systems and organizations and their relationship to society. In so far as questions of content arise, the focus is likely to be on the effect of social structure and media systems on patterns of content. In so far as questions of media use and effect are concerned, the approach favours the analysis of representative aggregate data derived from surveys or complete sets of statistics. Fundamental dynamics of media phenomena are sought in differences of power and life-chances in society (cf. the social-materialist perspective in Figure 1.1).

The **behavioural** approach has its principal roots in psychology and social psychology but is also represented by a sociological variant. In general, the object of interest is individual human behaviour, especially in matters to do with choosing, processing and responding to communication messages (thus mass media use and effect). Psychological approaches are more likely to use experimental methods. The sociological variant focuses on the behaviour of members of socially defined populations and favours the multi-variate analysis of representative survey data collected in natural conditions. Individuals are classified according to relevant variables of social position, disposition and behaviour, and the variables can be statistically manipulated. In the study of organizations, participant observation is commonly adopted. Content analysis is often practised as a form of behavioural research, treating media documents (texts) as the equivalent of populations which can also be sampled and submitted to statistical variable analysis.

The **cultural** approach has its roots in the humanities, in anthropology and in sociolinguistics. While very broad in potential, it has been mainly applied to questions of meaning and language, to the minutiae of particular social contexts and cultural experiences. It is more likely to be 'media-centric' (although not exclusively), sensitive to differences between media and settings of media making and reception, more interested in the in-depth understanding of particular or even unique cases and situations than in generalization. Its methods favour the qualitative and depth analysis of social and human-signifying practices.

Mass communication defined

The term 'mass communication', which was coined at the end of the 1930s, has too many connotations to allow of a simple agreed definition (see Chapter 2). The word 'mass' is itself value laden and controversial, and the term 'communication' still has no agreed definition — although Gerbner's (1967) 'social interaction through messages' is hard to beat. Nevertheless, there is sufficient commonality in widely held 'common-sense' perceptions to provide a working definition and a general characterization. The term 'mass' denotes great volume, range or extent (such as of people or production), while 'communication' refers to the giving and taking of meaning, the transmission and reception of messages. One definition (Janowitz, 1968) reads as follows: 'mass communications comprise the institutions and techniques by which specialized groups employ technological devices (press, radio, films, etc.) to disseminate symbolic content to large, heterogeneous and widely dispersed audiences'. In this and similar definitions, the word 'communication' is really taken to mean 'transmission', as viewed by the sender, rather than in the fuller meaning of the term which includes the notions of response, sharing and interaction.

The **process** of 'mass communication' is not synonymous with the 'mass media' (the organized technologies which make mass communication possible). There are other common uses of the same technologies and other kinds of relationships mediated through the same networks. For instance, the basic forms and technologies of 'mass' communication are the same as those used for very local newspapers or radio. Mass media can also be used for individual, private or organizational purposes. The same media that carry public messages to large publics for public purposes can also carry personal notices, advocacy messages, charitable appeals, situations-vacant advertisements and many varied kinds of information and culture. This point is especially relevant at a time of convergence of communication technologies, when the boundaries between public and private and large-scale and individual communication networks are increasingly blurred.

Everyday experience with mass communication is extremely varied. It is also voluntary and usually shaped by culture and by the requirements of one's way of life and social environment. The notion of mass (and homogeneous) communication experience is abstract and hypothetical; and where, on occasions, it does seem to become a reality, the causes are more likely to be found in particular conditions of social life than in the media. The diversity of technology-mediated communication relationships is increasing as a result of new technology and new applications. The general implication of these remarks is that mass communication was, from the beginning, more of an idea than a reality. The term stands for a condition and a process which is theoretically possible but rarely found in any pure form. It is an example of what the sociologist Max Weber called an 'ideal type' — a concept which accentuates key elements of an empirically occurring reality. Where it does seem to occur, it turns out to be less massive, and less technologically determined, than appears on the surface.

The mass media institution

Despite changing technology, the mass communication phenomenon persists within the framework of the mass media institution. This refers broadly to the set of media organizations and activities, together with their own formal or informal rules of operation and sometimes legal and policy requirements set by the society. These reflect the expectations of the public as a whole and of other social institutions (such as politics, governments, law, religion and the economy). Media institutions have developed gradually around the key activities of publication and wide dissemination of information and culture. They also overlap with other institutions, especially as these expand their public communication activities. Media institutions are internally segmented according to type of technology (print, film, television, etc.) and often within each type (such as national versus local press or broadcasting). They also change over time and differ from one country to another (see Chapter 6). Even so, there are several typical defining features, additional to the central activity of producing and distributing 'knowledge' (information, ideas, culture) on behalf of those who want to communicate and in response to individual and collective demand. The main features are as follows.

- The media institution is located in the 'public sphere', meaning especially that it is open in principle to all as receivers and senders; the media deal with public matters for public purposes — especially with issues on which public opinion can be expected to form; the media are answerable for their activities to the wider society (accountability takes place via laws, regulations and pressures from state and society).

- By virtue of their main publishing activity on behalf of members of a society, the media are institutionally endowed with a large degree of freedom as economic, political and cultural actors.
- The media institution is formally powerless (there is a logical relation between this absence of power and media freedom).
- Participation in the media institution is voluntary and without social obligation; there is a strong association between media use and leisure time and a dissociation from work or duty.

The mass media institution

- Main activity is the production and distribution of symbolic content
- Media operate in the 'public sphere' and are regulated accordingly
- Participation as sender or receiver is voluntary
- Organization is professional and bureaucratic in form
- Media are both free and powerless

The rise of the media: origins of media definitions

The aim of this section is to set out the approximate sequence of development of the present-day set of mass media — to indicate major turning points and to tell briefly something of the circumstances of time and place in which different media acquired their public definitions in the sense of their perceived utility or role in society. These definitions have tended to form early in the history of any given medium and to have become 'fixed' by circumstances as much as by any intrinsic properties as means of communication. As time has passed, definitions have also changed, especially by becoming more complex and acquiring more 'options', so that it eventually becomes difficult to speak of a single, universally current and consistent definition of a medium.

In summarizing the history and characteristics of different media, as a further step towards typifying mass communication, a convergence on an original Western (European) form tends to be assumed. This does some violence to the diversity of media in the world, but can also be justified on grounds of the similarity of many global media phenomena.

In the history of mass media we deal with four main elements: a technology; the political, social, economic and cultural situation of a society; a set of activities, functions or needs; and people — especially as formed into groups, classes or interests. These four elements have interacted in different ways and with different orders of primacy, sometimes one seeming to be the driving force or precipitating factor, sometimes another.

Print media

The book The history of modern media begins with the printed book — certainly a kind of revolution, yet initially only a technical device for reproducing the same, or rather a similar, range of texts to what was already being extensively copied by hand. Only gradually does printing lead to a change in content — more secular, practical and popular works (especially in the vernacular languages), as well as political and religious pamphlets and tracts — which played a part in the transformation of the medieval world. Thus there occurred a revolution of society in which the book played an inseparable part.

The book medium

- Technology of movable type
- Bound pages
- Multiple copies
- Commodity form
- Multiple (secular) content
- Individual in use
- Publication freedom

The early newspaper It was almost two hundred years after the invention of printing before what we now recognize as a prototypical newspaper could be distinguished from the handbills, pamphlets and newsletters of the late sixteenth and early seventeenth centuries. Its chief precursor seems, in fact, to have been the letter rather than the book — newsletters circulating through the rudimentary postal service, concerned especially with transmitting news of events relevant to international trade and commerce. It was thus an extension into the public sphere of an activity which had long taken place for governmental, diplomatic or commercial purposes. The early newspaper was marked by its regular appearance, commercial basis (openly for sale), multiple purpose (for information, record, advertising, diversion and gossip) and public or open character.

The seventeenth-century commercial newspaper was not identified with any single source but was a compilation made by a printer-publisher. The official variety (as published by Crown or government) showed some of the same characteristics but was also a voice of authority and an instrument of state. The commercial paper was the form which has given most shape to the newspaper institution, and its development can be seen in retrospect as a major turning point in communication history — offering first of all a service to its anonymous readers rather than an instrument to propagandists or potentates.

In a sense the newspaper was more of an innovation than the printed book — the invention of a new literary, social and cultural form — even if it might not have been so perceived at the time. Its distinctiveness, compared to other forms of cultural communication, lies in its individualism, reality-orientation, utility, secularity and suitability for the needs of a new class: town-based business and professional people. Its novelty consists not in its technology or manner of distribution, but in its functions for a distinct class in a changing and more liberal social-political climate.

The later history of the newspaper can be told either as a series of struggles, advances and reverses in the cause of liberty or as a more continuous history of economic and technological progress. The most important phases in press history which enter into the modern definition of the newspaper are described in the following paragraphs. While separate national histories differ too much to tell a single story, the elements mentioned, often intermingling and interacting, have generally been factors in the development of the press institution to a greater or lesser degree.

The newspaper medium

- Regular and frequent appearance
- Commodity form
- Informational content
- Public sphere functions
- Urban, secular audience
- Relative freedom

The press as adversary   From its beginning, the newspaper was an actual or potential adversary of established power, especially in its own self-perception. Potent images in press history refer to violence done to printers, editors and journalists. The struggle for freedom to publish, often within a broader movement for freedom, democracy and citizen rights, is emphasized. The part played by underground presses under foreign occupation or dictatorial rule has also been celebrated. Established authority has often confirmed this self-perception of the press by finding it irritating and inconvenient (although also often malleable and, in the extreme, very vulnerable to power).

There has also been a general progression historically towards more press freedom, despite major setbacks from time to time. This progress has sometimes taken the form of greater sophistication in the means of control applied to the press. Legal restraint replaced violence, then fiscal burdens were imposed (and later reversed). Now institutionalization of the press within a market system serves as a form of control, and the modern newspaper, as a large business enterprise, is vulnerable to more kinds of pressure or intervention than its simpler forerunners were.

Rise of a newspaper-reading public   The extension of newspaper reach to the 'masses', beyond the circle of an educated elite or business class, is a familiar feature of press history in many countries, although the causes are disputed (Williams, 1958). Improved technology, rising literacy, commerce, democracy and popular demand all played a part and they largely coincided in their timing. Few countries experienced majority penetration by the newspaper until well into the twentieth century, and there are still large variations in rates of newspaper reading between countries at the same level of development. In assessing the significance of the rise of the newspaper, we should distinguish between the growing market penetration of the commercial press (as a vehicle for advertising and entertainment) and the reading of the newspaper for mainly political purposes. The enhanced role of the newspaper in political movements or at times of national crisis is also a striking feature of press history.

The political press   It is not surprising that the newspaper should often have been used as an instrument for party advantage and political propaganda. One common form of the newspaper was the party-political paper dedicated to the task of activation, information and organization. This type is now largely unknown in North America and has been in general decline elsewhere for some time (although alive once more in Central and Eastern Europe). The party newspaper has lost ground to commercial press forms, both as an idea and as a viable business enterprise. The commercial newspaper promotes itself as more objective, less manipulative and more fun, and has been able to appeal more to more readers more of the time. The idea of a party press, even so, still has its place as a component in democratic politics. Where it does survive in Europe (and there are examples elsewhere), it is typically independent from the state (though possibly subsidized), professionally produced, serious and opinion-forming in purpose. In these aspects it is not far removed from the prestige liberal newspaper, but its uniqueness lies in the attachment of its readers by way of party allegiance, its sectionalism and its mobilizing function for party objectives.

The prestige press   The late-nineteenth-century bourgeois newspaper was a high point in press history and contributed much to our modern understanding of what a newspaper is or should be. The 'high-bourgeois' phase of press history, from about 1850 to the turn of the century, was the product of several events and circumstances: the triumph of liberalism and the absence or ending of direct censorship or fiscal constraint; the emergence of a progressive capitalist class and several new professions, thus forging a business-professional establishment; and many social and technological changes favouring the rise of a national or regional press of high information quality.

The chief features of the new prestige or 'elite' press which was established in this period were: formal independence from the state and from vested interests; recognition as a major institution of political and social life (especially as a self-appointed former of opinion and voice of the 'national interest'); a highly developed sense of social and ethical responsibility and the rise of a journalistic profession dedicated to the objective reporting of events. Many current expectations about what a 'quality' newspaper is still reflect several of these ideas and provide the basis for criticisms of newspapers which deviate from the ideal, by being either too partisan or too 'sensational'.

Commercialization of the newspaper press   The mass newspaper has been called 'commercial' for two main reasons: it is operated for profit by monopolistic concerns, and it is heavily dependent on product advertising revenue (which made it both possible and advantageous to develop a mass readership). The commercial aims and underpinnings of the mass news-paper have exerted considerable influence on content, in the direction of political populism as well as support for business, consumerism and free enterprise (Curran, 1986; Curran and Seaton, 1988). For present purposes, it is more relevant to see, as a result of commercialization, the emergence of a new kind of newspaper: lighter and more entertaining, emphasizing human interest, more sensational in its attention to crime, violence, scandals and entertainment, and having a very large readership in which lower-income and lower-education groups are overrepresented (Hughes, 1940; Schudson, 1978; Curran et al., 1981).

While this may now appear to be the dominant (in the sense of the most read) newspaper form in many countries, it still effectively derives its status as a newspaper from the 'high-bourgeois' form (especially by claiming to give current political and economic information), although it is otherwise most clearly defined by its contrast with the prestige newspaper.

Film

Film began at the end of the nineteenth century as a technological novelty, but what it offered was scarcely new in content or function. It transferred to a new means of presentation and distribution an older tradition of entertain-ment, offering stories, spectacles, music, drama, humour and technical tricks for popular consumption. As a mass medium, film was partly a response to the 'invention' of leisure — time out of work — and an answer to the demand for economical and (usually) respectable ways of enjoying free time for the whole family. Thus it provided for the working class some of the cultural benefits already enjoyed by their social 'betters'. To judge from its phenomenal growth, the latent demand met by film was enormous; and if we choose from the main formative elements named above, it would not be the technology or the social climate but the needs met by the film for a class (urban lower-middle and working) which mattered most — the same elements, although a different need and a different class, which produced the newspaper.

The characterization of the film as 'show business' in a new form for an expanded market is not the whole story. There have been three other significant strands in film history. First, the use of film for propaganda is noteworthy, especially when applied to national or societal purposes, based on its great reach, supposed realism, emotional impact and popularity. The practice of combining improving message with entertainment had been long established in literature and drama, but new elements in film were the capacity to reach so many people and to be able to manipulate the seeming reality of the photographic message without loss of credibility. The two other strands in film history were the emergence of several schools of film art (Huaco, 1963) and the rise of the social documentary film movement. These were different from the mainstream in having either a minority appeal or a strong element of realism (or both). Both have a link, partly fortuitous, with film-as-propaganda in that both tended to develop at times of *social crisis*.

There have also been thinly concealed ideological and implicitly propagandist elements in many popular entertainment films, even in politically 'free' societies. This reflects a mixture of forces: deliberate attempts at social control; unthinking adoption of populist or conservative values; and the pursuit of mass appeal. Despite the dominance of the entertainment function in film history, films have often displayed didactic-propagandistic tendencies. Film is certainly more vulnerable than other media to outside interference and may be more subject to conformist pressures because so much capital is at risk.

Two turning points in film history were the coming of television and the 'Americanization' of the film industry and film culture in the years after the First World War (Tunstall, 1977). The relative decline of nascent, but flourishing, European film industries at that time (reinforced by the Second World War) probably contributed to a homogenization of film culture and a convergence of ideas about the definition of film as a medium. Television took away a large part of the film-viewing public, especially the general family audience, leaving a much smaller and younger film audience. It also took away or diverted the social documentary stream of film development and gave it a more congenial home in television. However, it did not do the same for the art film or for film aesthetics, although the art film may have benefited from the 'demassification' and greater specialization of the film/ cinema medium.

One additional consequence of this turning point is the reduced need for 'respectability'. The film became more free to cater to the demand for violent, horrific or pornographic content. Despite the liberation entailed in becoming a less 'mass' medium, the film has not been able to claim full rights to political and artistic self-expression, and many countries retain an apparatus of licensing, censorship and powers of control.

A last concomitant of film's subordination to television in audience appeal has been its integration with other media, especially book publishing, popular music and television itself. It has acquired a certain centrality (Jowett and Linton, 1980), despite the reduction of its immediate audience, as a showcase for other media and as a cultural source, out of which come books, strip cartoons, songs, and television 'stars' and series. Thus film is as much as ever a mass culture creator. Even the loss of the cinema audience has been more than compensated by a new domestic audience reached by television, video recordings, cable and satellite channels.

The film medium

- Audiovisual technology
- Public performance
- Extensive (universal) appeal
- Predominantly narrative fiction
- International character
- Public regulation
- Ideological character

Broadcasting

Radio and television have, respectively, a seventy-plus- and a forty-plus-year history as mass media, and both grew out of pre-existing technologies — telephone, telegraph, moving and still photography, and sound recording. Despite their obvious differences, now wide in content and use, radio and television can be treated together. Radio seems to have been a technology looking for a use, rather than a response to a demand for a new kind of service or content, and much the same is true of television. According to Williams (1975, p. 25), 'Unlike all previous communications technologies, radio and television were systems primarily designed for transmission and reception as abstract processes, with little or no definition of preceding content.' Both came to borrow from existing media, and most of the popular content forms of both are derivative — film, music, stories, news and sport.

Perhaps the main genre innovations common to both radio and television have been based on the possibility of direct observation, transmission and recording of events as they happen. A second distinctive feature of radio and television has been their high degree of regulation, control or licensing by public authority — initially out of technical necessity, later from a mixture of democratic choice, state self-interest, economic convenience and sheer institutional custom. A third and related historical feature of radio and television media has been their centre–periphery pattern of distribution and the association of national television with political life and the power centres of society, as they have become established as both popular and politically important. Despite, or perhaps because of, this closeness to power, radio and television have hardly anywhere acquired, as of right, the same freedom that the press enjoys, to express views and act with political independence.

The broadcast media

- Very large output, range and reach
- Audiovisual content
- Complex technology and organization
- Public character and extensive regulation
- National *and* international character
- Very diverse content forms

Recorded music

Relatively little attention has been given to music as a mass medium in theory and research, perhaps because the implications for society have never been clear, nor have there been sharp discontinuities in the possibilities offered by successive technologies of recording and reproduction/transmission. Recorded and replayed music has not even enjoyed a convenient label to describe its numerous media manifestations, although the generic term 'phonogram' has been suggested (Burnett, 1990) to cover music accessed via record players, tape players, compact disc players, VCRs (video cassette recorders), broadcasting and cable, etc.

The recording and replaying of music began around 1880 and were quite rapidly diffused, on the basis of the wide appeal of popular songs and melodies. Their popularity and diffusion were closely related to the already established place of the piano (and other instruments) in the home. Much radio content since the early days has consisted of music, even more so since the rise of television. While there may have been a gradual tendency for the 'phonogram' to replace private music-making, there has never been a large gap between mass mediated music and personal and direct audience enjoyment of musical performance (concerts, choirs, bands, dances, etc.). The phonogram makes music of all kinds more accessible at all times in more places to more people, but it is hard to discern a fundamental discontinuity in the general character of popular musical experience, despite changes of genre and fashion.

Even so, there have been big changes in the broad character of the phonogram, since its beginnings. The first change was the addition of radio broadcast music to phonogram records, which greatly increased the range and amount of music available and extended it to many more people than had access to gramophones. The transition of radio from a family to an individual medium in the post-war 'transistor' revolution was a second major change, which opened up a relatively new market of young people for what became a burgeoning record industry. Each development since then — portable tape players, the Sony Walkman, the compact disc and music video — has given the spiral another twist, still based on a predominantly young audience. The result has been a mass media industry which is very interrelated, concentrated in ownership and internationalized (Negus, 1993). Despite this, music media have significant radical and creative strands which have developed despite increased commercialization (Frith, 1981).

While the social significance of music has received only sporadic attention, its relationship to social events has always been recognized and occasionally celebrated or feared. Since the rise of the youth-based industry in the 1960s, mass-mediated popular music has been linked to youthful idealism and political concern, to supposed degeneration and hedonism, to drug-taking, violence and antisocial attitudes. Music has also played a part in various nationalist independence movements (e.g. Ireland or Estonia). While the content of music has never been easy to regulate, its distribution has predominantly been in the hands of established institutions, and its perceived deviant tendencies subject to some sanctions. Aside from this, most popular music has continued to express and respond to rather enduring and conventional values and personal needs.

Recorded music (phonogram) media

- Multiple technologies of recording and dissemination
- Low degree of regulation
- High degree of internationalization
- Younger audience
- Subversive potential
- Organizational fragmentation
- Diversity of reception possibilities

New electronic media

The so-called *telematic media* ('telematic' because they combine telecommunications and informatics) have been heralded as the key component in the latest communication revolution which will replace broadcast television as we know it. The term covers a set of developments at the core of which is a visual display unit (television screen) linked to a computer network. What are sometimes referred to as the 'new media', which have put in an appearance since the 1970s, are in fact a set of different electronic technologies with varied applications which have yet to be widely taken up as *mass* media or to acquire a clear definition of their function.

Several kinds of technology are involved: of transmission (by cable or satellite); of miniaturization; of storage and retrieval; of display (using flexible combinations of text and graphics); and of control (by computer). The main features, by contrast with the 'old media' as described, are: decentralization — supply and choice are no longer predominantly in the hands of the supplier of communication; high capacity — cable or satellite delivery overcomes the former restrictions of cost, distance and capacity; interactivity — the receiver can select, answer back, exchange and be linked to other receivers directly; and flexibility of form, content and use.

Aside from facilitating the distribution of existing radio and television, new telematic media have been offered to the general public in two main forms, one known as teletext, the other as videotex. The former makes available much additional textual information by way of over-air broadcasting to supplement normal television programming on adapted receivers, and it can be called up at the viewer's initiative. The second provides, usually via the telephone network, a much larger and more varied supply of computer-stored information which can be consulted and/or interrogated by users equipped with a terminal and television screen. It also offers a wide range of interactive services, including a form of visual communication between centres and peripherals and in principle between all those connected on the same network. Videotex can also be used to supply printed material.

The new media also include computer video games, virtual reality and video recordings of all kinds. Home video may be considered as an extension of television and cinema, with greatly increased flexibility in use. It is thus a hybrid medium (like television itself), borrowing essential features from film and television for content and forms and from the book and music industries for means of distribution (separate items of content rented or sold). Yet another innovation, CD-ROM (standing for compact disc, read only memory), provides flexible and easy access to very large stores of information, by way of computer-readable discs. In general, the new media have bridged differences both between media (convergence of technology), and also between public and private definitions of communication activities. The same medium can now be used interchangeably for public and private purposes and both for receiving and self-production (for example, the video 'camcorder'). In the long run this has implications not only for definitions of separate media but also for the boundaries of the media institution.

Although the 'new media' were, in their initial stages, taken up mainly as extensions of existing audiovisual media, they represent a challenge to the production, distribution and basic forms of the latter. Production, for example, need no longer be concentrated in large centrally located organizations (typical of film and television), nor linked integrally with distribution (as with most television and radio), nor so centrally controlled. Nor are print media immune to fundamental change, as direct electronic delivery of print to households becomes a reality, and as the organization of production and the work of journalists and authors become increasingly computerized.

```
┌─────────────────────────────────────────┐
│             The telematic media           │
│                                           │
│   •  Computer-based technologies          │
│   •  Hybrid, flexible character           │
│   •  Interactive potential                │
│   •  Private and public functions         │
│   •  Low degree of regulation             │
│   •  Interconnectedness                    │
│                                           │
└─────────────────────────────────────────┘
```

Inter-media differences

The different branches of communication activity which belong to the 'mass media institution' could once be conveniently distinguished and separately described. This is becoming increasingly difficult as a result of changes in communication technology and in the organization of production and distribution. These changes have tended to accelerate, tending towards a condition which has been characterized in terms of both 'convergence' and 'fragmentation'. This sounds inconsistent, but in fact the convergence referred to is primarily that of means of distribution, while the fragmentation relates to the services and content offered and to the differentiation of audiences.

Convergence occurs because the same content can be distributed through more than one 'channel'. For instance, films are released via cinemas, video recordings, broadcast or cable television, and even the telephone network. The physical and institutional barriers between channels are increasingly unclear. There is also convergence between 'mass communication' offered from a central point and the networks of communication available to individuals to choose their own media supply. Between them, multiplication of channels and increased individual access to stores of media products (such as by way of video recorders) have reduced the distinctiveness and perhaps the (shared) public character of the mass media.

This process can be described as one of fragmentation and it is also a result of the technological possibility of offering many more different forms of media product to many different groups or markets of consumers at low cost. The term 'fragmentation' contrasts the situation of today with an earlier condition of homogeneity and integration in which large 'mass' audiences could be readily reached by a few sources or a few kinds of popular media product.

The distinctions between one medium and another are now harder for audiences to discern and still declining. Even so, there continue to be differences of perception, of purpose and of value which are often both institutionally embedded as well as familiar to audiences. In the following paragraphs some of the persisting differences between media channels and products are discussed in terms of two broad questions: first, what sort of relations of freedom and control exist between a medium and the society?;

and secondly, what is a medium seen to be 'good for' and how it is experienced by the audience?

Freedom versus control

Relations between media and society usually have both a political dimension and a normative or social-cultural aspect. Central to the political dimension is the question of freedom and control. As noted above, near-total freedom was claimed and eventually gained for the **book**, for a mixture of reasons, in which the requirements of politics, religion, science and art all played some part. This situation remains unchallenged in free societies, although the book has lost some of its once subversive potential as a result of its relative marginalization. The influence of books has to a large extent to be mediated through other more popular media or other institutions (education, politics, etc.).

The **newspaper** press bases its historical claim to freedom of operation much more directly on its political functions of expressing opinion and circulating political and economic information. But the newspaper is also a significant business enterprise for which freedom to produce and supply its primary product (information) is a necessary condition of successful operation. The rather limited political freedom enjoyed by broadcast **television** and **radio** derives from a claim to perform some of the same functions as the newspaper press and to serve a general 'public interest'. Formal political control has tended to diminish, as the television industry expands and becomes more like a normal business, in which market disciplines replace open political control. This does not yet seem to have led to any greater politicization of the medium.

The variety of new means of distribution, some using **cable** or **telecommunications** networks, still await clear definitions of their appropriate degree of political freedom. Freedom from control may be claimed on the grounds of privacy or the fact that these are not media of indiscriminate mass distribution but directed to specific users. They are so-called 'common-carriers' which generally lack control over their content. They also increasingly share the same communicative tasks as media with established editorial autonomy. The question remains in dispute for a number of reasons, among them the need for regulation for technical reasons or to prevent abuse of monopoly power. The question of political freedom does not generally arise in the case of media channels which primarily carry fiction, entertainment or music, despite the political potential of all three. In free societies these media are left largely to the free market, while in totalitarian societies their political potential is usually harnessed to official aims.

These differences of perception and institutional definition relating to *political* control (where there is freedom, there are few regulations and little supervisory apparatus) follow a general pattern. First, where the communication function involved closely affects the exercise of power in society (as with newspapers and television informational services), there is a stronger motive for scrutiny if not direct control (political control can be exercised by ownership). In general, activities in the sphere of fiction, fantasy or entertainment are more likely to escape attention than are activities which touch directly on social reality.

Virtually all media of public communication have a radical potential, in the sense of being potentially subversive of reigning systems of social control: they can provide access for new voices and perspectives on the existing order; new forms of organization and protest are made available for the subordinate or disenchanted. Even so, the institutional development of successful media has usually resulted in the elimination of the early radical potential, partly as a side-effect of commercialization, partly because authorities fear disturbance of society (Winston, 1986). According to one theory of media development, the driving logic of communication has been towards more effective social management and control, rather than towards change and emancipation (Beniger, 1986).

The *normative* dimension of control operates according to the same general principles, although sometimes with different consequences for particular media. For instance, film, which escapes direct political control because it has not usually been seen as politically relevant, has often been subject to control of its content, on grounds of its potential moral impact on the young and impressionable (especially in matters of violence, crime or sex). The widespread restrictions applied to television in matters of culture and morals stem from the same (generally unstated) assumptions. These are that media which are very popular and have a potentially strong emotional impact on many people need to be supervised in 'the public interest'.

Supervision often includes positive support for 'desirable' cultural communication objectives as well as for restrictions on the undesirable. The more communication activities can be defined as either educational or 'serious' in purpose — or, alternatively, as artistic and creative — the more freedom from normative restrictions can usually be claimed. There are complex reasons for this, but it is also a fact that 'art' and content of higher moral seriousness do not usually reach large numbers and are seen as marginal to power relations.

The degree of control of media by state or society may depend on the feasibility of applying it. The most regulated media have typically been those whose distribution is most easily supervised, such as centralized national radio or television broadcasting or local cinema distribution. In the last resort, books and print media generally are much less easy to monitor or to suppress. The same applies to local radio, while new possibilities for desktop publishing and photocopying and all manner of ways of reproducing sound and images have made direct censorship a very blunt and ineffective instrument. The impossibility of policing national frontiers to keep out unwanted foreign communication is another consequence of new technology which promotes more freedom. While technology in general seems to increase the promise of freedom of communication, the continued strength of institutional controls, including those of the market, over actual flow and reception should not be underestimated.

Social control of media

Types of control

- On content for political reasons
- On content for cultural and/or moral reasons
- On infrastructures for technical reasons
- On infrastructures for economic reasons

Associated conditions

- More politically subversive potential
- More moral, cultural and emotional impact
- More feasibility of applying control
- More economic incentive to regulate

Issues of use and reception

The increasing difficulty of typifying or distinguishing media channels in terms of content and function has undermined once stable social definitions of media. The newspaper, for instance, may now be as much an entertainment medium, or a consumers' guide, as it is a source of information about events and society. Cable-delivered television systems are no longer confined to offering balanced programming for all. Even so, a few dominant images and definitions of what media 'are best for' do appear to survive, the outcome of tradition, social forces and the 'bias' of certain technologies.

For instance, television, despite the many changes and extensions relating to production, transmission and reception, remains primarily a medium of family entertainment (Morley, 1986), a focus of public interest and a shared experience in most societies. It has both a domestic and a collective character which seems to endure. The traditional conditions of family living (shared space, time and conditions) may account for this, despite the technological trend to individuation and specialization of content. The expected diffusion of high definition television is likely to reinforce rather than undermine the established pattern.

Differentiating media use

- Inside or outside the home?
- Individual or shared experience?
- Public or private in use?
- Interactive or not?

These remarks about television indicate three relevant dimensions of media perception and reception: whether within or outside the home; whether an individual or shared experience; and whether more public or more private. Television is typically shared, domestic and public. The newspaper, despite its changing content, conforms to a different type. It is certainly public in character, but is less purely domestic and is individual in use. Radio is now many things but often rather private, not exclusively domestic and more individual in use than television. Both the book and the music phonogram also largely follow this pattern. In general, the distinctions indicated have become less sharp as a result of changes of technology in the direction of proliferation and convergence of reception possibilities.

The newer telematic and computer-based media have added to the vagueness about which medium is good for what, but they have also added a new dimension according to which media can be distinguished: that of degree of interactivity. The more interactive media are those which allow continual motivated choice and response by users. While the video game, CD-ROM computer database and telephone chat-line are clear examples where interaction is the norm, it is also the case that multi-channel cable or satellite television increases interactive potential, as do the recording-and-replay facilities of the domestic VCR.

Changes in society

Internationalization

Since the Second World War, commerce and industry have been increasingly globalized, multinational corporations have increased in relative significance, and forms of international co-operation in politics, economics and social-cultural affairs have increased. Nation states are less autonomous and more subject to worldwide trends in matters of security, strategic resources and environmental hazards. National politics may often be driven by international circumstances.

Informatization

Under various definitions, the notion of an 'information society' has been advanced to describe some key features of modern societies — referring particularly to the growth of service- and information-based occuptions, the great increase in the flow of information within and across national frontiers, the rise of knowledge as a source of wealth and power and the great dependence of modern political and economic systems on information and on communication technologies. Mass communication is only one component of the information society, but it is an important one and it shares in the rapidity of change and increased salience of information and communication in society.

Rise of postmodern culture

The notion of a 'postmodern condition' (Harvey, 1989) has widely captured the imagination of social and cultural theorists, often forcing both traditionalist and critical theorists on the defensive. Postmodernism seems to be very much a theory of or for the 'information society'. It is a complex and obscure concept which has received no satisfactory statement, but it involves several ideas which are relevant to the present subject. Its political implication is to the effect that the 'Enlightenment project' has now reached its historic end, especially the emphasis on material progress, egalitarianism, economic and social rationality and the application of bureaucratic means to achieve socially planned objectives.

As a social-cultural philosophy, postmodernism undermines the traditional notion of culture as something fixed and hierarchical. It fundamentally opposes the notion of fixed standards and canons of art and culture. It favours forms of culture which are transient, of the moment, superficial, appealing to sense rather than reason. Postmodernist culture is volatile, illogical, kaleidoscopic and hedonistic. In mass media terms, it favours audio-visual media over print, and current fashion over tradition.

Individuation

The virtues of individualism and of the free market are more in vogue than was the case a decade or two ago. Class systems are also said to be weaker, under the impact of more democratic cultural and political arrangements and the move to service-based occupational structure, although clear evidence of the growth of an 'underclass', consisting mainly of the new poor, has marred celebrations of the new prosperity. The same can be said of the growing global gap between rich and poor countries, which has an even more explosive potential. In many countries, there is said to be less social solidarity, more privatization, weaker collective ties and more interpersonal crime and disorder. Religion and family institutions are said to be in decline.

Social trends relevant to mass communication

- Informatization
- Internationalization
- Postmodern culture
- Individuation

Changes in the media

It is easier to give an objective description of changes in the media than of changes in society. These can be located under relevant main headings, describing interrelated trends which echo several of the lines of social change sketched above. Most obvious is the sheer volume of media and of media products: more kinds of media, more channels, more words, pictures and images produced and distributed (even if not proportionately more 'consumed'). The explanation for growth lies in increased prosperity, growing population and demand, and new distribution and production technologies which lower costs and increase the attractiveness of media products.

The main technological changes involve leaps forward in the possibilities for electronic recording, storing, reproducing and transmitting all kinds of images and sounds, as well as developments of computerization and the use of satellites for transmission. As far as the mass media are concerned, the most obvious change has been the rise of television to a pre-eminent position as a media institution of global as well as national significance, complementing the print media and radio but 'outranking' them by some criteria: certainly by measures of reach and popularity, and possibly in public prestige and credibility.

The more recent advances in distribution by cable and satellite have largely removed the technical scarcity of distribution imposed by limited transmission range and wavelength interference. This has allowed more alternative organizations to have access to television and radio channels as suppliers of information and culture, as well as seeming to have increased choice for receivers. While not yet accountable as 'mass media', the interactive electronic media (videotex) have opened up a very large potential for quite different kinds of information provision and exchange, especially possibilities for individual access to a very large range of electronic media services and to all kinds of content satisfactions, whether in personal networks or as general public provision.

The technical possibility (in some degree realized) of greater media 'abundance' has a good many implications for the 'traditional' media institutions of the nation state. They are, first of all, less confined within national frontiers, where reception is effectively under the control of the national political system. Not only technical changes but also international agreements (on standards, content regulations, rights to communicate, intellectual property and more) and transnational media business arrange- ments (multinational multimedia companies and vertical integration of activities) make the media increasingly international in character.

Coincident with the growth of an international media industry, based on global corporate ownership, markets and transnational production arrange- ments, we see evidence of an international 'media culture'; this can be recognized in similar professional standards worldwide, as well as in content forms, genres and the actual substance of communication. This is true not only of radio (especially music and news) and television, but also of newspapers, books and magazines, where stories, authors, marketing strategies, fashions and trends are no longer restricted by a particular language and national culture. This comment reflects the inextricable and worldwide 'intertextuality' of the main mass media of books, newspapers, phonogram, film, television, radio and magazines. They overlap and feed each other in content and commercial arrangements.

Conclusion: implications for the public interest in media

This summary version of trends affecting the media also has implications for changes in the requirements of society from its media. For instance, the features of postmodernism described above seem to make it a very appropriate theory for the electronic media age, but they also challenge traditional theories about the effects and social role of the mass media in society. Postmodernist thinking is fundamentally in tension with the very idea of storing valued information and culture and redistributing it according to some agreed notions of public interest, which involve assumptions of utility, justice, equality and rationality. Postmodernism also challenges theories of direct and mechanistic effect-processes from message to audience.

The changes described suggest that, in general, there is less need for the kind of close supervision and regulation of media which prompted many of the concerns underlying earlier media research. These concerns often stemmed from the wish to assert collective control over newly developing media, to protect vulnerable individuals, to limit the power of private capital, to guarantee fair access to opposed ideological factions or political parties and generally to ensure adequate distribution of scarce and valued social and cultural goods. Greater prosperity, openness, value-relativity, individual consumerism and economic liberalism all seem to weigh in this direction, leaving aside any changes occurring in the media themselves.

Against this, it can also be argued that more complex social arrangements, nationally and globally, the greater abundance of information flows and their centrality for the commerce, progress and social-cultural life of modern society have established new requirements of adequate performance on the part of the media. The decline of some older structures of political and social control and sources of guidance for individuals (political parties, churches, family, community) may well be thought to increase the need for effective institutions in the public sphere to compensate for these losses. The 'public sphere' may appear to have contracted, as a result of 'privatization', individualism and secularization, but it has also been extended by globalizing trends which touch almost every aspect of daily experience.

Conditions of individualism, relativism and volatility are precisely those which increase the dependence and vulnerability of most people and thus also their need for information. This may imply a greater rather than a diminishing public interest in mass media. On the other hand, the nature of any 'public interest' may well now be more variable and uncertain, and it will need continuing redefinition. What we cannot yet discern, among the many patterns of change, is any sign of the imminent demise of the mass media in their central character as sketched in this chapter.

PART I
THEORIES

2
CONCEPTS AND MODELS

Early perspectives on media and society

We are approaching the end of a century which can be described as the 'first age of mass media', and which has certainly been marked by continuous and vocal speculation about the influence of the mass media. Despite the enormous changes in media institutions and technology and in society itself, and also the rise of a 'science of communication', the terms of public debate about the potential social significance of 'the media' seem to have changed remarkably little. A description of the issues which emerged during the first two or three decades of the century is of more than just historical interest, and early thinking provides a point of reference for understanding the present. Three sets of ideas were of particular importance from the outset. One concerned the question of the **power** of the new means of communication, a second the question of **social integration** or disintegration and the third the question of public **enlightenment** or its opposite.

The power of mass media

A belief in the power of mass media was based on observation of their apparent great reach and impact, especially those of the new popular newspaper press (newspaper penetration peaked in 1910 in the USA — DeFleur and Ball-Rokeach, 1989 — a good deal later in Europe), with its advertising and sensational news stories and with control often concentrated in the hands of powerful press barons. The First World War, which saw the mobilization of press and film in most of Europe and the United States for the nationalist war aims of contending states, seemed to leave little doubt of the potency of media influence on the 'masses', when effectively managed and directed.

This impression was yet further reinforced by what happened in the Soviet Union and, later, in Nazi Germany, where the media were pressed into the service of propaganda on behalf of ruling party elites. Before the century had passed a third of its course, there was already a strongly held and soundly based view that mass publicity had power to rule peoples and to influence the shape of international relations and alliances. The conditions for media power were usually assumed to be: a national media industry capable of reaching most people; a degree of monopolistic or authoritative control at the top or centre; and a public that was strongly attached and attracted to media and also susceptible to manipulative appeals.

Communication and social change

Social theorists in the late nineteenth and early twentieth centuries were very conscious of the 'great transformation' which was taking place, as slower, traditional and communal ways gave way to fast-paced, secular, urban living and to a great expansion in the scale of social activities. Many of the themes of European and North American sociology (for example, in the work of Tönnies, Spencer, Weber, Durkheim and Park) reflect this collective self-consciousness of the problems of change from small- to large-scale and from rural to urban societies. The social theory of the time posited a need for new forms of integration in the face of the problems caused by industrialization and urbanization. Crime, prostitution, dereliction and dependency were associated with the increasing anonymity, isolation and uncertainty of modern life.

While the fundamental changes were social and economic, it was possible to point to newspapers, film and other forms of popular culture (music, books, magazines, comics) as potential contributors both to individual crime and declining morality and also to rootlessness, impersonality and lack of attachment or community. In the United States, where attention to communication was first most clearly articulated (for example, in the sociological work of the Chicago School and the writings of Robert Park, G.H. Mead, Thomas Dewey and others) large-scale immigration from Europe in the first two decades of the century highlighted questions of social cohesion and integration (Rogers, 1993). Hanno Hardt (1979, 1991) has reconstructed the main lines of early theory concerning communication and social integration, both in Europe and in North America.

The links between popular mass media and social integration were readily open to conceptualization in terms both negative and individualistic (more loneliness, crime and immorality), but it was also possible to envisage a positive contribution from modern communications to cohesion and community. Mass media were a potential force for a new kind of cohesion, able to connect scattered individuals in a shared national, city and local experience. They could also be supportive of the new democratic politics and of social reform movements. How the influence of media came to be interpeted was often a matter of an observer's personal attitude to modern society and the degree of optimism or pessimism in their social outlook. The early part of the century, as well as (or perhaps because of) being a high point of nationalism, revolution and social conflict, was also a time of progressive thinking, democratic advance and scientific and technological progress.

The potential benefits of mass communication

This underlines the third set of ideas about mass communication — that the media could be a potent force for mass enlightenment, supplementing and continuing the new institutions of universal schooling. Political and social reformers saw a positive potential in the media, taken as a whole, and the media also saw themselves as, on balance, making a contribution to progress by spreading information and ideas, exposing political corruption and also providing much harmless enjoyment for ordinary people. In many countries, journalists were becoming more professional and adopting codes of ethics and good practice. The newly established radio institutions of the 1920s and 1930s, especially in Europe, were often given a cultural, educational and informative mission, as well as the task of promoting national unity. Each new mass medium has been hailed for its educational and cultural benefits, as well as feared for its disturbing influence. The potential for communication technology to promote enlightenment has been invoked once again in respect of the latest communication technologies — those based on the computer and telecommunications (for example, Neuman, 1991).

The passing of decades does not seem to have changed the tendency of public opinion both to blame the media (see Drotner, 1992) and also to look to them for solutions to society's ills. Perhaps the most constant element has been negative — the inclination to link media portrayals of crime, sex and violence with the seeming increase in social disorder. However, new ills have also been found to lay at the door of the media, especially such phenomena as violent political protest and demonstration, international terrorism and sometimes also just old-fashioned rioting and the breakdown of civil order. At the same time, the media (by now largely coterminous with television) have been hailed as the best hope for uniting a divided world in the effort to preserve global peace and to solve looming environmental problems.

The 'mass' concept

While such views about media tendencies and effects in society are not the same as scientific theories, they have largely formed the background against which research has been commissioned, hypotheses have been formulated and tested, and more precise theories about mass communication have been developed. And while the interpretations of the direction (positive or negative) of mass media influence show much divergence, the most persistent element in public estimation of the media has been a simple agreement on their strong influence. In turn, this perception owes much to various meanings of the term 'mass'. Although the concept of 'mass society' was not fully developed until after the Second World War, the essential ideas were circulating before the end of the nineteenth century. The key term 'mass' in fact unites a number of concepts which are important for understanding how the process of mass communication has often been understood, right up to the present.

Early uses of the term usually carried negative associations. It referred initially to the multitude or the 'common people', usually seen as uneducated, ignorant and potentially irrational, unruly and even violent (as when the mass turned into a mob of rioters) (Bramson, 1961). It could also be used in a positive sense, however, especially in the socialist tradition, where it connotes the strength and solidarity of ordinary working people when organized for collective purposes or when having to bear oppression. The terms 'mass support', 'mass movement' and 'mass action' are examples whereby large numbers of people acting together can be seen in a positive light. As Raymond Williams (1961, p. 289) commented: 'there are no masses, only ways of seeing people as masses'.

The different valuations of the idea of a mass depend on a chosen political or personal perspective, but they also relate to whether or not the mass in question is legitimately constituted and acting in a rational and orderly manner. Even so, the predominant tendency has been negative towards mass phenomena, even when they pose no threat to the established social order. The dominant social and cultural values of 'the West' have been individualist and elitist, unsupportive of collective action. Aside from its political references, the word 'mass', when applied to a set of people, also has unflattering implications. It suggests an amorphous collection of individuals without much individuality. One standard dictionary definition defines the word as an 'aggregate in which individuality is lost' (*Shorter Oxford English Dictionary*). This is close to the meaning which early sociologists sometimes gave to the media audience. It was the large and seemingly undifferentiated audience for the popular media which provided one of the clearest examples of the concept.

The concept of mass

- Large aggregate
- Undifferentiated
- Mainly negative image
- Lacking order
- Reflective of mass society

The mass communication process

It is easy to see why the early media of popular press and the cinema were readily labelled with the term 'mass', even if the term 'mass communication' does not seem to have emerged until the late 1930s. These new means of communication were certainly designed for the *many* — whether one takes a negative, neutral or positive view of large social aggregates. Moreover, the actual *process* of communication via the mass media seems to lead unavoidably to mass-like relations between senders and receivers. This relation is necessarily one-directional and impersonal, and most mass communication originates in centralized industrial or bureaucratic organizations remote from their intended 'receivers'. The process is often calculative or manipulative on the part of the sender, who takes a distanced and undifferentiating view of the public, which cannot be known in any real sense. Whether accurately or not, the media receiver was often conceived as a passive spectator, if only because opportunities to participate in the process in any other way (for instance, by response or interaction) are very small or totally absent.

This description can be filled out by noting some essential features of the mass communication process, as compared with other kinds of communication (see also Chapter 1). Senders in mass communication are nearly always either professional communicators (journalists, producers, entertainers etc.) employed by formal media organizations or others (such as advertisers, artists and politicians) who have been chosen for access by the organizations. The symbolic content or 'message' carried in mass communication is often 'manufactured' in standardized ways (mass production) rather than being unique, creative or unpredictable. It is a 'product' of a work process with an exchange value (in the media marketplace) as well as a use value (for receivers) and is thus a marketable commodity. The relationship between sender and receiver is often essentially 'non-moral', a service delivered or a market deal, voluntarily entered into, with no obligations on either side.

While many different kinds of relationship between media senders and their audiences are possible, the 'ideal-typical' or paradigm case is established by the nature of the technology of multiple reproduction and transmission, as well as by the social organization and the economics of the operation. Most mass media messages are not addressed to particular people, and there is a physical distance between sender and receiver which is almost unbridgeable. This is compounded by a social gap, since the sender usually has more prestige, power, resources, expertise and authority than the receiver. The *asymmetry* of relationships can be modified by media diversity and expanded access, but the typical case is as indicated. Reception of mass communication messages is also distinctive. The receiver of mass communication is part of a large aggregate audience, but has little or no contact with fellow-audience members and little direct knowledge or awareness of who they are. Mass communication often involves simultaneous contact between one sender and many receivers, with a potential for immediate and uniform impact which other forms of communication do not have.

The mass communication process

- Large scale
- One-directional flow
- Asymmetrical
- Impersonal and anonymous
- Calculative relationship
- Standardized content

The mass audience

Herbert Blumer (1939) was the first to define the 'mass' formally as a new type of social formation in modern society, by contrasting it with other formations, especially the group, crowd and public. In a small group, all its members know each other, are aware of their common membership, share the same values, have a certain structure of relationships which is stable over time and interact to achieve some purpose. The crowd is larger but still restricted within observable boundaries in a particular space. It is, however, temporary and rarely re-forms with the same composition. It may possess a high degree of identity and share the same 'mood', but there is usually no structure or order to its moral and social composition. It can act, but its actions are often seen to have an affective and emotional, often irrational, character.

The third collectivity named by Blumer, the public, is likely to be relatively large, widely dispersed and enduring. It tends to form around an issue or cause in public life, and its primary purpose is to advance an interest or opinion and to achieve political change. It is an essential element in democratic politics, based on the ideal of rational discourse within an open political system and often comprising the better-informed section of the population. The rise of the public is characteristic of modern liberal democracies and related to the rise of the 'bourgeois' or party newspaper described earlier.

The term 'mass' captured several features of the new audience for cinema and radio which were not covered by any of these three concepts. The new audience was typically much larger than any group, crowd or public. It was very widely dispersed, and its members were usually unknown to each other or to whoever brought the audience into existence. It lacked self-awareness and self-identity and was incapable of acting together in an organized way to secure objectives. It was marked by a shifting composition within changing boundaries. It did not act for itself but was, rather, 'acted upon' (thus an object of manipulation). It was heterogeneous, in consisting of large numbers, from all social strata and demographic groups, but also homogeneous in its choice of some particular object of interest and according to the perception of those who would like to manipulate it.

The mass audience

- Large numbers
- Widely dispersed
- Non-interactive and anonymous
- Heterogeneous
- Not organized or self-acting

The audience for mass media is not the only social formation that can be characterized in this way, since the word is sometimes applied to consumers in the expression 'mass market' or to large bodies of voters (the 'mass electorate'). It is significant, however, that such entities also often correspond with media audiences and that mass media are used to direct or control both consumer and political behaviour.

Within the conceptual framework sketched, media use was represented as a form of 'mass behaviour', which in turn encouraged the application of methods of 'mass research' — especially large-scale surveys and other methods for recording the reach and response of audiences to what was offered. A commercial and organizational logic for 'audience research' was furnished with theoretical underpinnings. It seemed to make sense, as well as being practical, to discuss media audiences in purely *quantitative* terms. In fact, the methods of research tended only to reinforce a biased conceptual perspective (treating the audience as a mass market). Research into ratings and the reach of press and broadcasting reinforced a view of readerships and audiences as a mass market of consumers. There has been a theoretical opposition to this view which has gradually gained ground (see Chapter 9) and led to revised views of the nature of audience experience (Ang, 1991). Even the relevance of viewing the audience as a mass has been undermined by the changes in the media of the kind sketched above (see Chapter 1).

Mass culture and popular culture

The typical **content** which flowed through the newly created channels to the new social formation (the mass audience) was from the start a very diverse mixture of stories, images, information, ideas, entertainment and spectacles. Even so, the single concept of 'mass culture' was commonly used to refer to all this (see Rosenberg and White, 1957). Mass culture had a wider reference to the tastes, preferences, manners and styles of the mass (or just the majority) of people. It also had a generally pejorative connotation, mainly because of its associations with the assumed cultural preferences of the 'uncultivated' or non-discriminating. However, in socialist discourse, mass culture could refer positively to the 'culture of the masses', taking its value from the idea of the mass of ordinary people as the main agent of progressive social change. In such cases the reference has to be to the 'culture of the people' rather than culture **for** the people (as mass consumers).

Definitions and contrasts

Attempts to define mass culture often contrasted it (unfavourably) with more traditional forms of (symbolic) culture. Wilensky, for instance, compared it with the notion of 'high culture', which

> will refer to two characteristics of the product: (1) it is created by, or under the supervision of, a cultural elite operating within some aesthetic, literary, or scientific tradition . . . (2) critical standards independent of the consumer of their product are systematically applied to it. . . . 'Mass culture' will refer to cultural *products manufactured solely for the mass market*. Associated characteristics, not intrinsic to the definition, are *standardization* of product and *mass behaviour* in its use. (1964, p. 176)

Mass culture

- Non-traditional
- Non-elite
- Mass produced
- Popular
- Commercial
- Homogenized

Mass culture was also defined by comparison with an earlier cultural form — that of folk culture or a traditional culture which more evidently comes from the people and usually pre-dates (or is independent of) mass media and the mass production of culture. Original folk culture (especially expressed as dress, customs, song, stories, dance, etc.) was being widely rediscovered in Europe during the nineteenth century (sometimes for reasons connected with the rise of nationalism, otherwise as part of the 'arts and crafts' movement and the romantic reaction against industrialism) at the very time that it was rapidly disappearing because of social changes.

Folk culture was originally made unselfconsciously, using traditional forms, themes, materials and means of expression and had usually been incorporated into everyday life. Critics of mass culture often regretted the loss of the integrity and simplicity of folk art, and the issue is still alive in parts of the world where mass-produced culture has not completely triumphed. The new urban industrial working class of Western Europe and North America were the first customers for the new mass culture and the first to be cut off from the roots of folk culture. No doubt the mass media drew on some popular cultural streams and adapted others to the conditions of urban life to fill the cultural void created by industrialization, but intellectual critics could usually see only a cultural loss.

Dynamics of cultural forms

Subsequently, Bauman (1972) took issue with the idea that mass communication media *caused* mass culture, arguing that they were more a tool to shape something that was happening in any case as a result of the increasing cultural homogeneity of national societies. In his view, what is often referred to as mass culture is more properly just a more universal or standardized culture. Several features of mass communication have contributed to the process of standardization, especially dependence on the market, the supremacy of large-scale organization and the application of new technology to cultural production. This more objective approach helps to defuse some of the conflict which has characterized debate about mass culture. In some measure, the 'problem of mass culture' reflected the need to come to terms with new possibilities for symbolic reproduction (Benjamin, 1977) which challenged established notions of art. The issue of mass culture was fought out in social and political terms, without being resolved in aesthetic terms.

Despite the possibility of finding a seemingly value-free conception of mass culture in terms of social change, the issue remains conceptually and ideologically troublesome. As Bourdieu (1986) and others have clearly demonstrated, different conceptions of cultural merit are strongly connected with social class differences. Possession of economic capital has usually gone hand in hand with possession of 'cultural capital', which in class societies could also be 'encashed' for material advantages. Class-based value systems once strongly maintained the superiority of 'high' and traditional culture against much of the typical popular culture of the mass media. The support for such value systems (though maybe not for the class system) has weakened, although the issue of differential cultural quality remains alive as an aspect of a continuing cultural and media policy debate (see pages 151–2).

The rise of a dominant paradigm for theory and research

The ideas about media and society and the various subconcepts of 'mass' which have been described helped to shape a model of research into mass communication which has been described as 'dominant' in more than one sense. First, the model is still widely taught and applied. It has also been seen as somewhat hegemonic and oppressive by its critics (for example, Gitlin, 1978; Real, 1989). The description of a 'dominant paradigm' offered here is rather eclectic and mixes different elements. It is inevitably an oversimplification of a complex and not very coherent set of ideas. A somewhat similar version is to be found in other textbooks and overviews (for example, Rogers, 1986; DeFleur and Ball-Rokeach, 1989). It is counterbalanced by the description of an 'alternative paradigm' which can be compiled from various critical views of society and of the media.

A view of the good society

The 'dominant paradigm' (or dominant meaning structure) combined a view of powerful mass media in a mass society with the typical research practices of the emerging social sciences, especially social surveys, social-psychological experiments and statistical analyis. The paradigm is both an outcome of and a guide to communication research. The underlying, though rarely explicated, view of society in the dominant paradigm is essentially normative. It presumes a certain kind of normally functioning 'good society' which would be democratic (elections, universal suffrage, representation), liberal (secular, free-market conditions, individualistic, freedom of speech), pluralistic (institutionalized competition between parties and interests) and orderly (peaceful, socially integrated, fair, legitimate).

The potential or actual good or harm to be expected from mass media has largely been judged according to this model, which happens to coincide with one version of Western society. The contradictions within this view of society and its distance from social reality were largely ignored. We can only make sense of most media theory and research if it is assumed to be the norm, or at least an ideal to be aimed for. It is by reference to this model that research has been undertaken into the socializing, informing, mobilizing and opinion-shaping activities of the media. The same is true in relation to crime, ethnic conflict and other problematic features of mass media content and effects. Most early research oriented to the media in developing or Third World countries was guided by the assumption that these societies would gradually converge on the same (more advanced and progressive) Western model.

Early international communication research was also influenced by the notion that the model of a liberal, pluralist and just society was threatened by an alternative, totalitarian form (communism), where the mass media were distorted into tools for suppressing democracy. The awareness of this alternative helped to identify and even reinforce the norm described. This point of view could be largely shared between the media and theorists/ researchers. The media often saw themselves as playing a key role in supporting and expressing the values of the 'Western way of life'.

Scientific origins

The theoretical elements of a dominant paradigm were not invented for the case of the mass media but largely taken over from sociology, social psychology and an applied version of information science, especially in the decade after the Second World War, when there was a largely unchallenged North American hegemony over both the social sciences and the mass media (Tunstall, 1977). The model of a good society described above leans to the mid-century US ideal. Sociology, as it matured theoretically, offered a functionalist framework of analysis for the media as for other institutions. Lasswell (1948) was the first to formulate a clear statement of the 'functions' of communication in society — meaning essential tasks performed for the maintenance of society (see Chapter 3). The general tendency of functional analysis is to assume that communication works towards the integration, continuity and normality of society, although also recognizing that mass communication can have dysfunctional (disruptive or harmful) consequences. There are many ramifications and variants of functional analysis, and, despite a much reduced intellectual appeal, the language of functions has proved difficult to eliminate from discussions of media and society.

The other important theoretical element influential in the dominant paradigm guiding media research stemmed from information theory, as developed by Shannon and Weaver (1949), which was concerned with the technical efficiency of communication channels for carrying information. They developed a model for analysing information transmission which visualized communication as a sequential process beginning with a **source** which selects a **message**, which is then **transmitted**, in the form of a **signal**, over a **communication channel**, to a **receiver**, who transforms the signal back into a message for a **destination**. The model was designed to account for differences between messages as sent and messages as received, these being considered as **noise or interference** affecting the channels. This model was not directly concerned with **mass** communication, but it was popularized as a versatile way of conceiving many human communication processes, despite its original non-human applications.

These theoretical origins were very much in line with methodological developments of the mid-century period, when a combination of advances in 'mental measurement' (especially applied to individual attitudes and other attributes) and in statistical analysis appeared to offer new and powerful tools for achieving generalized and reliable knowledge of previously hidden processes and states. The methods were especially valued because they seemed able to answer questions about media effects.

Bias of the paradigm

According to Rogers (1986, pp. 86–7) this model 'was the single most important turning point in the history of communication science' and it 'led communication scientists into a linear, effects-oriented approach to human communication in the decades following 1949'. Rogers also notes that the result was to head communication scientists into 'the intellectual cul-de-sac of focusing mainly upon the *effects* of communication, especially mass communication' (1986, p. 88). This view of communication is compatible with, though more flexible than, the stimulus–response model, which in one variant or another was equally influential in educational research. Although Rogers and others have long recognized the blindspot in this model, and more recent thinking about communication research has often taken the form of a debate with the model, it is also true that the linear causal approach was what many wanted, and still do want, from communication research.

Mass communication is often seen (by those with power to transmit) primarily as an efficient device for getting a message to many people — whether as advertising, political propaganda or public information. The fact that communication does not usually look that way from the point of view of receivers has taken a long time to register. The theoretical materials for a very different model of (mass) communication were actually in place relatively early — based on the thinking of several earlier (North American) social scientists, especially G.H. Mead, C.H. Cooley and Robert Park. Such a 'model' would have represented human communication as essentially human, social and interactive, concerned with sharing of meaning, not impact (see Hardt, 1991). That this alternative was not taken up reflects the greater appeal of the dominant paradigm because of its assumed relevance and practicality and also the power of its methods.

Concentration on effects

Against this background, the path taken by 'mainstream' mass media research is not difficult to describe and understand. Research has mostly been concerned with the measurement of the effects of mass media, whether intended (as with political campaigns) or unintended (as with crime and violence), or with studying aspects of the process which could aid in the interpretation of effects — for instance, the content of media messages, or the motivations, attitudes and different characteristics of the audience. Even the study of media organizations has been justified by the light it sheds on what messages are likely to be selected for transmission. Traces of functional thinking and of the linear causal model are ubiquitous. The methodological preferences of most communication researchers within the mainstream have also been for precise measurement and quantification, usually based on observations of individual behaviour.

Mainstream research has built around this basic approach several extra elements which have helped it to retain its credibility and to resolve conflicts with the ideal model of liberal-pluralist society described above. On the face of it, the one-way model of effect appears mechanistic and deterministic, in line with the conception of mass society in which a small elite with power and money could use the powerful instruments of media channels to achieve persuasive and informational ends. The images of a hypodermic syringe or 'magic bullet' have been used to capture part of this idea (DeFleur and Ball-Rokeach, 1989). In fact, the rejection by researchers of this notion of powerful direct effect is almost as old as the idea itself (Chaffee and Hochheimer, 1982). It has been clear for fifty years that mass media simply do not have the direct effects suggested. It has always been rather difficult to prove **any** effects (cf. Klapper, 1960).

The simple transmission model does not work for a number of reasons which empirical research made clear. The main reasons are as follows: signals do not reach receivers, or not the ones intended; messages are not understood as they are sent; there is much more 'noise' in the channels than can be overcome; and there is little unmediated communication — it is often filtered through other channels or open to checking with personal contacts. All this undermines the notion of powerful media and casts doubt on the transmission model. On the other hand, the model still helps in posing and testing (null) hypotheses, and the findings which have accumulated around its failure have helped to sustain the positive image of the liberal-pluralist society as still in good shape and not subject to subversion by a few powerful or wealthy manipulators (Gitlin, 1978). Out of 'failed' (= no measured effect) research comes a positive message of health for the status quo and also a vindication of the empirical research tradition.

The dominant paradigm

- A liberal-pluralist ideal of society
- A functionalist perspective
- A linear transmission model of effects
- Powerful media modified by group relations
- Quantitative research and variable analysis

An alternative paradigm

What follows is also a composite picture, woven from different voices at different times and expressing different objections to the dominant paradigm, but nevertheless reasonably coherent. Of course, 'the' critical perspective has itself developed and changed over time, but its origins are as old as its chief object of attack. In varying degrees the alternative (or 'critical') perspectives involve objections to a set of disparate but interrelated ideas and practices. The objects of criticism include: an unacknowledged liberal-pluralist ideology of society (for example, Hall, 1989); the linear model of effect and general mechanicalism; the influence of market and military demands on research and the media (Mills, 1956); the too rosy interpretations of research findings about media effects and audience motivations (for example, Gitlin, 1978); the potentially dehumanizing effects of technology (for example, Carey, 1988); the excessively quantitative and individual-behaviourist methodologies and the prevailing 'scientism' of research and theory (for example, Smythe, 1972; Real, 1989); and the neglect by communication research of vast areas of culture and human experience (Carey, 1988).

A different view of society and media

Most broadly, an 'alternative paradigm' rests on a different view of society, one which does not accept the prevailing liberal-capitalist order as just or inevitable or the best one can hope for in the fallen state of humankind. Nor does it accept the rational-calculative, utilitarian model of social life as at all adequate or desirable. There is an alternative, idealist and sometimes Utopianist ideology, but nowhere a worked-out model of an ideal social system. Nevertheless, there is a suffcient common basis for rejecting the hidden ideology of pluralism and of conservative functionalism.

There has been no shortage of vocal critics of the media themselves, from the early years of the century, especially in relation to their commercialism, low standards of truth and decency, control by unscrupulous monopolists and much more. More relevant here are the theoretical grounds for approaching the mass media in a way different from that proposed in the dominant paradigm. The main ideological inspiration for a well-grounded alternative has been socialism or Marxism in one variant or another. The first significant impulse was given by the *émigrés* from the Frankfurt School who went to the USA in the 1930s and helped to promote an alternative view of the dominant commercial mass culture (Jay, 1973; Hardt, 1991). Their contribution was to provide a strong intellectual base for seeing the process of mass communication as manipulative and ultimately oppressive.

C. Wright Mills followed them (in the 1950s) by articulating a clear alternative view of the media, drawing on a native North American radical tradition, eloquently exposing the liberal fallacy of pluralist control, describing the media as organized in the post-war USA (now often portrayed as a golden age) as one powerful instrument of an interlocked 'power elite' (Mills, 1956) and a means of inducing total conformity to the state and the economic order. He had himself worked on the research (Katz and Lazarsfeld, 1955) which purported to establish the importance of personal relations in insulating individuals from media power, but came to reject the results as potentially manipulative knowledge.

Diverse sources of challenge

Despite the influence of the social-critical perspective of Mills, and later, of Marcuse (1964), a second wave of influence from Europe (where the dominant paradigm also held sway until well into the 1960s) has perhaps done most to promote the alternative paradigm internationally. This has occurred since the 1970s and has different driving forces and objectives. The main components of, and supports for, an alternative paradigm are as follows. First is a much more sophisticated notion of ideology in media content which has allowed researchers to 'decode' the ideological messages of mass-mediated entertainment and news (which tend towards legitimating established power structures and defusing opposition).

Secondly, a related development has denied the notion of fixed meanings embedded in media content and leading to predictable and measurable impact. Instead, we have to view meaning as constructed and messages as decoded according to the social situation and interests of those in the receiving audience. In particular, it is argued that the ideology of the 'power elite' disseminated by the media can be read in an 'oppositional' way and exposed for the propaganda which it is. This is an alternative version of the 'active' or obstinate audience discovered in the course of empirical media-effect research.

The economic and political character of mass media organizations and structures nationally and internationally has been re-examined. These institutions are no longer taken at face value but can be assessed in terms of their operational strategies, which are far from neutral or non-ideological. As the critical paradigm has developed, it has moved from an exclusive concern with working-class subordination to a wider view of other kinds of domination, especially in relation to youth, alternative subcultures, gender and ethnicity. These changes have been matched by a turn to more 'qualitative' research, whether into culture, discourse or the ethnography of mass media use, which has provided alternative routes to knowledge and forged a link back to the neglected pathways of sociological theory of symbolic interactionism and phenomenology (see Jensen and Jankowski, 1992). This is part of a more general development of cultural studies, within which mass communication can be viewed in a new light.

The concern with communication relations between the First World and the Third World, especially in the light of changing technology, has defined fresh tasks and also encouraged new ways of thinking about mass communication. For instance, the relationship is no longer seen as a matter of the enlightened transfer of development and democracy to 'backward' lands. It is at least as plausibly seen as economic and cultural domination. Lastly, although it does not necessarily lead in a *critical* direction, the new means of communication have forced a re-evaluation of earlier thinking about media effects, if only because the model of one-directional mass communication can no longer be sustained.

The status of the alternative paradigm

The alternative perspective which emerges from these developments of thought and enquiry, briefly summarized, is not just the mirror image of the dominant paradigm or a statement of opposition to the mechanistic and applied view of communication. It is complementary as well as being an alternative. It offers its own viable avenues of enquiry, but following a different agenda. The main points on that agenda are: to engage critically with the political and economic activities of the media; to better understand the language (or the meanings) of media and the ways of media culture; to discover how meaning is constructed, out of the media materials offered, by groups differently situated socially and culturally; and to explore the diverse meanings of the practices of using mass media. The interaction and engagement between media experiences and social-cultural experiences are central to all this.

The alternative paradigm

- A critical view of society and rejection of value neutrality
- Rejection of the transmission model of communication
- A non-deterministic view of media technology and messages
- Cultural and qualitative methodology
- A preference for cultural or political-economic theories
- Wide concern with inequality and sources of opposition in society

---

These are lines which go back to the social and intellectual concerns and problems noted at the start of this chapter (which are still to be found in public debate); but, despite the continuing suspicion of the media, the agenda outlined is generally divergent from that of the mainstream. The success of the alternative approach to media research, backed by strong reinforcements from cultural studies and humanistic research (drawn by the magnetism of media power and centrality in cultural life), has not caused its old opponent to expire. It too has its sources of renewed vigour (for instance, the impulse to apply media to political and other forms of campaigning and the growing economic and industrial significance of media technology). There is also evidence of some overlapping and *rapprochement* (Curran, 1990). In particular, ideological (as opposed to intellectual) differences are no longer so salient.

Implications for the study of communication

The differences of approach between dominant and alternative paradigms are too deep-rooted to disappear, and their existence underlines the difficulty of having any unified 'science of communication'. The differences are also rooted in the very nature of (mass) communication, which has to deal in ideology, values and ideas and cannot escape from being interpreted within ideological frameworks. While the reader of this book is not obliged to make a choice between the two paradigms, knowing about them will help to make sense of the diversity of theories and of disagreements about the supposed 'facts' concerning mass media.

The dominant paradigm was never proclaimed as such by its practitioners, who simply assumed that there was one valid scientific approach. It was more a construct of those who were dissatisfied with, or critical of, it. It is not surprising if it is liable to fragment under close inspection, since its cohesion was always loose. The alternative paradigm sketched is barely more unified, although it is more likely to be self-proclaimed, as is the nature of an opposition. It too is liable to decay, if its unifying intellectual bases shift or fragment. It was originally held together by its critical commitment to a notion of a more just and equal society, in opposition to the centralized and bureaucratized capitalist and communist states and empires. One element has been a continual revision of the original mass society theory. What seems to be happening is not just a collapse of one pillar of that edifice (the communist 'empire', based on the former Soviet Union), but a weakening of the force of political ideology in general (at least in its older forms) and a diffusion of the critical spirit into diverse directions. This seems to be one of the implications of postmodern thinking (Gitlin, 1989), as well as a correlate of the resurgence of free-market philosophy in many places.

The mass society thesis can fairly safely be proclaimed to be exhausted (Neuman, 1991), but what is of interest is what is now coming to replace it. The outlines of an alternative vision of society may well be found, with much detail, under the provisional name of 'the information society'. As with the mass society theory before it, there are many prophets, apostles and competing gospels. As the name tells us, it is a view of society in which communication and even mass communication have a significant place.

Four models of communication

The original definition of mass communication as a process (see pages 36–7) depended on objective features of mass production, reproduction and distribution which were shared by several different media. It was very much a technologically and organizationally based definition, subordinating human considerations. Its validity has long been called into question, especially as a result of the conflicting views just discussed and, more recently, by the fact that the original mass production technology and the factory-like forms of organization have themselves been undermined by social and technological change. We have to consider alternative, though not necessarily inconsistent, models (representations) of the process of public communication. At least four such models can be distinguished, aside from the question of how the 'new media' should be conceptualized.

A transmission model

At the core of the dominant paradigm can be found (see page 43) a particular view of communication as a process of *transmission* of a fixed 'quantity' of information — the **message** as determined by the sender or source. Simple definitions of mass communication often follow Lasswell's (1948) observation that the study of mass communication is an attempt to answer the question, 'Who says what to whom, through what channel and with what effect?' This represents the linear sequence already mentioned which is largely built into standard definitions of the nature of predominant forms of mass communication. A good deal of early theorizing about mass communication (see, for example, McQuail and Windahl, 1993) was an attempt to extend and to improve on this simplistic version of the process. Perhaps the most complete and most highly regarded early version of a model of mass communication, in line with the defining features noted above and consistent with the dominant paradigm, was offered by Westley and MacLean (1957).

Their achievement was to recognize that mass communication involves the interpolation of a new 'communicator role' (such as that of the professional journalist in a formal media organization) between 'society' and 'audience'. The sequence is thus not simply: (1) sender, (2) message / (3) channel, (4) many potential receivers; but rather: (1) events and 'voices' in society, (2) channel/communicator role, (3) messages, (4) receiver. This revised version takes account of the fact that mass communicators do not usually originate 'messages' or communication. Rather they *relay* to a potential audience their own account (news) of a selection of the events occurring in the environment, or they give *access* to the views and voices of some of those (such as advocates of opinions, advertisers, performers and writers) who want to reach a wider public. There are several important features of the complete model as drawn by Westley and MacLean. One is the emphasis on the selecting role of mass communicators; secondly, the fact that selection is undertaken according to an assessment of what the audience will find interesting; thirdly, that communication is not purposive, beyond this last goal: the media themselves typically do not aim to persuade or educate or even to inform.

According to this view, mass communication is a self-regulating process which is guided by the interests and demands of an audience which is known only by its selections and responses to what is offered. Such a process can no longer be viewed as linear, since it is strongly shaped by 'feedback' from the audience both to the media and to the advocates and original communicators. This view of the mass media sees them as relatively open and neutral service organizations in a secular society, contributing to the work of other social institutions. It remains essentially a transmission model (from senders to receivers), although much less mechanistic than earlier versions. It also substitutes the satisfaction of the audience as a measure of efficient performance for that of information transfer.

A ritual or expressive model

The transmission model remains a useful representation of the rationale and general operation of some media in some of their functions (especially general news media and advertising). It is, however, incomplete and misleading as a representation of many other media activities and of the diversity of communication processes which are at work. One reason for its weakness is the limitation of communication to the matter of 'transmission'. This version of communication, according to James Carey (1975),

> is the commonest in our culture and is defined by such terms as sending, transmitting or giving information to others. It is formed off a metaphor of geography or transportation. . . . The centre of this idea of communication is the transmission of signals or messages over time for the purpose of control.

The version implies instrumentality, cause-and-effect relations and one-directional flow. Carey pointed to the alternative view of communication as 'ritual', according to which

> communication is linked to such terms as sharing, participation, association, fellowship and the possession of a common faith. . . . A ritual view is not directed towards the extension of messages in space, but the maintenance of society in time; not the act of imparting information but the representation of shared beliefs.

This alternative can equally be called an 'expressive' model of communication, since its emphasis is also on the intrinsic satisfaction of the sender (or receiver) rather than on some instrumental purpose. Ritual or expressive communication depends on shared understandings and emotions. It is celebratory, consummatory (an end in itself) and decorative rather than utilitarian in aim and it often requires some element of 'performance' for communication to be realized. Communication is engaged in for the pleasures of reception as much for any useful purpose. The message of ritual communication is usually latent and ambiguous, depending on associations and symbols which are not chosen by the participants but made available in the culture. Medium and message are usually hard to separate. Ritual communication is also relatively timeless and unchanging.

Although, in natural conditions, ritual communication is not instrumental, it can be said to have consequences for society (such as more integration) or for social relationships. In some planned communication campaigns — for instance, in politics or advertising — the principles of ritual communication are sometimes taken over and exploited (use of potent symbols, latent appeals to cultural values, togetherness, tradition, etc.). Ritual plays a part in unifying and in mobilizing sentiment and action. Examples of the model can be found in the spheres of art, religion and public ceremonials and festivals.

Communication as display and attention: a publicity model

Besides the transmission and ritual models, there is a third perspective which captures another important aspect of mass communication. This can be summarily labelled a 'publicity model'. Often the primary aim of mass media is neither to transmit particular information nor to unite a public in some expression of culture, belief or values, but simply to catch and hold visual or aural attention. In doing so, the media attain one direct economic goal, which is to gain audience revenue (since attention = consumption, for most practical purposes), and an indirect one, which is to sell (the probability of) audience attention to advertisers. As Elliott (1972, p. 164) has pointed out (implicitly adopting the transmission model as the norm), 'mass communication is liable not to be communication at all', in the sense of the 'ordered transfer of meaning'. It is more likely to be 'spectatorship', and the media audience is more often a set of spectators than participants or information receivers. The *fact* of attention often matters more than the *quality* of attention (which can rarely be adequately measured).

While those who use mass media for their own purposes do hope for some effect (such as persuasion or selling) beyond attention and publicity, gaining the latter remains the immediate goal and is often treated as a measure of success or failure. A good deal of research into media effect has been concerned with questions of image and awareness. The fact of being known is often more important than the content of what is known and is the only necessary condition for celebrity. Similarly, the supposed power of the media to set political and other 'agendas' is an example of the attention-gaining process. A good deal of effort in media production is devoted to devices for gaining and keeping attention by catching the eye, arousing emotion, stimulating interest. This is one aspect of what has been described as 'media logic' (see page 265), with the *substance* of a message often subordinated to the devices for presentation (Altheide and Snow, 1979, 1991).

The attention-seeking goal also corresponds with one important perception of the media by their audiences, who use the mass media for diversion and passing time. They seek to spend time 'with the media', to escape everyday reality. The relationship between sender and receiver according to the display–attention model is not necessarily passive or uninvolved, but it is morally neutral and does not in itself necessarily imply a transfer or creation of meaning.

Going with the notion of communication as a process of **display and attention** are several additional features which do not apply to the transmission or ritual models:

- Attention-gaining is a *zero-sum* process. The time spent attending to one media display cannot be given to another, and available audience time is finite. By contrast, there is no quantifiable limit to the amount of 'meaning' that can be transferred or to the satisfactions that can be gained from participating in ritual communication processes.
- Communication in the display–attention mode exists only in the present. There is no past that matters, and the future matters only as a continuation or amplification of the present. Questions of cause and effect relating to the receiver do not arise.

- Attention-gaining is an end in itself and in the short term *value neutral* and essentially *empty of meaning*. Form and technique take precedence over message.

These three features can be seen as underlying, respectively, the **competitiveness**, the **actuality/transience** and the **objectivity/detachment** which are pronounced features of mass communication, especially within commercial media institutions.

Encoding and decoding of media discourse: a reception model

There is yet another version of the mass communication process, which involves an even more radical departure from the transmission model than the two variants just discussed. This depends very much on the adoption of the critical perspective described above, but it can also be understood as the view of mass communication from the position of many different receivers who do not perceive or understand the message 'as sent' or 'as expressed'. This model has its origins in critical theory, semiology and discourse analysis. It is located more in the domain of the cultural than the social sciences. It is strongly linked to the rise of 'reception analysis' (see Holub, 1984; Jensen and Rosengren 1990), which questions the predominant methodologies of empirical social scientific audience research and also the humanistic studies of content because both fail to take account of the 'power of the audience' in giving meaning to messages.

The essence of the 'reception approach' is to locate the attribution and construction of meaning (derived from media) with the receiver. Media messages are always open and 'polysemic' (having multiple meanings) and are interpreted according the context and the culture of receivers. Among the forerunners of reception analysis was a persuasive variant of critical theory formulated by Stuart Hall (1980) which emphasized the stages of transformation through which any media message passes on the way from its origins to its reception and interpretation. It drew from, but also challenged, the basic principles of structuralism and semiology which presumed that any meaningful 'message' is constructed from signs which can have denotative and connotative meanings, depending on the choices made by an 'encoder'.

Semiology emphasizes the power of the encoded text and sees the location of meaning as firmly embedded in it. Hall accepted some elements of this approach but challenged the basic assumption, on two grounds. First, communicators choose to encode messages for ideological and institutional purposes and manipulate language and media for those ends (media messages are given a 'preferred reading', or what might now be called 'spin'). Secondly, receivers ('decoders') are not obliged to accept messages as sent but can and do resist ideological influence by applying variant or oppositional readings, according to their own experience and outlook.

In Hall's (1980) model of the process of encoding and decoding, he portrays the television programme (or any equivalent media text) as a **meaningful discourse** which is encoded according the **meaning structure** of the mass media production organization and its main supports, but decoded according to the different meaning structures and frameworks of knowledge of differently situated audiences. The path followed through the stages of the model is simple in principle. Communication originates within media institutions whose typical frameworks of meaning are likely to conform to dominant power structures. Specific messages are 'encoded', often in the form of established content genres (such as 'news', 'pop music', 'sport reports', 'soap operas', 'police/detective series') which have a face-value meaning and in-built guidelines for interpretation by an audience. The media are approached by their audiences in terms of 'meaning structures', which have their origin in the ideas and experience of the audience.

While the general implication is that meaning as decoded does not necessarily (or often) correspond with meaning as encoded (despite the mediation of conventional genres and shared language systems), the most significant point is that decoding can take a different course than intended. Receivers can read between the lines and even reverse the intended direction of the message. It is clear that this model and the associated theory embody several key principles: the multiplicity of meanings of media content; the existence of varied 'interpretative' communities; and the primacy of the receiver in determining meaning. While early effect research recognized the fact of selective perception, this was seen as a limitation on, or a condition of, the transmission model, rather than part of a quite different perspective.

Comparisons

The discussion of these different models shows the inadequacy of any single concept or definition of mass communication which relies too heavily on what seem to be intrinsic characteristics or biases of the *technology* of multiple reproduction and dissemination. The human uses of technology are much more diverse and more determinant than was once assumed. Of the four models, summarized in comparative terms in Figure 2.1, the transmission model is largely taken over from older institutional contexts — education, religion, government — and is really appropriate only to media activities which are instructional, informational or propagandist in purpose. The expression or ritual model is better able to capture elements which have to do with art, drama, entertainment and the many symbolic uses of communication. The publicity or display–attention model reflects the central media goals of attracting audiences (high ratings and wide reach) for purposes of prestige or income. The reception model reminds us that the seeming power of the media to mould, express or capture is partly illusory, since the audience in the end disposes.

| | Orientation of | |
	Sender	Receiver
Transmission model	Transfer of meaning	Cognitive processing
Expression or ritual model	Performance	Consummation/ shared experience
Publicity model	Competitive display	Attention-giving/ spectatorship
Reception model	Preferential encoding	Differential decoding/ construction of meaning

Figure 2.1 *Four models of the mass communication process compared: each model involves differences of orientation on the part of sender and receiver*

New patterns of information traffic

Changes in communication technologies have forced a much more radical rethinking about communication than is represented by the above discussion of variant models. Mass communication itself is declining in its relative significance compared to other communication processes and is no longer easy to demarcate. The main cause is the rise of new electronic or 'telematic' media, which have been defined as 'a set of services . . . which can be provided to the users by the telecommunications net and which allow public and private information and data to be sent and received' (Mazzoleni, 1986, p. 100). The archetypal new telematic medium has the general name 'videotex' and involves a service, delivered by the telephone network, which enables individuals to consult and interact at will with data banks as well as with all other individuals connected to the net. The most essential capacity is that of **interactivity** (Rogers, 1986). There are more 'passive' forms of telematic media, such as teletext, which provide a large amount of broadcast (or cabled) information, from which a user can select according to wish or need. The number of electronic consultative media forms is increasing, as are the possibilities for interpersonal interaction (electronic mail, telefax, teleconferencing, mobile phones, etc.). In principle, the changes promote a shift from **mass** media to small-scale media and of control from sender to receiver.

A useful way of considering the implications of these changes is to think in terms of alternative types of **information traffic** and the balance between them. Two Dutch telecommunication experts, J.L. Bordewijk and B. van Kaam (1986), have developed a model which helps to make clear and to investigate the changes under way. They describe four basic communication patterns and show how they are related to each other.

Allocution

With allocution, information is distributed from a centre simultaneously to many peripheral receivers. This pattern applies to several familiar communication situations, ranging from a lecture, church service or concert (where listeners or spectators are physically present in an auditorium) to the situation of broadcasting, where radio or television messages are received by large numbers of scattered individuals at the same moment. Allocution (a word derived from the Latin for the address by a Roman general to assembled troops) is typically *one-way* communication to many, with relatively little personal 'feedback' opportunity (especially in the mass media situation). Another characteristic is that time and place of communication are determined by the sender or at the 'centre'. Although the concept is useful for this comparison, the gap between personal address to many and impersonal mass communication is a very large one and is not really bridgeable by a single concept.

Conversation

With conversation, individuals (in a potential communication network) interact directly with each other, bypassing a centre or intermediary and choosing their own partners as well as the time, place and topic of communication. This pattern also applies in a wide range of situations, from that of an exchange of personal letters to use of electronic mail. The electronically mediated conversation does, however, often imply a centre or intermediary (such as the telephone exchange), even if this plays no active or initiatory role in the communication event.

Characteristic of the conversational pattern is the fact that parties are *equal* in the exchange. In principle, more than two can take part (for example, a small meeting or telephone conference). However, at some point, increased scale of participation leads to a merger with the allocutive situation.

Consultation

Consultation refers to a range of different communication situations in which an individual (at the periphery) looks for information at a central store of information — data bank, library, reference work, computer disc, etc. As noted, such possibilities are increasing. In principle, this pattern can also apply to the use of a newspaper (otherwise considered an allocutive mass medium), since the time and place of consultation and also the topic are determined by the receiver at the periphery and not by the centre.

Registration

The pattern of information traffic termed registration is, in effect, the consultation pattern in reverse, in that a centre 'requests' and receives information from a participant at the periphery (usually without their awareness). This applies wherever central records are kept of individuals in a system and to all systems of surveillance. It relates, for instance, to the automatic recording at a central exchange of telephone calls, to electronic alarm systems and to automatic registration of television set usage in 'people–meter' audience research or for purposes of charging consumers. The accumulation of information at a centre often takes place without reference to, or knowledge of, the individual. While the pattern is not historically new, the possibilities for registration have increased enormously because of computerization and extended telecommunication connections. Typically, in this pattern, the centre has more control than the individual at the periphery to determine the content and occurrence of communication traffic.

An integrated typology

These four patterns complement and border upon (or overlap with) each other. The authors of the model have shown how they can be related in terms of two main variables: of central versus individual control of information; and of central versus individual control of time and choice of subject (see Figure 2.2).

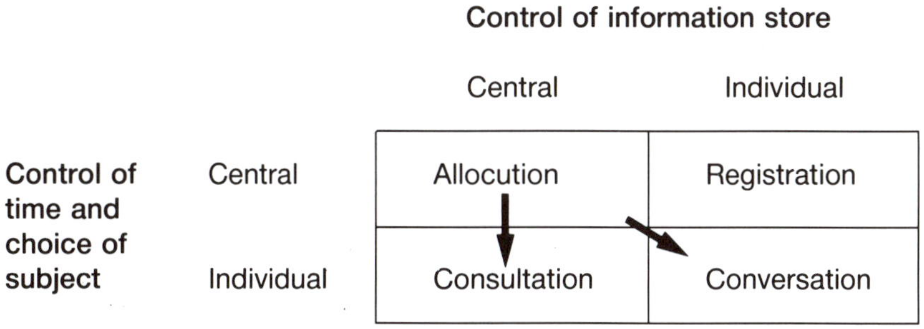

Control of information store

		Central	Individual
Control of time and choice of subject	Central	Allocution	Registration
	Individual	Consultation	Conversation

Figure 2.2 *A typology of information traffic: communication relationships are differentiated according to the capacity to control the supply and the choice of content; the trend is from allocutory to consultative or conversational modes*

The allocution pattern stands here for the typical 'old media' of mass communication and conforms largely to the transmission model — especially broadcasting, where a limited supply of content is made available to a mass audience. The consultation pattern has been able to grow, not only because of the telephone and new telematic media, but because of the diffusion of video and sound recording equipment and the sheer increase in the number of channels as a result of cable and satellite. The new media have also differentially increased the potential for 'conversational' or interactive communication between widely separated individuals. As noted, 'registration' becomes both more practicable and more likely to occur, although it is not a substitute for other types of communication traffic. It can be viewed as extending the powers of surveillance in the electronic age.

The arrows inserted in Figure 2.2 reflect the redistribution of information traffic from allocutory to conversational and consultative patterns. In general, this implies a broad shift of balance of communicative power from sender to receiver, although this may be counterbalanced by the growth of registration and a further development of the reach and appeal of mass media. Allocutory patterns have not necessarily diminished in volume, but they have taken new forms, with more small-scale provision for segmented audiences based on interest or information need ('narrowcasting'). Finally, we can conclude from this figure that patterns of information flow are not as sharply differentiated as might appear, but are subject to overlap and convergence, for technological as well as social reasons. The same technology (for example, the telecommunications infrastructure) can provide a household with facilities for each of the four patterns described.

New theoretical perspectives on media and society

The bare facts of media change have already been alluded to in Chapter 1. In the light of the changing balance of communication forms and processes, we can appreciate that the mass media are, in general, likely to be viewed differently in relation to society than they were a century or so ago. Much has also changed in social thinking since the turn-of-the-century heyday of industrialism in Western Europe. The story has many strands and can only be dealt with by an extreme over-simplification. There are now several competing or overlapping concepts of society in circulation, including the postindustrial, postmodern and poststructural. The shared implication is that at some point a break occurred with the era which saw the establishment and rise of the industrial nation state.

The term 'modern' has been widely used by social theorists since the mid-nineteenth century to refer to a form of society characterized by urban concentration, mass production based on physical energy applied to mechanization, capitalist economics and associated political and social relations. A modern society was also assumed to be involved in a process of progressive material improvement. The formerly socialist Eastern Europe and Soviet Union offered a competing version of modernity, based on collective ownership and a planned economy. The modern society was seen to have replaced the traditional or medieval society, in which religion, family, community and personal ties governed social and cultural life, landownership and agriculture dominated economic life, and politics was largely the preserve of princes and the aristocracy.

The information age

The transition from modern to 'postindustrial' (Bell, 1973; Dordick and Wang, 1993) conditions is generally defined in terms of 'information work' (the service sector, management, etc.) overtaking physical industrial production of goods as the primary economic activity. Information becomes the most valuable resource and is the main *economic* component of the supposed shift. The transition is clearly related in time, perhaps causally, to a change in *communication technology* which has provided much faster, cheaper and more efficient means of production, transmission, handling and storage of information of all kinds. The political, social and cultural characteristics of the postindustrial society are less easy to define or to account for than the economic and technological components. The concept which seems best able to organize this aspect of current change is that of postmodernism.

Postmodernism

Postmodernism has many exponents (and critics) and many different points of reference (see, for example, Gitlin, 1989), but it does help to describe: (a) the dominant ethos or spirit of our times; (b) certain aesthetic and cultural trends; and (c) several influential political and moral notions. In some versions (for example, Docherty, 1993), postmodern cultural and social philosophy is seen to have been born in response to the post-1968 reappraisal of revolutionary aspirations which, in their time, had been based on the premise of an end to capitalism and the birth of a new Utopia. This dream had been originally founded on the ideas of material progress, reason and enlightenment which were embedded in the idea of modern society.

Viewed like this, postmodernism stands for a retreat from political ideology, a disengagement from and abandonment of Utopia, a certain loss of faith in the gods of reason and science. This shapes the *Zeitgeist* (spirit of the age): our time is one of no fixed beliefs or commitments and no certain standards, but also one of relaxation, hedonism, individualism, living in the present moment (especially if there is no future project to strive and sacrifice for). The cultural aesthetics of postmodernism involve a rejection of respect for tradition, a search for novelty and invention, momentary enjoyment, euphoria, nostalgia, self-indulgence, playfulness, pastiche and inconsistency. Jameson (1984) refers to postmodernism as 'the cultural logic of late capitalism', although there is no logic to be found. Gitlin (1989) suggests that postmodernism is specifically North American, especially capturing features of US culture. Amongst other things, there is no longer any basis for distinguishing between 'high' and 'mass' culture or for making valid ethical distinctions within cultural contents.

The political and moral implications are not hard to distil from this. The general tendency is apolitical and amoral. There are no longer fixed goals for political progress, except perhaps to create more opportunities for fun for more people. The postmodern ethos is much more favourable than past perspectives were to commerce, since opposition to capitalism as a political system is undermined, and commerce can be seen as responding to consumer wants or as actively promoting innovation and change of fashion, style and products. (Commerce may, however, be subverted by postmodern attitudes, since commercial logic belongs to modernism.) No appeal can be made to the supposedly fixed moral and political principles on which political thinking at least has usually been based.

Conclusion: implications for mass media theory

Communication research and theory have, from the beginning, been driven by several different logics: moral and political, commercial/industrial and cultural. Postmodernist thinking undermines both the 'dominant' and the 'alternative' paradigms. It is easier to see how the dominant paradigm can be adapted to the new information age, even if the postmodern spirit is not very close to the ideas of communication as information transfer. The main problem for holders of the critical perspective is the fracturing of any overarching commitment or belief. Even so, some elements of the alternative paradigm (especially the methodological principles) are in accord with the changed social circumstances and with a postmodern *Zeitgeist*, since they are sensitive to context and to diversity of use, response and interaction.

As to the critical purpose, it is possible that the seeming current condition of 'normlessness' and loss of faith is temporary and superficial. The old problems to which critical theory was addressed have not been solved, and there are plenty of new causes to fill the gap left (temporarily) by the decline of the class struggle. The mass media themselves are organized in no postmodern spirit, whatever may be said of their content. Issues of gender definition, cultural identity, inequality, racism, environmental damage, world hunger and social chaos are examples of problems of rising salience and concern in which the media are deeply implicated, just because of their enhanced role in the organization of national and global society.

3
THEORY OF MEDIA AND THEORY OF SOCIETY

Media, society and culture: connections and conflicts

In this chapter, we look at ideas concerning the relation between mass media and society, reserving the implications for culture for Chapter 4. This separation is intellectually indefensible but helpful in making sense of a very diverse and fragmentary body of theory concerning mass communication. If warning of the dangers can help, the reader is reminded that society and culture are inseparable, and the one cannot exist without the other; that treating society first implies a primacy for society which cannot be sustained; and that most media theory relates to both 'society' and 'culture' together and has to be explained in relation to both.

For present purposes, the domain of 'society' refers to the material base (economic and political resources and power), to relationships in various social collectivities (national societies, communities, families, etc.) and to social roles and occupations which are regulated (formally or informally) by the structures of collective social life. The domain of 'culture' refers primarily to other essential aspects of collective social life, especially to **meanings** and **practices** (social customs, institutional ways of doing things and also personal habits) (see Chapter 4).

While it is incorrect to view culture as secondary to, and dependent on, society, the history of modern society has usually been written (and is now hard to interpret otherwise) in terms of a materially driven process, with society as the 'base' and culture as 'superstructure'. In fact, this is an example of a 'cultural' bias in the interpretation of experience which illustrates the impossibility of separating the two concepts. We (that is, all of us) can reflect on society only through ideas which have their location (as defined above) in the sphere of culture. Society, as we experience it, is constituted out of the meanings we give to material experience.

A typology of society–culture relations

The conundrum of the relation between culture and society is no easier to resolve in this context than in any other. In fact it may even be more difficult, since mass communication can be considered as both a 'societal' and a

Social structure
influences culture

		Yes	No
Culture influences social structure	Yes	*Interdependence* (two-way influence)	*Idealism* (strong media influence)
	No	*Materialism* (media are dependent)	*Autonomy* (no causal connection)

Figure 3.1 *Four types of relation between culture (media content) and society*

'cultural' phenomenon. The mass media institution is part of the structure of society, and its technological infrastructure is part of the economic and power base, while the ideas, images and information disseminated by the media are evidently an important aspect of our culture (in the sense defined above).

In discussing this problem, Rosengren (1981b) has offered a simple typology which cross-tabulates two opposed propositions: 'social structure influences culture' and its reverse, 'culture influences social structure'. This yields four cells, as shown in Figure 3.1.

The terms used in Figure 3.1 identify the four main options available for describing the relation between mass media and society. If we consider mass media as an aspect of society (base or structure) then the option of **materialism** is presented. There is a considerable body of theory which sees culture as dependent on the economic and power structure of a society. It is assumed that whoever owns or controls the media can choose, or set limits to, what they do.

If we consider the media primarily in the light of their contents (thus more as culture), then the option of **idealism** may be indicated. The media are assumed to have a potential for significant influence, but it is the particular ideas and values conveyed by the media which are seen as the primary causes of social change, irrespective of who owns and controls. The influence is thought to work through individual motivations and actions. This view leads to a strong belief in various potential media effects for good or ill. Examples include the promotion by the media of peace and international understanding (or having the opposite effect), of pro- or antisocial values and behaviour, and of enlightenment or the secularization and modernization of traditional societies. A form of idealism or 'mentalism' concerning media also lies behind the view that changes in media forms and technology can change our experience in essential ways and even our relations with others (as in the theories of McLuhan).

The two options remaining — of interdependence and of autonomy — have found less distinctive theoretical development, although there is a good deal of support in common sense and in evidence for both. **Interdependence** implies that mass media and society are continually interacting and influencing each other (as are society and culture). The media (as cultural industries) respond to the demand from society for information and entertainment and, at the same time, stimulate innovation and contribute to a changing social-cultural climate, which sets off new demands for communication. Clark (1969) explains how the French sociologist Gabriel Tarde, writing about 1900, envisaged a constant interweaving of influences: 'technological developments made newspapers possible, newspapers promote the formation of broader publics, and they, by broadening the loyalties of their members, create an extensive network of overlapping and shifting groupings'.

Today, the various influences are so bound together that neither mass communication nor modern society is conceivable without the other, and each is a necessary, though not a sufficient, condition for the other. From this point of view we have to conclude that the media may equally be considered to mould or to mirror society and social changes. The option of **autonomy** in the relations between culture and society is not necessarily inconsistent with this view, unless interpreted very literally. It is at least very likely that society and mass media can vary independently up to a point. The autonomy position supports those who are sceptical about the power of the media to influence ideas, values and behaviour — for instance, in promoting a conformist ideology.

The autonomy option also calls into question the theory that Western media content is likely either to stimulate modernity or to damage the cultural identity of poorer or less powerful countries. There are different views about the degree of autonomy (or lack of interaction between media and society) which can be sustained. The debate is especially relevant to the discussion of 'internationalization' or globalization, which implies a convergence and homogenization of a worldwide culture, as a result of the media. The autonomy position would suggest that media culture is superficial and need not significantly touch the local culture. It follows that 'cultural imperialism' is not likely to happen simply by chance or against the will of the culturally 'colonized'.

An inconclusive outcome

As with many of the issues to be discussed, there are more theories than there is solid evidence, and the questions raised by this discussion are much too broad to be settled by empirical research. According to Rosengren (1981b, p. 254), surveying what scattered evidence he could find, research gives only 'inconclusive, partly even contradictory, evidence about the relationship between social structure, societal values as mediated by the media, and opinions among the public'. There is a strong possibility that different theories hold under different conditions and at different levels of analysis. This applies to each of the three main issues of society which are discussed below: those relating to power, integration and change.

It seems that the media can serve to repress as well as to liberate, to unite as well as to fragment society, both to promote and to hold back change. What is also striking in the theories to be discussed is the ambiguity of the role assigned to the media, since they are as often presented in a 'progressive' as in a 'reactionary' light, according to whether the dominant (pluralist) or alternative (critical, radical) perspective is adopted. Despite the degree of uncertainty, there can be little doubt that the media, whether moulders or mirrors of society, are the main messengers *about* society, and it is around this observation that the alternative theoretical perspectives can best be organized.

Mass communication as a society-wide process: the mediation of social relations

A central presupposition, relating to questions both of society and of culture, is that the media institution is essentially concerned with the production and distribution of *knowledge* in the widest sense of the word. Such knowledge enables us to make some sense of our experience of the social world, even if the 'taking of meaning' occurs in relatively autonomous and very diversified ways. The information, images and ideas made available by the media may, for most people, be the main source of an awareness of a shared past time (history) and of a present social location. They are also a store of memories and a map of where we are and who we are (identity) and may also provide the materials for orientation to the future. As noted at the outset, the media to a large extent constitute social reality and normality for purposes of a public, shared social life, and are a key source of standards, models and norms.

The main point to emphasize is the degree to which the different media have come to interpose themselves between us and any experience of the world beyond our direct sense observation. They also provide the most continuous line of contact with the main institutions of the society in which we live. In a secular society, in matters of values and ideas, the mass media tend to 'take over' from the early influences of school, parents, religion, siblings and companions. We are consequently very dependent on the media for a large part of our wider 'symbolic environment' (the 'pictures in our heads'), however much we may be able to shape our own personal version. It is the media which are likely to forge the elements which are held in common with others, since we now tend to share much the same media sources and 'media culture'. Without some degree of shared perception of reality, whatever its origin, there cannot really be an organized social life.

The mediation concept

These comments can be summed up in terms of the concept of mediation of contact with social reality. Mediation involves several different processes. As noted already, it refers to the relaying of second-hand (or third-party) versions of events and conditions which we cannot directly observe for ourselves. Secondly, it refers to the efforts of other actors and institutions in society to contact us for their own purposes (or our own supposed good). This applies to politicians and governments, advertisers, educators, experts and authorities of all kinds. It refers to the indirect way in which we form our perceptions of groups and cultures to which we do not belong.

Mediation also implies some form of *relationship*. Relationships which are mediated through mass media are likely to be more distant, more impersonal and weaker than direct personal ties. The mass media do not monopolize the flow of information we receive and intervene in all our wider social relations, but their presence is inevitably very pervasive. Early versions of the idea of 'mediation of reality' were inclined to assume a division between a public terrain in which a widely shared view of reality was constructed by way of mass media messages and a personal sphere, where individuals could communicate freely and directly. More recent developments of technology have undermined this simple division, since a much larger share of communication and thus of our contact with others and our environment reality is mediated via technology (telephone, computer, fax, e-mail, etc.), although on an individual and private basis. The implications of this change are still unclear and subject to diverse interpretations.

Mediation metaphors

In general, the notion of mediation in the sense of media intervening between ourselves and 'reality' is no more than a metaphor and one which invites the use of other metaphors to characterize the nature of the role played by the media. Several different terms are used to describe this role, reflecting different attributions of purposefulness, interactivity and effectiveness. Mediation can mean different things, ranging from neutrally informing, through negotiation, to attempts at manipulation and control. The variations can be captured by the following communication images, which express different ways in which the media may connect us with reality. The media have been variously perceived as:

- a **window** on events and experience, which extends our vision, enabling us to see for ourselves what is going on, without interference from others;
- a **mirror** of events in society and the world, implying a faithful reflection (albeit with inversion and possible distortion of the image), although the angle and direction of the mirror are decided by others, and we are less free to see what we want;

- a **filter** or **gatekeeper**, acting to select parts of experience for special attention and closing off other views and voices, whether deliberately or not;
- a **signpost**, **guide** or **interpreter**, pointing the way and making sense of what is otherwise puzzling or fragmentary;
- a **forum** or **platform** for the presentation of information and ideas to an audience, often with possibilities for response and feedback;
- a **screen** or **barrier** , indicating the possibility that the media might cut us off from reality, by providing a false view of the world, through either escapist fantasy or propaganda.

Some of these images are to be found in the media's own self-definition — especially in the more positive implications of extending our view of the world, providing integration and continuity and connecting people with each other. Even the notion of filtering is often accepted in its positive sense of selecting and interpreting what would otherwise be an unmanageable and chaotic supply of information and impressions. Among these different versions of the mediating process, there is scope for choice concerning the role assigned to the media: it can range from a model of openness and diversity to one of direction and control; or from a neutral and reflective to a participant and active version of the media task. It is notable that the various images discussed do not refer to the interactive possibilities of newer media, in which the 'receiver' can become a 'sender' and make use of the media in interaction with the environment. This indicates the degree to which new technology may indeed lead to revolutionary changes, with 'intermediation' replacing or supplementing the mediation process.

Mediation metaphors

- Window
- Mirror
- Filter/gatekeeper
- Signpost/guide/interpreter
- Forum/platform
- Screen/barrier

A frame of reference for connecting media with society

The very general notion that mass communication (and now also less massified media) interposes in some way between 'reality' and our perceptions and knowledge of it can be useful in orienting us to the very different kinds and levels of theory about media and society. The Westley and MacLean (1957) model (see page 50) suggests some of the additional elements needed for a more detailed frame of reference. Most significant is the idea that the media are sought out by institutional advocates as channels for reaching the general public (or chosen groups) and for conveying their chosen perspective on events and conditions. This is broadly true of competing politicians and governments, advertisers, religious leaders, some thinkers, writers and artists, etc. This reminds us that experience has always been mediated by the institutions of society (including the family), and what has happened is that a new mediator (mass communication) has been added which can extend, compete with, replace or even run counter to the efforts of social institutions.

The simple picture of a 'two-step' (or multiple) process of mediating reality is complicated by the fact that mass media are not completely autonomous in relation to the rest of society. They are also institutionalized — subject to rules, convention, economic and political influence, formal and informal control — and also have their own non-communication objectives. Thus a more complete, though very abstract, view of the 'mediation of reality' can be sketched as in Figure 3.2. Within the space in which reality is played out, as it were, the media institution (comprising a complex sphere of social action and organization) provides media audiences with information, images, stories and impressions, sometimes according to its own purposes and logic, sometimes guided by other social institutions. It is unlikely that mediation can ever be a purely neutral process and probable that it will have consistent biases. These will reflect especially the differential power in society for gaining media access and the influence of 'media logic' in constituting reality.

Briefly, the figure represents a situation in which audiences (people) acquire information and meaning about 'reality' in four main ways: via direct observation and experience; from the institutions of society directly; from the institutions by way of the media; and from the media autonomously. None of the elements indicated (institutions, media and people) are independent of each other. The influence of larger events and of economic and political forces is partly channelled though the mass media.

Types of media–society theory

In the light of this, the main varieties of theory about media and society can be accounted for as follows. First, there are 'macro-theories' concerning the relations between media and other social institutions, which bear on the extent to which the media might compete with or simply reinforce otherwise dominant lines of power and influence. Secondly, there is theory which focuses more directly on media institutions and organizations and on how they interpret and carry out their chosen or given tasks, especially under conditions of changing technology and competition for resources and

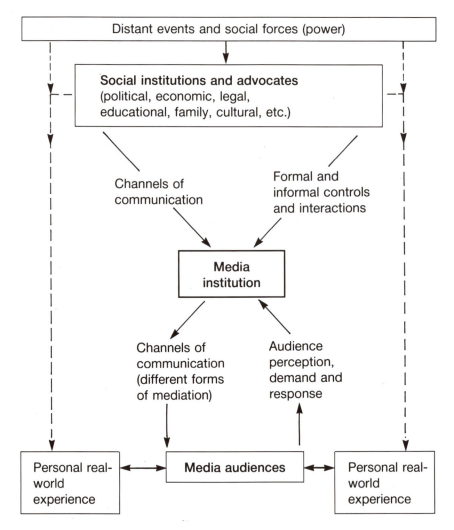

Figure 3.2 *A frame of reference for theory-formation about media and society: media interpose between personal experience and more distant events and social forces*

support. Thirdly, other theory focuses on the perspective of the audience and the consequences of their using media to gain social experience. This also covers the question of the everyday-life experience of audience members and the social context of media reception.

Of course, there is no neat system for categorizing the available theories. These are fragmentary and selective, sometimes overlapping or inconsistent, often guided by conflicting ideologies and assumptions about society. Theory-formation does not follow a systematic and logical pattern but responds to real-life problems and historical circumstances. Before describing some of the theory which has been formulated, it is necessary to consider what some of these problematic issues have been been during the 'first age of mass communication'.

Main issues for theory: power and inequality

Since media operate in societies in which power is unevenly distributed between individuals, groups and classes, and since media are invariably related in some way to the prevailing structure of political and economic power, several questions arise about this relationship. It is evident, first of all, that media have an economic cost and value, are an object of competition for control and access and are subject to political, economic and legal regulation. Secondly, mass media are very commonly regarded as effective instruments of power, with the potential capacity to exert influence in various ways.

Mass media power potential

- Attracting and directing public attention
- Persuasion in matters of opinion and belief
- Influencing behaviour
- Structuring definitions of reality
- Conferring status and legitimacy
- Informing quickly and extensively

These propositions give rise to the following sub-questions:

- Who controls the media and in whose interest?
- Whose version of the world (social reality) is presented?
- How effective are the media in achieving chosen ends?
- Do mass media promote more or less equality in society?

In discussions of media power, two models are usually opposed to each other — one a model of dominant media, the other of pluralist media (see Figure 3.3). The former model sees media as subservient to other institutions, which are themselves interrelated. Media organizations, in this view, are likely to be owned or controlled by a small number of powerful interests and to be similar in type and purpose. They disseminate a limited and undifferentiated view of the world shaped by the perspectives of ruling interests. Audiences are constrained or conditioned to accept the view of the world offered, with little critical response. The result is to reinforce and legitimate the prevailing structure of power and to head off change by filtering out alternative voices.

The pluralist model is, in nearly every respect, the opposite, allowing for much diversity and unpredictability. There is held to be no unified and

	Dominance	Pluralism
Societal source	Ruling class or dominant elite	Competing political, social, cultural interests and groups
Media	Under concentrated ownership and of uniform type	Many and independent of each other
Production	Standardized, routinized, controlled	Creative, free, original
Content and world view	Selective and uniform, decided from 'above'	Diverse and competing views, responsive to audience demand
Audience	Dependent, passive, organized on large scale	Fragmented, selective, reactive and active
Effects	Strong and confirmative of established social order	Numerous, without consistency or predictability of direction, but often no effect

Figure 3.3 *Two models of media power: mixed versions are more likely to be encountered*

dominant elite, and change and democratic control are both possible. Differentiated audiences are seen to initiate demand and are able to resist persuasion and react to what media offer. In general, the 'dominance' model is that preferred both by conservatives pessimistic about the 'rise of the masses' and by critics of capitalist society disappointed by the failure of the revolution to happen. The pluralist view is an idealized version of what liberalism and the free market will lead to. While the models are described as total opposites, it is possible to envisage there being mixed versions, in which tendencies towards mass domination (such as through concentration of ownership) are subject to limits and counter-forces and are 'resisted' by their audiences. In any free society, minorities and opposition groups should be able to develop and maintain their own alternative media.

Main issues for theory: social integration and identity

A dual perspective on media

Theorists of mass communication have often shared with sociologists an interest in how social order is maintained and in the attachment of people to various kinds of social unit. The media were early on associated with the problems of rapid urbanization, social mobility and the decline of traditional communities. They have continued to be linked with social dislocation and a supposed increase in individual immorality, crime and disorder. Mass communication as a process has often been typified as predominantly individualistic, impersonal and anomic, thus conducive to lower levels of social control and solidarity. The media have brought messages of what is new and fashionable in terms of goods, ideas, techniques and values from city to country and from the social top to the base. They have also portrayed alternative value systems, potentially weakening the hold of traditional values.

An alternative view of the relation between mass media and social integration has also been in circulation, based on other features of mass communication. It has a capacity to unite scattered individuals within the same large audience, or integrate newcomers into urban communities by providing a common set of values, ideas and information and helping to form identities. This process can help to bind together a large-scale, differentiated modern society more effectively than would have been possible through older mechanisms of religious, family or group control. In other words, mass media seem in principle capable both of supporting and of subverting social cohesion. The positions seem far apart, the one stressing centrifugal and the other centripetal tendencies, although in fact in complex and changing society both forces are normally at work at the same time, the one compensating to some extent for the other.

Ambivalence about social integration

The main questions which arise for theory and research have thus (much as in the case of power) to be grouped according to either an optimistic or a pessimistic expectation about the working of mass media (including the direction of 'new media' developments). There is an additional dimension of valuation or perspective in that both social integration and fragmentation can themselves appear in either a favourable or an unfavourable light. One person's desirable social control is another person's denial of freedom, one person's non-conformity is another's individualism, and one person's evidence of social fragmentation is another's proof of the benefits of privatization. At issue is a contrast between the notions of change, freedom, diversity and fragmentation (**centrifugal** tendencies), on the one hand, and those of order, control, unity and cohesion (**centripetal** tendencies), on the other. For theory formulation much depends on whether one takes a positive or negative view of the different outcomes of these alternative tendencies (McCormack, 1961; Carey, 1969).

In order to make sense of this complicated situation, it helps to think of the two versions of media theory — centrifugal and centripetal — each with its own dimension of evaluation, so that there are, in effect, four different theoretical positions relating to social integration (see Figure 3.4).

The positive version of the centripetal effect stresses the media as integrative and unifying (essentially the functionalist view). The negative

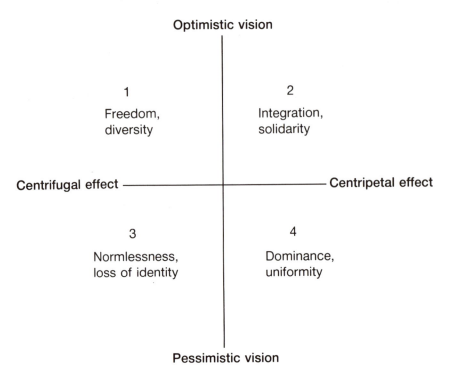

Figure 3.4 *Four images of social integration, both positive and negative*

version represents this effect as one of homogenization and manipulative control (critical theory or mass society view). The positive version of centrifugalism stresses modernization, freedom and mobility as the effects to be expected from media (individualism in general), while the negative version points to isolation, alienation, loss of values and vulnerability (a 'dysfunctional' view of change as social disorder — for example, Janowitz, 1981).

Media and integration

- Do mass media increase or decrease the level of social control and conformity?
- Do media strengthen or weaken intervening social institutions, such as family, political party, local community, church, trade union?
- Do media help or hinder the formation of diverse groups and identities based on subculture, opinion, social experience, social action, etc.?

Different types and levels of integrative media effects

We need to take account of different levels at which integration might be observed (such as the level of a whole society, or a local community, or the individual sense of identity). We may also have to distinguish between 'functional integration' (absence of conflict, co-operation for common tasks) and 'normative integration' (the sharing of norms and values). One can have one without the other, and communication is relevant to both (Allen, 1977).

A good deal of early media theory and research focused on questions of integration. For instance, Hanno Hardt (1979) has described the concerns of nineteenth- and early twentieth-century German theorists with the integrative role of the press in society. Among the functions of the press he encountered were: those of 'binding society together', giving leadership to the public, helping to establish the 'public sphere', providing for the exchange of ideas between leaders and masses, satisfying needs for information, providing society with a mirror of itself and acting as the 'conscience of society'.

In the United States, members of the Chicago School, who pioneered research into mass communication (Rogers, 1993), especially in the person of Robert Park and his pupil Herbert Blumer, emphasized the potentially positive role of mass media — for instance, in the assimilation of immigrants into their new nation (Clark, 1969). McCormack (1961) has argued that a modern, changing society is necessarily segmented, and the 'unique function of mass media is to provide both to industry and to society a coherence, a synthesis of experience, an awareness of the whole'.

The media may also be expected to help forge minority identities or to help resolve social conflicts. Much of the early literature on 'modernization', development and nation-building in the post-colonial era emphasized the contribution of media to forging a new national identity (Pye, 1963). More recently, attention has focused on the opposite effects, as increasingly internationalized media threaten to undermine national and cultural autonomy in many media-dependent societies.

Mass communication and social change

A core question concerns the direction and strength of the relationship between mass communication and other changes taking place in society — in brief, are media a cause or an effect of social change? Many issues of change have already been raised in relation to power and integration: where media exert influence they also cause change; the options of social centralization or dispersal are two main kinds of change. As we have seen, no simple answer can be expected, and different theories offer alternative versions of the relationship. At issue are the alternative ways of relating three basic elements: (a) the technology of communication and the form and content of media; (b) changes in society (social structure and institutional arrangements); and (c) the distribution among a population of opinion, beliefs, values and practices. All consequences of mass media are potentially questions about social change, but most relevant for theory have been the issue of 'technological determinism' (the effect on society of changing communications media) and the more practical question of whether or not (and how) mass media might be applied to economic and social development (as an 'engine of change' or 'multiplier of modernity') (see page 84).

Mass society theory

In the following pages, several distinctive theoretical approaches to these issues of social power, integration and change are discussed. They are presented more or less in chronological order of their formulation and they span the range from optimistic to pessimistic, critical to neutral. Mass society theory is more interesting for historical reasons than for its current relevance, and its elements are built around the concept of 'mass' which was discussed on pages 35–6. There is an extensive literature on the subject, including the work of Mills (1951, 1956), Kornhauser (1959, 1968), Bell (1961), Bramson (1961), Giner (1976), Beniger (1986) and Neuman (1991). The theory emphasizes the interdependence of institutions that exercise power and thus the integration of the media into the sources of social power and authority. Content is likely to serve the interests of political and economic power-holders. The media cannot be expected to offer a critical or alternative definition of the world, and their tendency will be to assist in the accommodation of the dependent public to their fate.

The 'dominant media' model sketched above reflects the mass society view. The type of society which developed out of industrialization and urban immigration is one characterized by family privatization, competitiveness and low levels of solidarity and participation. Mass society theory gives a primacy to the media as a causal factor. It rests very much on the idea that the media offer a view of the world, a substitute or pseudo-environment, which is a potent means of manipulation of people but also an aid to their psychic survival under difficult conditions. According to C. Wright Mills (1951, p. 333), 'Between consciousness and existence stand communications, which influence such consciousness as men have of their existence.'

This vision of society is pessimistic and more a diagnosis of the sickness of the times than a social theory, mixing elements of critical thought from the political left with a nostalgia for a golden age of community and democracy. As a theory of the media, it strongly envokes images of control and portrays the direction of influence as flowing from above. Mass society is, paradoxically, both 'atomized' and centrally controlled. The media are seen as significantly contributing to this control in societies characterized by largeness of scale, remoteness of institutions, isolation of individuals and lack of strong local or group integration.

The theory posits that media will be controlled or run in a monopolistic way and will be an effective means of organizing people in masses — as audiences, consumers, markets, electorates. Mass media are usually the voice of authority, the givers of opinion and instruction and also of psychic satisfaction. The media establish a relation of dependence on the part of ordinary citizens, in respect not only of opinion but also of self-identity and consciousness. According to the most influential and articulate theorist of mass society, C.W. Mills (1951, 1956), the mass media lead to a form of non-democratic control 'from above', with few chances to answer back.

The mass society as described is certainly integrated but not in any 'healthy' way. According to Kornhauser (1968), the lack of strong social organization and the relative isolation of individuals encourage efforts of leaders to mobilize and manipulate. Mills (1951, 1956) also pointed to the decline of the genuine public of classic democratic theory and its replacement by shifting aggregates of people who cannot formulate or realize their own aims in political action. This regret has been echoed more recently by arguments about the decline of a 'public sphere' of democratic debate and politics, in which large-scale, commercialized mass media have been implicated (Elliott, 1982; Garnham, 1986).

One solution to increased massification and privatization that has been proposed has been by way of emancipatory uses of new media from below (for example, Enzensberger, 1970), or as a result of new developments of technology (Neuman, 1991). Research has helped to modify some of the large claims of mass society theory by reasserting the potential resistance of the audience to manipulation and control and demonstrating the persistence of strong influences from group, subculture, class, locality and other sources as a limitation on the power of the media.

Mass society theory of media

- Large-scale society
- Atomized public
- Centralized media
- One-way transmission
- People depend on media for identity
- Media used for manipulation and control

Marxism and mass media

While Karl Marx only knew the press before it was effectively a mass medium, it is possible to analyse modern media according to his ideas. The media as an industry conform to a general capitalist type, with factors of production (raw materials, technology and labour) and relations of production. They are likely to be in the monopolistic ownership of a capital-owning class, and to be nationally or internationally organized to serve the interests of that class. They do so by materially exploiting workers (extracting surplus labour value) and consumers (making excess profits). Media work ideologically by disseminating the ideas and world views of the ruling class, denying access to alternative ideas which might lead to change or to a growing consciousness on the part of the working class of its interests, and by hindering the mobilization of such consciousness into active and organized political opposition. The complexity of these propositions has led to several variants of Marxist-inspired analysis of modern media, merging into the present-day 'critical political economy' (Golding and Murdock, 1991; and see pages 82–3).

The classic position

The question of power is central to Marxist interpretations of mass media. While varied, these have always emphasized the fact that ultimately they are instruments of control by a ruling class. The founding text is Marx's *German Ideology*, where he states:

> The class which has the means of material production has control at the same time over the means of mental production so that, thereby, generally speaking, the ideas of those who lack the means of mental production are subject to it. . . . Insofar, therefore, as they rule as a class and determine the extent and compass of an epoch, it is self-evident that they . . . among other things . . . regulate the production and distribution of the ideas of their age: thus their ideas are the ruling ideas of the epoch. (cited in Murdock and Golding, 1977)

Marxist theory posits a direct link between economic ownership and the dissemination of messages which affirm the legitimacy and the value of a class society. These views are supported in modern times by evidence of tendencies to great concentration of media ownership by capitalist entrepreneurs (for example, Bagdikian, 1988) and by much correlative evidence of conservative tendencies in content of media so organized (for example, Herman and Chomsky, 1988).

Neo-Marxist variants

Revised versions of Marxist media theory which concentrate more on ideas than on material structures emphasize the ideological effects of media in the interests of a ruling class, in 'reproducing' the essentially exploitative relationships and manipulation, and in legitimating the dominance of capitalism and the subordination of the working class. Louis Althusser (1971) conceived this process to work by way of what he called 'ideological state apparatuses' (all means of socialization, in effect), which, by comparison with 'repressive state apparatuses' (such as the army and police), enable the capitalist state to survive without recourse to direct violence. Gramsci's (1971) concept of hegemony refers to a ubiquitous and internally consistent culture and ideology which are openly or implicitly favourable to a dominant class or elite, although less closely and consciously organized.

Marcuse (1964) interpreted the media, along with other elements of mass production systems, as engaged in 'selling' or imposing a whole social system which is at the same time both desirable and repressive. The main contribution of the media is to stimulate and then satisfy 'false needs', leading to the assimilation of groups who have no real material interest in common into a 'one-dimensional society'.

All in all, the message of Marxist theory is plain, except perhaps in respect of how the power of the media might be countered or resisted, and of how to accommodate forms of media which are not clearly in capitalist ownership or in the power of the state (such as independent newspapers or public broadcasting). The original Leninist model of the vanguard press leading the revolutionary class struggle is no longer realistic, and critics in the Marxist tradition either rely on the weapon of critical disclosure of propaganda and manipulation (for example, Herman and Chomsky, 1988) or pin their hopes on some form of collective ownership of alternative media as a counter to the media power of the capitalist class. This is not to rule out the possibilities for change (not necessarily in directions endorsed by Marxists) by way of micro- or grass-roots media, especially under conditions of open repression and denial of legitimate alternative media (Downing, 1984).

Marxist theory of media

- Mass media owned by bourgeois class
- Media operated in their class interest
- Media promote working-class false consciousness
- Media access denied to political opposition

Functionalist theory of media and society

Functionalism claims to explain social practices and institutions in terms of the 'needs' of the society and of individuals (Merton, 1957). As applied to the media institution, the presumed 'needs' have mainly to do with continuity, order, integration, motivation, guidance, socialization, adaptation, etc. Society is viewed as an ongoing system of linked working parts or subsystems, of which the mass media are one, each making an essential contribution to continuity and order. Organized social life is said to require the continued maintenance of a more or less accurate, consistent, supportive and complete picture of the working of society and of the social environment. It is by responding to the demands of individuals and institutions in consistent ways that the media achieve unintended benefits for the society as a whole.

Thus, structural-functional theory requires no assumption of a particular ideological direction from the media (although it does assume ideological consistency) but depicts media as essentially self-directing and self-correcting. While apolitical in formulation, it suits pluralist and voluntarist conceptions of the fundamental mechanisms of social life and has a conservative bias to the extent that the media are likely to be seen as a means of maintaining society as it is rather than as a source of major change.

Conceptual basics

The functionalist approach has been beset with difficulties, partly because of confusion over the meaning of 'function' (Wright, 1960, 1974; McQuail, 1987) and over the question of who is really likely to benefit (as distinct from society in the abstract). Thus, function can mean a purpose, an effect, or simply a correlate. More fundamentally, an agreed version of media functions would require an agreed version of society, since the same media activity (such as mass entertainment) can appear in a positive light in one formulation and negatively in another. Much has also been written about the circularity of functionalism. Its starting point is an assumption that any recurrent and institutionalized activity must serve some long-term purpose and contribute to the normal working of society (Merton, 1957); yet beyond the fact of its occurrence there is no independent way of verifying either the utility or the indispensability of the activity in question (here mass communication). At root, whatever persists is assumed to be necessary.

Despite the many difficulties, a functional approach still seems useful for some purposes of description. It offers a language for discussing the relations between mass media and society and a set of concepts which have proved hard to escape from or to replace. This terminology has the advantage of being to a large extent shared by mass communicators themselves and by their audiences and being widely understood. A definition of media function as an explicit task, purpose or motive (whether for communicators or receivers) seems to provide most common ground and to avoid the worst of the conceptual difficulties noted above. Media function can refer both to more or less objective tasks of the media (such as news or editorializing) and to purposes or utilities as perceived by a media user (such as being informed or entertained).

Specifying the social functions of media

The main functions of communication in society, according to Lasswell (1948), were surveillance of the environment, correlation of the parts of the society in responding to its environment and the transmission of the cultural heritage. Wright (1960) developed this basic scheme to describe many of the effects of the media and added 'entertainment' as a fourth key media function. This may be part of the transmitted culture but it has another aspect — that of providing individual reward, relaxation and reduction of tension, which makes it easier for people to cope with real-life problems and for societies to avoid breakdown (Mendelsohn, 1966). With the addition of a fifth item — mobilization, designed to reflect the widespread application of mass communication to political and commercial propaganda — we can name the following set of basic ideas about media tasks (= functions) in society:

Information
- providing information about events and conditions in society and the world;
- indicating relations of power;
- facilitating innovation, adaptation and progress.

Correlation
- explaining, interpreting and commenting on the meaning of events and information;
- providing support for established authority and norms;
- socializing;
- co-ordinating separate activities;
- consensus building;
- setting orders of priority and signalling relative status.

Continuity
- expressing the dominant culture and recognizing subcultures and new cultural developments;
- forging and maintaining commonality of values.

Entertainment
- providing amusement, diversion and the means of relaxation;
- reducing social tension.

Mobilization
- campaigning for societal objectives in the sphere of politics, war, economic development, work and sometimes religion.

We cannot give any general rank order to these items, nor say anything about their relative frequency of occurrence. The correspondence between function (or purpose) and precise content is not exact, since one function overlaps with another, and the same content can serve different functions. The set of statements refers to functions for society and needs to be reformulated in order to take account of the perspective of the individual user of mass media, as in 'uses and gratifications' theory and research (see Chapter 12).

Uses and disuses of functionalism

Functionalist theory has often been criticized for its inadequacy in dealing with questions of power and conflict, although the media are presumed to play a necessary part in processes of social control, and it is easy to see how media are functional in the exercise of power. What part the media play and how it is performed vary according to the type of society. An essentially functionalist theory of 'media dependency' formulated by DeFleur and Ball-Rokeach (1989) treats the relative dependency of audiences on mass media sources (compared to other information sources) as a variable to be empirically determined. The theory posits that the more an audience is reliant on the mass media for information *and* the more a society is in a state of crisis or instability, then the more power the media are likely to have (or be credited with).

Media and social integration

Functionalist theory is really only useful for considering questions of social integration. Without integration there can be no agreement on goals and means and no co-ordinated activity to achieve them. Both 'functional' and 'normative' integration, according to the meanings noted above (page 73), are indispensable. However, in a complex society there will be a number of different ways for societies to achieve a required degree of control and consensus, and mass media are only one institution among several with overlapping tasks in this respect.

The effects of mass media have often been studied in terms of the contribution made to informal control or the formation of consensus (sometimes from a critical perspective). Media institutions ensure that major media conform to a 'national' or 'general public' interest or, at least, operate within limits of what is considered broadly acceptable in terms of criticism of government and society or matters of public morals and behaviour (see Chapter 5). Often these limits are set by unwritten convention rather than by law or censorship. At the level of media organizations, there is also pressure, reinforced by direct or informal means, to ensure that personnel conform to the policy and tradition of the organization concerned (for example, Breed, 1956; Burns, 1977). Cohesion and loyalty within media organizations are likely to contribute to integration into the society and to support for wider processes of social control and cohesion. Often media take it upon themselves to speak up for and express what they believe to be the dominant values of their own society (Gans, 1979).

Media tend to support the values not only of society as a whole but also of segments within it, defined in various ways. For instance, local community media have consistently been portrayed, following the work of Janowitz (1952), as helping to promote identity and social organization within the anonymity of large urban societies (Stamm, 1985). They generally support the values of the community and the maintenance of a local order (Jackson, 1971; Cox and Morgan, 1973; Murphy, 1976).

Functionalist theory of media

Mass media are essential to society for:
- Integration
- Co-operation
- Order, control and stability
- Adaptation to change
- Mobilization
- Management of tension
- Continuity of culture and values

An example of a selective integration function was offered by Ferguson (1983), who drew an analogy between Durkheim's concept of a religious cult and the relationship between magazines and their female readers, based on the notion of a 'cult of femininity', of which the editors are the priestesses and readers the devotees. The women's magazine press is the mainstay of this cult, giving it legitimacy, defining norms, giving shape and cementing a common culture based on the importance of gender and female solidarity. Radway (1984) found a somewhat similar media function for women readers of romance fiction. This sub-theory can be extended to a variety of subcultural audiences — especially perhaps in respect of music (Lull, 1992).

Studies of content have often found that large-audience media tend to be conformist and supportive rather than critical of dominant values. This support takes several forms, including: avoidance of fundamental criticism of key institutions such as business, the justice system and democratic politics; giving differential access to the 'social top'; symbolically rewarding those who succeed according to the approved paths of virtue and hard work; and symbolically punishing those who fail or deviate. Media are generally found to give disproportionate attention either to those who exemplify the aspirations of the majority or to those who reject the values of society, usually by way of crime or 'extremist' politics.

Functionalist analysis suggests (along with most criticial theory) that news and information are always normative, despite the objective format adopted. There is evidence from audience research to show that one motivation for media use is to reinforce attachment to society and its values, or at least to find security and reassurance (Katz et al., 1973). Katz and Dayan (1986) argue that major social events portrayed on television (public or state ceremonies, major sporting events) and often drawing huge audiences help to provide social cement in otherwise atomized societies.

Not surprisingly, in the light of these observations, research on effects has failed to lend much support to the proposition that mass media, for all their attention to crime, sensation, violence and deviant happenings, are a significant cause of social, or even individual, crime and disorganization. The more one holds to a functionalist theory of media, the less logical it is to expect socially disintegrative effects.

Critical political-economic theory

Political-economic theory is an old label that has been revived to identify a socially critical approach which focuses primarily on the relation between the economic structure and dynamics of media industries and the ideological content of media. It directs research attention to the empirical analysis of the structure of ownership and control of media and to the way media market forces operate. From this point of view, the media institution has to be considered as part of the economic system with close links to the political system. The predominant character of what the media produce can be largely accounted for by the exchange value of different kinds of content, under conditions of pressure to expand markets, and by the underlying economic interests of owners and decision-makers (Garnham, 1979). These interests relate to the need for profit from media operations and to the relative profitability of other branches of commerce as a result of monopolistic tendencies and processes of vertical and horizontal integration (such as into or from oil, paper, telecommunications, leisure, tourism and property).

The consequences are to be observed in the reduction of independent media sources, concentration on the largest markets, avoidance of risks, reduced investment in less profitable media tasks (such as investigative reporting and documentary film-making), neglect of smaller and poorer sectors of the potential audience and often a politically unbalanced range of news media. The effects of economic forces are not random, but (according to Murdock and Golding) work consistently to exclude

> those voices lacking economic power or resources . . . the underlying logic of cost operates systematically, consolidating the position of groups already established in the main mass-media markets and excluding those groups who lack the capital base required for successful entry. Thus the voices which survive will largely belong to those least likely to criticize the prevailing distribution of wealth and power. Conversely, those most likely to challenge these arrangements are unable to publicize their dissent or opposition because they cannot command resources needed for effective communication to a broad audience. (1977, p. 37)

The main strength of the approach lies in its capacity for making empirically testable propositions about market determinations, although the latter are so numerous and complex that empirical demonstration is not easy. While the approach centres on media activity as an economic process leading to the commodity (the media product or content), there is a variant of the political-economic approach which suggests that media really produce **audiences**, in the sense that they deliver audience attention to advertisers and shape the behaviour of media publics in certain distinctive ways (Smythe, 1977). While Marxism has been the main inspiration for the political-economic analysis of media, the approach has a much wider base in the critical analysis of media structure and economics, the tools for which are widely available in sociology, political science and economics. (See, for example, Hirsch and Gordon, 1975; Murdock and Golding, 1977; Curran, 1986; Bagdikian, 1988; Curran and Seaton, 1988; Ferguson, 1990.)

The relevance of political-economic theory has been greatly increased by several prominent trends in media business and technology (perhaps also enhanced by the fall from grace of a strictly Marxist analysis). First, there has been a growth in media concentration worldwide, with more and more power of ownership being concentrated in fewer hands and with tendencies for mergers between electronic hardware and software industries (Murdock, 1990). Secondly, there has been a growing global 'information economy' (Melody, 1990), involving an increasing convergence between telecommunication and broadcasting. Thirdly, there has been a decline in the public sector of mass media and in direct public control of telecommunication (especially in Western Europe), under the banner of 'deregulation', 'privatization' or 'liberalization' (McQuail, 1990; Siune and Truetszchler, 1992). The essential propositions of political-economic theory have not changed since earlier times, but scope for application is much wider.

Critical political-economic theory

- Economic control and logic is determinant
- Media structure tends towards concentration
- Global integration of media develops
- Contents and audiences are commodified
- Diversity decreases
- Opposition and alternative voices are marginalized
- Public interest in communication is subordinated to private interests

---

Golding and Murdock (1991) indicate several tasks for the application of theory of political economy. One has to do with the impact of forms of ownership and commercial strategies (both state and commercial) on cultural production. They argue that the increasing share of large corporations in cultural production leads to a further reduction of the 'public sphere' (the open space for rational political discourse between economy and state — Garnham, 1986) and more pressure on the autonomy of those who work within the media industries. A second task is to shed light on the political economy of cultural consumption, with particular reference to material and cultural barriers to benefits from the communication 'abundance' of our time and to the potentially widening information 'gaps' between richer and poorer (see also Golding, 1990).

Theory of media and development: rise and decline

The present overview of theory would be incomplete without reference to a body of thinking and research activity which flourished in the years after the Second World War. This approach was based on the belief that mass communication could be a potent instrument in world economic and social development by effectively spreading the message of modernity and transferring the institutions and practices of democratic politics and market economics to economically backward and socially traditional nations of the world, especially those outside the control of the communist sphere of influence. The global development project cannot really be understood outside the context of the Cold War, but it had several independent streams, among them a genuine wish to improve conditions in the 'underdeveloped world' and a belief in the power of mass communication to teach and to lead by example and by the stimulation of consumer demand for industrial goods.

Theory of media and development has several variants, but most assume the superiority of modern (that is, secular, materialist, Western, individualist, etc.) ways and of individual motivation as the key to change. People need to want to 'get on' (McLelland, 1961; Hagen, 1962). The contribution of mass media can take several forms. They can help to promote the diffusion and adoption of many technical and social innovations which are essential to modernization (Rogers, 1962, 1976; Rogers and Shoemaker, 1973). They can teach literacy and other essential skills and techniques. They can encourage a 'state of mind' favourable to modernity (Lerner, 1958), especially the possibility to imagine an alternative way of life. Lerner described the Western-inspired media as 'mobility multipliers'. Thirdly, mass communication was seen as essential to the development of national unity in new nations (ex-colonies) (Pye, 1963) and of participant democratic politics, especially by way of elections.

Much of this thinking has now been set aside or re-evaluated, in the light of very limited success in terms of the original development goals and increasing doubts about the underlying purpose (Hamelink, 1983; Schiller, 1989; Tomlinson, 1991). The model of media influence deployed was very much a mechanistic transmission model which did not take account of the realities of social context. Rogers (1976) has described the 'passing of a dominant paradigm' and suggested an alternative, based on participation and convergence (1986). In general, the much greater significance of local power structures, traditional values and economic constraints, relative to what mass communication can achieve, has been recognized. Media remain one tool for implementing change in 'developing' countries, but they may in fact have less rather than more potential compared to already 'modernized' contexts.

Mass media and development theory

Mass media serve as agents of development by:
- Disseminating technical know-how
- Encouraging individual change and mobility
- Spreading democracy (= elections)
- Promoting consumer demand
- Aiding literacy, education, health, population control, etc.

Communication technology determinism

There is a long and still active tradition of searching for links between the dominant communication technology of an age and key features of society, bearing on all three of the issues outlined (power, integration and change). To label this body of thinking 'determinist' does not do justice to the many differences and nuances, but there is a common element of 'media-centredness' (see page 3), a tendency to concentrate on the potential for (or bias towards) social change of a particular communication technology and to subordinate other variables. Otherwise, there may be little in common between the theories.

The Toronto School

The first significant theorist in this tradition seems to have been the Canadian economic historian H.M. Innis, who founded the 'Toronto School' of thinking about the media in the period after the Second World War. Innis (1950, 1951) attributed the characteristic features of successive ancient civilizations to the prevailing and dominant modes of communication, each of which will have its own 'bias' in terms of societal form. For example, he regarded the change from stone to papyrus as causing a shift from royal to priestly power. In ancient Greece, an oral tradition and a flexible alphabet favoured inventiveness and diversity and prevented the emergence of a priesthood with a monopoly over education. The foundation and endurance of the Roman empire was assisted by a culture of writing and documents on which legal-bureaucratic institutions, capable of administering distant provinces, could be based. Printing, in its turn, challenged the bureaucratic monopoly of power and encouraged both individualism and nationalism.

There are two main organizing principles in Innis's work. First, as in the economic sphere, communication leads over time to monopolization by a group or a class of the means of production and distribution of knowledge. In turn this produces a disequilibrium which either impedes changes or leads to the competitive emergence of other forms of communication, which tend to correct the disequilibrium. This can also be taken to mean that new communication technologies undermine old bases of social power.

Secondly, the most important dimensions of empire are **space** and **time**, and some means of communication are more suitable for one than for the other (this is the main so-called bias of communication). Thus, empires can persist either through time (such as ancient Egypt) or extensively in space (such as Rome), depending on the dominant form of communication.

McLuhan's (1962) developments of the theory offered new insights into the consequences of the rise of print media, although his main purpose of explaining the significance of electronic media for human experience has not really been fulfilled (McLuhan, 1964) (see also Chapter 4). Of printing, McLuhan wrote: '. . . the typographic extension of man brought in nationalism, industrialism and mass markets and universal literacy and education'.

Technology and ideology

The sociologist Gouldner (1976) interpreted key changes in modern political history in terms of communication technology. He connects the rise of 'ideology', defined as a special form of rational discourse, to printing and the newspaper, on the grounds that (in the eighteenth and nineteenth centuries) these stimulated a supply of interpretation and ideas (ideology). He then portrays the later media of radio, film and television as having led to a decline of ideology because of the shift from 'conceptual to iconic symbolism', revealing a split between the 'cultural apparatus' (the intelligentsia), which produces ideology, and the 'consciousness industry', which controls the new mass public. This anticipates a continuing 'decline in ideology' as a result of the new computer-based networks of information (see also pages 88–9).

Media technological determinism (pre-new technology)

- Communication technology is fundamental to society
- Each technology has a bias to particular communication forms, contents and uses
- The sequence of invention and application of communication technology influences social change
- Communication revolutions lead to social revolutions

An interactive alternative

Most informed observers are now wary of single-factor explanations of social change and do not really believe in direct mechanistic effects from new technology. Effects occur only when inventions are taken up, developed and applied, usually to existing uses at first, then with a great extension and change of use according to the capacity of the technology and the needs of a society (see page 108). Development is always shaped by the social and cultural context. It no longer makes sense to think in terms of a single dominant medium with some unique properties, although this may have been justifiable in the case of the book or, in some respects, later, the telegraph and telephone. At present, very many different new media forms coexist with many of the 'old' media, none of which has disappeared. At the same time, the argument that media are converging and linking to comprise an all-encompassing network has considerable force and implications (Neuman, 1991). It may also be true that new media forms can have a particular social or cultural 'bias' (see Chapter 4) which makes certain effects more likely. These possibilities are discussed in the following section.

The information society: new theory of media–society linkages

While several historians (for example, Eisenstein, 1978) have shared with Innis and McLuhan a belief in the great influence of the printed word on social change, and while television has had its own prophets of revolutionary effect, there has, if anything, been even more agreement on the implications of the 'new technology', for good or ill. The assumption of a revolutionary social transition is, even so, not without its critics (for example, Leiss, 1989; Ferguson, 1992). Ferguson (1986a) treats this 'neo-technological determinism' as a *belief system* which now tends to operate as a self-fulfilling prophecy.

The term 'communications revolution', along with the term 'information society', has almost come to be accepted as an objective description of our time and of the type of society which is emerging. It is hard to escape from the deterministic element in much current thinking about the 'new media', with societal effects again being attributed to intrinsic features of technology. Rogers, who sees himself as a 'soft technological determinist', views 'technology along with other factors, as causes of change' (1986, p. 9) and identifies three crucial features of the new technology as their interactivity, their individualized, demassified nature and the 'asynchronous nature of the new communication systems' (they are no longer time-bound). Most commentators seem to agree on the relevance of these points, if not about the strength of influence.

Conceptual underpinnings

The term 'information society' itself seems to have originated in Japan (Ito, 1981), although a concept of 'postindustrial' society (Bell, 1973) was developed independently to describe a society in which the service sector had overtaken manufacturing as the main form of employment. In the information society, 'information work' predominates, and information is the most valuable resource, tending to displace capital in this respect (Rogers, 1986; Dordick and Wang, 1993). Melody (1990, pp. 26–7) describes information societies simply as those which have become 'dependent upon complex electronic information and communication networks and which allocate a major portion of their resources to information and communication activities'.

Characteristic of information societies (in effect, of all modern economies) is an exponential increase in the production and flow of information of all kinds (van Cuilenburg, 1987). Miniaturization and computerization have made enormous differences to the costs involved. The mass media are only one kind of information production, but they are increasingly integrated with other flows, especially by way of shared infrastructures. Information society theory involves a break with earlier theory of society and is a further development of media technological determinism. Its most essential point is that the means of production of information are more important than the specific contents which are distributed (such as particular ideologies or bodies of information).

Neuman (1991), also a 'soft determinist', has claimed that there is an underlying 'logic behind the cascade of new technologies'. He refers to this as their 'interconnectedness' (p. 48), the fact that they lend themselves to forming an integrated electronic network. In addition these networks increasingly show: lower sensitivity to distance and cost and increasing speed, volume, flexibility, interactivity, interconnectivity and extensibility. Neuman writes:

> The quintessential characteristic of the new electronic media is that they all connect with one another. We are witnessing the evolution of a universal, interconnected network of audio, video and electronic text communication that will blur the distinction between interpersonal and mass communication and between public and private communications. . . . The ultimate result . . . will be intellectual pluralism and personalized control over communication. (1991, p. 12)

Out of the ongoing revolution, he also sees the potential for a more vital democratic pluralism.

Logic of change

Any history of communication (as of other) technologies testifies to the accelerating pace of invention and of material potential as an outcome, and some theorists are inclined to identify distinct phases. Rogers (1986), for instance, locates turning points at the invention of writing, the beginning of printing in the fifteenth century, the mid-nineteenth century start to the telecommunication era, and the age of interactive communication beginning in 1946 with the invention of the mainframe computer. Schement and Stout (1988) provide us with a detailed 'timeline' of communication technology inventions, which they classify according to their being either 'conceptual/

institutional' (such as writing) or 'devices for acquisition and storage' (such as paper and printing), or being related to processing and distribution (such as computers and satellites). History shows several apparent trends but especially a shift over time in the direction of more speed, greater dispersion, wider reach and greater flexibility. They underline the capacity for communication more readily to cross barriers of time and space.

The marked consensus about the significance of changes occurring in communication technology is not accompanied by unanimity about the social consequences. Neuman's views, cited above, represent an informed optimism about the benefits which will follow from new communication technology if they are allowed to develop freely (see also Pool, 1983). These views are a decisive rejection of the gloomy prophecies of mass society theory (see above), in which new and more powerful mass media were represented as tools for a greater degree of subordination of the masses by powerful elites in societies characterized by homogeneity, privatization, loneliness and conformity.

'Videotopia' versus 'dystopia'

There are 'video-Utopians' who think that the communicative potential which is being unleashed can promote a more participatory and active social life. Voices from the political left as well as the right can be heard with a similar message. An early and eloquent prophet of change was the poet and social critic H.M. Enzensberger (1970), who hailed the socialistic and emancipatory potential of the then developing new media — helping to decentralize, mobilize, interconnect and free the individual from bureaucratic control. In the wake of such visions, more down-to-earth democrats have hoped that more abundant, free, participant, flexible and democratic local communication systems could arise on the basis of new media and feed local democracy. To some extent these expectations have been fulfilled, at least in terms of institutional possibilities (Jankowski et al., 1992). Currently, postmodernist thinking is also inclined to promote visions of new escape routes from beneath the weight of centralization, tradition and control (see below).

There are still a good many doubters, especially theorists of the political economy school who still see the hand of (now global) monopoly capitalism behind the impulse to promote and spread the new technology, others who are simply more inclined towards 'society-centric' explanations and expect change to be determined by more fundamental social and political factors. For these critics, it is not the theoretical potential of social renewal but the actual structure of ownership and control of the new media which matters and the way the technologies are implemented.

The critique of 'videotopia' has several strands, but three points are probably most significant. First, the new technologies extend the power and reach of large multinational corporations much more readily than they enlarge the freedom of individual citizens. Secondly, the individual benefits of access to interactive communication technology are very unevenly distributed (Golding, 1990). Most who gain access are already economically and socially privileged, and their greater communicative empowerment only widens social gaps, leading to a new information underclass. Thirdly, the new electronic networks are potentially just as effective means of supervision and control (through monitoring and information) in a modern society as they are individually emancipating. The new potential indication by the 'registration' pattern described on page 57 has been referred to as an 'Electronic Panopticon' (echoing Jeremy Bentham's model prison). According to Jansen (1988), the privacy of the home and of interpersonal relations is eroded. The system of surveillance operates around the clock, monitoring almost all human activity. She writes, 'Once the wires are in place, the Electronic Panopticon works automatically. Only the minimal supervision for the Tower is required' (1988, pp. 23–4).

There is a resistance to 'videotopian' visions on humanistic grounds as well. They are the tools for a new spurt to rationalism as much as a basis for a return to community. According to James Carey:

> Electronics has the potential for the perfection of a utilitarian attitude and the indefinite expansion of the administrative mentality and imperial politics. Electronics, like print, in its early phases, is biassed towards supporting one kind of civilization: a powerhouse society dedicated to wealth, power and productivity, to technical perfectionism and ethical nihilism. (1988, p. 10)

Progressive or conservative direction?

More sober assessments tend in the same direction. For instance, Beniger's (1986) interpretative history of communication innovations since the early nineteenth century finds that they fit within a pattern, not of increasing liberation, but of increasing possibilities for management and control. He uses the term 'control revolution' to refer to the communications revolution, and it is easy to appreciate why. Whatever the potential, the needs of commerce, industry, the military and bureaucracy have done most to promote development and determine how innovations are actually applied.

Another chronicler of communication innovation, Brian Winston (1986), recognizes that most new technologies have innovative potential, but the actual implementation always depends on two factors: one is the operation of 'supervening social necessity', which tends to dictate the degree and form of development of inventions; secondly, there is the ' "law" of the suppression of radical potential', which acts as a brake on innovation to protect the social or corporate status quo. In general, he argues for theories of 'cultural' rather than technological determination. If the institutionalization of all technologies has led until now to the suppression of any radical tendency, there is no particular reason to suppose that this will be different with the latest inventions.

Bias to globalization

One major societal bias which does seem to follow from several characteristics of new technology (especially the transcendence of time and space barriers) is the 'bias to internationalization' or globalization, which affects social structures and relations as well as cultures. The transnationalization of mass media is not in itself new if we consider the history of news agencies (Boyd-Barrett, 1980) or film (Tunstall, 1977), but most mass media institutions have been rather firmly rooted in their own national soil. Changes in communication technology (such as satellites) have made it much more feasible for mass media to distribute worldwide as cheaply and quickly as within the locality or country, and the same applies to telecommunication links between individuals and organizations.

There is a rapidly extending global communication infrastructure, as well as a network of interconnected ownership and management of communication businesses. Under current conditions, the internationalization of politics and of trade and commerce both supports and is stimulated by communication globalization (Frederick, 1992). The effects of such changes may be experienced most directly in respect of culture. But they also have a strong effect on international political and economic relations (Hamelink, 1983; Mowlana, 1986; Schiller, 1989). There are some clear implications for social experience and for political life. It might seem, for instance, that while 'globalization' can open new horizons, it also detaches people more certainly than did the old national mass media from their local and community roots. Internationalization of communication would seem to create new kinds of dependency and actually to reduce autonomy.

Information society theory

New media technology leads to an information society, characterized by:
- Predominance of information work
- Great volume of information flow
- Interactivity of relations
- Integration and convergence of activities
- Globalizing tendencies
- Postmodern culture

Conclusion: conflict versus consensus, and media-centric versus society-centric approaches

These theoretical perspectives on the relation between media and society are diverse in several respects, emphasizing different causes and types of

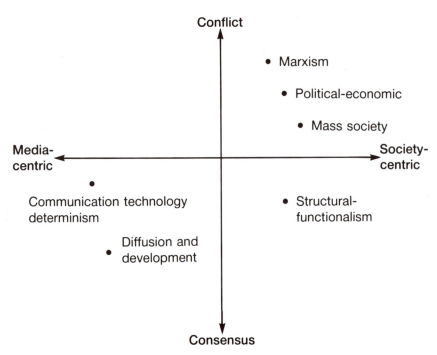

Figure 3.5 *An overview of theories of media and society: the main choices are between conflict and consensus and between media as moulder and media as mirror of society*

change and pointing to different paths into the future. They cannot all be reconciled, since they represent alternative philosophical positions and opposed methodological preferences. Nevertheless, we can make sense of them in terms of two main dimensions of approach: one contrasting a critical with a consensual view of society; another focusing on the difference between a 'media-centric' and a 'society-centric' view. In general, the critical approach implies a view of society as in a continual state of conflict or power struggle between (mainly) 'haves' and 'have-nots', while the consensual approach implies a pluralistic view of society as governed by forces of equilibrium and the hidden hand of the market and leading to the best that can be hoped for.

The second dimension is more self-explanatory, representing the difference between those who see media technology (and content) as primary movers in social change and those who consider the roots of change to lie with the society. Rosengren (1983) has drawn attention to a somewhat similar mapping of differences in sociological theory (Burrell and Morgan, 1979), which also identified four alternative paradigms on much the same lines as in Figure 3.5.

The six types of theory discussed in this chapter are given an approximate location in terms of the two dimensions. The 'map' is really incomplete without some of the theory relating to culture which will be discussed in Chapter 4, but it gives some idea of the general structure of thinking about mass media and society. The picture is complicated by the fact that some theories are expressed in optimistic and others in pessimistic terms. This applies especially to thinking about new information technology. Both the predicted interconnectedness and the globalization of society which are seen to develop have been viewed as either positive or negative, depending on outlook. The general division of theory into a dominant paradigm and an alternative/critical view (see pages 41–8) lies at the root of this ambivalence and inconsistency.

4

MASS COMMUNICATION AND CULTURE

Setting the scene: the culturalist approach

This chapter sets out to explore the more 'cultural' dimensions of the theories already discussed in Chapter 3 and to introduce some additional perspectives. The general framework of 'mediation' (see pages 65–6) remains relevant, but here the emphasis shifts to *what* is mediated (the particular meanings) and to the process by which meaning is given and taken (sometimes referred to as 'signification'). Since the earlier days of mass communication research, a distinctive 'culturalist' perspective on mass media has been developing, especially under the influence of the humanities (literature, linguistics, philosophy), as distinct from the more social scientific emphasis of 'mainstream' communication science. At some points, or on some issues, the two traditions have merged, although there remain substantial differences of thinking and method. This book, and this chapter, is written primarily from a social scientific perspective, but it aims also to benefit from some of the insights and ideas of the 'culturalists'.

It is not easy to give a simple definition of the essence of their approach, but it has generally to do with the notion of a **text** and with the construction and taking of meaning from texts. Fiske (1989, p. 1) defines culture as 'the constant process of producing meanings of and from our social experience'. This view of culture as an ongoing process contrasts with older versions equating culture with fixed patterns or with the *results* of cultural practices — especially valued cultural artefacts. The taking of meaning involves the 'reading' of texts, a term which encompasses a wide range of symbolically encoded items, including commodities, clothes, language and structured social practices, as well as the more conventional notion of all kinds of media products (television programmes, books, songs, films, etc.). The culturalist approach takes in all aspects of the production, the forms and the reception of texts in this sense and the discourses which surround them. While mass media necessarily fall within the range of cultural studies, the latter has a much wider range of reference, and there is only a limited overlap of issues and theory.

Communication and culture

James Carey (1975) proposed an alternative to the dominant view of communication as **transmission** in the form of a 'ritual' model (see page 50), and he has also advocated an approach to communication and society in which culture is allotted a more central place. 'Social life is more than power and trade . . . it also includes the sharing of aesthetic experience, religious ideas, personal values and sentiments, and intellectual notions — a ritual order' (Carey, 1988, p. 34). Accordingly, he defined communication as 'a symbolic process whereby reality is produced, maintained, repaired and transformed' (p. 23).

In order to take the question of the relation between *mass* communication and culture in this sense further, we need to be more precise about what presents itself as an object of study. This is made difficult by the many senses in which the term 'culture' is used — itself a reflection of the complexity of the phenomenon. Culture is defined by Carey as a *process*, but it can also refer to some *shared attribute* of a human group (such as their physical environment, tools, religion, customs and practices, or their whole way of life). Culture also can refer to *texts and symbolic artefacts* which are encoded with particular meanings by and for people with particular cultural identifications.

Towards defining culture

If we extract essential points from these different usages, it seems that culture must have all of the following attributes. It is something collective and shared with others (there is no purely individual culture); it must have some symbolic form of expression, whether intended as such or not; it has some pattern, order or regularity, and therefore some evaluative dimensions (if only degree of conformity to a culturally prescribed pattern); there is (or has been) a dynamic continuity over time (culture lives and changes, has a history and potentially a future). Perhaps the most general and essential attribute of culture is communication, since cultures could not develop, survive, extend and generally succeed without communication. Finally, in order to study culture we need to be able to locate it, and essentially there are three places to look: in people, in things (texts, artefacts) and in human practices (socially patterned behaviours).

There are some obvious implications for the study of mass communication, since every aspect of the production and use of mass media has a cultural dimension. We can focus on *people* as producers of culturally meaningful media texts, or people as 'readers of texts', from which they take cultural meanings, with implications for the rest of social life. We can focus on the texts and artefacts themselves (films, books, newspaper articles) and on their symbolic forms and possible meanings. We may want to study the *practices* of makers of media products or of *users* of the media. Media

---

Characteristics of culture

- Collectively formed and held
- Open to symbolic expression
- Ordered and differentially valued
- Systematically patterned
- Dynamic and changing
- Communicable over time and space

---

audience composition and behaviour (practices around the choice and use of media) are always culturally patterned, before, after and during the media experience.

Research issues

This broad terrain can be narrowed down by identifying some of the main questions and theoretical issues which have arisen. Historically, the first 'cultural' question on the agenda of media theory was that of the character of the new **mass culture** made possible by mass communication. It was usually posed in respect of the content (cultural texts), but it extended to the question of the *practice* of mass media use and it nearly always involved a view of *people* as a mass — the new form of social collectivity, which was otherwise often perceived as without any other culture of its own.

The rise of a distinctive 'media culture' has also stimulated rethinking about the nature of 'popular culture', which has now to be seen not just as a cheap alternative, mass-produced for mass consumption, but as a vital new branch of cultural creativity and enjoyment (Schudson, 1991; McGuigan, 1992). The issue of mass culture also stimulated the rise of **critical cultural theory**, which, among other things, has been extended to consider issues of **gender** and of **subculture** in relation to mass communication.

A second key theme, following the line opened up in Chapter 3, relates to the potential consequences of the new **technologies** themselves for the experience of meaning in the emerging modern world, according to the 'mediation' perspective outlined above. There are large implications in communication technology for the way we may come to know our own social world and our place in it.

Thirdly, there are political-economic aspects of the organized production of culture represented by mass media industries. We have come to think of the media as a 'consciousness industry', driven by economic logic as well as by cultural changes. An important aspect is the **commodification** of culture in the form of the 'software' produced by communication 'hardware' which is sold and exchanged in enlarging markets. Another consequence of this (and of technology) has been the **internationalization** of production and distribution.

The typical culture (in the sense of media texts) produced by the major media industries is often globalized in form, even when it appears in the local or national variants and languages. This has led to theory and research concerning the consequences for **cultural identity** and for the autonomy and distinctiveness of pre-existing ways of life and belief systems. Similar questions of cultural identity and autonomy also arise at the level of subcultures and extend to cover the way media use and reception are integrated into and adapted according to the immediate lived cultural and social experience.

Issues for media cultural theory

- Mass culture and popular culture
- Communication technology effects
- Commodification of culture
- Globalization
- Cultural identity
- Gender and subculture

The beginnings: the Frankfurt School and critical theory

A socially based critical concern with the rise of mass culture (see pages 40–1) goes back at least to the mid-nineteenth century and in the mid-twentieth century was represented in England in the work of F.R. Leavis and his followers in the field of social literary criticism. The latter movement has also been (indirectly) influential in the rise of more radical (and populist) critical theory as expressed in the work of Richard Hoggart, Raymond Williams and Stuart Hall. The continuing thrust of these critics has been to attack the commercial roots of cultural 'debasement' and to speak up for the working-class consumer of mass culture as the victim (and not only that) rather than the villain of the story. The initial aim was to redeem the people on whose supposedly 'low tastes' the presumed low quality of mass culture was often blamed. Since then, 'mass culture' itself has largely been rescued from the stigma of low quality (see page 103), although in the course of this the original concept of mass culture has been largely abandoned.

For the wider development of ideas about mass communication and the character of 'media culture', within an internationalized framework, the various national debates about cultural quality have probably been less influential than a set of ideas, owing much to Marxist thinking, which developed and diffused in the post-war years. The term 'critical theory' serves to refer to this long and diverse tradition which owes its origins to the work of a group of post-1933 *émigré* scholars from the Marxist School of Applied Social Research in Frankfurt. The most important members of the group were Max Horkheimer and Theodor Adorno, but others, including Leo Lowenthal, Herbert Marcuse and Walter Benjamin, played an important role (see Jay, 1973; Hardt, 1991).

The school had been established originally to examine the apparent failure of revolutionary social change as predicted by Marx, and in explanation of this failure they looked to the capacity of the superstructure (especially ideas and ideology represented in the mass media) to subvert historical forces of economic change (and also the promise of the Enlightenment). History (as interpreted by Marx) seemed to have 'gone wrong', because ideologies of the dominant class had come to condition the economic base, especially by promoting a 'false consciousness' among the working masses and helping to assimilate them to capitalist society. The universal and commercialized mass culture was seen as one important means by which this success for monopoly capital had been achieved. The whole process of mass production of goods, services and ideas had more or less completely sold the system of capitalism, along with its devotion to technological rationality, consumerism, short-term gratification and the myth of 'classlessness'.

The **commodity** is the main instrument of this process since it appeared that both art and oppositional culture could be marketed for profit at the cost of losing critical power. Marcuse later (1964) gave the description 'one-dimensional' to the mass consumption society founded on commerce, advertising and spurious egalitarianism. The media and the 'culture industry' as a whole were deeply implicated in this critique. Many of these ideas were launched during the 1940s by Adorno and Horkheimer (1972, in translation), which contained a sharp and pessimistic attack on mass culture, for its uniformity, worship of technique, monotony, escapism and produc-tion of false needs, its reduction of individuals to customers and the removal of all ideological choice (see Hardt, 1991, p. 140). According to Shils (1957), the very jaundiced Frankfurt School view of mass culture was not only anti-capitalist but also anti-American and mainly reflected the first impact of modern mass media on a group of displaced European intellectuals. In several respects, the critique of mass culture outlined is very close to that found in different versions of the then contemporary mass society theory.

The emphasis in critical theory on the culture of the mass media as a powerful influence for preventing fundamental change has lived on in several different lines of theory. In general, the 'consciousness industry' has been an object of sustained critical attention. More particularly, a concept of cultural 'commodification' was developed as a tool for examining the commercialization of culture and the working of advertising, while a broader notion of 'hegemony' evolved to account for the effects of media on consciousness.

The theory of commodification originates in Marx's *Grundrisse*, in which he noted that objects are commodified by acquiring an exchange value, instead of having merely an intrinsic use value. In the same way, cultural products (in the form of images, ideas and symbols) are produced and sold in media markets as commodities. These can be exchanged by consumers for psychic satisfactions, amusement and illusory notions of our place in the world, often resulting in the obscuration of the real structure of society and our subordination in it (false consciousness). This is an ideological process largely conducted via our dependence on commercial mass media. The theory of commodification applies especially well to the interpretation of commercial advertising (Williamson, 1978), but it has a wider reference. In general, the more art and culture are commodified, the more they lose any critical potential, and intrinsic value distinctions are replaced by or equated with market criteria of cost and demand.

Hegemony

The concept of 'hegemony', borrowed by critical theorists from Gramsci's (1971) term for a ruling ideology, helps to bring together a lot of different ideas about how the culture of media (news, entertainment, fiction) helps to maintain the class-divided and class-dominated society. Hegemony refers to a loosely interrelated set of ruling ideas permeating a society, but in such a way as to make the established order of power and values appear natural, taken-for-granted and common-sensical. A ruling ideology is not imposed but appears to exist by virtue of an unquestioned consensus. Hegemony tends to define unacceptable opposition to the status quo as dissident and deviant. In effect, hegemony is a constantly reasserted definition of a social situation, by way of discourse rather than political or economic power, which becomes real in its consequences (Hall, 1982). The mass media do not define reality on their own but give preferential access to the definitions of those in authority. This is a 'culturalist' correlate of the political-economy theory of control described in Chapter 3.

Ideology, in the form of a distorted definition of reality or, in the words of Althusser (1971), as 'the imaginary relationships of individuals to their real conditions of existence', is not dominant in the sense of being imposed by force by a ruling class, but is an all-pervasive and deliberate cultural influence which serves to interpret experience of reality in a covert but consistent manner. According to Hall:

> That notion of dominance which meant the direct imposition of one framework, by overt force or ideological compulsion, on a subordinate class, was not sophisticated enough to match the complexities of the case. One had also to see that dominance was accomplished at the unconscious as well as the conscious level: to see it as a property of the system of relations involved, rather than as the overt and intentional biases of individuals in the very activity of regulation and exclusion which functioned through language and discourse. (1982, p. 95)

This approach directs attention at the way the relationships of capitalism have to be reproduced and legitimized according to the more or less voluntary consent of the working class itself. The tools for analysing these processes have been provided by developments in semiological and structural analysis which offer methods for the exposing of covert and underlying structures of meaning.

Later developments of critical cultural theory: the Birmingham School

Critical cultural theory has now extended well beyond its early concerns with ideological domination, although in one way or another the study of ideology in media culture remains central, as does the significance of media culture for the experience of particular groups in society such as youth, the working class, ethnic minorities and other marginal categories. Theory posits a drive towards the assimilation and subordination of potentially deviant or oppositional elements in society. Research carried out, in particular, at the Centre for Contemporary Cultural Studies at the University of Birmingham during the 1970s led to the identification of the 'Birmingham School' as the main locus for the approach.

The person most associated with the work of this school, Stuart Hall, has written that the cultural studies approach:

> stands opposed to the residual and merely reflective role assigned to the 'cultural'. In its different ways it conceptualizes culture as interwoven with all social practices; and those practices, in turn, as a common form of human activity. . . . It is opposed to the base–superstructure way of formulating the relationship between ideal and material forces, especially where the base is defined by the determination by the 'economic' in any simple sense. . . . It defines 'culture' as both the means and values which arise amongst distinctive social groups and classes, on the basis of their given historical conditions and relationship, through which they 'handle' and respond to the conditions of existence . . . (quoted in Gurevitch et al., 1982, pp. 26–7)

The social-cultural approach seeks to attend to both messages and public, aiming to account for patterns of choice and response in relation to the media by a careful and critically directed understanding of the actual social experience of sub-groups within society. The whole enterprise has also been informed by an appreciation of the efforts of power-holders to manage the recurrent crises of legitimacy and economic failure held to be endemic in industrial capitalist society (Hall et al., 1978).

The critical approach associated with the Birmingham School was also responsible for an important shift from the question of ideology embedded in media texts to the question of how this ideology might be 'read' by its audience. Stuart Hall (1980) proposed a model of 'encoding–decoding media discourse' which represented the media text as located between its producers, who framed meaning in a certain way, and its audience, who 'decoded' the meaning according to their rather different social situations and frames of interpretation.

Drawing on the political sociology of Parkin (1972), Hall suggested that there are three basic codes in circulation — one of dominant meanings associated with power, a second 'negotiated' code, which is essentially the code of the media in their role as neutral and professional carriers of information, and a third 'oppositional' code, which is available to those who choose, or who are led by circumstances, to view messages about reality differently and can 'read between the lines' of official versions of events. This simple model recognizes that ideology as **sent** is not the same as ideology as **taken**. While there may be so-called 'preferred' readings offered from above, they can either be treated with some distance and subjected to objective analysis (as they may be by journalists) or be perceived as 'propaganda' and resisted or subverted accordingly.

These ideas proved a considerable stimulus to rethinking the theory of ideology and of false consciousness. They led to research on the potential for 'differential decoding' (for example, Morley, 1980), with a view, especially, to finding evidence of working-class resistance to dominant media messages. The direct results were meagre in this respect, but indirectly the theory was very effective in 're-empowering' the audience and returning some optimism to the study of media and culture. It also led to a wider view of the social and cultural influences which mediate the experience of the media, especially ethnicity, gender and 'everyday life' (Morley, 1986, 1992).

Gender and mass media

One area where the theory of differential cultural reading of media texts has made important advances, in collaboration with feminist research, is in relation to gender. While communication studies, even of the radical critical tendency, have long seemed to be largely 'gender-blind' (perhaps more a matter of unwillingness to see), one can now justifiably speak of a 'cultural feminist media studies project' (van Zoonen, 1991), which goes far deeper and wider than the original limited agenda of matters such as sex-role socialization. The amount of gender-related media research is now very large and, although in part it follows lines of theory pioneered with reference to social class and race, it has several new dimensions, especially those based on psychoanalytic theory and drawing on the wider field of feminist studies (Long, 1991; Kaplan, 1992).

The question of gender touches almost every aspect of the media–culture relationship. Most central is probably the question of gender definition. Van Zoonen (1991, p. 45) writes that the meaning of gender 'is never given but varies according to specific cultural and historical settings . . . and is subject to ongoing discursive struggle and negotiation'. Partly at issue is how gender differences and distinctiveness are signified (see Goffman, 1976). Another general aspect of the struggle is over the differential value attaching to masculinity and to femininity and over the related question of an all-pervasive 'patriarchal' ideology in many mass-mediated cultural forms.

Feminist perspectives on mass communication open up numerous lines of analysis, often largely neglected in the past (Rakow, 1986; Dervin, 1987). One concerns the fact that many media texts are deeply and persistently *gendered* in the way they have been encoded, usually according to a view of the anticipated audience. Fiske (1987) provides extensive evidence of what 'gendered television' means, from detailed deconstructions of numerous popular television programmes. A prominent example in his and other work is that of the soap-opera genre (see Brown, 1990), which may arguably be regarded as following a 'feminine aesthetic'. According to Fiske (1987, p. 197), soap operas 'keep patriarchy under constant interrogation, they legitimate feminine values and thus produce self-esteem for the women who live by them. They provide, in short, the means for a feminine culture . . . in constant struggle to establish and extend itself within and against a dominant patriarchy.' Livingstone (1991) refers to the theory that the typical structure of soap operas parallels the typical routine of a housewife's day (see also Modleski, 1982). The gendering of content may also be studied at the point of production, since most media selection and production work is carried out by men (see Chapter 9).

Attention to the construction of gender in media texts is only one aspect of the relevance of gender for communication theory. Studies of media audiences and the reception of media content have shown that there are relatively large differences according to gender in the manner of use of media and the meanings attached to the activity. A good deal of the evidence can be accounted for by patterned differences in social roles, by typical everyday experience and concerns, and by the way gender shapes the availability and use of time. It also relates to power roles within the family and the general nature of relationships between women and male partners or of women in the wider family (Morley, 1986). There may also be deep roots in psychological differences between male and female (Williamson, 1978). Different kinds of media content (and their production and use) are also associated with expressions of common identity based on gender (Ferguson, 1983; Radway, 1984) and with different pleasures and meanings acquired (Ang, 1985).

A gender-based approach also raises the question of whether media choice and interpretation can provide some lever of change or element of resistance for women in a social situation still generally structured by inequality. The potential for oppositional reading and resistance has been invoked both to explain why women seem attracted to media content with overtly patriarchical messages (such as romance fiction) and to help re-evaluate the surface meaning of this attraction (Radway, 1984). One can say, in summary, that differently gendered media culture, whatever the causes and the forms taken, evokes different responses, and that differences of gender lead to alternative modes of taking meaning from media. There are also differences in selection and context of use which have wider cultural and social implications (Morley, 1986). While the greater attention to gender has been widely welcomed, there have also been warnings about reading too much into gender differences and about assuming the presence and influence of gender identity (Ang and Hermes, 1991).

The 'redemption' of the popular

The mass media are largely responsible for what we call either mass culture or popular culture, and they have 'colonized' other cultural forms in the process. The most widely disseminated and enjoyed symbolic culture of our time (if it makes any sense to refer to it in the singular) is what flows in abundance by way of the media of films, television, newspapers, phonogram, video, etc. It makes little sense to go on supposing that this flood can in some way be dammed in, turned back or purified, or to view the predominant culture of our time as a deformed offspring of commerce from a once pure stock.

There is even little possibility of distinguishing an elite from a mass taste, since nearly everyone is attracted to some of the diverse elements of popular media culture. Tastes will always differ, and varying criteria of assessment can be applied, but we should at least accept the media culture of our time as an accomplished fact and treat it on its own terms. The term 'mass culture' is likely to remain in circulation, but the alternative form 'popular culture' (meaning essentially 'culture which is popular' — much enjoyed by many people) seems preferable and no longer carries a pejorative association. Popular culture in this sense is a hybrid product of numerous and never-ending efforts for expression in contemporary idiom aimed at reaching people and capturing a market, and an equally active demand by people for what Fiske (1987) would call 'meanings and pleasures'.

The (semiotic) power of the people

John Fiske (1987, 1989) has been one of the most eloquent and convincing in the effort to vindicate popular culture. An important source of his attachment to popular culture is the line of thinking, outlined above, according to which the same cultural product can be 'read' in different ways, even if a certain dominant meaning may seem to be built in. Fiske defines a media text as the *outcome* of its reading and enjoyment by an audience. He defines the plurality of meanings of a text as its 'polysemy'. The associated term 'intertextuality' refers partly to the interconnectedness of meanings across different media artefacts (blurring any line between elite and popular culture) but also to interconnectedness of meanings across media and other cultural experiences. An example of both terms is provided by the fact that a cultural phenomenon like the pop singer Madonna can appeal to, yet have quite different meanings for, both young girls and ageing male readers of *Playboy* magazine (Schwichtenberg, 1992).

There are entirely different readings of much popular media content in different subcultures, opening the way for escape from potential social control. Fiske writes:

> The preferred meanings in television are generally those that serve the interests of the dominant classes; other meanings are structured in relations of dominance–subordination . . . the semiotic power of the subordinate to make their own meanings is the equivalent of their ability to evade, oppose, or negotiate with this social power. (1987, p. 126)

Much of this thinking is derived originally from Hall's theory of decoding and from new critical theory in general, according to which all texts can be read in an oppositional way and their encoded ideology readily subverted.

For Fiske, the primary virtue of popular culture is precisely that it is popular — both literally 'of the people' and dependent on 'people power'. He writes: 'Popularity is here a measure of a cultural form's ability to serve the desires of its customers . . . For a cultural commodity to become popular it must be able to meet the various interests of the people amongst whom it is popular as well as the interests of its producers' (1987, p. 310). Popular culture must be relevant and responsive to needs or it will fail, and success (in the market) may be the best test that culture is both (in practice the criterion of success supersedes any notion of intrinsic quality). Fiske rejects the argument that lines of division of cultural capital follow the lines of division of economic capital (Bourdieu, 1986). Instead he argues that there are two economies, with relative autonomy — one cultural and the other social. Even if most people in a class society are subordinated, they have a degree of 'semiotic power' in the former economy (the cultural one) — that is, the power to shape meanings to their own desires.

Links to postmodernism

This general line of thinking about popular culture is relatively close to ideas found in postmodernism theory about culture generally (see page 27). Many features of (commercial) popular media culture reflect postmodernist elements. Music video on television was hailed as the first postmodern television service (Lewis, 1992). Old ideas of quality of art and serious messages cannot be sustained, except by reference to authority, and are seen as inescapably 'bourgeois'. This is a potent set of ideas which goes much further than providing a defence for the once much maligned and patronized 'culture of the masses'. It is an entirely new representation of the situation which has turned some of the weapons of cultural critics against themselves (for instance, their claim to speak on behalf of the masses). It gains strength both from a real shift of social values and from a re-evaluation of popular culture and the probability that there has also been a real cultural revolution within the mass media, leading towards a new aesthetic. Television and popular music have become the dominant arts of the time and have shown enormous inventiveness and power to change.

Unanswered questions

Despite this, several charges of the kind made by Frankfurt School critics remain on the table. Much of the content offered by media that is both popular and commercially successful still looks to many critics as if it is, variously, repetitive, infantile, thematically limited, undisturbing, ideologically tendentious, empty, nasty, anti-intellectual and subordinating content to form and technique. Most popular culture is produced by large corporations with an overriding view to their own profits, rather than to enriching the cultural lives of the people, who are treated as consumer markets to be manipulated and managed. Popular formulas and products tend to be used until threadbare, then discarded when they cease to be profitable, whatever the audience might demand in the cultural economy.

It seems strange to social critics that critical theorists can celebrate cultural forms which are acknowledged to have a structured tendency to support an oppressive form of society. The new 'cultural populism' has produced its own backlash (McGuigan, 1992). Semiotic liberation has a very limited effect on material conditions. It may even seem very like the old idea of 'escape' in new clothing. One of the difficulties with the 'redemption' arguments is that they largely ignore the continuing semiotic inequality whereby a more educated and better-off minority has access both to popular culture *and* to 'unpopular' culture (such as classical music, great literature and modern and avant-garde art), while the majority are limited to popular forms alone and totally dependent on the commercial media market (Gripsrud, 1989). There is nothing in the redemption arguments presented which really addresses this point or indicates how this difference can be bridged. Nor is there anything which allows one to discriminate between cultural productions in terms of any intrinsic value.

There has always been a possibility (and an actuality) of culture which is both popular *and* 'on the side of' (or even genuinely *of*) the people, while most 'mainstream' (commercial) mass media culture does not seem to qualify (though some does). This idea at least offers one criterion of cultural value which might still be relevant and one which survives in normative and policy discourse about the mass media (see Chapter 5), as well in commonsense notions held by the general public (the audience) about what is of more or less cultural value, more or less time-wasting, more or less exploitative and propagandist (see page 310).

The idea of 'quality' of mass media cultural provision also remains on the agenda of applied media theory, although its meaning has shifted. Quality no longer refers exclusively to the degree of conformity to a traditional cultural canon, but may be defined in terms of creativity, originality, diversity of cultural identity and various ethical or moral principles (Schrøder, 1992), depending on whose perspective is chosen. It can certainly no longer be assumed that what has most appeal has less 'quality', but the material economic dynamic of cultural production cannot be so easily distinguished from the 'semiotic' cultural economy.

Commercialization

Embedded in the early critique of mass culture, and still alive at the fringes of the discussion (certainly in the context of media policy), is the notion of 'commercialism' (the condition) or 'commercialization' (the process). In some uses, this is a watered-down version of the Marxist critique and may verge on the 'bourgeois' (implying, for instance, a disdain for trade) and on the elitist (a disdain for the mass), but it expresses some ideas which are still relevant to current media industry dynamics and media-cultural change. Being watered down, it may more easily survive the decline or demise of the full-blooded Marxist critique of mass culture. It is closely related to the critique of commodification (see page 98). The critique of commercialism is particularly difficult to reconcile with the redemption of the popular, since popularity is usually a condition of commercial success.

While at one level the term 'commercialism' may refer objectively to particular free-market arrangements, it has also come to imply consequences for the type of media content which is mass-produced and 'marketed' as a commodity, and also consequences for the relations between the suppliers and the consumers of media. The term 'commercial', applied as an adjective to some types of media provision, identifies correlates of the competitive pursuit of large markets. Aside from an abundance of advertising matter (commercial propaganda), commercial content is likely, from this perspective, to be more oriented to amusement and entertainment (escapism), more superficial, undemanding and conformist, more derivative and standardized. These at least are features which are related to success in large market terms (although there are many differentiated markets).

This was the view of early radical critics of mass culture. It generally ignores the fact that essentially the same market arrangements can just as easily support the supply and consumption of greatly varied and high-quality cultural products. Closer to the core of the relevant critical notion is the view that commercial relationships in communication are intrinsically distancing and potentially exploitative. The commercial variant of a communicative relationship does not support the formation of ties of mutual attachment or lead to shared identity or community. It is calculative and utilitarian on both sides, reflecting essential features of the 'transmission' or 'publicity' rather than the 'ritual' model of communication in society (see page 50). The commercial environment of media production also provides a straitjacket which closes off many possibilities for innovation and creativity (Blumler, 1991, 1992).

Critique of media commercialization

- Low cultural quality
- Exploitation of 'weaker' consumers
- Alienative relationships
- Utilitarian and calculative relations
- Propaganda for consumerism
- Commodification of culture and of relations with the audience

---

Communication technology and culture

It has already been made clear that the historical innovations in communication technology, although undoubtedly often revolutionary in their implications, cannot really be traced as causes of specific shifts in the form of society (Slack, 1984). Innovations are always taken up and adapted according to some more compelling social imperative (Winston, 1986). There are too many other powerful forces involved in social change. (If proof were needed, the failure of mass media to 'modernize' large parts of the less developed world in the last fifty years is relevant evidence.) It is, however, more plausible to suppose that communication technology will have an effect on the process of communication itself and that culture and communication are intertwined. If our experience of the world is technologically mediated, then technology itself must have a direct relevance.

McLuhan's view of cultural change

McLuhan's (1964) advance on Innis (see page 85) was to look at the process by which we experience the world through different media of communication and not just at the relation between communication and social power structures. He proclaimed that all media (by which he meant anything which embodies cultural meaning and can be 'read' as such) are 'extensions of man', thus extensions of our senses. Like others, he drew attention to the implications of a shift from a purely *oral* communication to one based on a written language (by about 5000 BC). Much of cultural experience remained predominantly oral until comparatively recent times.

McLuhan also focused on *how* we experience the world, not on *what* we experience (thus not on the content). Each new medium transcends the boundaries for experience reached by earlier media and contributes to further change. McLuhan correctly saw different media working together, while perhaps less plausibly he predicted the attainment of a 'global village' in which information and experience would be freely available for all to share.

A general proposition was that as more of our senses are engaged in the process of taking meaning (as media become increasingly 'cool', or frictionless, as against single-sense or 'hot' media), the more involving and participant the experience is. According to this view, experiencing the world by reading printed text is isolating and non-involving (encouraging the rational, individual attitude). Television viewing is involving, although not very informing, and also conducive of a less rational and calculative attitude. No proof (or disproof) has ever been offered, and the ideas were described by McLuhan himself only as perceptions or 'probes'. As he wished, they stimulated much speculation in an era in which audiovisual media have seemed in many respects to take over from print media.

A model of technology and cultural change

Most other relevant theory of communication technology has focused on possible influences on the form or content of given media messages and thus on the meanings they make available. Even so, no technology–culture effect can be established, because the technologies themselves are also cultural artefacts, and there is no way of breaking into the circle. Such theory as we have is little more than description of observable patterns in the cultural meanings offered via mass media which may be influenced by various characteristics, not only technological, of a given medium. A general view of the process by which changing technology can influence media culture is given in Figure 4.1. Perhaps the most important point which it illustrates is that technologies are unlikely to have a direct impact on cultural

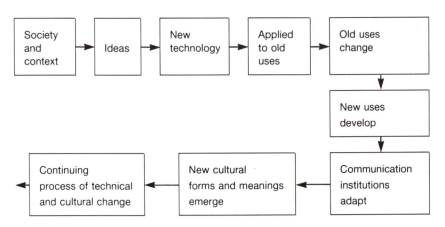

Figure 4.1 *Interactive sequence of communication and technological and cultural change: technologies arise from society and have effects on society depending on the form of application developed*

practices, but only as mediated through a relevant institution (in this case, the mass media).

Media logic and the bias of communication

Further to the question of technological determinism, a concept which has proved useful is that of 'media logic', developed by Altheide and Snow (1979) to refer to the influence of media (considered both as cultured technology and formal organization) on 'real world' events themselves, as well as on their portrayal and constitution. More recently, Altheide and Snow (1991) have described media logic as 'a way of seeing and interpreting social affairs. . . . Elements of this form (of communication) include the various media and the formats used by these media. Formats consist, in part, in how material is organized, the style in which it is presented, the focus or emphasis . . . and the grammar of media communication' (p. 10).

Because of the increased centrality of mass media for other institutions, there is a also growing need for public people and events relating to public (and commercial) life to require high and appropriate media visibility if they are to have their full effect (the requirement of appearing frequently in the symbolic, ritual sphere and being salient in public opinon, esteem and recognition — the publicity model at work). There is an imperative to conduct affairs and stage events in ways which conform to the needs and routines of the mass media (in respect of timing and form). The idea of a staged 'media event' belongs to the theory of media logic (Boorstin, 1961; Katz and Dayan, 1986). It has an obvious relevance to predominant modes of news coverage, in which familiar formats and routines predictably frame certain categories of event (Altheide, 1985). The general notion of media logic extends to include the influence of media requirements on a wide range of cultural happenings, including sport, entertainment and public ceremonies. There are also many examples of new kinds of format which the media have made part of everyday cultural experience (such as radio phone-ins, television talk-shows, music video films, advertising spots and never-ending serials).

In trying to account for technological influence on (media) culture, we may extend the notion of 'bias' introduced by Innis and recognize several tendencies which follow from the characteristics of a particular media technology (and its institutional development). We can name five types of media bias as follows, without exhausting the possibilities. There is a bias of **sense experience**, following McLuhan, so that we may experience the world in more or less visual imagery (see Hartley, 1992) or in more or less of an involving and participant way. Secondly, there is a bias of **form** and representation, with 'messages' strongly coded (as in print) or essentially uncoded, as in photographs (Barthes, 1967). Thirdly, there is the bias of message **content** — for instance, in terms of more or less realism or polysemy, more open or closed formats (other dimensions are possible).

Fourthly, there is a bias of **context of use**, with some media lending themselves to private and individualized reception, others being more collective and shared. Fifthly, there is a bias of **relationship**, contrasting one-way with interactive media. Bias does not mean determinism, but it contains a prediction towards certain kinds of experience and ways of mediation. Ellis's (1982) comparison of broadcast television with cinema film is an instructive example of how the (unintended) bias of a medium can work in subtle but systematic and multiple ways, affecting content and probable ways of perception and reception.

Five types of media technology bias

- Of sense experience
- Of content
- Of form
- Of context of use
- Of sender–receiver relationships

Cultivation and the mediation of identity

The rise of television and its enormous appeal were the source of much theorizing about the consequences for social experience. A recurring theme has been the degree to which most of our experience is literally mediated through the words and images of the dominant medium of our time. Giddens (1991) has emphasized this as one of the key features of 'high modernity'. He writes:

> In high modernity, the influence of distant happenings on proximate events, and even on the intimacies of the self, becomes more and more commonplace. The media, printed and electronic, obviously play a central role in this respect. Mediated experience, since the first experience of writing, has long influenced both self-identity and the basic organization of social relations ... With the development of mass communications, the interpenetration of self-development and social systems ... becomes ever more pronounced. (1991, pp. 4–5)

Earlier, Gerbner (1967) had identified the significance of mass communication, in terms not of the concept of 'masses', but of the transformation of society brought about by the 'extension of institutionalized public acculturation beyond the limits of face to face and any other personally mediated interaction'. He writes of 'publication' (the main action of mass media) as a transformation of private systems of knowing into public systems — creating new bases of collective thought. McLuhan (1964) wrote similarly of the 'retribalizing' effects of television. Implied in this is the view that identities are drawn from the systematic and widely shared messages of the mass media.

According to Gerbner and colleagues, television is responsible for a major 'cultivating' and 'acculturating' process, according to which people are exposed systematically to a selective view of society on almost every aspect of life, a view which tends to shape their beliefs and values accordingly. The environment is so monopolized by television that its lessons are continually learned and relearned. In a more critical vein, C.W. Mills had earlier drawn a similar lesson. He wrote: 'Between consciousness and existence stand communications which influence such consciousness as men have of their existence' (1951, p. 333). Subsequently (1956), he expounded on the almost total dependency of individuals on the media for their sense of identity and aspirations. This transformation brings publics into being.

The shifting boundaries of social space

A more recent theory of mass media and social change which owes something to McLuhan (with help from Goffman) also attributes great cultural influence to television. Meyrowitz's (1985) thesis is that the all-pervasiveness of electronic media has fundamentally changed social experience by breaking down the compartmentalization between social spaces which was typical of earlier times. Human experience, in his view, has traditionally been segmented by role and social situation and sharply divided between private ('backstage') and public ('onstage') domains. Segmentation was by age, gender and social status, and the 'walls' between zones of experience were high. Television appears to put all aspects of social experience on show to all, without distinction. There are no longer any secrets — for instance, about adulthood, sex, death or power.

Older bases for identification and for authority are weakened or blurred, sometimes to be replaced by new group identities (such as for women, for homosexuals, and in radical movements) made possible by mediated experience and by the overcoming of limits of space (social and physical). Everyone tends to move in the same information environment, but the result is a culture without any distinct sense of socially or physically bounded place. The theory tends to explain rather too much of what has seemed to happen to (North American) society in modern times, and it cannot be tested, except mentally, but it sheds some extra light on the meaning of the 'mediation of experience'.

Globalization of culture

Structural trends towards transnationalization

One of the few effects of new communication technology on which there is wide agreement is the trend towards internationalization of mass communication. The question of potential cultural effects flowing from this trend has been much debated. The movement towards a global media culture has several sources, most notably the greatly increased capacity to transmit sounds and (moving) images at low cost across frontiers and around the world, overcoming limits of time and space, and the rise of global media businesses (and global markets for media products), which provides the organizational framework and driving force for globalization. Neither of these conditions has arrived suddenly, nor is the idea of transnational culture itself novel (it long predates the very idea of the national), but what may be new is the increased transcultural communicative potential of pictures and music. The relevant changes in the structure of media industries and global media flow, especially in relation to television, have been extensively studied (for example, Varis, 1974, 1984; Tunstall, 1977; Mowlana, 1985; Sepstrup, 1989; Wallis and Baran, 1990; Negus, 1993). However, the cultural consequences are much less open to observation and have led to much speculation and more sound than light.

The process of cultural 'transnationalization' which is assumed to be taking place has a variety of meanings, aside from the observable trend towards interconnected infrastructures for reception and towards multi-national ownership and operation. It refers both to the dissemination of certain broad *kinds* of media cultural content and also to some potential effects on a receiving culture. The typical content of transnational media channels will have been chosen expressly with a view to international transmission, even if it is originally designed primarily for a domestic market. This will usually imply a downgrading of cultural specificity in themes and settings and a preference for formats and genres which are thought to be more universal. Because of the influence of the United States in audiovisual and music production, transnational content is sometimes considered as culturally North American or 'mid-Atlantic' in character. The general direction of effect is assumed to be towards displacing the original culture of receiving countries and/or causing it to imitate the international model.

Transnational media flow as a process

Sepstrup (1989) has warned against drawing conclusions about cultural **effects** from the different character of the product transmitted and consumed. He points to the distinction between 'international' media content as sent, content as actually received and actual consequences for the receiving culture. The step from the first to the third is a long one. Even the first aspect is more complex than it seems, since international content can be transmitted in different ways: multilaterally, as when there is no specific direction and the same content is received in many different countries (as with much film, video and music); bilaterally, as when content flows across frontiers to a neighbouring country (such as from the USA to Canada, or from France to Belgium), or to a former colony (such as from Britain to

Nigeria); and nationally, as when the domestic supply contains a proportion of imported material (as with most television systems world-wide). These distinctions may matter considerably for the type and degree of transnational flow that occurs and for its consequences. Some aspects of transnationalization are not easy to observe, especially the widespread adoption of, or adaptation to, foreign cultural models in domestic media production. This accelerates global homogenization, although it is also a normal aspect of cultural change.

The process of global flow (or exchange) is shaped and modified by many factors. Differences or affinities of language and culture between partners to any exchange can either discourage or encourage flow. The media production capacity and relative wealth of national media systems are also relevant, since smaller, poorer countries are more vulnerable to foreign media reception, and vice versa. In other words, there are still many different barriers to the transnationalization of media culture, some of them deliberately erected by national cultural policy. But in general the terms of flow and exchange are far from fair or balanced. The process can also vary from one medium to another, some media being more or less immune to transborder effects.

Globalizing effects: pro and con

Theorizing about the cultural impact of transnational flow has been shaped by different value perspectives, and there are different issues involved. Commentators have broadly divided into critics and celebrators of ongoing trends (see Ferguson, 1992). The positive view of transnationalization has taken several forms, beginning with the notion (see page 84) that mass communication could be the primary 'mobility multiplier' to spread modern ways and democracy. Global communication may seem to exend the shared symbolic space, helping to liberate people from the constraints of place and time — thus extending 'semiotic power'. It may be regarded as potentially culturally enriching. It can be viewed positively compared with the possible ethnocentricism, nationalism and even xenophobia of restricted national systems. More recently, international communication has been celebrated (gaining strength from a 'globalist' variant of 'videotopia') as the potential basis for a new world order of international peace and understanding, in the wake of the proclaimed end of the Cold War.

For critics, the earliest doubts about media-cultural internationalization probably stemmed from its being framed in terms of worldwide US imperialism (Schiller, 1969). During the 1970s an influential movement of resistance developed on behalf of developing countries in their struggle to retain their cultural integrity and political autonomy, said to be threatened by Western media-cultural imperialism (Boyd-Barrett, 1977, 1982). The term 'cultural imperialism' implies invasion and an element of coercion, although the latter was largely confined to the pressures of a market system whose terms favoured the dominant suppliers of media culture. In this debate, the interests of the poorer 'South' were posed against those of the developed 'North' in media matters.

Concepts of cultural identity

A new issue has been added by the concern with a European cultural identity (in the context of European political and economic unification) (Schlesinger, 1987). It has been suggested that European culture (and different national cultures within Europe) might be undermined by transnational (especially North American) cultural importation (Thomsen, 1989). On the other hand, cultural transnationalization *within the boundaries of Europe* would support the unification project, helping to create a more distinctive and homogeneous European culture. The framing of the issue and the motivations (in part economic and political) behind it are not so very different in essence from the case of North–South cultural flow just described. Cultural relations between Canada and the USA have also long been treated in similar terms.

Within Europe, the relations of inequality or dependency which exist between the different nations have given rise to a further dimension of the debate — an issue highlighted by the ending of the division between Eastern and Western Europe, since there are now sharper divisions between the haves and have-nots in the material resources needed to support cultural identities. The situation is further complicated by the fact that a more international media culture is also likely to be a more *commercialized* culture, often meaning less control by national cultural policies (see below). The accelerating trend to more commercialism in Europe is also seen by many to work against both national and European cultural identity.

Underlying the above issues is a strong 'belief system' holding that cultures are both valuable collective properties of nations and places and also very vulnerable to alien influences. The value attributed to a national culture is rooted in ideas developed during the nineteenth and twentieth centuries, when national independence movements were often intimately connected with the rediscovery of distinctive national cultural traditions (for example, in Greece, Ireland and Finland). The frequent lack of correlation between newly established national boundaries (often invented) and 'natural' cultural divisions of peoples has done little to modify the rhetoric about the intrinsic value of national culture. 'National identity' is thus a different and more questionable concept than cultural identity in general, and the notion of a 'European cultural identity' is even weaker and even more an 'imagined community' — the term applied by Anderson (1983) to the idea of nation, since it is promoted for political reasons.

The notion of an imperilled cultural identity as a result of 'cultural imperialism' was first developed to apply to the more or less traditional societies of the developing world. This fear appears more justified than in the case of Europe versus the USA, but cultural imperialism in any case turns out to be a somewhat insubstantial concept when subjected to close analysis. This is not just because of the enormous cultural diversity and varying vulnerability of what we call the 'Third World', but also because of the mixture of different discourses embedded in the concept. According to Tomlinson (1991), 'cultural imperialism' refers to several different things almost interchangeably: a ccmmunication flow imbalance; a threat to national identity; a consumer/capitalist assault on older ways; and the growth of 'modernity' and its challenge to traditional culture.

In view of this degree of conceptual confusion, it is not surprising that the question of the cultural *impact* of the international flow remains unsettled. Schlesinger (1987) recommends starting at the other end, with a clearer idea of what cultural identity means, before trying to assess the effect of mass media on it, although he is sceptical about the whole business, at least in the European context. He suggests an approach by way of a general concept of 'collective identity'. A collective identity, in this sense, persists in *time* and is resistant to change, although survival also requires that it be consciously expressed, reinforced and transmitted. For this reason, having access to and support from relevant communications media is evidently important. The concept could well apply to what are called cultural identities in the debate about transnationalization, since there is assumed to be a set of people sharing some significant cultural features of ethnicity, language, way of life, etc., and also sharing the same place and time.

However, while it is useful for some purposes (such as determining if a cultural identity exists or not), this conceptualization may be too *strong* for the problem at issue (media transnationalization). Most of the collective identities which qualify according to this concept are enduring, have deep roots and are resistant to the relatively superficial 'impact' of, for example, watching or listening to foreign (especially Anglo-American) media. They depend on shared histories, religion and language. The media are more likely to have an influence, for good or ill, on cultural identities of a more voluntary, transient and also multiple (overlapping) kind.

These may be collectively held but are based on taste, lifestyle and other transient features. These are more like *subcultural* identities, which are not necessarily *exclusive* and whose growth may even be stimulated and helped by (international) media.

Cultural invasion: resistance and subversion

From this perspective, the media may appear even to help in the process of cultural growth, diffusion, invention and creativity, and are not just undermining existing 'culture'.

Much modern theory and evidence supports the view that media-cultural 'invasion' can sometimes be *resisted* or redefined according to local culture and experience. Often the 'internationalization' involved is self-chosen and not the result of imperialism (in Western Europe, for instance). Lull and Wallis (1992) use the term 'transculturation' to describe a process of 'mediated cultural interaction' in which Vietnamese music was crossed with North American strains to produce a new cultural hybrid. There are likely to be many examples of a similar process. Secondly, alternative 'readings' of the same 'alien' content are, as we have seen, quite possible. 'Semiotic power' can also be exercised in this context, and media content can be decoded differentially according to the culture of receivers (Liebes and Katz, 1986). This is probably too optimistic a view to bear much weight, and the evidence is not yet very strong. Foreign cultural content may also be received with a different, more distant attitude (Biltereyst, 1992) than home-made media culture.

The 'problem' of potential cultural damage from transnationalized media may well be exaggerated (in Europe at least). In the case of Europe, most cultural imports are from cultures with historic affinity to European culture, and the media do relatively little to diffuse the really different cultures (of Asia, Islam, etc.). Many distinct national (and sub-national) cultures within Europe are still strong and resistant. Audiences can probably tolerate several different and inconsistent worlds of cultural experiences (such as local, national, sub-group and global), without the one having to destroy the other. The media can extend cultural choices in a creative way, and internationali-zation can work creatively. Cultural 'invasion' of Third World cultures is different because it is accompanied by other material changes and occurs in situations of dependence and less free choice. Many parts of the Third World, even so, have still not yet been reached very significantly by the international media 'invasion'; large parts of Asia can and do look after themselves, or are protected by cultural distinctiveness.

This debate reflects the two contradictory trends at work, globally as well as nationally — one (centripetal) towards cohesion, the other (centrifugal) towards fragmentation (see page 71). The media can promote both, and which effect is stronger depends on the particular context and circum-stances. Strong cultural identities will survive and weaker ones give way. A weak cultural identity such as that of 'Europe' is not likely to be much affected one way or another by current levels of 'Americanization', though, if it is to get any stronger, it may need media recognition and policy support. This is to suggest that media may be a necessary, but are unlikely to be a sufficient, condition for cultural resistance or submission. This relativizing of the problem does not abolish it and there are circumstances under which cultural loss does occur.

Towards a global media culture?

One cultural consequence of media globalization may be overlooked because it is obvious — the rise of a globalized media culture as such. Media internationalization probably does lead to more homogenization or 'cultural synchronization'. According to Hamelink (1983, p. 22), this process 'implies that the decisions regarding the cultural development of a given country are made in accordance with the interests and needs of a powerful central nation and imposed with subtle but devastating effectiveness without regard for the adaptive necessities of the dependent nation'. As a result, cultures are less distinctive and cohesive and also less exclusive.

Another commentator observes that we increasingly encounter a form of culture which is

> tied to no place or period. It is contextless, a true melange of disparate components drawn from everywhere and nowhere, borne upon the chariots of the global telecommunications system. . . . There is something equally timeless about the concept of a global culture. Widely diffused in space, a global culture is cut off from any past . . . it has no history. (Smith, 1990, p. 177)

Some of these points can be seen to connect with the characterization of a postmodern culture, of which McLuhan has been hailed as precursor (Docherty, 1993). Postmodern culture is also detached from any fixed time and place, and has no moral standpoint or even meaning, except to be destructive of meaning and anti-Utopian (Harvey, 1989). Not by chance, the international media are given some credit (or blame) for promoting this type of culture, and, in turn, the preferred style of media culture may sometimes be described as postmodernistic.

While such a global media culture may appear value free, in fact it embodies a good many of the values of Western capitalism, including individualism and consumerism, hedonism and commercialism. It may add to the cultural options and open horizons for some, but it may also challenge and invade the cultural space of pre-existing local, indigenous, traditional and minority cultures.

Conclusion: time, space and the media

In conclusion, we can map out the relations between media and cultural identity in terms of two main dimensions, **time** and **space** (Figure 4.2). Time is chosen because endurance can be considered a central aspect of all cultures and degree of endurance the test of salience and significance. The most enduring identities are those based on language, religion, nationhood, etc., the most ephemeral those based on taste, fashion and style. In this context, the capacity of media to extend in space is also the most relevant criterion of globalizing tendencies. Media channels and content can range from the very local (and nearest to home) to the most global, carrying geographically and culturally remote messages.

In the space so mapped out by plotting one dimension against another there are many possibilities of different, but not necessarily inconsistent, relations between media and identity. Different types of media can have

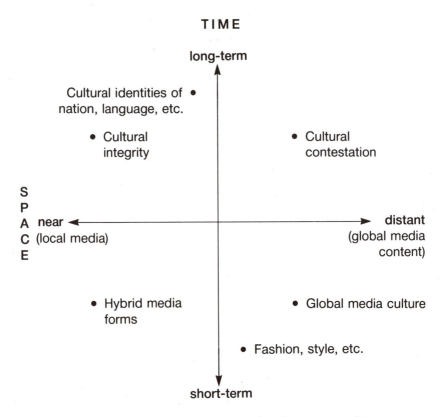

Figure 4.2 *Media and cultural identity: the dimensions of time and space between them locate the main variants and conditions of the relationship*

different types of impact on the decay, endurance or flourishing of cultural identity and experience. In general, local, ethnic and more personal media help to support enduring identities and cultural autonomy, while international media content has more impact on superficial and short-term cultural phenomena, such as fashion, style and taste. There is no longer a single dominant media technology, so that different media can compensate for (or reinforce) each other's cultural influence. Actual effects cannot be predicted and will depend on circumstances of case, time and place.

PART II
STRUCTURES

5

NORMATIVE THEORIES OF MEDIA PERFORMANCE

Media–society linkages

The links between mass media and society have already been approached in several different ways. The media are both a product and also a reflection of the history of their own society and have played a part in it. Despite the similarities of mass media institutions across societies, the media are by origin, practice and convention very much *national* institutions and respond to domestic political and social pressures and to the expectations of their audiences. They reflect, express and sometimes actively serve the 'national interest', as determined by other, more powerful actors and institutions.

Here we turn to another way in which the idea of linkage is very clearly expressed and to another kind of theory, one already referred to as 'normative theory'. This deals with ideas of how media *ought* to, or are *expected* to, operate. While each national society is likely to have its own more or less distinctive and differentiated version of normative media theory, we can also identify some general principles of 'media performance' which apply to modern mass communication often across different national systems, as discussed in Chapter 6. Normative theory relates to what is desirable in relation to both structure and performance.

Structure concerns such matters as freedom from the state or the multiplicity of independent channels, while **performance** refers to the manner in which the media carry out their chosen (or allotted) informative or entertaining tasks. There are also many conventions, professional guidelines and ethical rules which apply to what the media do, in terms of which they may be held accountable. Sometimes these have more to do with personal *conduct* within media organizations than with either the structure or the general performance of the media in public life.

Media may be subject to extensive forms of legal or administrative control, protection or regulation, which often have a normative character (or justification). Because of the complexity and fragmentation of most national media arrangements, no actual media 'system' is likely to be governed by any one 'pure' or consistent body of normative theory, nor does practice always follow very closely what the norms seem to call for. Most systems reflect the working of different (even inconsistent) sets of normative expectations.

In recent decades (mainly since the Second World War), the mass media, newly grown to maturity, have developed features which have been considered problematic for the rest of society and have stimulated guidance or policy-making from governments or even supra-national bodies. Examples of problems which have provoked a re-examination of normative principles or proposals for reform include: the concentration of press or other media ownership, threatening the diversity and independence of information and opinion; the rise of a section of the media devoted to sensation and scandal; an increase in transnational and multi-media operations which may weaken national cultural integrity or even political sovereignty; the rise of television as a social force, by-passing or supplanting other agencies of socialization and control and believed to be exceptionally influential; and the rise of computer-based new media with implications for freedom and privacy.

The response to perceived problems or challenges has taken a wide variety of forms, ranging from the commissioning of social research to enacting new laws. The possible social purposes of media and the standards against which they should be judged have been continuously debated. All this effort has contributed to a process of reformulating social theory about the position of media in society.

The status of normative theory

Normative media theory still has a rather uncertain and contested position within the field of 'communication science', partly because it leads inevitably into questions of ideology, politics, law or ethics, which are not easy to deal with in a 'scientific' way, according to the 'dominant paradigm'. There has been a tendency to take the media institution and its way of working as an empirical given and proceed from there, leaving normative or ethical matters to other specialists. In this way, the stance of value neutrality is best upheld. A 'liberal' bias in the Anglo-American tradition which has been very influential in defining the field of study of mass media has also tended to delegitimate most principles of would-be media social theory aside from that of freedom of communication. This is often defined as lack of legal, government or public interference in the media business — essentially the principle enshrined in the First Amendment to the US Constitution (see, for example, Lichtenberg, 1990). The libertarian view is that media social theory and media policy are both inconsistent with media freedom defined in this way.

Normative issues are often dealt with descriptively under such headings as 'communication policy', 'media law' or 'professional ethics', which allow some distancing from value judgements. Most of what passes for 'mass communication theory' seems to exist in a wider theoretical and normative vacuum, socially and historically decontextualized, aside from largely unacknowledged assumptions about the naturalness of liberal-pluralist arrangements in a capitalist economy. This state of affairs is unsatisfactory at a time of considerable change and reconstruction of media institutions, when normative questions need to be faced. This chapter is mainly concerned with the expectations from 'society' (the organized political community) relating to media structure and performance.

Varieties of theory for the press and other media: social responsibility

Origins

The main origins of such theory as we have for public communication (defined by Ferguson, 1990, p. ix, as 'those processes of information and cultural exchange between media institutions, products and publics which are socially shared, widely available and communal in character') lie in the role frequently attributed to the newspaper press in the rise of 'modern' society (capitalist, industrialized, ruled by democratically elected governments). From the seventeenth century onwards, in Europe and its colonies, the newspaper (or similar print publications) was widely seen as either a tool for political liberation and social/economic progress, or a legitimate means of opposition to established orders of power (often both at the same time). This perception of the part played by the press in society has understandably left an enduring stamp on questions of the rights and duties of the press itself and on the attitude of civil authorities to the press.

While the press in most places most of the time was engaged in activities other than advancing and protecting the liberty of citizens, the primacy allotted to its liberating role (and its claims to freedom), especially in the Anglo-American tradition and under the influence of the press itself, obscured as well as downgraded ideas about its many other tasks and effects in society. When modern communication science was being 'invented', about fifty years ago, the development of press theory was greatly influenced by various accidents of circumstance and history.

The 'commercialization' of the press, especially in Britain and the USA in the late nineteenth century, had been made possible by a greatly increased potential for mass production and distribution, financially aided by mass advertising. This development was, in turn, associated by critics of the press with sensationalism, scandal-mongering and declining informational standards. The growth of press empires, often with real or assumed right-wing political leanings, provided another dimension of critique. All around the pre-war world, in Germany, Japan and the Soviet Union, authoritarian regimes were also seen to be using the press and other media for purposes of political exploitation and control. The earlier optimistic and democratic visions conjured up by the spread of literacy and the potential abundance of information and culture were distinctly clouded.

The 1947 US Commission on the Freedom of the Press

The press was one of the institutions whose reconstruction (in Europe) after the Second World War owed a good deal to the Anglo-American liberal model. Significant in this process, at least in an intellectual history of it, was the outcome in the United States of the privately financed but publicly influential Commission on the Freedom of the Press (Hutchins, 1947). When it reported in 1947, the commission not only reaffirmed the principle of freedom but added to it the notion of **social responsibility**, which the press was called upon to accept, in recognition of its essential role in political and social life (Blanchard, 1977). The report also specified the main standards which a responsible press should observe. This meant, first of all, providing a 'full, truthful, comprehensive and intelligent account of the day's events in a context which gives them meaning'. Secondly, the press should serve as a 'forum for the exchange of comment and criticism' and be 'common carriers of the public expression'. Thirdly, the press should give a 'representative picture of constituent groups in society' and also present and clarify the 'goals and values of society'.

The report criticized 'sensationalism' and the mixing of news with editorial opinion. In general, the report supported the concept of an unbiased, informative and independent press institution, which would avoid causing offence to minorities or encouraging crime, violence and civil disorder. Social responsibility should be reached by self-control, not government intervention, although in the last resort even that might be justifiable. The message about desirable performance was not far out of line with leading professional and editorial aspirations within the US press of the kind that were already incorporated in codes of ethics and editorial prospectuses. The influence of the report may have been more on press theory than on practice.

Social responsibility theory

- The media have obligations to society, and media ownership is a public trust
- News media should be truthful, accurate, fair, objective and relevant
- The media should provide a forum for ideas
- The media should be free but self-regulated
- Media should follow agreed codes of ethics and professional standards
- Under some circumstances, society may need to intervene in the public interest

---

Social responsibility theory involved the view that media ownership and operation are a form of public trust or stewardship, rather than an unlimited private franchise. For the privately owned media, social responsibility theory has been expressed and applied mainly in the form of codes of professional journalistic standards, ethics and conduct or in various kinds of council or tribunal for dealing with individual complaints against the press, or by way of public commissions of inquiry into particular media. Most such councils have been organized by the press media themselves, a key feature of the theory being its emphasis on self-regulation.

Media codes of conduct

There are many different codes of ethical conduct, depending on the conventions and traditions of the country concerned and on who formulates the code — whether it is publishers, editors, journalists or an external regulatory body. Most codes concentrate on matters to do with the provision of reliable information and on avoiding distortion, suppression, bias, sensationalism and the invasion of privacy, but some codes go further. Journalistic codes may try to protect the independence of journalists from undue pressure from publishers or advertisers and often also call for protection of the confidentiality of sources (Harris, 1992).

Codes of practice drawn up by publishers and editors have usually emphasized the need for freedom to publish and independence from vested interests. An example of a comprehensive code, which also has an international reference, is the International Principles of Professional Ethics in Journalism, drawn up under the auspices of UNESCO (Traber and Nordenstreng, 1993). Unlike most industry codes, it does not use the word 'freedom', but refers frequently to rights and responsibilities. There are ten clauses, headed and summarized as follows:

I.   People's Right to True Information. This is formulated to include the right of people to express themselves freely through the media of communication.
II. The Journalist's Dedication to Objective Reality. This aims to provide the public with 'adequate material to facilitate the formation of an accurate and comprehensive picture of the world'.
III. The Journalist's Social Responsibility. This emphasizes the fact that journalistic information is a social good, not just a commodity.
IV. The Journalist's Professional Integrity. This deals especially with rights not to work against personal conviction and other matters of personal ethics.
V.   Public Access and Participation. This includes the right of rectification and reply.
VI. Respect for Privacy and Human Dignity.
VII. Respect for the Public Interest. This relates to respect for the 'national community, its democratic institutions and public morals'.
VIII. Respect for Universal Values and Diversity of Cultures. Calls for respect for human rights, social progress, national liberation, peace, democracy.
IX. Elimination of War and Other Great Evils Confronting Humanity. Calls for abstention from justifying aggression, arms proliferation, violence, hatred, discrimination.
X.   Promotion of a New World Information and Communication Order. This is directed especially at the need for decolonization and democratization of information and communications.

It is clear that attempts to codify press responsibility cannot overcome the fundamental differences of perspective and interests between the various participants in the media institution and between the different social and political systems in the world. Nor, in practice, has it proved easy to reach effective self-regulation. Despite the variety of formulation and wide range of application, most codes of media ethics focus on a limited number of principles for good professional conduct in relation to news journalism.

Journalistic ethics

- Truth and accuracy
- Impartiality and fairness
- Respect for individual privacy
- Independence from vested interests
- Responsibility to society and the public good
- Respect for law
- Moral decency and good taste

The public broadcasting idea

A different variety of social responsibility theory has been applied by the many and varied institutional arrangements for licensing or monitoring the activities of broadcasting, according to some notion of a 'public interest'. The nature of public expectations from broadcasting has varied considerably, from the minimal or voluntary to the detailed and obligatory (as in many European public broadcasting systems). An example of limited obligations is those which are applied by the US Federal Communications Commission (FCC) in allocating and supervising broadcasting licences. These regulations are now very weak but originally called for broadcasters to serve the public interest, especially by providing locally relevant information, balance or fairness on controversial and political issues, and diversity of programmes and services (Krugman and Reid, 1980). In general, the FCC was supposed to protect the right of the public to be informed by way of broadcasting. The safeguarding of children, public decency and maintaining order were generally left to be dealt with by voluntary codes of practice.

There has never been a generally accepted version of the theory of 'public service broadcasting' (as it is widely referred to in Europe), and the diversity of forms is now greater than ever before. A government-appointed committee in Britain (Peacock, 1986) endorsed a view of the 'public service idea' as involving eight principles: geographical universality of provision and reception; the aim of providing for all tastes and interests; catering for minorities; having a concern for national identity and community; keeping broadcasting independent from government and vested interests; having some element of direct funding by the public (thus not only from advertisers); encouraging competition in programmes and not just for audiences; and encouraging the freedom of broadcasters. There are many variations according to national priorities and traditions (see Blumler, 1992), but the general notion is one which tries, 'in the public interest', to advance 'quality' of service (variously defined) and which usually deploys some notion of diversity and also of a national political or cultural interest. The meaning of some of the principles and concepts of the public service idea is developed later in this chapter, especially in relation to independence, diversity and cultural quality.

The public service idea

- Universal service
- Diversity
- Editorial independence
- Social responsibility and accountability
- Cultural quality and identity
- Public financing and/or non-profit operation

Four Theories of the Press

The 1947 US Commission on the Freedom of the Press did more than lay the foundation for social responsibility theory. It also stimulated a sequence of attempts to describe the varieties of normative media theory, starting with the work of Frederick Siebert and colleagues (1956) in a book entitled *Four Theories of the Press*. They suggested that media systems around the world could be classified according to four main types of theory. One was that of a socially responsible press, as just described. Of the other three, the first was labelled authoritarian theory and emphasized the subordination of the press to state control, as in the monarchic system from which early North American colonists had tried to escape, or as in contemporary totalitarian (and some developing country) regimes. The last of the four was Soviet theory.

Authoritarian theory can justify advance censorship and punishment for deviation from rules laid down by political authorities. Aside from historic examples, the theory was likely to be observed in dictatorial regimes, under conditions of military rule or foreign occupation and even during states of extreme emergency in democratic societies. Authoritarian principles may even express the popular will under some conditions (such as in a nation at war or in response to terrorism). The application of authoritarian theory is generally designed to protect the established social order and its agents, setting clear and close limits to media freedom.

Soviet theory, which held an influential position in the post-war era and could not be ignored, assigned the media a role as collective agitator, propagandist and educator in the building of communism. The principles of the theory were established by Lenin after the 1917 Revolution (see Hopkins, 1970) and the theory was extended in essentials to most of Eastern Europe after the Second World War. The main principle was the subordination of the media to the Communist Party — the only legitimate voice and agent of the working class. Not surprisingly, the theory did not favour free expression, but it did propose a positive role for the media in society and in the world, with a strong emphasis on culture and information and on the task of economic and social development.

In many respects Soviet theory was authoritarian in the way it was exercised, but it could claim a popular legitimation as long as the political theory of communism could also be maintained. The media were expected to be responsible and serious and to reflect the diversity of social structure and culture. The results did not always compare badly with the performance of free-market media, but the theory had no appeal to free societies and has been largely abandoned in its homeland since the fall of communism.

Libertarian theory and press freedom

The libertarian ideal

The second of the Four Theories (in historical succession to authoritarianism) was labelled **libertarian**, drawing on the ideas of classical liberalism and referring to the idea that the press should be a 'free marketplace of ideas' in which the best would be recognized and the worst fail. In one respect it is a simple extension to the (newspaper) press of the fundamental individual rights to freedom of opinion, speech, religion and assembly. Libertarian theory had its early (seventeenth-century) origins in the writing of Milton (*Areopagitica*) but was developed in the North American colonies and in the new nation of the United States. Philosophical support was found in the writings of John Stuart Mill, who argued, in *On Liberty*, that

> the peculiar evil of silencing the expression of an opinion is, that it is robbing the human race, posterity as well as the existing generation, those who dissent from the opinion, even more than those who hold it. If the opinion is right, they are deprived of the opportunity of exchanging error for truth; if wrong, they lose what is almost as great a benefit, the clearer perception and livelier impression of truth, produced by its collision with error.

A free press has thus been seen as an essential component of a free and rational society. The nearest approximation to truth will emerge from the competitive exposure of alternative viewpoints, and progress for society will depend on the choice of 'right' over 'wrong' solutions. Political theories of the Enlightenment posited, in any case, a convergence between the good of society, the general welfare and the good of the individuals. The advantage of a free press is that it allows individuals free expression and enables 'society' to know what its members aspire to. Truth, welfare and freedom must go together, and control of the press can only lead ultimately to irrationality or repression, even if it may seem justifiable in the short term.

Questions about press freedom

Libertarian theory would seem to need no elaboration beyond a simple statement such as is contained in the First Amendment to the US Constitution, to the effect that 'Congress shall make no law . . . abridging the freedom of speech or of the press.' It is thus simply an absolute right of the citizen. In practice the application of press freedom has been far from straightforward. The question of whether it is an end in itself, a means to an end or an absolute right has never been settled, and there are those, from the time of Milton to the present, who have argued that if freedom is abused to the extent of threatening good morals and the authority of the state, it must be restrained. Even an American libertarian, de Sola Pool (1973), wrote that 'No nation will indefinitely tolerate a freedom of the press that serves to divide the country and to open the floodgates of criticism against the freely chosen government that leads it.' Libertarian theory finds it difficult to cope with extreme situations of war and revolution, when the overthrow of the state can be interpreted as the end of liberty.

For the most part, in societies which have recognized press freedom, the solution has been to free the press from advance censorship but to leave it answerable to the law for any consequences of its activities that infringe other individual rights or the legitimate claims of society. The protection (of their reputation, property, privacy and moral development) of individuals, of groups and minorities and the security or even dignity of the state have at times taken precedence over the absolute value of freedom to publish.

Freedom of expression and freedom of property

Much difficulty has also arisen over the institutional forms in which press freedom has been embodied. In many contexts, press freedom has become identified with property rights and has been taken to mean the right to own and use means of publication without restraint or interference from government. Freedom to publish is, accordingly, seen as a property right that will safeguard as much diversity as exists and is expressed by free consumers bringing their demands to the marketplace. Not only have monopoly tendencies in press and other media made this a very doubtful proposition, but the extent of external financial interests in the press seems to many as potent a source of constraint on liberty of expression as does any governmental action. Moreover, under modern conditions, the notion that private ownership guarantees to the individual a realistic possibility as well as the right of publishing looks absurd. The pure theory of press freedom presupposes that some tangible benefits of liberty will actually be delivered.

The dilemma has been expressed (for example, in Glasser, 1986) as a conflict between a 'negative' and a positive or 'affirmative' concept of press freedom. The first sees press freedom as simply absence of restraint; the second endows it with some purposes and benefits beyond those that accrue to owners of the press. Glasser writes:

> From the perspective of a negative conception of freedom, the press is under no obligation to extend its liberty or to accommodate the liberty of others. Press freedom and press responsibility, it follows, stand on opposite ends of a continuum; because responsibility ordinarily involves accountability, and because the essence of libertarianism is the denial of obligation, a 'responsible press' is regarded as a contradiction in terms. From the perspective of an affirmative understanding of the First Amendment, in contrast, freedom and responsibility stand side by side — distinct and yet inseparable . . . [and] an individual's ability to gain the benefits of liberty must be included among the conditions definitive of liberty. Further 'the tyranny of private transactions poses as much of a threat to individual liberty as the tyranny of government regulation'. (1986, p. 93)

Other problems and inconsistencies have arisen (see Lichtenberg, 1990; Curran, 1991; Keane, 1991). First, it is very unclear to what extent the theory can apply to broadcasting, which now accounts for a large part of media activity in many societies which remain attached to ideals of individual liberty. It is also unclear how far it applies to other important spheres of communication activity where freedom may be equally important — as in education, culture and the arts. Secondly, the theory seems designed to protect opinion and belief and has much less to say on 'information', especially in matters to do with access, privacy and publication, where personal or property interests are involved. Thirdly, the theory has been most frequently formulated to protect the owners of media and cannot give equal expression to the arguable rights of editors and journalists within the press, or to audiences, or to other potential beneficiaries, or victims, of free expression. Fourthly, the theory outlaws compulsory control but indicates no obvious way of handling the many pressures to which media are subject, especially, but not only, arising from market circumstances (Wintour, 1973; Shoemaker and Reese, 1991).

Having said all this, the notion of a free press is unsuppressable and provides a firm defence against censorship, licensing, political control and victimization of journalists for reporting unpopular opinions, telling the truth or refusing to tell lies. Indirectly, it may support the rights of the public to receive information and ideas and of the media to collect information necessary to their task. It also defends the right of the press to be 'irresponsible' — to show no respect for authority, privacy or decency, the possibility for which can be one small safeguard against conspiracies of the rich and powerful, whatever the more direct consequences.

Beyond 'theories of the press'

The Four Theories of the Press have often been invoked as a framework of discussion, sometimes modified by additions or subtractions. In the 1983 edition of this book I proposed two more — 'development' and 'democratic-participant' theories — to take account of other realities and other models.

Development media theory

Development theory was intended to recognize the fact that societies undergoing a transition from underdevelopment and colonialism to independence and better material conditions often lack the infrastructure, the money, the traditions, the professional skills and even the audiences needed to sustain media institutions comparable to those of the First World or Second World, in which the Four Theories could take root.

The media of many developing countries are subject to economic dependence, foreign domination and arbitrary authoritarianism. In so far as we can identify a media theory for development (see McBride et al., 1980; Altschull, 1984), it emphasizes the following goals: the primacy of the national development task (economic, social, cultural and political); the pursuit of cultural and informational autonomy; support for democracy; and solidarity with other developing countries. Because of the priority given to these ends, limited resources available for media can legitimately be allocated by government, and journalistic freedom can also be restricted. The responsibilities of the media are emphasized above their rights and freedoms.

Democratic-participant media theory

A 'democratic-participant' type of media theory was proposed in recognition of new media developments and of increasing criticism of the dominance of the main mass media by private or public monopolies (Enzensberger, 1970). From the 1960s onwards calls could be heard for alternative, grass-roots media, expressing the needs of citizens. The theory supports the right to relevant local information, the right to answer back and the right to use the new means of communication for interaction and social action in small-scale settings of community, interest group or subculture. Both theory and technology have challenged the necessity for and desirability of uniform, centralized, high-cost, commercialized, professionalized or state-controlled media. In their place should be encouraged multiple, small-scale, local, non-institutional, committed media which link senders to receivers and also favour horizontal patterns of interaction.

The practical expressions of the theory are many and varied, including the underground or alternative press, pirate radio, community cable television, 'samizdat' publication, micro-media in rural settings, neighbourhood media, wall posters, and media for women and ethnic minorities. The theory rejects the market as a suitable institutional form, as well as all 'top-down' professional provision and control. Participation and interaction are key concepts.

The term 'democratic-participant' expresses a sense of disillusionment with established political parties and with media systems, which are seen as having broken faith with the people. There is also an element of reaction against the 'mass society', which is over-organized and alienating. Free press theory is seen to fail because of its subversion by the forces of capitalism, while 'social responsibility' ends up as just another form of complicity with the bureaucratic state (Burgelman, 1986) or a mere self-serving by entrenched media professionals. Both freedom and self-regulation are seen to have failed.

Other models

Merrill (1974) argued that there were really only two fundamental kinds of theory of state–press relations, authoritarian and libertarian, although with gradations in between. Hachten (1981) added the concepts of 'revolution-ary', 'developmental' and 'Western' to two of the original four (authoritarian and Soviet). Altschull (1984) said there were basically three models: 'market', 'Marxist' and 'advancing', corresponding to the division into three 'worlds' — First, Second and Third. In his view, each kind of system, in different ways, ensured that media were responsive to their paymasters and each had somewhat different versions of what might constitute freedom and responsibility. More recently, Picard (1985) distinguished, within the category of 'Western' press models, a distinctive 'social democratic' version of press theory which, in contrast to 'social responsibility' and 'libertarian' (free-market) theory, provides legitimation for public intervention, or even for collective ownership, so as to ensure true independence from vested interests, access and diversity of opinion.

Limitations of the press theory approach

While most of the ideas discussed in these pages are still relevant to the general debate about the role of the media in society, the attempt to formulate consistent 'theories of the press' is nevertheless bound to break down. This is not just because of underlying differences of interest and political ideology which are present in any society. The frameworks offered have generally derived from a simple and outdated notion of 'the press' as providing (mainly political) news and information. They have failed to come to terms with the great diversity of mass media types and services and with changing technology and times.

There is, for instance, little of relevance in any of the variants of theory named which might realistically be applied to the cinema, to the music industry, to the video market or even to a good deal of sport, fiction and entertainment on television, thus to much of what the media are doing most of the time. It is unsatisfactory to leave all this entirely outside the scope of social-normative thinking. In fact, these are often the aspects of media performance that have been especially the subject of normative discourse, without much benefit of theory of any kind.

The four (or more, or less) 'theories' were also formulated in very general terms and did not describe or underlie any actual media system (except, perhaps, in the case of the Soviet model, which has largely been abandoned). Most national media institutions and practices and most relations between state and media display a mixture of several elements: libertarian, 'responsible' and authoritarian. The framework of theory was formulated largely from a North American perspective at one point in history, taking little note, for example, of the distinctive features of public service broadcasting as found in Western Europe. Despite their uncertain future, these institutions have contributed a great deal to notions of media responsibility and accountability. In most countries, in any case, the media do not constitute any single 'system', with a single purpose or philosophy, but are composed of many separate, overlapping, often inconsistent elements, with appropriate differences of normative expectation and actual regulation.

Media change: new normative theory needed for new times?

Apart from the relative decline of print media and the rise of electronic media, other changes are under way in the media landscape which undermine the validity of any unitary, holistic or even consistent framework of norms applying to a particular national 'media system'. The media are proliferating in their technical and institutional forms as much as in the volume of content produced and disseminated. This **abundance**, whatever its substance, defies any attempt to grapple with it in a comprehensive way. We can never do more than focus on a small part or sample of the reality of media practice. The more media channels there are, the less easy it is to judge what counts as an indispensable service and what the respective roles of different media in society might be.

An additional dimension of media proliferation has been the phenom- enon of **convergence** between media, referring to the fading of once clear boundaries between print-, broadcast- and telecommunication-based media which provided the basis for different kinds and degrees of public regulation (see page 172; also Pool, 1983). The original technological basis for the distinction is rapidly disappearing as electronic transmission becomes capable of delivering all forms of communication — print, voice, film, text, music. While this seems to open the way to more consistent policies and to a similarity of norms for performance across media, in practice this has not yet been the result, nor is it likely to occur as long as media vary greatly in their communicative functions. Some media forms and activities will, for instance, continue to claim more freedom to operate than others, on grounds of their political, artistic or scientific significance, while others will be subject to limitations for social or cultural reasons.

The media not only are proliferating but are becoming rapidly more **transnational** — in ownership, financing, organization, production, distribution, content, reception and even regulation. This trend reduces the distinctiveness of media experience in any country and makes the application of a normative framework to one particular *national* media system less relevant. There is, *de facto*, less sovereignty over media operations, and perceived problems and solutions extend over an area wider than the nation state. Internationalization also raises new normative issues or highlights older ones, especially matters to do with diversity, access and cultural 'integrity' and 'identity' (Tomlinson, 1991). The gap between issues of national and of international structure and performance has narrowed, since one overlaps with the other.

A related trend is that of growing **conglomeration** and the formation of large multi-media enterprises which not only cross national boundaries but also lead to vertical (between stages and factors in the production process) and horizontal (between different types of media and different types of business) concentration (Murdock, 1990). Worldwide conglomeration leads to fears of loss of creative independence and of cultural diversity. It may make it more difficult for a society to choose and implement a media policy of its own.

Often the trends described, which stem mainly from business and technology, have been accompanied by a loss of any clear national consensus about what to expect from the media in their public role. There has also been a general decline of public regulation of media and an increased role for the market in shaping the media (McQuail and Siune, 1986; Siune and Truetszchler, 1992). This is most observable in Europe, West and East, formerly the home of strict regulation of electronic media and careful protection of newspapers. The trend is only partly a result of greater 'commercialization', since it also reflects a general decline in normative certainties and an increase in libertarian thinking.

Even so, the challenge to the very foundations of European public service broadcasting systems has led indirectly to more conscious thought about the rationale of public intervention and support (see Blumler, 1992). The growth of the media as an industry has also been accompanied by greater professionalization, expanded media education and new, albeit less legalistic, forms of accountability. Taken together the changes referred to, all of which imply an increasing centrality of media, have also tended to stimulate thought about the role of media in society, even if the forms of accountability have also changed. Despite continuing and deep changes, the basic normative as well as theoretical issues have not yet needed redefinition even if some norms are weaker or less relevant.

The concept of a 'public interest' in media

The revised framework of normative principles for media structure and performance which follows is still based on the presumption that the media are widely expected to serve the 'public interest' or 'general welfare', whether by design or not. This means, in practice, that mass media are not the same as any other business or service industry, but often carry out some tasks which contribute to the wider and longer-term benefit of society as a whole, especially in cultural and political matters, over and above their own ostensible organizational goals (Smith, 1989; Melody, 1990; McQuail, 1992). This presumption is sometimes invited by the media themselves when they claim, however selectively or conditionally, to exercise a significant public role and expect some rights or privileges as a result. Although this view has its opponents on libertarian grounds, it also has good credentials, and in modern times it has been acted on in many democratic societies, sometimes leading to public intervention of various kinds (legal or economic) (for example, Picard, 1985).

An assumption of potential media accountability to society does not entail the view that there is a single known form which the media should take, or that some particular goals or effects are more 'in the public interest' than others. It does not imply, either, that the media can legitimately be obliged to conform to some version of the 'popular will' or, alternatively, be directed to carry out some particular mission, as determined by the state or politicians. The idea of subordinating an institution to the popular will has been called a 'majoritarian' view of the public interest (Held, 1970), because it equates the public interest with the outcome of a popular vote or of preponderant consumer demand in a market. In the case of the media it would lead to the view that more popular services and contents should always take priority (the public interest = what interests the public). The alternative view has been called 'unitarian' or absolutist, since the public interest is decided by reference to a single overriding value or ideology (such as Marxism, fundamentalist religion, or free-market ideology).

Another version of the public interest, and the one preferred here, views it as the outcome of a process of democratic debate and decision-making. It is thus never fixed but always changing, developing and subject to negotiation. In the end it comes down to the view that in democratic societies there are likely to be grounds on which an argued claim can be made, by reference to some widely held values and according to specific circumstances, that media should do or should not do some particular thing, for reasons of wider or longer-term benefit to the society (McQuail, 1992).

Although the general concept of the public interest has been slippery and controversial, without the possibility of making a guiding assumption of this kind about the public task of the media there is little point in bothering to discuss social-normative principles. Once the assumption is made, however, it becomes useful, even necessary, to have some ordered version, however provisional, of the relevant performance criteria that might be deployed. The problem, even so, is to move from the notion of a public interest in general to its interpretation in terms of particular media realities.

In keeping with the provisional character of the public interest notion, the criteria for assessing the media which are proposed below are not universal. The countries from whose experience they derive (mainly North American and Western European) happen to share some characteristics: they are politically pluralistic and predominantly capitalist and often have mixed media institutions. The structure and operation of the media in most of these countries have often been hotly debated, and public control of media has been applied or advocated on grounds of the 'public interest', as have deregulation and the further extension of the free market. This has led to wide-ranging enquiry and debate. In general, the limits of action, if not of debate and advocacy, have been set by the status quo of property ownership and the guidelines of electoral democracy.

Within these limits, a diverse set of expectations from, or on behalf of, 'society' has been articulated in different political arenas. The expression of these expectations has provided the materials from which to construct the framework offered below. The rather diverse set of principles making up this framework may be the nearest we can get to a body of social theory for the media. In the nature of things, no definitive version can be offered and there is at work a continuing process of evolution and change.

Issues for social theory of the media

The type of media theory under discussion has, for reasons given, been actively forged in the course of changes in media and society, often in a context of great political controversy and debate. Principles of media operation have been invoked, developed and adapted. The principles can best be introduced by summarizing the main different **issues** on which controversy has centred, as follows.

Concentration and monopoly

The earliest challenge to the new industrialized media order of the twentieth century concerned the danger to democracy and freedom contained in the concentrations of power in the hands of press 'barons', especially in the USA and Britain. This trend has continued and spread worldwide. The mainly North American phenomenon of 'one-newspaper cities' and the formation of large 'chains' provoked a fear of reduced freedom and independence of news and views (Bagdikian, 1988). In general, press concentration also threatened the balanced representation of opposed political views, especially where media proprietors belonged, by definition, to the propertied classes. If nothing else, concentration seemed to spell a loss of political choice for the reader, reduced opportunities for access to media channels and, generally, reduced media diversity (Picard et al., 1988).

News quality

A long-standing theme of debate, although a less politically sensitive one, which has surfaced in many discussions of the social role of the press, concerned the general quality of the news about events of the day and of the world as supplied to the average citizen, who depends on the media in order to reach informed choices and judgements. The press is often accused of sensationalism and superficiality, of omission, inaccuracy and even falsification and lying. The need for objective and balanced reporting and for diversity of opinion has been a recurrent issue. Another common theme of criticism has been the failure to cover international news in a comprehensive and balanced way (Kivikuru and Varis, 1985). The UNESCO Media Declaration of 1978 underlined the responsibilities of the press to resist warlike, nationalist and racist propaganda (Nordenstreng, 1984). While television, under public scrutiny, promised higher standards of news journalism, the proliferation of channels has led to new fears of sensationalism and lowered informational quality.

Security and social order

Perhaps the oldest and most controversial issue of all is that of the relationship of media to the security and authority of the state. The media are often thought to have a responsibility not to undermine the social order in any fundamental or violent way. While the issue might appear to be settled in favour of the media by constitutional guarantees of press freedom, some reserve powers could usually be invoked by the state in extreme situations, and the modern period has offered numerous instances where the temporary breakdown of civil order, or the actions of terrorists, or the fear of crime, or the pursuit of some minor war, or an issue of government confidentiality, has reawakened controversy about press freedom and its limitation. In general, authorities everywhere have shown a consistent inclination to want to manage the news, even if they stop short of censorship. They usually have more opportunity for control in the case of regulated broadcasting than with the printed press.

Morals and decency

There has been a continued debate in many countries over another issue of control — that concerning morals, decency and portrayals of matters to do with pornographic sex, crime and violence. While direct censorship and legal limitations have diminished in proportion to more relaxed moral standards in most societies, there remain limits to media freedom on grounds of the protection of minors from undesirable influences (see, for instance, clauses in the European Community Television Directive governing cross-border transmission). The issue has become further complicated by similar claims on behalf of women, who may either be portrayed in degrading circumstances or risk becoming the object of media-induced pornographic violence.

Commercialism

A long-standing expectation that media should contribute to education, culture and the arts has come increasingly into conflict with actual or perceived imperatives of the media marketplace, under conditions of heightened competition for audiences. The term 'commercialism' has many meanings, but in one influential view it stands opposed to a number of key social-cultural values. Commercialization has been associated with manipulation, consumerism, lack of integrity and lack of originality and creativity (Blumler, 1991, 1992). It is said to lead to homogeneity and neglect of minorities who do not provide profitable audience or advertising markets. In Western Europe, a key feature of public policy for electronic media has always been to keep commercial influences under firm control (McQuail and Siune, 1986).

Media issues of normative concern

- Concentration and monopoly
- News and information quality
- Security and social order
- Morals and decency
- Cultural quality and commercialism
- Cultural autonomy and integrity

Cultural issues

At different levels of social life, from village to nation state, a claim has increasingly been heard on behalf of cultural autonomy and integrity, something which is also threatened by current media-industrial trends. In brief, it is argued that media are ceasing to reflect the culture and the circumstances of their intended publics and may undermine the local language and cultural identity, as a result of the transnational flow of content (Sepstrup, 1989; Thomsen, 1989). The problem of cultural 'dependency' is most acute for poorer, less developed countries, but it arises as a potential problem for countries which are under the influence of a foreign media flow for other reasons (for instance, Canada and some small European countries).

Response to the issues

The outcome of political struggles over these different issues can be found in many laws and regulations. In most European countries, for instance, there are laws limiting press concentration and cross-ownership, and in some places subsidy systems exist in order to secure press diversity (Picard, 1985). There are also widespread regulations applied to television which require political balance and general neutrality of news. Other regulations call for attention to minorities and to different regions and localities. The national cultural integrity may be protected by import quotas, controls on foreign ownership of media and positive measures to stimulate home production of media.

The European Union has regulations of a similar kind for its member states. In varying degrees, efforts are made to apply controls on morally or culturally sensitive content (Blumler, 1992). While no two countries are the same, and the regulatory climate and regime frequently change, we can argue with conviction that the media operate nearly everywhere within frameworks of normative expectation or actual accountability which imply a set of relatively familiar principles for dealing with the issues raised.

Principles of structure and performance: an interpretative overview

It is a risky step to take from the description of such issues and of the regulations and interventions which they have generated to a general statement of the principles involved. There are many reasons for caution. The principles exist in so many specific variants, in such sensitive terrain, often with deep historical and cultural roots, that no single short account can be satisfactory. In addition, the outcome of such an exercise has the appearance of constituting something like a coherent and comprehensive set of standards for the media, when no such thing exists in any society, and if it did it would probably be inconsistent with fundamental freedoms. It also seems to advance a claim for increased control of the media (certainly it tends in this direction), even if this is not the intention.

There is still a lot of disagreement about the standards presented below, and they are not all fully consistent with each other. They also apply in different ways to different media phenomena. Some, for instance, relate to structure and organization (such as concentration of ownership), others to actual service and performance (such as diversity as choice for consumers).

Despite these reservations, it seems worthwhile trying to summarize the most commonly accepted ideas, if only to provide a starting point for criticism and discussion (for a fuller treatment, see McQuail, 1992). Where relevant, the normative ideas are discussed in terms both of what they call for in respect of media structure and performance and also of the benefits they should deliver for society — the 'public interest', as discussed above. The discussion is structured according to five main headings: freedom, equality, diversity, information quality, social order and solidarity, and cultural order.

Media freedom

Overuse has made the term 'freedom' difficult to discuss in any fresh way, but it has an obvious claim to be considered as the basic principle of any theory of public communication, from which other benefits should flow. Nevertheless, there are many versions of freedom, and the word does not speak for itself, as the earlier discussion (see page 128) has made clear. Freedom is a condition, rather than a criterion of performance, and does not readily lend itself to either prescriptive or proscriptive statements. It refers primarily to rights to free expression and the free formation of opinion. However, for these rights to be realized there must also be access to channels and opportunities to receive diverse kinds of information.

Freedom of communication has a dual aspect: offering a wide range of voices and responding to a wide-ranging demand or need. Similar remarks apply to the cultural provision of media, where independence will be associated, other things being equal, with creativity, originality and diversity. These ideas bring us to an interface and overlap with benefits offered under the heading of 'equality'. This brief discussion has sought to make a connection between the following: structural conditions (legal freedom to transmit/publish); operating conditions (real independence from economic and political pressures and relative autonomy for journalists and other 'communicators' within media organizations); opportunities for 'voices' in society to gain access to channels; and benefits of quality of provision for 'receivers' — according to criteria of relevance, diversity, reliability, interest, originality and personal satisfaction. The main elements discussed can now be expressed as logically related components in a larger normative framework, as summarized in Figure 5.1.

Freedom requirements

In the institutional arrangements and in the public interest discourse referred to above, freedom of communication calls for:

- (*very clearly*) absence of censorship, licensing or other controls by government so that there is an unhindered right to publish and disseminate news and opinions and no obligation to publish what one does not wish to;

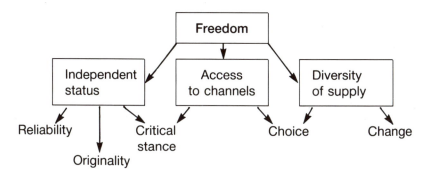

Figure 5.1 *Freedom as a media performance principle,
together with related criteria*

- (*also clearly*) the equal right and possibility for citizens of free *reception* of
  (and access to) news, views, education and culture (this is part of what
  has come to be known as a 'right to communicate');
- (*less clearly*) freedom for news media to obtain information from relevant
  sources;
- (*less clearly*) absence of concealed influence from media owners or
  advertisers on news selection and on opinions expressed;
- (*desirable but optional*) an active and critical editorial policy in presenting
  news and opinion and a creative, innovative and independent publishing
  policy in respect of art and culture.

These prescriptions assume that the only legitimate interests to be served
are those either of communicators (whoever has some public message to
transmit) or of citizens (all those who want to attend), or both. The freedom
of these two parties is paramount. There are several potential conflicts and
inconsistencies embedded in these requirements. First of all, freedom of
public communication can never be absolute but has to recognize limits
sometimes set by the private interests of others or by the higher collective
good of a society. Secondly, there is a potential conflict of interest between
owners or controllers of media channels and those who might want access to
the channels but have no power (or legal right) to secure it (either as senders
or receivers). Thirdly, there may be an imbalance between what communicators want to say and what others want to hear: the freedom of one to send
may not coincide with the freedom of another to choose. Finally, it may be
necessary for government or public power to intervene to secure some
freedoms which are not, in practice, delivered by the unfettered system.

Benefits of media freedom

Media freedom also leads to positive benefits for the everyday needs of
social institutions — especially a flow of reliable information and diverse

points of view. Press independence is also a precondition of the exercise of the 'watchdog' role — exercising public vigilance in relation to those with most power, especially government and big business. Free media will be prepared, when necessary, to offend the powerful, express controversial views and deviate from convention and from the commonplace.

Although no ideal state of communication freedom can be attained, the public benefits expected of freedom in a democratic society are easier to state and involve less inconsistency (see, for example, Curran, 1991). Most important are:

- systematic and independent public scrutiny of those in power and an adequate supply of reliable information about their activities (this refers to the 'watchdog' or critical role of the press);
- stimulation of an active and informed democratic system and social life;
- the chance to express ideas, beliefs and views about the world;
- continued renewal and change of culture and society;
- increase in the amount and variety of freedom available.

Media equality

The principle of equality has to be translated into more specific meanings when it is applied to the mass media. As a principle, it underlies several of the normative expectations which have already been referred to. In relation to communication and political power, equality requires that no special favour be given to power-holders and that *access* to media should be given to contenders for office and, in general, to oppositional or deviant opinions, perspectives or claims. In relation to business clients of the media, equality requires that all legitimate advertisers be treated on the same basis (the same rates and conditions). Equality implies, in such matters, that the normal principles of the market should operate freely and fairly.

Equality supports policies of universal provision in broadcasting and telecommunication and of sharing out the costs of basic services. Equality will support the expectation of fair access, on equivalent terms, for alternative voices (the diversity principle in another form) that meet relevant criteria. In short, equality calls for an absence of discrimination or bias in the amount and kind of access available to senders or receivers, as far as is practicable. The real chances of equality are likely to depend on the level of social and economic development of a society and the capacity of its media system. There will have to be *enough* space on different and mutually independent channels for any degree of equality to be realized in practice. A consideration of equality as an evaluative principle also takes us into the territory of objectivity, although this has other meanings and potential sources of support, especially those provided by the value of *independence* and by trends to professionalism and autonomy (see below). The main sub-

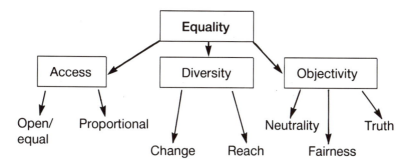

Figure 5.2 *Equality as a media performance principle, together with related concepts*

principles related to the value of equality can be expressed as shown in Figure 5.2.

Media diversity

The principle of diversity (also identified as a major benefit of freedom and linked with the concept of access) is especially important because it underpins the normal processes of progressive change in society (the periodic replacement of ruling elites, the circulation of power and office, the countervailing power of different interests) which pluralistic forms of democracy are supposed to deliver. In accounting for diversity of *provision*, the extent to which real alternatives are on offer can be registered according to several alternative yardsticks: type of media (such as press, radio or television); function or type (such as entertainment or information); the level of operation (national, regional, local, etc.); the audience aimed at and reached (differentiated by income, age, etc.); language, ethnic or cultural identity; and politics or ideology. In general, a media system is more equal in character the more diverse the provision according to the criteria mentioned.

Two basic variants of the 'diversity-as-equal-treatment' principle have been identified. According to one version, a literal equality should be on offer — everyone receives the same provision or chances for access as sender. This applies, for instance, where contending parties receive equal time in an election, or in those countries (such as Canada or Belgium) where separate language groups receive an equivalent media service. An alternative and more usual version means only a 'fair', or appropriate, allocation of access and treatment. Fairness is generally assessed according to the principle of proportional representation. Media provision should proportionately *reflect* the actual distribution of whatever is relevant (topics, social groups, political beliefs, etc.) in the society, or reflect the varying distribution of audience demand or interest. The differentiation of media provision (content) should approximately correspond to the differences at source or to those at the receiving end.

Diversity requirements

Diversity stands very close to freedom as a key concept in any discussion of media theory (Glasser, 1984). It presupposes, most generally, that the more, and the more different, channels of public communication there are, carrying the maximum variety of (changing) content to the greatest variety of audiences, the better. Put like this, it seems rather empty of any value direction, or prescription about *what* should actually be communicated. Indeed, this is a correct interpretation, since diversity, like freedom, is neutral as to content. It is a valuation only of variety, choice and change in themselves. Nevertheless, the diversity principle applied to actual media systems and content does become more specific in its normative requirements, and the following are the main elements:

- Media should **reflect** in their structure and content the various social, economic and cultural realities of the societies (and communities) in which they operate, in a more or less proportional way.
- Media should offer more or less equal chances of **access** to the voices of various social and cultural minorities which make up the society.
- Media should serve as a **forum** for different interests and points of view in a society or community.
- Media should offer relevant **choices** of content at one point in time and also **variety** over time of a kind which corresponds to the needs and interests of their audiences.

Again, we can point to some inconsistencies and problems in these normative requirements. The degree of diversity that is possible is limited by media channel capacity and by editorial selections which have to be made. The more that media are *proportionally* reflective of society, the more likely it is that small minorities will be effectively excluded from mass media, since a small proportion of access will be divided between many claimants. Similarly, catering properly for dominant and consistent expectations and tastes in mass media limits the chance to offer a very wide choice or much change. However, the full range of many different media in a society can help to compensate for the limitations of 'traditional' *mass* media.

Benefits of media diversity

While diversity is sometimes regarded as a good in itself, it is also often perceived as a means to other benefits. These include:

- opening the way for social and cultural change, especially where it takes the form of giving access to new, powerless or marginal voices;

- providing a check on the misuse of freedom (for instance, where the free market leads to concentration of ownership);
- opening the opportunity for minorities to maintain their separate existence in a larger society;
- limiting social conflicts by increasing the chances of understanding between potentially opposed groups and interests;
- adding generally to the richness and variety of cultural and social life.

Information quality

While the expectation that media should provide information of reasonable quality has a more practical than philosophical or normative foundation, it is hardly less important in modern thinking about media standards than the principles of freedom or diversity. Freedom and diversity do not necessarily produce more informative public communication. Informational require-ments have a dual origin — relating to the desirability of an informed society and a skilled work-force, on the one hand, and, on the other, having a body of citizens who are in a position to participate in the choice of leaders and in democratic decision-making (Keane, 1991).

The objectivity concept

The most central concept in relation to information quality has probably been that of objectivity. Objectivity is a particular form of media *practice* and also a particular attitude to the task of information collection, processing and dissemination. The main features are: adopting a position of detachment and neutrality towards the object of reporting (thus an absence of subjectivity or personal involvement); lack of partisanship (not taking sides in matters of dispute or showing bias); attachment to accuracy and other truth criteria (such as relevance and completeness); and lack of ulterior motive or service to a third party. The process of observing and reporting should, thus, not be contaminated by subjectivity, nor should it interfere with the reality being reported on. In some respects it has an affinity, in theory at least, with the ideal of rational, 'undistorted' communication advocated by Habermas (1989).

This version of an ideal standard of reporting practice has many advocates and has become the dominant ideal for the role of professional journalist (Weaver and Wilhoit, 1986). It has links with the principle of **freedom**, since independence is a necessary condition of detachment and truthfulness. Under some conditions (such as political oppression, crisis, war and police action), the freedom to report can only be obtained in return for a guarantee of objectivity. On the other hand, freedom also includes the right to be biased or partisan.

The link with **equality** is also strong: objectivity requires a fair and nondiscriminatory attitude to sources and to objects of news reporting — all should be treated on equal terms. Additionally, different points of view on matters where the facts are in dispute should be treated as of equal standing and relevance, other things being equal. Objective treatment or presentation may in practice be achieved by allowing equal space or time for alternative perspectives on, or versions of, facts.

The benefits of objectivity

In the set of normative interactions which develop between media and their operating environments, objectivity may be crucial. Agencies of state and advocates of various interests are able to speak directly to their chosen audiences by way of the media, without undue distortion or intervention by the mediators themselves and without compromising the independence of channels. Because of the established conventions of objectivity, media channels can distance their editorial content from the advertising matter which they carry, and advertisers can do likewise in respect of editorial content.

In general, media audiences appear to understand the principle of objective performance well enough, and its practice helps to increase their credence and trust in the information and opinions which the media offer. The media themselves find that objectivity gives their own news product a higher and wider market value. Finally, because the objectivity standard has such a wide currency, it is often invoked in claims and settlements concerning bias or unequal treatment. Most modern news media set a lot of store by their claim to objectivity in its several meanings. Policies for broadcasting in many countries impose, by various means, a requirement of objectivity, on their public broadcasting systems, sometimes as a condition of their independence.

A framework for objectivity research and theory

It is not easy to define objectivity, but one version of its various components has been set out by Westerståhl (1983) in the context of research into the degree of objectivity shown by the Swedish broadcasting system. This version (Figure 5.3) recognizes that objectivity has to deal with **values** as well as with facts and that facts also have evaluative implications.

In this scheme, factuality refers, first of all, to a form of reporting which deals in events and statements which can be checked against sources and are presented free from comment, or at least clearly separated from any comment. Factuality involves several other 'truth criteria': completeness of an account, accuracy and an intention not to mislead or suppress what is relevant (good faith). The second main aspect of factuality is 'relevance'. This is more difficult both to define and to achieve in an objective way. It relates to the process of *selection* rather than to the form of presentation

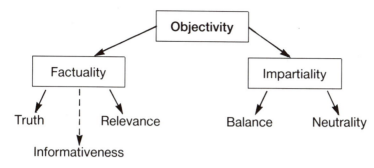

Figure 5.3　*Component criteria of objectivity (Westerståhl, 1983)*

and requires that selection take place according to clear and coherent principles of what is significant for the intended receiver and/or the society (Nordenstreng, 1974). In general, what affects most people most immediately and most strongly is likely to be considered most relevant (though there may be a gap between what the public perceives as of interest and what experts say is significant).

According to Westerståhl's scheme, impartiality presupposes a 'neutral attitude' and has to be achieved through a combination of balance (equal or proportional time/space/emphasis) as between opposing interpretations, points of view or versions of events, and neutrality in presentation. Under conditions of 'external diversity', as described above, the impartiality component of objectivity does not apply (although that of factualness does), since the assumption is that there will be alternative media to tell the story from another point of view. For instance, a strongly partisan newspaper in a partisan system is not expected to present the reader with all *points of view*, although the reader still expects reliable information.

The scheme in Figure 5.3 has been given an extra element, that of 'informativeness', which is important to the fuller meaning of objectivity. The reference is to qualities of informational content which are likely to improve the chances of actually getting information across to an audience: being noticed, understood, remembered, etc. This is the pragmatic side of information, which is often undervalued or neglected in normative theory but essential to the fuller notion of good informational performance.

Main information quality requirements

Some of the expected benefits of objectivity are self-evident, while others are subsumed under freedom and diversity requirements. The main 'information quality' standards which are encountered in policy prescriptions or codes of practice can be formulated as follows:

- Media (especially press and broadcasting) should provide a *comprehen-*

sive supply of *relevant* news and background information about events in the society and the world around.

- Information should be objective in the sense of being accurate, honest, sufficiently complete, true to reality, reliable, and separating fact from opinion.
- Information should be balanced and fair (impartial) — reporting alternative perspectives in a non-sensational, unbiased way.

Limits of objectivity

Several potential difficulties are embedded in these norms, especially because of uncertainty about what constitutes an adequate or relevant supply of information and about the very nature of 'objectivity' (Hemánus, 1976; Westerståhl, 1983; Hackett, 1984). More serious are the possible inconsistencies with claims of media freedom (which does not distinguish between 'true' and 'false' expression) and diversity (which emphasizes the multiplicity and inconsistency of reality). We can also note that such criteria are more appropriate to the *totality* of media information in a society, rather than to any particular channel or sector. Not all media are equally expected by their own audiences to provide full and objective information on 'serious' topics.

Objectivity (and related standards of factuality, etc.) is far from unanimously regarded as either necessary, virtuous or even possible to achieve, but there is a good deal of force in Lichtenberg's (1990, p. 230) argument that 'insofar as we aim to understand the world we cannot get along without assuming both the possibility and value of objectivity'.

Social order and solidarity

The normative questions which belong under this heading are those which relate to the integration and harmony of society, as viewed from different (even opposed) perspectives. On the one hand, there is a rather consistent tendency on the part of those in authority to look to public communication media for at least tacit support in the task of maintaining order. On the other hand, pluralistic societies cannot be conceived as having one single dominant order which has to be maintained, and mass media have mixed and divided responsibilities, especially with reference to alternative social groups and subcultures and to the expression of the conflicts and inequalities of most societies. Problems also arise over how far the media can go in their support for opposition or potential subversion (as it may seem from 'the top'). The relevant principles concerning the media are mixed and not mutually compatible but can be expressed in something like the following way.

The concept of order is used here in a rather elastic way, to apply to symbolic (cultural) orders such as religion, art and customs, as well as

Perspective

Domain		From 'above'	From 'below'
Social		Control/ compliance	Solidarity/ attachment
Cultural		Conformity/ hierarchy	Autonomy/ identity

Figure 5.4 *Ideas concerning mass media and order depend on whose order and what kind of order is involved*

to forms of social order (community, society and established structures of relations). This broad distinction is also cut across by a distinction of perspective — from 'above' and 'below', as it were. This distinction is essentially that between established authority of society, on the one hand, and individuals and minority groups, on the other. It also corresponds approximately to the distinction between order in the sense of control and order in the sense of solidarity and cohesion — the one 'imposed', the other voluntary and self-chosen. These ideas about order can be arranged as shown in Figure 5.4.

Any complex and viable social system will exhibit all the sub-aspects of order shown here. There will be mechanisms of social control as well as voluntary attachments, often by way of membership of component groups in society. There will be a sharing of common meanings and definitions of experience, as well as much divergence of identity and actual experience. Shared culture and solidaristic experience tend to be mutually reinforcing. The relationship between mass communication and these different concepts has been handled in theories of media and society in divergent, though not logically inconsistent, ways (see Chapter 3). Functionalist theory attributes to mass media a latent purpose of securing the continuity and integration of a social order (Wright, 1960) by promoting co-operation and a consensus of social and cultural values.

Critical theory has usually interpreted mass media as agents of a dominant, controlling class of power-holders who seek to impose their own definitions of situations and their values and to marginalize or delegitimize opposition. The media are often seen as serving conflicting goals and interests and as offering conflicting versions of an actual or desirable social order. The question *'Whose* order?' has first to be settled. Relevant normative theory cannot be concerned only with the disruption of order (such as with conflict, crime or deviance) but should also relate to the failings of the established order as perceived by more marginal, or minority, social and cultural groups.

Expectations and norms relating to order

From the perspective of social control, the relevant norms are often applied to condemn positive portrayals of conflict, disorder and deviance or to support differential access and positive symbolic support for established 'order' institutions and authorities — the law, church, school, police, military, etc. The second sub-principle (that of solidarity) involves a recognition that society is composed of many sub-groups, different bases of identity and different interests. There is no consensual good order in a modern nation state, and there can be a number of alternative ideas about what is a desirable social order. From this perspective, a viable normative expectation from mass media is that they should sympathetically recognize the alternatives and provide access and symbolic support for relevant minority groups and views. In general, this (normative) theoretical position will encompass an outward-looking and empathic orientation to social groups and situations which are marginal, distant or deviant from the point of view of a dominant national society.

To summarize a very mixed set of normative perspectives concerning social order:

- In respect of the relevant public which they serve (at national or local level, or as defined by group and interest), the media should provide channels of intercommunication and support.
- The media may contribute to social integration by paying concerned attention to socially disadvantaged or injured individuals and groups.
- The media should not undermine the forces of law and order by encouraging or symbolically rewarding crime or social disorder.
- In matters of national security (such as war, threat of war, foreign subversion or terrorism), the freedom of action of media may be limited by considerations of national interest.
- On questions of morals, decency and taste (especially in matters of the portrayal of sex and violence and the use of language), the media should in some degree observe the reigning norms of what is broadly publicly acceptable and avoid causing grave public offence.

It is clear that these prescriptions and proscriptions are mutually inconsistent and are very much subject to variations in time and place and in the details of the case and point of view. The norms also apply very differently to different kinds of media.

Cultural order

The domain of the 'cultural' is not easy to keep separate from that of the 'social', but here it refers to any set of symbols organized by way of language or in some other meaningful patterning. Normative media theory has typically been concerned either with matters of cultural 'quality' (of media content) or with its 'authenticity' in respect of real-life experience.

The subdivision of the sphere of the cultural for present purposes of representation in a normative framework follows a similar line to that applied in the social domain: between a 'dominant', official or established culture and a set of possible alternatives or subcultures. In practice, the former implies a hierarchical view of culture, according to which cultural values and artefacts which have been 'certified' by established cultural institutions will be relatively privileged, compared to 'alternative' cultural values and forms. Typically, such an established culture will imply a set of absolute cultural values and certifiable quality standards. The cultural virtues of the 'alternative' perspective will, in contrast, be diverse and relative, based only on personal perceptions of attractiveness, relevance and familiarity.

Cultural quality norms

Normative theory, often expressed in wider cultural policies, gives support for very different kinds of cultural quality in the mass media. First, it often protects the 'official' cultural heritage of a nation or society, especially in education and science, art and literature. This may extend to support for innovation in the traditional arts. Secondly, it supports distinctive regional and local variants of cultural expression, on grounds of authenticity as well as of tradition (sometimes for political reasons). Thirdly, some theory recognizes the equal rights of all cultural expressions and tastes, including 'popular culture'.

Although there have been many heated discussions about the possible cultural responsibilities of mass media, there is little agreement on what to do about them and less action. The norms involved are not usually very compelling and are always selectively applied. Even so, much the same principles tend to be invoked in different contexts. The most commonly encountered are the following:

- Media content should reflect and express the language and contemporary culture (artefacts and way of life) of the people which the media serve (nationally, regionally and locally); it should be relevant to current and typical social experience.
- Some priority should be given to the educational role of the media and to the expression and continuity of the best in the cultural heritage of a country.
- Media should encourage cultural creativity and originality and the production of work of high quality (according to aesthetic, moral, intellectual and occupational criteria).

The very uneven application of these normative principles in any form of control reflects both the primacy of freedom and also the strength of commercial imperatives. Principles of cultural quality are likely to be advanced as desirable but are rarely enforceable. There is rarely enough consensus on what criteria of cultural quality mean. Almost the only empirically demonstrable criterion of cultural quality is that of cultural *relevance* to the audience, especially as expressed in familiar, realistic and contemporary settings, events and themes. The more that media (for instance, public broadcasting institutions) are subject to policy in the interests of the public as a whole, the more likely are cultural criteria to be invoked as a guide to performance. Sometimes, national and economic self-interest can lead to support for some of the cultural principles described.

The range of application of normative media theory

Aside from the shrinking sector of public broadcasting (see Blumler, 1992), most media operate on a day to day basis with little conscious regard for the norms described above. The desirable goals are reached or not, and the evils are avoided or not, according to the working of particular media market circumstances, the pulls and pushes of organizational circumstance, and the professional ethics, creative goals and routine decisions of those who work in the media. There are more immediate rules of law, ethics or good practice which are more likely to preoccupy people in the media on a day-to-day basis (Meyer, 1987). Only occasionally is it necessary for those within or outside the media to reflect systematically on the application of one or more of the principles outlined. Only rarely, if ever, would consideration be given to the whole range of ideas which has been summarized.

The set of principles outlined is simply one attempt to describe a universe of discourse which is available within the Western liberal-pluralist tradition as it has developed during the last forty or so years. It cannot be said to represent a consensus on what the media ought to do or not do 'in the public interest' (as defined above), although an attempt has been made to avoid extreme or controversial propositions. What may well be controversial is the degree to which a given principle is relevant to a given situation or medium. In any case, the freedom principle provides a let-out from most obligations, short of extreme antisocial forms of publication. The application of any given principle has also to be established in a relevant political forum, before it can have much weight or consequence.

Conclusion: a changing normative environment

The changes in the media reviewed earlier have not yet fundamentally changed the *content* of the norms described, but they have affected their relative force and the priorities among them. The increasing number of alternative media channels, in particular, has reduced the pressure on seemingly 'dominant' media (for instance, the national newspaper press or broadcast television) to fulfil some perceived public roles. There is probably less fear of media monopoly, despite concentration tendencies, because the potential for competition is greater. More media channels also seem to promise more diversity, although the quality of that diversity is far from assured.

Several of the norms outlined have recently come to be invoked in debates about the future of public broadcasting and about the standards to be applied when allocating new television or radio operating licences, especially to private operators. Some of the norms are also still relevant to judging whether press concentration, or cross-media ownership, works against the public interest. There is also continued pressure for media with seeming increasing influence in cultural, social and political matters to show a degree of self-regulation. Some of the standards discussed are relevant to this matter.

We can expect that, as media institutions are reshaped in former communist states of Central and Eastern Europe, models will be sought in the West, perhaps even some coherent media 'philosophy' to replace one that has been discarded. No doubt some will find this in an unfettered libertarianism, which promises to open windows and dispose of the trappings of paternalism and control. Others will find continued value in a modified version of the former doctrines of social(ist) responsibility. The universe of ideas described above offers something to both parties, although (because of the nature of the exercise) it tends to stress the responsibilities of mass media and implicitly diminish the libertarian viewpoint. No general recommendation can be made. It will be up to the varied publics and to those who frame the new institutions to decide what they want, what is viable and what can be afforded. In respect of the last point social theory of the media does not have to be subordinate to commerce, but it has to take account of economic reality.

6

MEDIA STRUCTURES AND INSTITUTIONS

Media 'not just any other business'

So far, mass media have been discussed as if they were a social institution rather than an industry. They have become increasingly more of the latter without necessarily becoming less of the former, and to understand the main principles of structure and dynamics of the media calls for an economic as well as a political and a social-cultural analysis. Although the media have grown up in response to the social and cultural needs of individuals and societies, they are largely run as business enterprises (in the sense of being financed by private investment and consumption). A trend in this direction has accelerated in recent years for several reasons, especially in terms of the increasing industrial economic significance of information and communication hardware and the declining share of public intervention in media production as the media industry expands (also in terms of the shift to free-market economies in former communist states). Even where media are run as public bodies, they are subject to financial discipline and operate in competitive environments.

A book about mass communication theory is not the place for a thorough analysis of these matters, but it is impossible to understand the social and cultural implications of mass media without at least a sketch of the wider political and economic forces at work shaping media institutions. The public regulation, the control and the economics of media embody certain general principles which belong to the sphere of theory, and the aim of this chapter is to concentrate on these principles, avoiding detail of local and temporary circumstances.

The key to the unusual character of the media institution is that its activities are inextricably both economic and political as well as being very dependent on continually changing technologies of distribution. These activities involve the production of goods and services which are often both private (consumption for individual personal satisfaction) and public (viewed as necessary for the working of society as a whole and also in the public domain). The public character of the media relates, for instance, to the political function of the media in a democracy and to the fact that information and ideas cannot acceptably be monopolized by private individuals. Nor, as with other public goods like air and daylight, does their use diminish their availability for others.

More specifically, mass media have grown up historically with a strong and widely shared image as having an important part to play in public life and being, in a certain sense, if not public property, then within the public domain. Certainly, this was and remains true of the newspaper, but it applies in different ways to most of the newer mass media. What media do or do not do has mattered to societies, and this has been reflected in complex systems of ideas about what they should or should not be doing (see Chapter 5) and also in equally complex and varied mechanisms to encourage, protect or limit them on behalf of a supposed 'public interest'. Despite this, the media generally have to operate wholly or partly according to the dictates of market economics. Even in this aspect, they may attract the attention of governments for the same reasons that private businesses are also subject to various forms of legal and economic regulation.

Alternative perspectives

Not surprisingly, there is no agreed objective description of the media institution that can be separated from the varying national/societal circumstances in which they operate. One option is to apply an **economic/ industrial** perspective (see Tunstall, 1991), looking at the distinctive and varying characteristics of the media as economic enterprises, as between different media and different contexts. An alternative perspective is that offered by critical **political-economic** theory (as introduced on page 82), which provides some concepts derived especially from the critique of capitalism, with particular reference to the processes of concentration and the powers of ownership, but also to the cultural and social implications of 'commercialization'.

A third main possibility is to examine media structures according to a **public interest** perspective and in the light of normative criteria of conduct and performance which are deployed in the relevant national (and international) political fora. There is a fourth possibility — to look at the media institution from an internal or **media professional** point of view, as distinct from either the business perspective or outsiders' ideas of how the media ought to operate. Each of these perspectives will be drawn on for some purposes in the following pages.

We can represent the unusual position of media as at the centre of three main forces — political, economic and technological — and thereby requiring alternative modes of analysis (Figure 6.1).

The main issues

A theoretical analysis is only possible if certain general issues or problems are first identified. At a descriptive level, we focus mainly on the question of

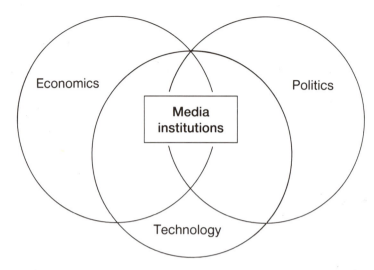

Figure 6.1 *Pressures on the media: media are at the centre of three overlapping areas of influence*

differences: how media differ from each other in economic and policy terms; how and why the economics and regulation of media are untypical both of normal business and of normal public services; and how and why national media institutions vary in structure and control. This last aspect of the comparison is important precisely because media are not only businesses, responding to economic forces, but also deeply rooted (usually nationally based) social and cultural institutions.

There is also relevant theory concerning the current *dynamics* of media industries, especially the trends towards expansion, diversification and convergence of media, mainly on the basis of new technology and new economic opportunities. There are trends towards concentration, integration and internationalization of media activity. Implicated in this last point is the question of global communicative relations between the main 'media powers', mostly in the North, and the relatively dependent South. Not all the trends mentioned seem logically consistent, and some framework is needed within which they can be made sense of.

Media policy and regulation are also both characterized by seemingly opposed trends, especially as between deregulation (and privatization) and some significant kinds of reregulation, especially at the transnational level. While it is tempting to regard our own time as a moment of communications 'revolution', the mass media have been continuously changing since their earliest days, following one technological revolution after another, and many of the forces at work are constant. They reflect two basic dynamics: the first, a wish to make money; and the other, a struggle for power in society, in which the media are deeply implicated.

The basics of media structure and levels of analysis

The scene can be set by a reminder of the main features of media structures in economically developed media systems. The term 'media system' refers to the actual set of mass media in a given national society, despite the fact that there may be no coherence or connection between the elements. Most media systems, in this sense, are the result of chance historical growth, with one new technology after another being developed and leading to the adaptation of existing media.

Sometimes a media system is linked by a shared political-economic logic — as with the free-enterprise media of the United States or the state-run media of China. Many countries have 'mixed' systems, with private and public elements, and these may well be organized according to a set of national media policy principles, leading to a degree of integration. Occasionally, there may be a single Ministry of Communications which has some responsibilities across a range of different media, private or public, which adds another 'systemic' component.

The media may also be *regarded* as a coherent system (or just very similar) by their audiences or by their advertisers, and certainly the term 'the media' is often used in this collective sense. The more that free-enterprise mass media are held in relatively few corporate hands, the more these may be thought of as a single system, although even the highest levels of concentrated private ownership still allow for some structural diversity and competition. Lastly, one may consider the media as a system in a broader sense, as not only integrating the political regulators, media producers and distributors, but also interconnected with the industries of advertising, public relations, marketing and, often, opinion and audience research as well.

Within the media system, specific different media types are to be found: newspapers, television, radio, music, telecommunications, etc. These may also be described as media 'sectors', especially in policy discourse or for purposes of economic analysis. In fact, the unity of such 'sectors' is often as illusory as is that of the whole system. There are many differentiating as well as integrating factors (especially through separate or shared distribution systems). For instance, the medium of film can refer to the cinema, video hire or sale, broadcast or subscription television, etc. These are different means of distribution, often different businesses and organizations, although there is usually some form of vertical integration. As a result of media conglomeration, we need to distinguish another unit of analysis: that of the firm or enterprise, which may comprise a significant part of a sector or have holdings which cut across boundaries of media type or geography (the multi-media, and often multinational, firm).

Major media like newspapers and broadcasting are often geographically fragmented. The 'daily newspaper' can be any one of the following: a national mass circulation paper, a business paper, a political or religious publication, a regional morning or a city evening newspaper. Other media, such as magazines, are ranged across a wide spectrum of type, defined by topic and readership. Below the level of medium or sector we find the single-medium organization — for instance, the particular 'title' in the case of a newsaper or magazine, or the network, channel or station in the case of radio or television. Because of horizontal integration, these may well not be independent. For some purposes of structural analysis, it may also be necessary to identify a particular media product — for example, a book, film or television show — as a separate unit.

There is no standard terminology to describe the many varieties of national circumstances of media systems. In general, we can do little more than try to distinguish by the medium of distribution or delivery, the type of content and the particular audience reached or aimed at (as identified by criteria such as income, location of residence, occupation, age or gender). In general, most national media systems are still clearly structured by regional level of provision (from national to local), a distinction which cuts across the media sector dimensions.

Media structure and levels of analysis

- Media system (all national media)
- Multi-media firm (with major holdings in several media)
- Media sector (newspapers, television, film, music, etc.)
- Circulation/distribution area (nation, region, city, locality)
- Unit medium (newspaper title, television channel, etc.)
- Unit media product (book, film, song, etc.)

Some economic principles of media structure

In economic terms, 'the media' show up as very disparate, although they do have some shared features (see below). Most obviously there are a number of different, often competing, media (newspapers, television, film, radio, etc.) within the same national 'media system', each with different advantages and disadvantages for producers and consumers. Equally obviously, media are structured geographically, with media provision geared to populations considered as national, regional, city, local, etc. (there is also an international level).

Different media markets and sources of income

The diversity can usefully be understood in terms of several different kinds of 'market'. According to Picard (1989, p. 17), 'A market consists of sellers that provide the same good or service, or closely substitutable goods or services, to the same group of consumers.' In general, markets can be defined according to place, people, type of revenue and the nature of the product or service. Different media and differences of geography often identify separate media markets.

A more fundamental line of economic division in the media business is between the **consumer market** for media products and services and the **advertising market**, in which a service is sold to advertisers in the form of access to the audience. This feature of media economics — reliance on two different sources of revenue — has far-reaching significance. One can note that within the first (consumer) market there is another division, between the market for 'one-off' products, like books, tapes, videos and newspapers, sold directly to consumers and that for continuous media services like cable or broadcast television or videotex.

Advertising versus consumer revenue — implications

The difference between the two main sources of revenue — direct consumer sales and advertising (there are other sources) — is an important tool for comparative analysis and for explaining media features and trends. The distinction cuts across the difference between media types, although some media are rather unsuitable for advertising (especially the 'one-off' media), while others can operate equally in both markets (especially television, radio, newspapers and magazines). There are some 'advertising only' media, with no consumer revenue — for instance, free newspapers, promotional magazines and sponsored television.

The distinction has both an economic and a non-economic significance. In respect of the latter, it is usually believed (from the critical or public interest and professional perspectives) that the higher the dependence on advertising as a source of revenue, the less independent the content from the interests of the advertisers and business generally. This implies less credibility as an information source and less creative autonomy. In the extreme case of totally advertising-financed publications or totally sponsored programming, the content is hard to distinguish from commercial propaganda or public relations. From the economic perspective, operation in the different markets raises other considerations. One is the question of financing, since advertising-supported media are usually paid for in advance of production, while in the consumer market the income has to follow the outlay, often with a considerable delay (as with the film industry).

Secondly, there are different criteria and methods for assessing market performance. Advertising-based media are assessed according to the number and type of consumers (who they are, where they live) reached by particular messages (for example, circulation, readership and reach/ratings). These measures are necessary for attracting would-be advertising clients and for establishing the rates which can be charged.

he market performance of media content which is paid for directly by sumers is assessed by the income received from sales and subscriptions to services. Ratings of (qualitative) satisfaction and popularity may be relevant to both markets, since they can be used in publicity for the media products and services, but they count for relatively more in the consumer income market.

Performance in one market can affect performance in another, where a medium operates in both. For instance, an increase in newspaper sales (producing more consumer revenue) can lead to higher advertising rates, provided that the increase does not lead to a lower average level of social-economic composition, with a reverse effect on unit advertising rates. It is also clear that the difference of revenue base can lead to different kinds of opportunity or vulnerability to wider economic circumstances. Media which are heavily dependent on advertising are likely to be more sensitive to the negative impact of general economic downturns than media which sell (usually low-cost) products to individual consumers. The latter may also be in a better position to cut costs in the face of falls in demand (but this depends on the cost structure).

Media market reach and diversity

The difference between the two revenue markets interacts with other features of the media market. As noted above, the social composition of the audience reached (and 'sold' to advertisers) is important, because of differences in purchasing power and in type of goods advertised. There is a logic in the advertising-based media which favours a convergence of media tastes and consumption patterns (less diversity). This is because homogeneous audiences are often more interesting to advertisers than heterogeneous and dispersed markets (unless they are very large mass markets). This is one reason for the viability of the free newspaper which provides homogeneous and complete coverage of a particular area.

This factor matters much less in the case of 'paid content', since it does not matter *whose* money it is as long as it is received. On the other hand, even paid content has to be marketed and distributed, and this raises the question of the location and social composition of intended audiences and markets. The success of advertising-based media may also depend on the geographical location and relative dispersion of audiences. It is important for some advertisers (such as local traders) to be able to reach a high proportion of their potential customers.

One result is that newspapers with a dispersed set of readers are often more at risk economically than those with a locally concentrated circulation. This is partly because of higher distribution costs, but it also stems from the relative capacity to 'cover' a particular market of consumers — especially the relevant so-called 'retail trading zone'. The general effect is to reward media concentration (almost by definition, the more newspapers — or other media

— which compete, the more dispersed their separate sets of readers are likely to be).

Competition for revenue

In line with this, it has been argued more generally that 'competition for a single revenue source results in imitative uniformity' (Tunstall, 1991, p. 182). Tunstall suggests that this is the reason for the perceived 'low taste' quality (or just 'imitative uniformity') of North American network television, which is financed almost entirely from mass *consumer* advertising (see DeFleur and Ball-Rokeach, 1989), and also for the low standards of the British tabloid newspapers which compete for much the same mass (down-) market. Tunstall also argues that this kind of large undifferentiated market 'maximizes the power of the powerful' (for instance, by the threat of advertising withdrawals, or simply pressure). Certainly one of the benefits argued for a public sector in European television has been that it avoids the situation where all broadcasting competes for the same revenue sources (for example, Peacock, 1986).

This argument mainly applies to a particular case (of national media financed by consumer advertising). The effects indicated would be modified according to the diversity of types of advertising and to any factor which tends to segment the market (such as diversity of social composition or taste of the audience). Although historically advertising for mass consumer products has been the mainstay of genuinely 'mass' media of the kind represented by US networks and British tabloid newspapers, this type of media is in relative decline, and there have always been differentiated advertising markets. For instance, there is a significant volume of personal advertising, or advertising for employment, business and finance, corporate images and public relations, or government and public information. Apart from this, the fact that different media often compete with each other for the same advertising income works against uniformity. The degree and kind of competition are an important modifying variable. Reliance on advertising as such need not lead to uniformity of provision.

The significance of the social-economic background of the would-be audience for media financing has already been mentioned, and the reasons are obvious enough. Aside from differences of content preferences and interests which may be linked with social class, the better-off can (and do) normally pay more for more media and are more interesting targets for high-value consumer products. There are also relations between occupational categories and media services.

Media cost structure

The issue of media cost structures was noted earlier as a variable in the economic fortunes of media. One of the peculiarities of mass media as compared with some other economic enterprises is the potential imbalance between the 'fixed costs' and the 'variable costs' of production. The former refer to such things as land, physical plant, equipment and distribution network. The variable costs refer to materials, 'software' and (sometimes) labour. The higher the ratio of fixed to variable costs, the more vulnerable a business is to a changing market environment, and mass media typically have a high ratio, with heavy capital investments which have to be recouped later by sales and advertising revenue.

It is in the nature of the typical media product that it has a very high 'first copy' cost. A single daily newspaper or the first print of a film carries all the burden of the fixed costs, while the marginal cost of additional copies may be very small. This makes traditional media like newspapers vulnerable to fluctuations in demand and in advertising revenue and also puts a premium on economies of scale and exerts a pressure towards agglomeration. It also exerts pressure towards the separation of production from distribution, since the latter often involves high fixed costs (for instance, cinemas, cable networks, satellites and transmitters). High fixed costs also erect a high barrier to would-be new entrants into the media business.

Ownership and control

Fundamental to an understanding of media structure is the question of ownership — who owns and how the powers of ownership are exercised. The belief that ownership ultimately determines the nature of media is not just a Marxist theory but virtually a common-sense axiom summed up in Altschull's (1984) second law of journalism: 'the contents of the media always reflect the interests of those who finance them'. Not surprisingly, there are several different forms of ownership of different media, and the powers of ownership can be exercised in different ways.

As implied by Altschull's remark, it is not just ownership which counts, it is a wider question of who actually pays for the media product. Although there are media whose owners do personally pay for the privilege, most media are financed from different sources. These include a range of private investors (among them other media companies), advertisers, consumers, various public or private subsidy-givers, and governments. It follows that the line of influence from ownership is often indirect and complex — and it is rarely the only line of influence.

Most media belong to one of three categories of ownership: commercial companies, private non-profit bodies and the public sector. However, within each of these three are significant divisions. For media ownership it will be relevant whether a company is public or private, a large media chain or conglomerate or a small independent. It may also matter whether or not a media enterprise is owned by a so-called 'media tycoon' or 'mogul', typified as wanting to take a personal interest in editorial policy (Tunstall and Palmer, 1991). Non-profit bodies can be neutral trusts, designed to safeguard independence of operations, bodies with a special cultural or social task, political parties, churches, etc. Public ownership also comes in many different forms ranging from direct state administration to elaborate and diversified constructions designed to maximize independence of decision-making about content.

The effects of ownership

For mass communication theory, it is nearly always the ultimate publication decision which matters most. Liberal theory rests on the assumption that ownership can be effectively separated from control of editorial decisions. Larger (allocative) decisions about resources, business strategy, etc., are taken by owners or boards of owners, while editors and other decision-makers are left free to take the professional decisions about content, which is their special expertise. In some situations and countries there are intermediatary institutional arrangements (such as editorial statutes) designed to safeguard the integrity of editorial policy. Otherwise, professionalism, codes of conduct, public reputation (since media are always in the public eye) and common (business) sense are supposed to take care of the seeming 'problem' of undue owner influence.

The existence of checks and balances cannot, however, obscure several facts of life of media operation. One is that, ultimately, commercial media have to make profits to survive, and this often involves taking decisions which directly influence content (such as cutting costs, closing down, shedding staff, investing or not, and merging operations). Publicly owned media do not escape an equivalent economic logic. It is also a fact that most private media have a vested interest in the capitalist system and are inclined to give support to its most obvious defenders — conservative political parties.

The overwhelming editorial endorsement by US newspaper editorials of Republican presidential candidates over the years (Gaziano, 1989) and similar phenomena in some European countries are not likely to be the result of either chance or natural wisdom. There are many less obvious ways in which a similar tendency operates, not least potential pressure from advertisers. Public ownership is thought to neutralize or balance these particular pressures, although that too means following a certain editorial line (albeit one of neutrality).

The conventional wisdom of liberal theory suggests that the best or only solution to such problems lies in multiplicity of private ownership — an ideal situation being one in which many small or medium-size media compete with each other for the interest of the public by offering a wide range of ideas, information and types of culture. The power which goes with ownership is not in itself seen as bad but only becomes so when concentrated or used selectively to deny access. This position tends to underestimate the fundamental tension between market criteria of size and profit and social-cultural criteria. They may simply not be reconcilable. The issue of concentration lies at the heart of the theoretical debate.

Competition and concentration

In the theory of media structure, much attention has been paid to the question of uniformity and diversity. Most social theory concerned with the 'public interest' places a value on diversity, and there is also an economic dimension involved — that of monopoly versus competition. Free competition, as noted, should lead to variety and to change of media structure, although critics point to a reverse effect: that it leads to monopoly, or at least oligopoly (undesirable on economic as well as social grounds). As far as media economics are concerned, there are three main aspects to the question: inter-media competition, intra-medium competition and interfirm competition. Inter-media competition depends chiefly on whether products can be substituted for one another (such as news on radio for news on television or in the newspaper) and on whether advertising can be substituted from one medium to another. Both substitutions seem possible only up to a certain point. There always appears to be some 'niche' in which a particular medium has an advantage (Dimmick and Rothebuhler, 1984). All media types also seem to be able to offer some distinctive advantages to advertisers: of form of message, timing, type of audience, context of reception, etc. (Picard, 1989).

Horizontal versus vertical concentration

In general, because units of the *same* medium sector are more readily substitutable than between media, the focus of attention is often directed at inter-media competition (such as of one newspaper with another in the same market, geographically or otherwise defined). This is where concentration has most tended to develop, within the same medium sector (this may also in part be the result of public policies to limit 'cross-media' monopoly). In general, media concentration has been distinguished according to whether it is 'horizontal' or 'vertical'. Vertical concentration refers to a pattern of ownership which extends through different stages of production and distribution (for instance, a film studio owning a cinema chain) or geographically (a national concern buying city or local newspapers, say).

Horizontal concentration refers to mergers within the same market (for example, of two competing city or national newspaper organizations or of a telephone and a cable network). Both of these processes have happened on a large scale in a number of countries, although the effects may have been modified by continuing inter-media choice and the rise of new media. Choice is often protected by public policies against 'cross-media ownership' (different media being owned and operated by the same firm, especially in the same geographical market). The media can also become involved in horizontal concentration through the merging of firms in different industries, so that a newspaper or television channel can be owned by a non-media business (see Murdock, 1990). This does not directly reduce media diversity but can add to the power of mass media and have wider implications for advertising.

Other types of concentration effect

Another relevant set of distinctions by type of concentration (de Ridder, 1984) relates to the *level* at which it occurs. De Ridder distinguishes between publisher/concern (ownership), editorial and audience levels. The first refers to increased powers of owners (for instance, the growth of large chains of separate newspapers, as in the USA and Canada) or of television stations (as has happened more recently in Italy). The units making up such media enterprises *can* remain editorially independent (as far as content decisions are concerned), although rationalization of business and organization often leads to sharing of certain services and reduces the difference between them. In any case, there is a separate question as to whether editorial concentration, as measured by the number of independent titles, rises or falls in line with publisher concentration. The degree of editorial independence is often hard to assess.

The third question — that of audience concentration — refers to the concentration of audience market share, which also needs to be separately assessed. A relatively minor change of ownership can greatly increase audience concentration (in terms of 'control' by a publishing group). A large number of independent newspaper titles does not in itself set limits to media power or ensure much real choice if most of the audience is concentrated on one or two titles. The condition of the system is certainly not very diverse in that case. The reasons for concern about concentration turn on these two points.

Degrees of concentration

The degree of media concentration is usually measured by the extent to which the largest companies control production, employment, distribution and audience. Although there is no ceiling beyond which one can say the degree is undesirable, according to Picard (1989, pp. 33–4) a 'traditional' threshold of acceptability is one where the top four firms in an industry control more than 50 per cent, or the top eight firms more than 70 per cent. There are several media instances where such thresholds are exceeded or approached — such as the daily newspaper press in the USA, the national daily press in Britain, Japan and France, television in Italy and the international phonogram industry.

The situation of concentration can vary from one of perfect competition to one of complete monopoly, with varying degrees in between. Different media seem inclined to take up different places on this continuum, for a variety of reasons. Perfect competition is rare, but a relatively high level of competition is shown in many countries by book and magazine publishing. Television and national newspapers are generally oligopolistic markets, while true monopoly is now mainly confined to unusual cases of more or less 'natural' monopoly — for instance, cable and telecommunication. A 'natural monopoly' is one where the consumer is best served, on grounds of cost and efficiency, by there being a single supplier (it is usually accompanied by measures to protect the consumer).

Transnationalization

The recent phase of the 'communications revolution' has been marked by a new phenomenon of media concentration — both transnational and multi-media, leading to the world media industry being increasingly dominated by a small number of very large media firms. In some cases, these developments are the achievement of a fairly traditional breed of media 'moguls' (Tunstall and Palmer, 1991), though with new names. The largest world media company was formed in 1989 out of Time and Warner (Steve Ross was the founding entrepreneur), but other named players have been the Italian press and television tycoon Silvio Berlusconi and Rupert Murdoch, head of News International, with large media holdings in the USA, Britain and Australia. In the same economic league belong the German publishing company Bertelsmann, Walt Disney, Paramount and Viacom.

The other transnational concentration phenomenon of note is the trend for media production (software) companies to be taken over by electronic (hardware) firms (especially Japanese, such as Sony and Matsushita). According to Murdock (1990, p. 6), the conglomerate has become the 'modal form of media enterprise'. He underlines the significance of conglomeration involving overlaps between communication and non-media businesses. Despite the high visibility of larger-than-life media moguls, it is likely that the trend is rather towards more impersonal patterns of ownership and operation, as befits such large global enterprises. The most internationally concentrated branch of the media industry is probably the music business, with five international companies (in 1990) controlling over 60 per cent of the global market for all kinds of music sales and income.

The reasons for increasing media concentration are the same as for other branches of business — especially the search for economies of scale and greater market power. In the case of the media it has something to do with the advantages of vertically integrated operation, since larger profits may be made out of distribution than from production. There is also an incentive for media companies to acquire media with a stable cash flow of the kind provided by conventional television channels and daily newspapers (Tunstall, 1991). Control of software production and distribution can be very helpful for electronic companies, which need to make heavy investments in product innovations (such as forms of recording) that depend for their take-off on a good supply of software.

There are also increasing advantages in sharing services and being able to link different distribution systems and different markets. This is generally known as 'synergy'. As Murdock (1990, p. 8) remarks: 'In a cultural system built around "synergy" more does not mean different; it means the same basic commodity appearing in different markets and in a variety of packages.' In this kind of environment, an upward spiral to concentration is continually being applied, since the only way to survive is by growth. The unification of the Single European Market since 1993 has played a part in this spiralling effect. Often, national restrictions on growth within a single country (because of anti-monopoly or cross-media ownership regulations) have stimulated cross-national monopoly-forming (Tunstall, 1991).

Policy issues arising

The trend towards greater media concentration, nationally and internationally, gives rise to three main kinds of public policy issues. One relates to pricing, another to the product and a third to the position of competitors. The main pricing issue has to do with consumer protection, since the more monopoly there is the greater the power of the provider to set prices. A media example is offered by the case of cable television, which can gradually acquire a distribution monopoly for the residents of a locality, where there is limited substitutability. Competition in most other media sectors is effective in keeping prices down. A separate question relates to rates charged to advertisers under conditions of monopoly, and similar considerations arise.

The main product issue has to do with the content of a monopoly-supplied media service, especially questions of adequate quality and choice, both for the consumer and for would-be providers of content. The third issue, concerning competitors, refers to the driving out of competitors as a result of economies of scale or advantages in the advertising market of high density of coverage or use of financial power to engage in 'ruinous competition'. Concentration will generally impinge only on competitors in the same market, but it can extend further.

For all the reasons given, there has been much research directed at the consequences of concentration (whether good or bad), especially for the newspaper sector of media where concentration has been greatest (see Picard et al., 1988). The results of research have been generally inconclusive, partly because of the complexity whereby the fact of concentration is usually only one aspect of a dynamic market situation. Most attention has focused on the consequences for content, with particular reference to the adequacy of **local news** and information, the performance of the **political and opinion-forming** functions of media, the degree of

access to different voices and the degree and kind of **choice and diversity** (McQuail, 1992). While, by definition, media concentration always reduces choice in some respects, it is possible that the profits of monopoly can be returned to the consumer or community in the form of better media. The profits can also be channelled to shareholders (Squires, 1992).

Distinctive features of media economics

This account of the main economic principles of media structure and dynamics can be concluded by pointing to some typical features of the economics of media, which at the same time distinguish them from other kinds of business. First, we can say that the media are typically 'hybrid' or mixed in character. Often they operate in a dual market — selling a product to consumers and a service to advertisers. They are also extremely diversified in terms of the type of product sold and the range of technologies and organizational means for distribution. Secondly, media cost structures are characterized by high labour intensiveness and high fixed costs (although both dependencies are diminishing as a result of technological change and media expansion).

Media economics

- Media are hybrid in respect of markets, product and technology
- Media have high fixed costs
- Media business involves creativity and uncertainty
- Products can be multiply used/recycled
- Media tend naturally to concentration
- Media business is difficult to enter
- Media are not just any other business because of public interest aspect

---

A third feature of the media is the high degree of uncertainty and also uniqueness of product. Uncertainty refers to consumer evaluation (it is still difficult to predict audience tastes for music, films or books, however much manipulation through publicity is tried). Fourthly, despite standardization, many media products can be, and have to be, endlessly differentiated on a day-to-day basis and can rarely be repeatedly sold in exactly the same form. Fifthly, the media seem especially prone to concentration tendencies, perhaps because the advantages of monopoly control of advertising markets are so evident, and perhaps because of the appeal of power and social prestige to would-be media 'tycoons'. Sixthly, many media businesses (at least those involving distribution) are unusually hard to enter without large capital resources (mainly because of high fixed costs and high launch costs). One cannot hope to start up a significant newspaper or a television channel 'in a small way', although there are always some specialist niche markets available. Finally, the media are different just because they are affected by a public interest (Melody, 1990), and thus 'not just any other business', and tend to be burdened with a considerable weight of public responsibility, whether they like it or not (sometimes they do).

Dynamics of media structure

Only a few brief remarks are possible about the dynamics of media structure, although it is a large topic. All media structures are temporary arrangements, with only the appearance of solidity, although this appearance is itself the result of some general forces which are continuously at work in a given society or a particular **market**. These forces are relatively stable and constant in the short term but produce change in the long term. The main enduring forces are: the pursuit of profit in a situation of supply and demand (market forces); the dominance of certain technologies for a period of time; social and economic changes in society; and the various political and policy goals which often shape the working environment of media. Of the four, the most generally predictable and unchanging are market forces, although the consequences are always dependent on other (more changeable) factors.

As far as market forces are concerned, commercial media are not so very different from any other business, although differences do arise when mass media have a semi-public status and role. The drive towards concentration, for reasons of market control and economies of scale, is probably the most obvious and ubiquitous process of change, affecting almost all mass media in one way or another. A second main process of change in media is also characteristic of all business environments: namely, the rise and fall of firms in a more or less cyclical pattern, reflecting variable commercial dynamism and investment as well as changes in conditions of operation. Media may be especially sensitive to changing social and cultural trends. The rise and fall of the general family weekly magazine in the United States over the period 1880-1940 are an example of change caused by changing social pattern rather than market or technological forces (van Zuylen, 1977).

That changing communication technology causes change needs little argument, since it is obvious that media institutions have developed around a succession of different technologies (as described in Chapter 1), which constantly open up the potential for new markets and undermine old ones. Even this process of change is usually managed, as far as possible, to avoid major disruption to the industry. DeFleur (1970) convincingly demonstrated that the diffusion of successive new media technologies, from the press through to television, followed a similar cumulative S-shaped curve, and we can expect the same pattern to apply to the many new electronic media forms. At some point a critical mass appears to be reached which is a precondition for take-off. The rise of new technology does not usually eclipse old media entirely but causes them to adapt to the new market conditions.

The role of public policy (in effect, politics) in relation to media change is ambiguous, sometimes seeking to hold back or firmly manage change, sometimes to encourage it for economic or ideological reasons. The history of broadcasting in Western Europe since about 1980 is illustrative of this (see Siune and Truetzschler, 1992). Until that point in time, for half a century the development of radio and television had been kept firmly in the hands of national governments and under conditions of legal monopoly. The broadcast media were deemed too important to society to be left to the marketplace, and the intrinsically monopolistic character of broadcasting was thought to need strong public control to protect consumers.

These political arrangements were fundamentally undermined by four main kinds of change which were largely outside the control of European national governments: technological advances in the means of transmission (satellite and cable) made the original justification of monopoly (shortage of airwaves and channels) obsolete and made it physically very difficult to maintain the system of national monopoly; there arose powerful economic arguments for opening up the market to encourage industrial development of new communication technology; moves towards European integration, political as well as economic, also implied trans-border freedom of communication and worked against tight national control; and the public service character of the 'old order' of broadcasting was inconsistent with a rising tide of free-market ideology.

The results can be seen in the ending of public broadcasting monopolies in Europe, the opening of frontiers to transnational television, the multiplication of television channels and the appearance of strong commercial competition for the public television and radio channels. Broadcast institutions have been radically adapted, and a new phase of (still limited) competition is under way, with further change to be expected, as the financial basis of public television is further undermined. In Central and Eastern Europe, for different reasons, there have been parallel movements from public to commercial arrangements.

The European case is illustrative both of the continuing strength and of the ultimate limits of public policy for managing media change. Richer societies with the will to do so can keep their media under control, but only so far as technology and the wider political environment allow. The much more economically dependent countries of the Third World are much more exposed to external forces outside their control. Salvaggio (1985) developed a model in which he compared four different types of society in relation to their communication policy goals and potential for implementation. The four types are: competitive, free-market; public utility (the mixed or social-market economies of Western Europe); communist (as in China or the former Soviet Union); and Third World (most developing countries). Salvaggio argues that the same general factors govern policy in all four types of society, but that each society will have a more or less constant guideline of its own (the **ideology** of the society, such as 'development' or 'free enterprise'), while at least one other variable factor will exert a dominant influence on what is done to promote or control change. In the case of free-market societies, this will be **economic forces**; and in the case of developing countries, it is **external forces** outside the control of the national society.

The regulation of mass media: alternative models

For reasons which have been explained, mass media institutions carry a heavy weight of rules, regulation and scrutiny. The shape and rationale of media regulation can only be sketched here. The normative basis for the principles underlying regulation has been discussed in Chapter 5. The simplest way of describing media regulation is in terms of three basic models (see Pool, 1983), which apply, approximately and respectively, to the newspaper press, to radio and television broadcasting and to telecommunication.

The free press model

The basic model for the press is one of freedom from any government regulation and control which would imply censorship or limits on freedom of publication. Press freedom is often enshrined as a principle in national constitutions and in international charters, such as the European Treaty on Human Rights. However, the press freedom model is often modified or extended by public policy in order to guarantee the expected public interest benefits of a free and independent press. Prominent among the reasons for public policy attention to newspapers are some of the economic tendencies noted above — especially the trend towards concentration which, although the result of free economic competition, effectively reduces access to press channels and choice for citizens. Because of this, the press often receives some legal protection as well as some economic benefits. Both imply some element of public scrutiny and supervision, however benevolent. Economic benefits can range from postal and tax concession to loan and subsidy arrangements. They may also involve anti-concentration laws and rules against foreign ownership.

The free press model (of no regulation) has not prevented some legal or institutional limits being set to press conduct, in the interests of public order and decency, security or the interests of minorities. The press freedom model applies in much the same way to book publishing (where it originates) and to most other print media. By default it also applies to music, although without any special privileges.

The broadcasting model

By contrast, radio and television broadcasting and, less directly, many newer means of audiovisual delivery have been subject from their beginning to high levels of restriction and direction, often involving direct public ownership. The initial reasons for regulation of broadcasting were mainly technical or to ensure the fair allocation of scarce resources and control of monopoly. However, regulation became deeply institutionalized, at least until the 1980s when new technologies and a new climate of opinion reversed the trend.

The general concept of public service lies at the core of the broadcasting model, although there are several variants, as well as weaker (as in the USA) or stronger forms (as in Europe). Public service broadcasting in a fully developed form (such as in Britain) generally has several main features, supported by policy and regulation (see pages 126–7). One is the provision of a universal service (a full service to all). A second is that the system should be financed by payments from all citizens (not just the consumers). Thirdly, there is public control of access as sender, in greater or less detail, to ensure 'fairness', political neutrality and independence from vested interests and the state. Fourthly, a public broadcasting service is democratically accountable to the society (or nation). Fifthly, a public service seeks to achieve various goals of quality of service, as determined according to local cultural and social priorities.

The broadcasting model can involve an enormous range of different kinds of regulation. Usually, there are specific media laws to regulate the industry and often some form of public service bureaucracy to implement the law. Quite often, the services of production and distribution may be undertaken by private enterprise concerns, operating concessions from the government and following some legally enforceable supervisory guidelines. Although public broadcasting nearly always involves some significant element of financing from public sources, there are often significant independent sources of revenue (especially from advertising).

The decline in strength of the broadcasting model has been marked by increasing tendencies towards 'privatization' and 'commercialization' of broadcasting, especially in Europe (see Siune and Truetszchler, 1992). This has involved, most notably, the transfer of media channels and operation from public to private ownership, increased levels of financing from advertising and the franchising of new commercial competitors for public broadcasting channels. Despite its relative decline, however, the broadcasting model shows no sign of being abandoned, for reasons related to the presumed communicative power of audiovisual media and broader public interest concerns (see Chapter 5), which are thought to require fair allocation and some public accountability.

The common carrier model

The third main model of regulation predates broadcasting and is usually called the common carrier model because it relates primarily to communication services such as mail, telephone and telegraph which are purely for distribution and intended to be open to all as universal services. The main motive for regulation has been for efficient implementation and management of what are (or were) 'natural monopolies' (see page 166) in the interests of efficiency and the consumer. In general, common carrier media have involved heavy regulation of the infrastructure and of economic exploitation but only very marginal regulation of content. This is in sharp contrast to broadcasting, which is characterized by a high degree of content regulation, even where infrastructure is increasingly in private hands.

While the three models are still useful for describing and making sense of the different patterns of media regulation which are found side by side, the logic, legitimacy and practicality of maintaining these different regimes are increasingly questioned (see Pool, 1983). The main challenge comes from the technological 'convergence' between modes of communication which makes the regulatory separation between print, broadcasting and telecommunication increasingly artificial and arbitrary. The same means of distribution, especially satellites and telecommunication, can be used to deliver all three kinds of media; and the monopolistic and regulatory arrangements which used, especially, to keep radio, television and telecommunication restricted to their own patch are widely being demolished or undermined. Cable systems are already legally permitted in some places to offer telephone services; broadcasting can deliver newspapers; and the telephone network can provide television services. For the moment, a political and regulatory logic survives, but it will not endure.

Three regulatory models compared			
	Print	Broad-casting	Common carrier
Regulation of infrastructure	None	High	High
Regulation of content	None	High	None
Sender access	Open	Closed	Open
Receiver access	Open	Open	Closed

Inter-country differences: the social and cultural specificity of media systems

In this account of media structure the emphasis has been on the combination of general economic and technological factors which shape and drive media industries in different parts of the world. While there are many similarities between countries, and these are likely to increase rather than to diminish, there are also enduring differences between media systems which have their origins in facts of history, geography, culture and politics. The media are still very much the institutions of particular nation states, and their particular character and mode of integration depend on factors which lie outside media systems. It is important not to underestimate this continued diversity, nor to assume that we can properly understand the media of a particular society in terms of a few more or less universal features of structure and dynamics. It is not only *systems* which differ markedly from country to country, but also patterns of cultural preference and of actual media use behaviour.

It is impossible to summarize the full diversity of media structure, but we can point to a few of the dimensions which differentiate national media systems. The main relevant dimensions relate to massification and centralization, the amount and kind of politicization, cultural profiling, diversity, public regulation and control, and the balance of funding. These dimensions are of interest because it is widely assumed that media systems are converging towards a common destination on these very points. In general, the media are thought to be becoming not only 'globalized' but also less massified, more decentralized, more oriented to popular taste and culture, less (or more) diverse (according to perspective), less politicized, less regulated and more commercial in funding. The reality is not so simple.

In relation to **massification**, there are large initial variations between countries in the degree of dominance by a few sources or media owners. This is especially true of the newspaper press. The United States, for instance, has no truly mass circulation newspaper (*pace USA Today*), unlike the United Kingdom, Germany or Japan. There is a similar range in respect of **centralization**. Some countries have media systems which are dominated by a metropolitan centre (examples are the United Kingdom and Japan), while others (most in fact) retain strongly regionalized print media (potentially extending to other media, despite internationalization). The causes of these differences are often circumstantial or culturally specific.

While a commonly told story describes the gradual 'secularization' of the press along with its **commercialization** and changing role in modern societies, there are very big differences in the degree and kind of *political* role played by the press (and sometimes other media) in society. The newspapers (and other media) of the United States tend, for instance, to be presented as the model of politically neutral information providers (despite evidence to the contrary) and the European press as partisan and advocative. In reality, virtually all newspapers are ideological, but with varying degrees of openness and acceptability. The open party-political commitment of many newspapers in Europe stems mainly from their particular history but has also to do with their being national (rather than city or local) in orientation. Politics is one way of identifying their loyal readership. Each country has its own particular model and its own story to tell. Broadcasting is often theoretically neutral(ized) but in practice highly politicized in diverse and subtle ways (especially in Europe) which are not easy to perceive or explain outside the particular national context.

The **cultural profile** of media systems refers to such matters as the balance between 'quality' and 'sensational' sections of the press or of television programming content, or to expectations and actual performance in matters of culture, whether relating to education, the traditional arts or the national 'cultural heritage'. It is probable that different systems measure up in different ways to what are often locally specific expectations. At the very least, there is endless room for argument about what is desirable and a mass of evidence is available demonstrating actual differences. Much the same can be said of **diversity**, since what counts as a desirable range is determined differently in each country, despite the widely current assumption that increasing the number of channels increases consumer choice. For many, diversity is defined not in these terms but according to relevant cultural divisions and the needs of minorities.

Despite the deregulatory trend and the increased dominance of market principles, there are strong pockets of resistance and new forms of control which respond to changed conditions. One example is provided by the European Union rules relating to the content of cross-border television transmission between member states (see page 181) and the more recent moves to assess the need for measures to protect the pluralism of the newspaper press in Europe. The new potential for telecommunication as a multi-media carrier has also had consequences for the extension of regulation as well as for deregulation and privatization. In respect of **financing** of media, it is still early to conclude that any particular form of financing will dominate or that public subsidies in their many forms will disappear.

All national media systems appear to be in a state of permanent flux, mainly as a result of the same technological changes. Even so, neither the media practices nor the established economic and regulatory patterns have yet converged on anything like a single model, despite superficially similar trends. A simple reason for this is that the technological changes imply very different consequences according to the specific national situation. The differences are rooted not only in politics, culture and history but also in varying market circumstances (reflecting the great complexity of the media business). Economics as much as culture inhibits the convergence which technology is supposed to produce. Media markets are still very culturally specific. The same forces which are at work nearly everywhere are as much inclined to differentiate as they are to unify in their consequences. Commonly experienced trends (such as that of media globalization) do not logically have to lead to the same outcomes.

International communication: structural aspects

Mass media institutions are still overwhelmingly *national* in character, although the international flow of mass communication is large and growing in volume. Some media organizations do have transnational communication as their primary objective, and others are organized largely towards international audiences. One of the most important origins of the newspaper was the channelling of information about events in Europe (and further afield) through the routes of the postal system, which was then published as news in the commercial centres of the early seventeenth century, especially Amsterdam and London. The most significant examples of international media organizations are still probably the global news and news-film agencies, even though these have a strong national base. Other media with an international task were the numerous radio stations designed to disseminate information and the cultural and political messages of various nation states. This media phenomenon continues, but it hardly counts as mass communication.

The film industry, especially under the domination of Hollywood (Tunstall, 1977), from early days took on an international character, even if distribution was in local hands. The pattern of producing for international markets has spread to recorded music and to television (especially fiction) in a large way, aided by the relative ease with which pictures and sound can cross barriers of culture, language and distance. It remains the case, nevertheless, that nearly all international media flow still has to have a strong national base, and there is relatively little media production purely for non-localized international markets.

This means that the originators of international communication flows continue to be countries (or companies) which have the strongest home markets (Hoskins and Mirus, 1988; Hoskins et al., 1989). In addition, because English has become established as the nearest to a lingua franca for film, television and popular music, English-speaking countries have an advantage in the richest global markets. The national base of international communication is being eroded by multinational media conglomeration, which tends towards the delocation of production, making national origin less easy to determine and also less significant as a distinguishing feature.

Satellite technology has made the worldwide distribution of television technically feasible and easily affordable, leading to a significant number of media services oriented to world markets (audience and advertising). These services take several forms. Some offer specific content services for reception by cable or satellite dish — for instance, in the form of music, news, art, sport, education or movies. Some are the television equivalent of the older radio 'world services', though more with linguistic and cultural than with political goals. Others are commercial companies which offer general services designed to cross more than one national frontier. Most examples of these are to be found in Europe.

Another important component of international mass communication is advertising, stemming from the globalization of product markets and the international character of many advertising agencies. One direct result is the appearance of the same advertising film spot in different countries, but there is also an indirect internationalizing effect on media seeking to carry such advertising. Technology is stimulating more international media communication in other ways than by direct satellite television broadcasting. The international telecommunication network is becoming increasingly important as the infrastructure for global communication.

The seeming confusion about the components of international mass communication can be simplified if we consider the stages of production and distribution separately (see Figure 6.2 below). As to the first, media content originates with particular sources or producers (such as film or music companies and television stations/networks), but the actual products can be more or less international in content (in language, theme, format, 'inscribed' audience, etc). Either the distribution stage can take place in one country, with transmission (and reception) across frontiers (as with typical 'world service' radio), or it can take place within one national media system, using media content produced in a foreign country. There are several different combinations.

Sepstrup (1989) has suggested that we classify transnational communication flow (in particular television) as either 'national', 'bilateral' or 'multilateral'. The first refers to all imported content (for instance, films, television series, advertisements or press or film news agency items) which are chosen for transmission within the national media system. The second refers to direct cross-border transmission from one country to a neighbour (such as from Britain to Ireland, the Netherlands to Belgium or the USA to Canada). Multilateral communication refers to flow which has no distinctive destination and sometimes no clear national origin (such as MTV or CNN International). The available evidence suggests that the first kind of internationalization of media is by far the most important in terms of volume of flow and reach, and, on the face of it, it remains within the control of the country at the receiving end (but see below).

Multinational media ownership and control

Certain types of media content lend themselves to globalization of ownership and control of production and distribution. These include 'foreign news', feature films, popular music recordings, television serials and books. Tunstall (1991) refers to these as 'one-off' media, by contrast with the 'cash-flow' media of newspapers and television stations, which have generally resisted multinational ownership. The 'one-off' product can be more easily designed for an international market and lends itself to more flexible marketing and distribution over a longer time span. 'News' was the first product to be 'commodified' in the way indicated, by way of the main international news agencies. These are, in effect, 'wholesale' suppliers of news as a commodity, and it is easy to see why national news media find it much more convenient and economical to 'buy in' news about the rest of the world than to collect it themselves.

The rise of the global news agencies of the twentieth century was made possible by technology (telegraph and radio-telephony) and stimulated by war, trade, imperialism and industrial expansion (Boyd-Barrett, 1980). For these reasons, the main press agencies in the post-war era were North American (UPI and Associated Press), or British (Reuters), French (AFP) or Russian (Tass). Since then, the US predominance has declined, with the virtual demise of UPI, while other agencies have grown (such as the German DPA and the Japanese Kyodo). According to Tunstall (1992), Europe is now the largest producer and consumer of foreign news, and the 'strongest single news entity' in the world is the 'loose Reuters–Visnews–BBC alliance'. It is clear that predominance is, as always, shaped by the domestic strength of the media organizations concerned, in terms of market size, degree of concentration and economic resources.

The foremost example of internationalization of ownership, production and distribution is that of the popular music industry (a development of the last fifty years), with a high proportion of several major markets being in the hands of the 'big five' companies (Burnett, 1990; Negus, 1993). These were (as of 1993): Columbia (a former US company bought by Sony of Japan), Time–Warner (the world's largest media conglomerate), RCA (now owned by the German company Bertelsmann), EMI (Britain's Thorn Electronics) and Polygram (now Dutch and German owned, by Philips and Siemens).

The pattern is the result of European and Japanese firms buying into leading US music companies, for reasons of 'synergy' between media hardware and software, and also reflecting the shift of consumer market strength from the USA to Europe, as a result of globalization. Contributing to what has happened is the lack of special protection of the US music industry from foreign ownership, of the kind enjoyed by press and television (the film industry is similarly open to normal international market trends).

International media dependency

While there is no international media *system* as such, many commentators have pointed to the fact that market forces have in practice led to the rise of a rather rigid and inescapable structure of global media ownership, production and distribution, which is dominated by the richer (and capitalistic) countries of the North (especially North America, Europe and Japan). The term 'cultural imperialism' (see Tomlinson, 1991; and see page 116) has been widely used to refer to the phenomenon. A few countries certainly do dominate the *international* flow of news and culture, supplying the other countries of the world (numerically greater) with what they cannot easily produce for themselves to fill domestic media. The main trends have already been explained: the rise of multinational business empires; attempts by competing power blocs to spread their power and influence; and the rise of

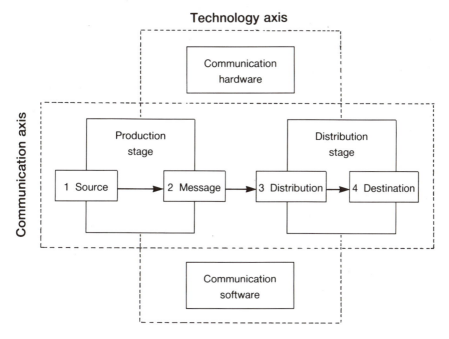

Figure 6.2 *International communication dependency (Mowlana, 1985): each stage in the mass communication process can be identified as having a hardware and a software aspect of potential dependency*

an international 'media culture' in which certain formats, languages and types of story have come to find wide acceptance in many different societies.

Mowlana (1985) made a general analysis of all forms of international communication (of which mass communication may be only a minor element) and drew a model in which two dimensions are shown to be determinant for these issues. These are the **technology axis** (hardware versus software) and the **communication axis** (production versus distribution). The main features of the model appear in Figure 6.2.

The model represents a familiar sequence from sender (1) to receiver (4), mediated by a technologically based production (2) and (3) distribution system. In international communication, the situation differs from that at national level, in that each of the four stages can be (and often is) spatially, organizationally and culturally separated from the other stages. As noted above, media products from one country may be incorporated in a message produced in another country (such as a news bulletin) and distributed in that or even a third country. More commonly, the whole production stage is carried out in one country and distributed and received in another. This is how the richer North is often related to the poorer South.

This typically extended and discontinuous process is cross-cut by the technology axis, which reminds us that each stage in the process is dependent on two kinds of expertise (and property), relating to hardware or software. Production hardware consists, for instance, of studios and printing presses, distribution hardware of transmitters, satellite links, home receivers, etc. Production software includes such elements as scripts, performance rights, management and professional norms. Distribution software includes publicity, research and marketing. At both stages (production and distribution) there are 'extra-' as well as 'intra-' media variables — on the production side facts of ownership and economics, for instance, and on the distribution side also social and economic factors which determine whether or not information actually flows through international channels.

The model portrays the condition of multiple dependency in the flow of communication from more developed to less developed countries. The latter are often dependent in respect of all four main elements in the sequence, and each may be controlled from the originating country. Self-sufficiency in media terms is, it seems, completely out of reach and even receding. The flow of news is both very selective and one-directional. Organizational gatekeeping and the application of news values (see Chapter 8) ensure that news is chosen to reflect the interests of the audiences of the large 'news-producing' countries. The dominance of the world news business by a few large news and news-film agencies reinforces the bias in the content of what is available for many news media around the world. News sources, actual news stories and the means of international transmission and delivery to audiences are concentrated in the North. For the media of dependent countries (mainly in the South), there is no practical alternative to making use of the international news facilities which serve the developed world.

The situation has been explained in terms of a 'centre–periphery' model of news flow (Galtung in Mowlana, 1985). According to this model, the world is divided into either dominant central or dependent peripheral lands, with a predominant news flow from the former towards the latter. The larger, 'central' news-originating lands have their own 'satellites', although these are much less dependent and have their own news-gathering and news-processing resources.

There is little or no flow between peripheral countries themselves, although there are *regional* (in the global sense) patterns of news flow and dependency, which lead to some intra-peripheral news relationships. For instance, there are patterns which interrelate some Far Eastern countries and the Caribbean, Latin American and North African sub-regions. This supports the view that there is no single centre, and changes under way in world power and economic relations will continually modify the reality. An additional feature of the situation is the fact that international news is often gathered in the South by correspondents from the North, where it returns to be processed and edited before its eventual return for distribution by the local media in the South.

The pattern of flow of international news cannot be fully understood just by looking at the structure of international media organizations. It is strongly shaped by other social, cultural, political and economic factors, especially affinities of culture, propinquity, patterns of trade between nations and political relations (as shown by treaties and alliances) (Ito and Koshevar, 1983).

International media regulation

The complex and disparate set of activities which makes up the 'system' of international mass communication is, of its very nature, subject to no coherent regulation, although some elements do come within the scope of various voluntary agreements for economic, legal or political purposes. There is an increasing degree of voluntary international regulation of technical matters, especially in relation to telecommunications, the radio spectrum and satellite communication. Some business matters come within the scope of international trade agreements, and there are extensive agreements covering copyright. As yet, the *content* of mass communication is not much directly affected by regulation, although there have been attempts to reach some codes of practice. These efforts go back a long way and were originally designed to respond to the use of mass media for national and militaristic propaganda (Nordenstreng, 1984).

The United Nations (especially via UNESCO) has been one forum in which the potential role of the mass media in development and in matters of war and peace has been debated and moves to regulation have been urged. In 1978 UNESCO introduced a Media Declaration concerning International Communication, with a view to getting governments to agree on certain standards in news reporting concerning other countries and ensuring respect for national communication sovereignty. The effort failed, largely because of the conflict with journalistic freedom which could be entailed.

Within Europe, there have been more successful attempts, within the context of the European Union and the Council of Europe, to establish a framework of good practice within which national broadcasting should operate in an age of easy trans-border penetration (by satellite and cable) and of more limited media sovereignty. The question of sovereignty was rarely seen as a problem in respect of print media, and for a long time the case of broadcasting presented no significant issue, because the normal range of transmission was limited. The European Union has established a legally enforceable framework relating to television which sets minimum standards concerning, *inter alia*, the permitted level and type of advertising and the protection of minors, which apply to any trans-border transmissions to other member countries of the EU. A similar, but voluntary, agreement applies to most of the countries affiliated to the Council of Europe. Despite this initiative in the direction of international control of the media, it seems likely that the regulation of international communication will continue to be by way of voluntary and informal agreement, with a large measure of market, artistic and journalistic freedom.

Conclusion

Despite the enormous variety of industrial and organizational media activities, there are some consistent lines of force and some patterns to be found. Even so, theory of media structure and organization (as distinct from economic theory) is hard to conceive without the application of critical or normative perspectives.

PART III
ORGANIZATIONS

7

THE MEDIA ORGANIZATION IN
ITS CONTEXT

Issues and perspectives

The media organization, where media content is 'made', is an essential link
in the process of mediation by which 'society', as it were, addresses itself.
While the work of media organizations belongs within the scope of any
theory of mass communication, it is so varied that it can be dealt with only
selectively. At best, we can hope to find empirical generalizations which
describe some of the recurring features of media production. There is now a
relatively large body of empirical research into mass communication which
in one way or another sheds light on the nature of media organizations, the
forces at work within them, the external influences upon their activity and
the influence of particular organizational features on what they produce and
disseminate in the way of 'media culture'.

One very simple and general framework within which questions can be
posed takes as its starting point the institutional structures as described in
Chapter 6. Accordingly, these **structures** (for instance, size, forms of
ownership and media-industrial function) can be seen as having direct
consequences for the **conduct** of particular media organizations (all the
systematic activities within them), which in turn affects **performance**, in the
sense of the relative amount and type of media content produced and
offered to audiences. We need to look not only at the media organization
but also at its relations with other organizations and with the wider society.
We also need to look *within* the organization, at its internal structure and
activities. This means paying attention to those who work in the media — the
'mass communicators' (see Ettema et al., 1987).

Research on media organizations goes back to the 1960s, although there
are earlier examples of attention being given to some categories of 'media
people' (for example, Rosten, 1937, on Washington correspondents, and
1941, on Hollywood film-makers). Organizational research reflects a gradual
shift of interest from media effects to the characteristic features of media
content and then to the organizational sources and 'causes' of these features.
At the same time, it reflects a concern to know how 'society' exerts an
influence on the media, something which can be uncovered only by
knowing how the media themselves operate.

Organizational influences on content

It is possible to channel nearly all the main theoretical questions about media and society through an examination of media organizations, although in the end this is not very helpful, and it is better to concentrate on a few central issues of media organizational structure and conduct. Two overarching issues can be identified:

- What degree of freedom does a media organization possess in relation to the wider society and how much freedom is possible within the organization?
- How do media-organizational routines and procedures for selecting and processing content influence what is produced?

These two questions roughly correspond to the duality noted above of structural effect on organizational conduct and effect of the latter, in its turn, on content produced. Between them they generate a large number of subsidiary issues. Both questions, for instance, lead to consideration of the perennial issue of the tensions between constraint and autonomy, routine production and creativity, commerce and art, bureaucracy and individual freedom, and profit and social purpose. The broad range of issues which arise can be appreciated when one takes an overview of theoretical perspectives organized around the question of 'influences on media content', as posed by Shoemaker and Reese (1991). Drawing on suggestions from Gans (1979) and Gitlin (1980), they name five main hypotheses:

1 Content reflects social reality (mass media as mirror of society);
2 Content is influenced by media workers' socialization and attitudes (a communicator-centred approach);
3 Content is influenced by media-organizational routines;
4 Content is influenced by social institutions and forces;
5 Content is a function of ideological positions and maintains the status quo (the hegemonic approach).

This chapter is not only concerned with direct influences on content, although ultimately this is what matters most. The most directly relevant of the five hypotheses are numbers 2 and 3, although we cannot understand the how and why of media organizations without attention to 4. Hypothesis 1 is also of interest, since organizational routines have helped most to explain why media content does *not* mirror social reality. Hypothesis 5 lies outside the scope of this chapter but can never be tested unless we know how media organizations work.

Alternative modes of analysis

Most of the research and theory discussed in the following pages is 'media-centric' rather than 'society-centric' (see Chapter 7), taking or recording the view from within the media, and this may lead to an overestimation of the significance of organizational influences on content. From a 'society-centric' point of view, much of what media organizations do is determined by external social forces, including, of course, the requirements of media audiences. The question of 'paradigm choice' (see page 41) has not been very sharply posed in relation to research on media organizations, since it tends to call for a mixture of both qualitative and quantitative methods and attracts critical as well as neutral perspectives. There is also scope for applying structural, behavioural and cultural analysis, since all three are relevant. The predominant method of research has been participant observation of media people at work or depth interviewing of involved informants. On some points, survey research has provided essential additional information (for instance, on questions of occupational role and work-force social composition).

In general, the theory which has been formulated on the basis of research into media organizations, while fragmentary, has been fairly consistent in supporting the view that content is systematically and distinctively influenced by organizational practices (and imperatives). It is for this reason that the first hypothesis stated above (content reflects reality) has been rejected. The fifth (hegemonic) hypothesis has found some support but has also been called into question, depending on the kind and the standard of evidence found acceptable.

The rise of a research tradition

There has been a gradual development in the research agenda relating to media organizations, starting with rather individualistic attention being given to the social background and personal attitudes of 'mass communicators' as the dominant influence on content, as if the media message was really the expression of particular individuals. The main step forward was to appreciate the degree to which the requirements of a formal work organization (a bureaucracy) take precedence over the personal leanings of the communicators within it. During the 1970s, in particular, there was a flood of research into 'news-making', stimulated initially by evidence of patterning and selective attention (sometimes called 'bias') in news content and by debates over news objectivity and the nature of 'news values'.

The largely consistent findings showed the news product to be, in one sense or another, an artificial and very predictable symbolic 'construction' of reality. However, this conclusion was itself open to alternative interpretations, since it could result either from a hegemonic ideology or simply from the standardization to be expected in any mass production process. It is here that the choice of critical perspective (and wider social theory) comes into play. Gradually, more attention began to be paid to the production of non-journalistic content, especially drama, music and entertainment (Ettema and Whitney, 1982; Turow, 1991; Tunstall, 1993), although this has remained an undeveloped and fragmentary field of research compared to the attention paid to journalism and news.

New life has been given to organizational research by major changes in the structure of media industries, especially the processes of globalization, ownership conglomeration and organizational fragmentation. New means of distribution (such as cable, satellite and telecommunication networks) have also given rise to new kinds of media organization. Perspectives based on questions of gender have also widened the range of critical inquiry.

Levels of analysis

It is increasingly difficult to speak of a 'media organization' as if there were a single ideal-typical form. The original term was largely based on the model of an independent newspaper, within which all the principal activities of management, financial control, news collection and processing, printing and distribution took place more or less under one roof. This model was always untypical of media in general, not applying, for instance, to the film, book publishing or music industries and applying only variably to radio and television. It is virtually impossible to apply it to cable television, which interrelates several separate and disparate organizational functions. As a model, it is best suited to studying news production, which takes place within a unity of time and space. It is least suited to the spheres of fiction, music and entertainment, where creation, selection, processing, production and distribution are often organizationally very separate from each other.

The diversity of organizational forms is matched by the diversity of occupational groups which might qualify as 'mass communicators'. These have been taken as including movie moguls and press tycoons, actors, television producers, film directors, script-writers, book authors, newspaper and broadcast journalists, song-writers, disc-jockeys, musicians, literary agents, newspaper and magazine editors, advertisers and public relations people, campaign managers, and many more. Most of these categories are also subdividable according to type of medium and size or status of the work organization, employment status, etc. A good deal of media work takes place on a freelance or entrepreneurial basis (such as film-making — Boorman, 1987), and many media workers (notably writers and actors) belong to no single production organization, even if they may belong to professional or craft associations. As a result, the concepts of 'mass communicator' and of 'media profession' are almost as leaky as that of media organization.

Despite this diversity, it still makes sense to try to contain questions of media production within a common framework of analysis. One useful step is to think in terms of levels of analysis, so that the different phases of media work and the significant relations between units of organizational activity and between media and the 'outside world' can be identified for study. Dimmick and Coit (1982), for instance, describe a hierarchy with nine

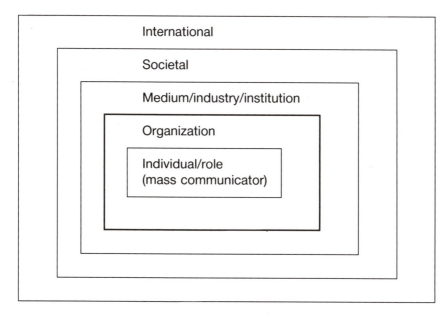

Figure 7.1 *Mass media organizations: levels of analysis*

different levels at which influence or power may be exercised. The main levels and associated sources of influence are: the supra-national (inter-national regulation agencies or multinational firms); society (for instance, government or national social institutions, such as political parties); that of industry (competing media firms, advertisers, etc.); the supra-organizational (chains, conglomerates); the community (city, local business); the intra-organizational (groups or departments within an organization); and the individual (role, social background, personal attitude, gender, ethnic origin). Shoemaker and Reese (1991) employ a somewhat similar hierarchy of levels of influences on media content, which they label (in descending order) as ideological, extra-media, organizational, media routines and individual.

For the purposes of this chapter, a similar but modified hierarchy is employed, as shown in Figure 7.1. The hierarchical presentation implies that the 'higher-order' influence has primacy in terms of strength and direction. This is not necessarily the case in reality, although it does serve to represent the society-centric perspective, according to which media are dependent on their society. It also corresponds to the most likely general balance of power in society. Even so, it is more appropriate to consider the relations between media communicators and their environment as, in principle, interactive and negotiable. It is also appropriate to emphasize that the media organization operates within and maintains its own 'boundaries' (however permeable) and has some degree of autonomy and freedom of choice.

The arrangement of entries recognizes the significance of the individual who carries out media work and is subject to the requirements of the organization, but also has some freedom to define his or her place in it. Most of the discussion which follows relates to the central area of the 'organizational level', but also takes account of the relations across the boundary between the work organization and other agents and agencies of the wider media institution and society. The nature of media institutions as providers and definers of the context of organizational activity has already been discussed (Chapter 6). It is also clear from Chapter 5 that media organizations in their relations with the wider society operate within a terrain which is formally or informally regulated or governed by normative expectations on either side. Such matters as the essential freedoms of publication and the ethical guidelines for many professional activities are laid down by the 'rules of the game' of the particular society.

This implies, for instance, that the relations between media organizations and their operating environment are governed not solely by naked market forces or political power but also by unwritten social and cultural guidelines. Nevertheless, as a further step in identifying and examining key issues of theory relating to media organizations it is useful to consider our notional media organization as an actor engaged in a web of interrelations which do involve exchanges of resources and influence and do depend on the particular balance of power in a particular case.

The media organization in a field of social forces

It follows from what has been said that any theoretical account of media organizations and occupations has to take account of a number of different relationships within and across the boundaries of the organization. These relationships are often active negotiations and exchanges and sometimes conflicts, latent or actual. The influential model of mass communication drawn by Westley and MacLean (1957), which has already been mentioned (page 50), represents the (news) communicator role as that of a broker between, on the one hand, would-be 'advocates' in society with messages to send and, on the other, the public seeking to satisfy its information and other communication needs and interests.

Gerbner (1969) portrayed mass communicators as operating under pressure from various external 'power roles', including clients (such as advertisers), competitors (other media in the main), authorities (especially legal and political), experts, other institutions and the audience. He wrote: 'While analytically distinct, obviously neither power roles nor types of leverage are in reality separate or isolated. On the contrary, they often combine, overlap and telescope . . . the accumulation of power roles and possibilities of leverage gives certain institutions dominant positions in the mass communication of their societies.'

Clearly, in the case of agents of government or business, these can represent powerful leverage and at the same time be 'advocates' in the sense used above (self-interested communicators) and also important *sources* for the media themselves. Not only are they often major would-be

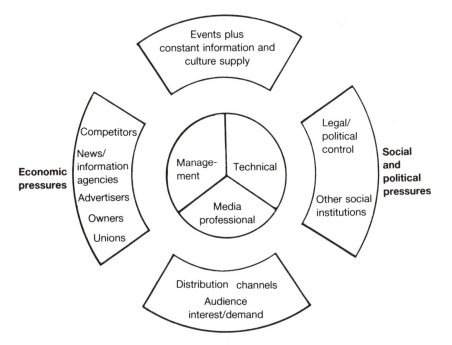

Figure 7.2 *The media organization in a field of social forces*

communicators, they are also *avoiders* of communication attention, except on their own terms. The media have to try to manage the supply of source material in competition with other would-be managers and in latent competition with some of their own sources.

Using these ideas and relying on the wide support for such a view in the research literature (see also Dimmick and Coit, 1982), we can sketch the position of the media organization and those within it as making decisions at the centre of a field of different constraints, demands or attempted uses of power and influence, as in Figure 7.2. The very general hierarchy shown in Figure 7.1 has been converted into a view of more specific actors and agencies in the environment of a media organization. This representation is primarily derived from research on news organizations (especially newspapers), but the picture would be much the same for many similar 'self-contained' and multi-purpose media organizations, including broadcast television (see, for example, Wallis and Baran, 1990).

The pressures and demands illustrated in Figure 7.2 are not all necessarily *constraining* on media organizations. Some can be sources of liberation (for instance, by way of alternative sources of income, or government policy protection for their task). Some of the forces cancel or balance each other (such as audience support against advertiser pressure, or media institutional prestige against external institutional or source pressure). Lack of external pressure would probably indicate social marginality or insignificance.

A further refinement of this scheme, based on the work of Engwall (1978), involves the internal division of the media organization into three dominant work cultures, indicating the main sources of tension and lines of demarcation which have been found to exist within media organizations (see page 194). This presentation allows one to identify five main kinds of relationship which need to be examined in order to gain some understanding of the conditions affecting organizational activity and the mass communicator role: relations with society; with owners, clients, and suppliers; with sources; within the organization; and with the audience. Each is discussed in this chapter, apart from source-relations, which is reserved for Chapter 8.

Types of media-organizational relations

- With society
- With owners, clients and suppliers
- With sources
- Within the organization
- With the audience

Relations with society

A good deal has already been said on this matter, especially in the preceding chapters, dealing with the institutional context and with normative media theory. In most capitalist-democratic societies, the media are free to operate within the limits of the law, but particular issues still arise concerning relations with government and with powerful social institutions and organized pressure groups. How these issues are defined and handled depends in part on the self-defined goals of the media organization. There are likely to be large differences, for instance, between media which adopt or are given a significant social, cultural or political task (true of many news organizations) and those which are primarily concerned with making profits from making and selling media products (generally true of the popular music and commercial cinema industries, for instance). Related to the question of the media's own goals is that of the kind of expectation about access to the media which 'society' may express, through its organized institutions (especially that of democratic politics).

Goals of media organizations

Most organizations have mixed goals, and rarely are they all openly stated. Mass media are no different, and they may even be particularly ambiguous in this respect, given the unclear boundaries and internal fragmentation of media institutions. In organizational theory, a differentiation is often made between utilitarian and normative organizational goals (for example, Etzioni, 1961). The utilitarian organization aims to produce or provide material goods or services for financial ends, while the normative organization aims to advance some value or achieve a valued condition, based on the voluntary commitment of its participants. The position of mass media organizations in respect of this typology is ambiguous, but they often have a mixture of utilitarian and normative goals and forms of operation. Most media are run as businesses but often with some 'ideal' goals, and some media are run primarily for 'idealistic' social or cultural purposes, without seeking profit. For instance, public broadcasting organizations (in Europe especially) have generally had a bureaucratic form of organization but with non-profit social and cultural goals.

Another suggested basis for organizational classification distinguishes according to **type of beneficiary**. Blau and Scott (1963) ask: 'Is it the society as a whole, a particular set of clients, the owners, the audience, or the employees of the organization, whose welfare or good is being served?' Again, no single answer can be given for the media as a whole, and particular organizations often have several actual or potential beneficiaries. Nevertheless, there is some reason to hold that the general public (not always the direct audience) should be the chief beneficiary (see the discussion of public interest on page 135).

A common element in all the normative press theories discussed (in Chapter 5) is that the media should meet the needs and interests of their audience in the first instance and the interests of clients and the state only secondarily. Since media depend on the continuous voluntary choices of their audiences if they are to be either effective or profitable, this principle has a common-sense basis, but the view that the audience comes first is also often expressed by mass communicators.

Drawing from evidence of newspaper journalists, Tunstall (1971) described the organizational goals in economic terms, distinguishing between revenue goals and non-revenue goals, the latter referring to purposes without a direct financial aspect, such as gaining prestige, exercising influence or power in society or achieving some normative end (for instance, serving the community). Revenue goals are of two main kinds — gaining income from direct sales to consumers and from selling space to advertisers. Different kinds of publication policy go with the variation of goals in these terms. While the audience appears to be subordinate in this typology, in practice the satisfaction of advertisers and the gaining of revenue from sales both depend on pleasing the audience, and non-revenue goals are often shaped by some conception of wider public interest. Furthermore, Tunstall indicates that in a case of conflict of goals within the newspaper, the audience revenue goals (increasing the circulation by pleasing the audience) provide the 'coalition goal' on which most can agree (especially management and journalists).

Internal diversity of purpose

The fact that mass media organizations have mixed goals is important for locating the media in their social context, understanding some of the pressures under which they operate and helping to differentiate the main occupational choices available to media workers. It is one essential aspect of a general ambiguity over social role which is discussed a little later. Some further light on this question is shed by the characterization of the newspaper as a 'hybrid organization' (Engwall, 1978), in the sense that it cannot be clearly placed on either of two key organizational dimensions: the manufacture-service dimension, and the dimension of variability of product and technology and use. The newspaper organization is engaged in both making a product and providing a service. It also uses a wide variety of production technology, from the simple to the complex.

In varying degrees, this holds true of other mass media organizations, certainly of broadcasting. Engwall found that several different 'work cultures' flourish, each justified according to a different goal or work task — namely, the news-oriented culture, the politically oriented, the economically oriented and the technically oriented. The first two tend to go together and are expressed by the professional or creative category, noted above (also closer to the 'normative' type), while the second two are essentially 'utilitarian'. Those holding to the news-oriented culture are likely to be journalists collecting and processing news, while the politically oriented will generally comprise editorial staff and senior political correspondents. The economically and technically oriented consist of those involved in financial management and in solving problems of production, and they will have much in common with their counterparts in other business organizations.

In so far as this situation can be generalized, it seems that media organizations are likely to be as internally divided as to purpose as they are different from each other. It is hard to think of another category of organization that is as likely to pursue simultaneously such diverse objectives and serve such divergent values. That this should happen without excessive conflict suggests some fairly stable forms of accommodation to the attendant problems. Such an accommodation may be essential in what Tunstall (1971) has characterized by the paradoxical term of 'non-routine bureaucracy'. It may also indicate the presence in media of an above-average degree of compromise, uncertainty and 'displacement of goals' by comparison with other types of complex organization.

The journalist's role: engagement or neutrality?

Some media organizations (especially public service media and those with an opinion-forming or informational purpose) clearly do seek to play some part in society, but the nature of this role is also open to diverse interpretations. Certain kinds of publication, especially prestige or elite newspapers (such as *Le Monde*, the *Financial Times* and the *Washington Post*) have set out deliberately to be influential through the quality of their information or the authority of their opinion (Padioleau, 1985), but there are several other options for the exercise of influence, and it is not the exclusive property of an internationally known elite press. Small-scale media can be influential in more restricted spheres, and influence can obviously be exercised by mass circulation newspapers and popular television.

There is, nevertheless, a broad choice to be made between a more active and participant, or a more neutral, role in society. Cohen (1963) was one of the first to make the critical distinction along these lines when he (p. 191) distinguished two separate self-conceptions of the reporter's role as that of 'neutral reporter', referring to ideas of the press as informer, interpreter and instrument of government (lending itself as channel or mirror), and that of 'participant', the traditional 'fourth estate' notion, covering ideas of the press as representative of the public, critic of government, advocate of policy and policy-maker. The weight of evidence (for example, Johnstone et al., 1976) is that the neutral, informative role is most preferred by journalists, and it goes with the importance attached by most journalists to objectivity as a core professional value (Lippman, 1922; Carey, 1969; Janowitz, 1975; Roshco, 1975; Phillips, 1977; Schudson, 1978; Tuchman, 1978; Hetherington, 1985; Morrison and Tumber, 1988). It is understandable that strong political commitment (and active engagement) is not easy to reconcile with even-handed neutral reporting, and many news organizations have guidelines designed to limit the influence of strong personal beliefs on reporting.

The underlying differentiation of press roles was clarified in a study of regional newspaper journalists in Sweden. Fjaestad and Holmlov (1976) identified two main kinds of purpose, each endorsed by over 70 per cent of respondents — those of 'watchdog' (such as control of local government) and of 'educator' (providing a forum, aid to consumers, social and political information, etc.). They also named some secondary or minor functions recognized by a third or fewer of respondents (especially 'political mobilization', 'entertainment' and 'forging a local consensus').

Studies of journalists and editors in the United States have tended to reveal a clear preference for non-engagement and objectivity; but even so, Johnstone et al. (1976) found that 76 per cent of US journalists thought it extremely important that media should 'investigate claims and statements made by government'. Although the date (1971) when these data were collected was favourable to the adoption of a somewhat critical role by the press, the finding is consistent with several elements in the North American journalistic tradition — for instance, the philosophy of reformism (Gans, 1979), the choice of an 'adversary role' vis-à-vis government (Weaver and Wilhoit, 1986) or, more generally, the idea that media should look out for the interests of their audience, whom they claim to represent. This is different from partisan advocacy of a particular point of view, which still seems to be in decline as a journalistic philosophy.

A survey of US journalists by Weaver and Wilhoit (1986), using the same

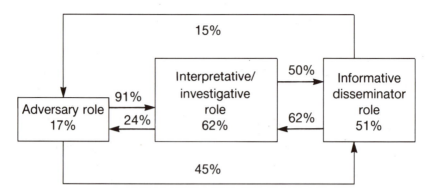

Figure 7.3 *Journalists' role perceptions (Weaver and Wilhoit, 1986): interpretation and information come first, with opposition a clear but distinctive third option*

questions and design as Johnstone et al. (1976), confirmed some enduring features of the situation and added some new elements. The research showed that in 1982–3 there had been some withdrawal from the critical perspective held by journalists of 1971, although they remained somewhat reformist in spirit and, on balance, politically more left-inclined than right. Endorsement of the questionnaire item on the 'extreme importance' of media investigating claims and statements made by government had dropped from 76 to 66 per cent, and there was more support for neutral-informative than for participant elements of the journalist's role. Nevertheless, there was also significant minority support for an 'adversary' role.

A similar enquiry in the early 1990s found approximately the same balance of views on journalists' roles (Weaver and Wilhoit, 1992). Perhaps the most interesting change from the early 1970s emerged from a reassessment of the 'neutral versus participant' dichotomy. Using similar survey material, Weaver and Wilhoit opted instead for a tripartite division of roles as interpreter, disseminator or adversary, in that order of prominence. The **interpreter** role involved the same items as were previously used to produce the label 'participant' — analysing and interpreting complex questions, investigating claims made by government and discussing national policy as it happens. The second type — that of **disseminator** — mainly relates to 'getting information to the public quickly' and 'concentrating on the largest possible audience'. The third, **adversary** role (applying to both government and business) was much weaker but was still recognized in some degree by a majority of journalists. The resulting scheme of role perceptions is reproduced in Figure 7.3, showing the main overlap between them.

The *plurality* of role conceptions held by journalists is also stressed by Weaver and Wilhoit (1986). They write (p. 116): 'only about 2 percent of the respondents are exclusively one-role oriented'. They also remind us that, on such matters as role perception and journalistic ethics, there seem to be large cross-cultural differences. For instance, Donsbach (1983) showed British journalists to be much more committed to a purely informative role than were German journalists, and they were much less particular about a range of dubious journalistic practices. Köcher (1986) offers more evidence on this matter, referring to the alternative roles of 'bloodhound' or 'missionary' which, respectively, typified British and German journalists.

Public broadcasting institutions, such as the BBC, are under a particular obligation to be neutral and balanced, and the chief aim of BBC decision-makers in news and actuality has been described as 'holding the middle ground' (Kumar, 1975), acting as a broker between disputants, rather than being a participant. The question as to whether this lends itself to supporting the established social order has often been discussed. Hall (1977) thought that it does, and we would not expect a public institution to undermine its own foundations. However, this does not prevent fundamental criticism being reported or carried. A wide-ranging investigation of the BBC by Burns (1977) reached a more cautious conclusion than Hall but spoke nevertheless (p. 209) of a 'collusion thus forged with both the establishment and the "silent (and invisible, perhaps imaginary) majority" . . . against any disturbance of the peace'. While times have changed, the forces at work are likely to be similarly balanced.

Professionalism

At the heart of Burns's study of the BBC is a discussion of 'professionalism' in broadcasting and of alternative orientations to the work task which forms one source of the statement of occupational dilemmas made above. Burns found three main attitudes to the occupational task. One was a deep loyalty to the traditional goals of public broadcasting as an instrument of cultural and social betterment and for the defence of 'standards'. The second was 'professionalism', sometimes 'television for television's sake', but always involving a deep commitment to the task and the craft of making 'good television'. This concept of media professionalism has several components — standing opposed to 'amateurism' and to external interference, resting on the judgement of work by fellow professionals and leading to some insulation from the pressures of both public and management.

For most members of professions, the appropriate wider social role which they perform is usually 'taken care of' by the institution — as in medicine or teaching — leaving individuals to concentrate on the practice of their skills. To a certain extent, this is true of mass communicators, but full professionalization has been held back, perhaps by the internal diversity of media and the recentness and flux of some of the occupations involved. There is also a continued uncertainty about what is actually the central professional skill of the journalist (and this is possibly even more in question for other media occupations). The sociologist Max Weber (1948) referred to the journalist as belonging to 'a sort of pariah caste' and, like the artist, lacking a fixed social classification. Schudson (1978) aptly characterized journalism as an 'uninsulated profession', because of the lack of clear boundaries.

The general import of Tuchman's (1978) study of news work is towards the conclusion that professionalism in news has largely come to be defined according to the needs of the news organization itself. The height of professional skill is the exercise of a practical craft, which delivers the required informational product, characterized by a high degree of **objectivity**, key marks of which are obsessive facticity and neutrality of attitude. The objectivity of news has become, in her view, the equivalent of a professional ideology. This analysis is consistent with other indications from media work that professionalism is a degree of accomplishment which cannot be measured by tests or examinations and can only be recognized by fellow professionals.

Media-occupational dilemmas

Media occupations are weakly 'institutionalized' compared, for instance, to law, medicine or accountancy, and professional success will often depend on unaccountable ups and downs of public taste or on personal and unique qualities which cannot be imitated or transmitted. Apart from skills of performance (for instance, making 'objective' news or film acting) and other artistic or technical accomplishments, the essential media skill is hard to pin down and may variously be presented as an ability to attract attention and arouse interest, assess public taste, be understood or 'communicate' well, be liked, 'know the media business' or 'have a nose for news'. None of these seems comparable to the skills, based on recognized and required training, that underlie most other professions. It may be that the freedom, creativity and critical approach that many media personnel still cherish, despite the bureaucratic setting of their work, are ultimately incompatible with full professionalization in the traditional sense.

It would, in any case, as noted above, be very difficult, even allowing for the division of labour in any complex organization, to identify a general occupational type or archetypal 'mass communicator' profession. There may well be a central core consisting especially of those with a directly creative or communicative task, such as editors, journalists, writers and film-makers. But even the core professionals rarely seem unanimous about how they see their professional task.

There is some general pattern to these divisions, one which connects with certain basic alternatives that are built into the media institution. These choices, in turn, may be thought to stem from the intermediary position of mass communication, as described in Chapter 3, between, on the one hand, sources of social power (other institutions) which exert leverage and, on the other, the public who are supposed to be the beneficiaries of mass communication work. The most fundamental dilemma is one of freedom versus constraint in an institution whose own ideology places a value on originality and freedom, yet whose organizational setting requires relatively strict control.

Media-occupational role dilemmas

- Active participatory versus neutral, informational
- Creative and independent versus bureaucratic, routine
- Communicative purpose versus meeting consumer demand

Internal diversity of communicator goals

The analysis made so far, in line with the scheme in Figure 7.1, points to a degree of internal division within the boundaries of the organization as it relates to its operating environment. The sources of division lie in: the diversity of function (such as news giving, entertainment or advertising) of many media organizations, with different interests competing for status and finance; the duality of purpose of many media (both material and ideal); and the endemic conflict between creative ends (which have no practical limits) and the need to organize, plan, finance and 'sell' media products. Most accounts of media-organizational goals point to differences of orientation and purpose which can be a source of latent conflict.

Latent conflicts

Muriel Cantor's (1971) study of a group of producers employed in making films for major television networks indicated the existence of three main types. First, there were 'film-makers', mainly younger, well-educated people ambitious to become feature film directors and comparable to the 'professional' category of broadcasters which Burns (1977) singled out. Secondly, there was a group of writer-producers, whose chosen purpose was to make stories with a worthwhile message and to communicate with a wide public. Thirdly, there were older, less well-educated career producers, whose main orientation was to the network and their career within it.

Not surprisingly, the last-mentioned group was least likely to have conflicts with management, since their main aim of reaching the biggest possible audience was shared by the networks. The film-makers, for different reasons, were prepared to accept network goals because they wanted to practise their craft, accumulate money and move on to feature films. It was the writer-producers who came most into conflict with the networks (management) because of their different attitude to the content which they were required to produce. Management wanted a saleable, risk-free product, while the writers still retained some ideals of the craft and wanted to convey a worthwhile message. The chance to reach a large audience was essential to their purpose, but the price, in terms of conforming to commercial goals, was a high one to have to pay.

The lessons of other research on communicators (mainly journalists) seem to lead to a similar conclusion — that where conflict occurs between media organization and employee, it is likely to be where the political tendency or economic self-interest of the organization gets in the way of individual freedom of expression. According to Sigelman (1973), the potential problem is usually avoided by selective recruitment and self-selection by entrants into media organizations with compatible work environments. Studies of newspapers indicate a strong sense on the part of journalists that editors and publishers have a 'policy', which tends to dictate either the kind of story to be chosen or the manner of treatment.

Aside from initial selection, the main way of achieving conformity seems to be by way of socialization 'on the job'. An early study by Breed (1955) detailed the (mainly informal) socializing mechanisms which helped to ensure the maintenance of policy. Young reporters would be expected to read the newspaper they work for and sit in on editorial conferences. Policy is also learned through informal gossip with colleagues. Deviations from publication 'policy' were discouraged by feelings of obligation to superiors, by the satisfactions of belonging to the in-group and sometimes by management sanctions and rewards in giving assignments. In general, according to Breed's research, what policy actually was remained covert. Perhaps most significant in news media is the fact that being able to handle the news according to the reigning policy becomes a skill and even a value in itself. The organizational objective of getting the news overrides personal feelings. Presumably similar processes occur in other media organizations.

It is less clear how much power lies with owners and chief editors to control the message directly. Gans's account of several US news media (1979, p. 95) is somewhat ambiguous about the power of corporate executives over reporters. On the one hand, they do make 'policy', conduct frequent and regular briefings, look after the commercial and political interests of the firm and can 'suggest, select and veto news stories whenever they choose'. On the other hand, they do not use their power on a day-to-day basis, and there are countervailing powers which lie with television news producers and editors, if not with individual reporters.

The survey evidence available tends generally to support the view that journalists mainly regard themselves as having a reasonable degree of autonomy, even if the problem of pressure from 'policy' does arise (see Meyer, 1987). Weaver and Wilhoit (1986) reported that 60 per cent of their journalists thought they had almost complete freedom in selecting stories they wanted to work on and 66 per cent in deciding which aspects of a news story to emphasize. There are so many considerations in any given case of news selection or treatment that the issue of influence or autonomy cannot be clearly settled on its own; nor is it easy to separate the issue of internal freedom of expression and reporting from the normal hierarchy of bureaucracy and from the external constraints discussed above.

Characteristics of mass communicators

Many studies of media organizations or occupations include, as a matter of course, an examination of the social background and outlook on society of the group of respondents under study (early examples are Rosten, 1937, 1941; a recent example is Tunstall, 1993). This is sometimes because of an assumption that the personal characteristics of those most directly responsible for media production will influence content. It is a hypothesis which accords well with the ideology or mythology of the media themselves and stands opposed to the notion of organizational or technological determinism. The expectation that media will 'reflect society' (the first hypothesis considered on page 186) can be supported on the grounds either that it is what their audiences want or that those who work in the media are a cross-section of society, at least in their values and beliefs.

However, both arguments may need to be modified to allow for the influence of organizational goals and settings. Shoemaker and Reese (1991) suggest that lines of influence can follow one or other of the paths shown in Figure 7.4. In essence, what is shown are two alternative paths — one in which organizational role subordinates or conceals personal characteristics, and another in which having power or status in an organization permits an individual communicator to express their personal beliefs and values in public communication.

The first question to arise is whether there is any distinctive pattern of social experience or personal values to be found among media communicators. Inevitably there are as many descriptions of social background as there are studies, and even though most concern journalists, there is no single pattern to report. However, a few general remarks are in order, taking as a starting point the findings of Weaver and Wilhoit concerning the social composition of their sample of US journalists in 1982–3 and using their definition of journalists as 'those who have editorial responsibility for the preparation or transmission of news stories or other information, including fulltime reporters, correspondents, columnists, newsmen and editors' (1986, p. 168). It is clear that US journalists, however marginal their role in society, are not marginal in income terms but belong on average to the middle category, thus within the economically secure sector of society, without being rich. This mirrors the earlier findings of Johnstone et al. (1976) and the data from Britain afforded by Tunstall (1971). More recent evidence from Weaver and Wilhoit (1992) suggests that US journalists are fairly average in respect of many aspects of social background.

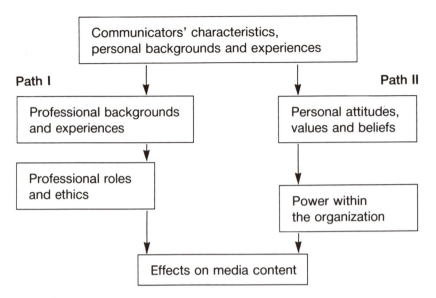

Figure 7.4 *How factors intrinsic to the communicator may influence media content: institutional versus professional pathways (Shoemaker and Reese, 1991)*

Secondly, there are evidently big variations between the stars of journalism and the ordinary salariat, as in other branches of media business. Lichter and Rothman (1986), for instance, painted a portrait of 240 personnel of elite US news media showing them to be not only well off but demographically unrepresentative in being more white and more male than the country as a whole and less likely to hold a religious belief. One can probably assume that people who work for less elite media are also less of an elite themselves, although they may still be demographically unrepresentative (for instance, in terms of gender and ethnicity). Johnstone et al. (1976) concluded that 'in any society those in charge of mass communication tend to come from the same social strata as those in control of the economic and political systems'.

Weaver and Wilhoit found that, since 1971, the composition of the corps of US journalists had changed remarkably in one respect — a much greater representation of women (from 20 to 34 per cent), although there were relatively fewer black and Hispanic journalists. There seems, however, to have been little further change up to the 1990s (Weaver and Wilhoit, 1992). The trends mentioned are supported by Shoemaker and Reese (1991). There seems little doubt about the general class position of the average media worker — it is a middle-class occupation, but less professionalized or well paid than other established professions (law, medicine, accountancy, etc.) and with a small elite of well-paid stars. Peters and Cantor's (1982) account of the movie acting profession stresses the extreme gap between the powerless and insecure many and the minority at the top.

The theoretical significance of such observations is less easy to establish. One view, advanced by Gans (1979), is that the middle-class position of the journalistic profession is a guarantee of their ultimate loyalty to the system. Therefore they are free, in the United States system, because they can be trusted to see and interpret the world in much the same way as the real holders of power, holding the same basic ideology and values. Gans concluded that news journalists generally hold what are called 'motherhood' values, including support for the family and a nostalgia for small-town pastoralism. They also tend to be ethnocentric, pro-Democratic, individualistic and in favour of 'responsible capitalism', moderatism, social order and leadership.

Such values, according to Gans, include elements of both conservative and liberal ideologies. It is a persuasive view, more so than the alternative idea that they are not only an elite but a left-leaning one, according to Lichter and Rothman (1986), with subversive motives and a penchant for supporting deviance and extremist movements. Their main argument was based on case studies of news reporting of controversial issues in elite media. Gans's view of journalists as 'safe' but not reactionary is also perhaps more convincing than the other extreme view that they are a conservative elite, mainly serving the interests of the state, the governing class and big business (as inferred by Herman and Chomsky, 1988).

More significant than evidence of the values of journalists (but not inconsistent with it) may be the finding that media personnel owe most of their relevant attitudes and tendencies to socialization from the immediate work environment (for example, Breed, 1955; Weaver and Wilhoit, 1986, pp. 127–8). This view, while not discounting the influence of social background and personal belief, returns us to the greater probability of organizational, rather than individual and subjective, determination. Even so, the possibility for personal influence by mass communicators varies according to the genre and the type of organization. Non-news genres offer more scope for expressing personal beliefs, and there is probably more scope where commercial and financial pressures are less (Tunstall, 1993).

Women in news organizations

There is an empirical correlation between the relatively low numbers and the lower occupational status of women in news media organizations (Gallagher, 1981; Thoveron, 1986; *Media Studies Journal*, 1993) and the underrepresentation or stereotyping of women in the news (for instance, in terms of topic and context, as well as the more obvious use of female 'sex symbols') (see, for example, Tuchman et al., 1978). The issue is not confined to the question of news, but news is often singled out as of particular significance for the wider question of gender inequality and construction in society. The correlation between male domination (in power positions if not always numerically) of virtually all media organizations and male-oriented themes or patriarchal values offers strong prima facie support for the view that greater media occupational equality would make a difference to content (see Chapter 8).

Van Zoonen (1988, 1991) argues, however, that a more fundamental approach to the construction of gender is needed. She points to basic inconsistencies in the assumption that having more women in the newsroom would change the news (for the better). For one thing, on closer inspection the available evidence does not give good empirical support for this assumption. There have been significant increases in female participation in the work-force (see, for example, Weaver and Wilhoit, 1986; *Media Studies Journal*, 1993) without any noticeable changes in the 'nature of news'. The theory takes for granted that journalists have enough autonomy to have influence as individuals, whereas this has to be treated as problematic and variable.

There are also divergent views as to what constitutes 'change'. Should the news become 'feminized', whatever that might mean (for instance, more attention to 'women's issues'), or should 'femininity' itself be redefined (perhaps in the direction of masculinity)? There are two distinct issues here: that of journalistic autonomy versus determination (by external forces or the organizational hierarchy or 'media logic') and that of the desirability of change in the nature of news and the direction which it might take. None of this is an argument against the fact of there being gender differences, or against more equal employment for women, or against change, but the various issues are separate and cannot all be bundled together under the general heading of having more women in news organizations. If the central matter is the way gender is constructed then a broader approach is needed.

The review of evidence by Shoemaker and Reese (1991) relating to the influence of personal beliefs and values is inconclusive. Even so, to conclude that there is no connection would seem to rule out any real degree of personal autonomy and to overestimate the power of work socialization. Shoemaker and Reese (1991, p. 72) see the relation as variable: 'it is possible that when communicators have more power over their messages and work under fewer constraints, their personal attitudes, values and beliefs have more opportunity to influence content' (see Figure 7.4). It is fairly evident, for instance, that individuals who reach high status in different media (journalism, film, television, music) do have and use opportunities for expressing personal opinions and beliefs. The 'logic of media', which favours personalization, often supports this tendency, as long as it does not also conflict with commercial logic.

It would follow that a necessary condition for more equitable treatment of women in news will be a gradual rise of women to positions of power within media organizations. Tunstall's (1993) evidence concerning television producers in Britain describes a situation of increasingly significant representation of women in production (and decision-making) roles (especially in the BBC), against a background of strong gender segmentation in television work. The producer role is also sketched as one which seems designed to suit men or unmarried women. The study produced some evidence of a belief on the part of producers themselves that, in several fields, gender could affect the choice of topics.

Pressure and interest groups

Relations between media and society are often mediated through a wide range of more or less informal, but often organized, pressure groups which seek to influence directly what the media do — especially by trying to set limits to what they publish. There are many examples of established bodies, such as religious, occupational or political bodies, complaining and lobbying on a range of issues, often to do with matters of morality, perceived political bias or minority representation (Shoemaker and Reese, 1991). In the United States and elsewhere there is much pressure on the media to be positive towards minorities of all kinds, including ethnic groups, women, gays and lesbians, and more sensitive to the needs of vulnerable groups like children, poor, disabled and homeless people and the mentally ill.

While the media are usually cautious in handling such pressures and are reluctant to yield their autonomy (the pressures often tend to cancel each other out), there is evidence of success by outside agencies in influencing content, especially where media's commercial interests might be threatened and where bad publicity is feared. According to an extensive study by Montgomery (1989), the most effective advocacy groups 'were those whose goals were most compatible with the TV network system and whose strategies were fashioned with a keen sense of how that system functioned' (p. 217). Success also depends on the degree of support among the general public for a particular advocacy position. The general effect is likely to show up in entertainment television as blandness, conformity and a blurring of controversy. In general, the media are less open to external pressures of this kind in relation to 'hard news'.

It is usually impossible to distinguish unacceptable pressure (or the act of yielding to it) from the general tendency of the media to try to please as many of their audiences (and advertisers) as possible and to avoid hurting minorities or encouraging antisocial activities. The media are also wary of legal reprisal (Tuchman, 1978) and inclined to avoid unnecessary controversy or departures from verifiable facts which are in the public domain. Organizational avoidance behaviour in response to social or legal pressure has to be accepted as legitimate, within the rules of the media-institutional 'game', but the general result is to ensure a differentially more positive treatment for the better-organized and more socially central minorities and causes (Shoemaker, 1984). Weaker and more deviant groups get a worse press and exert little influence. Paletz and Entman (1981) exemplified such marginal groups with little positive access to, or control over, media coverage as 'unofficial strikers, urban rioters, welfare mothers, student militants, radicals and impoverished reactionaries' (p. 125).

Relations with owners, clients and suppliers

The central issue which arises under this heading is the extent to which media organizations can claim to exercise autonomy in relation, first of all, to their owners and, secondly, to other direct economic agencies in their environment, especially those which provide operating funds: investors, advertisers, sponsors. According to Altschull's (1984) dictum that 'The content of the news media always reflects the interests of those who finance the press', the answer is fairly clear and also consistent with the principles of free press theory in its 'market' version. Nevertheless, there is usually some scope for autonomy on the part of 'communicators' employed by media owners (especially freedom based on professionalism or the requirements for creativity), and there are many different kinds of media and several different kinds of paymaster. Of the latter, the most important (leaving the paying audience aside) are media owners and advertisers.

Proprietor influence

There is no doubt that owners in market-based media have ultimate power over content and can ask for what they want to be included or left out. There is plenty of circumstantial evidence to show that this power is used (Curran and Seaton, 1988; Shoemaker and Reese, 1991). Even so, there are quite strong conventions relating to journalism which protect the decision-making autonomy of editors on particular news stories. Meyer's (1987) survey evidence confirms that US journalistic ethics frown on owner intervention and that editors report a fair degree of autonomy. Similar evidence was obtained in Britain by the Royal Commission on the Press (1977).

Nevertheless, there is a tendency for owners of news media to set broad lines of policy, which are likely to be followed by the editorial staff they employ. There may also be informal and indirect pressure on particular issues which matter to owners (for instance, relating to their other business interests). Much credible, but often anecdotal, evidence supports this conclusion, and, in the end, the theory of economically free press legitimates this state of affairs. Newspaper owners are entirely free to use their papers to make propaganda, if they wish to do so. There is a widely held view, though one difficult to prove, that increased size and conglomeration of the media industry have reduced the relevance of this issue. Media have simply become too big business to be run for personal whims, and decisions have to be taken impersonally on grounds of managerial and market considerations.

Aside from direct proprietorial intervention on particular matters, there are likely to be pressures which arise from the growth of chains and conglomerates. These often involve a high degree of co-operation between different editorial units and implementation of a group-wide policy on some issues. There is some evidence in the United States, for instance, that certain newspaper groups are more likely to consistently support Republican rather than Democratic candidates for the Presidency (most newspaper editorials do this anyway — Wackman et al., 1975; Gaziano, 1989). Giffard (1989) showed that reporting of UNESCO has consistently followed lines laid down by publishers' interests (see also Preston et al., 1989).

The general effect of monopoly media ownership has proved difficult to pin down (see, for example, Picard et al., 1988), but Shoemaker and Reese conclude (1991) that those who work for large chains are likely to have a lower attachment to and involvement in the community in which they work. For them, the (larger) media organization takes precedence over community influence. Correlatively, locally based media may gain strength and independence from ties with the community or city which they serve. The commercial newspaper business is, of course, not the only branch of the media industry. In the case of most entertainment industries — the non-news branch of broadcasting, popular music, film, etc. — there are few conventions which set limits to the power of owners, although organizational decisions are assumed to be largely driven by market considerations (including public demand and response).

The situation of public broadcasting is more complex. There are no owners, only managers, controllers and guardians appointed by democratically elected governments, who are usually accountable for their decisions according to a specific version of the public interest. The degree of freedom for journalists, producers, writers and entertainers may be less than in market-based media (although this is not necessarily so), but the limits are normally clear and not subject to arbitrary breach or suspension. There has usually been a relatively high degree of artistic and professional freedom, with limits from bureaucratic and budgetary control (and organization policy) rather than from market forces.

The influence of advertisers

The consequences of advertising financing for media content are perennially discussed. On the one hand, it is obvious that the *structure* of much of the mass media industry in most capitalist countries reflects the interests of advertisers — something that has developed historically along with other social and economic changes. It is no accident that media markets often coincide with other consumer divisions. Most free-market media are finely tuned to jointly maximizing the needs of advertisers and their own interests as a normal condition of operation. The 'normal' influence extends to the matching of media content patterns according to the consumption patterns of targeted audiences. Media design, layout, planning and scheduling often reflect advertiser interests. What is less *easy* to demonstrate is that particular advertisers can directly intervene to influence significant publication decisions in their own interests, beyond what is already provided for in the system.

As with proprietorial intervention in news, there is little doubt that it happens from time to time on a local or specific basis (for example, Shoemaker and Reese, 1991). It is also ethically discouraged when it affects news (Meyer, 1987), and in general it may not even be in the interests either of media (especially news media) or of advertisers to be seen to be too close to each other. Both can lose credibility and effectiveness if a form of conspiracy against the media public is suspected. In general it seems that economically strong and 'elite' media are best in a position to resist undue pressure (see Gans, 1979), as are media which are supported by balanced sources of revenue (that is, subscriber payments as well as advertisers, or, in Europe especially, broadcast licence revenue plus advertising income). Media organizations most likely to be influenced by advertiser pressure are those whose sole source of revenue is advertising, especially where there is heavy competition for it. The most striking example often cited is that of US network television (Blumler, 1991; Tunstall, 1991).

Several organizational factors limit the power of outside economic agencies and promote autonomy, although they offer only uncertain and variable protection (see Elliott, 1977). For instance, there are some sources of finance, whether public or private, which are intended to support non-profit, cultural or professional goals, most obviously in public media, but also through private sponsorship. Secondly, media as much as (if not more than) other business enterprises have to take risks, which means sometimes giving creative and professional people their own way. New ideas and an oversupply of products are continually needed to match an insatiable demand for products which rapidly become obsolescent (Hirsch, 1973). An important key to potential freedom lies in the most unpredictable of the sources of support — the audience. If media organizations succeed with the public, they attract other financial benefits. Since there is no known way of buying or predicting this success, the prediction or attainment of audience interest counts as a professional/organizational secret, whose possession gives leverage in economic bargaining.

Some organizational studies suggest an alternative view to that advanced above about financial constraints — namely, that a competitive commercial environment can have positive effects on creativity and innovation. Ettema and Whitney (1982), for instance, in a study of US public television, report the view that struggling against organizational and financial limits sets puzzles for solution by creative workers. Turow's (1982) comparison of 'unconventional' US television projects with 'conventional' projects also concluded that innovation was likely to come not from attempts to meet audience demand but from a series of essentially conflict-laden factors, such as aggressive competition from other media or channels, technical change, enforced internal economy or power struggles between individuals within media organizations.

Relations with the audience

Although the audience is, by conventional wisdom, the most important of the clients and influences in the environment of any media organization, research tends to show the audience as having a low salience for many mass communicators, however closely ratings and sales figures are followed by management. Media professionals display a high degree of 'autism' (Burns, 1969), consistent perhaps with the general attitude of professionals, whose very status depends on their knowing better than their clients what is good for them. Burns extended the comparison to service occupations in general, whose members 'carry with them a countervailing and ordinarily concealed posture of invidious hostility' (towards their clients).

Hostility to the audience

Altheide (1974, p. 59) comments that the pursuit of large audiences by the television stations which he studied 'led to a cynical view of the audience as stupid, incompetent and unappreciative'. Elliott (1972), Burns (1977) and Schlesinger (1978) found something of the same to be true of British television. Schlesinger (p. 111) attributed this partly to the nature of professionalism: 'a tension is set up between the professionalism of the communicator, with its implied autonomy, and the meeting of apparent audience demands and desires, with their implication for limiting autonomy'. Ferguson (1983) also reported a somewhat arrogant attitude to the audience on the part of women's magazine editors.

The situation may also stem from the fact that the mass communicator is offering a professional service and a product, while the dominant criterion applied by the organization is nearly always the ratings (= volume of sales of the product, the size of the audience sold to the advertiser). As Ferguson (1983) pointed out, editors in commercial media all agreed that professional success has to be demonstrated in terms of rising circulations and advertising revenues. However, most people in the media, with some justification, will not recognize ratings as a very reliable measure of intrinsic quality. For instance, Gans (1979, p. 232) notes that 'When a network audience-research unit presented findings on how a sample of viewers evaluated a set of television news films, the journalists were appalled because the sample liked the films which the journalists deemed to be low quality and disliked the "good stories".'

An alternative view

It is possible that hostility towards the audience is somewhat exaggerated by media respondents themselves, since there is contrary evidence that media people have a strong positive attitude to their audience in the abstract.

Ferguson, again, notes that women's magazine editors showed a strong sense of responsibility to their audience and want to provide a helpful service (1983, p. 140). Weaver and Wilhoit (1986) found that the single most important factor contributing to work satisfaction of journalists was the possibility of helping people (endorsed by 61 per cent). They also found that the single most frequent source of feedback to journalists is from individual members of the audience. The resistance to ratings and other audience statistics, which are largely a management tool with little to say about actual audiences (Ang, 1991), should not necessarily be equated with negative views of the audience.

Insulation and uncertainty

On a day-to-day or item-by-item basis, most mass communicators in established media do not need to be concerned about the immediate response of the audience, and they have to take decisions about content in advance of any response. This, coupled with the intrinsic difficulty of 'knowing' a large and very disparate audience, contributes to the relative insulation described above. The most common institutional device for making contact with the audience — that of audience research — serves an essential management function and relates media to the surrounding financial and political system, but seems to convey little that is meaningful to the individual mass communicator (Burns, 1977; Gans, 1979). Attitudes to the audience tend to be guided and differentiated according to the role orientations set out above.

Among communicators, if one follows the line of Burns's findings, the 'pragmatic' are happy with the ratings which also satisfy the organization. The craft-oriented are content with the judgements of their fellow-professionals. Those committed to the goals of the organization (for instance, carrying out a cultural mission, or political or commercial propaganda) are content with these goals as internally assessed. Those wishing to have influence in society look to their influential contacts in relevant social contexts. For everyone there are friends, relatives and casual contacts who can provide feedback of a more comprehensible kind.

Images of the audience

There remains a continuing problem of uncertainty for those who do want to communicate, who do want to change or to influence the general public and use media for this purpose, or who direct themselves at minorities or for minority causes where impact matters. One readily available solution is the construction of an abstract image of the kind of people they would like to reach (Bauer, 1958; Pool and Shulman, 1959). According to Gans (1957, p. 318), 'The audience participates in the making of a movie through the audience image held by the creator.' Shoemaker and Reese (1991, p. 96) conclude that 'Journalists write primarily for themselves, for their editors, and for other journalists.' Nevertheless, communicating to a large and amorphous audience 'out there' is bound to remain problematic for those who care about 'getting a message across'. Audiences are mainly just spectators, who observe and applaud but do not interact with the senders and performers (Elliott, 1972).

Media organizations, as distinct from the individual 'communicators' within them, are to a large extent in the business of producing spectacles as a way of creating audiences and generating profit and employment (see the 'publicity model' on pages 51–2). They need some firm basis on which to predict the interests and likely degree of attention of an audience. As Pekurny (1982) points out, feedback from ratings cannot tell you how to improve television programmes, nor are they often available until long after a programme is made. Pekurny says that the 'real feedback system' is not the home viewing audience but the writers, producers, cast and network executives themselves. In addition, there is strong reliance on 'track records' of particular producers and production companies and on reusing successful past formulas. This conclusion is supported by Ryan and Peterson (1982), who tell us that in popular music the most important factor guiding selection in the production process (see page 231) is the search for a good 'product image', which means essentially trying to match the characteristics of previously successful songs.

Conclusion

Media organizations, not surprisingly, share many characteristics with other formal organizations, just as they share a similar economic logic. But there are also some distinctive and also deviant features, stemming partly from the public role which the media fulfil, and partly from their dependence on creative talent and political ideas which cannot be confined and controlled.

8

THE PRODUCTION OF MEDIA CULTURE

Media-organizational activities: gatekeeping and selecting

Attention has so far been given to a range of more or less static or constant factors which shape the work of media organizations — especially the composition and internal social structure of the media workforce and the relations which are maintained, under a variety of economic and social pressures, with the world outside the organization. The situation of the media organization is never really static, but it may appear 'fixed' or balanced by the relative strength of alternative forces and of differing social and organizational goals. In the following sections we focus on two interrelated aspects of the work of media organizations, which can be described as 'selecting' and 'processing'. The first refers to the sequence of decisions which extends from the choice of 'raw material', as it were, to delivering the finished product. The second refers to the application of work routines which affect the nature of this product as it passes through the 'chain' of decision-making.

This way of describing media-organizational work originates primarily from research on news production, but it can apply more or less equally to a range of other media products and media settings (Hirsch, 1977). In the case of news, the chain extends from 'noticing' an event in the world, through writing about or filming it and preparing a news item for transmission. In the case of a book, a movie, a television show or a piece of popular music, a similar chain extends from an idea in someone's head, through an editorial selection process and many phases of transformation into the final product (Ryan and Peterson, 1982).

In most cases of industrialized media production, all phases in these chains involve a large volume of work which becomes routinized as a matter of necessity. Even the starting point — a news event or 'creative idea' — is strongly (perhaps most strongly) influenced by convention and prior experience. The regularities of behaviour and thinking which result from these routines give rise to empirical generalizations and to the possibility of theorizing about what is going on. The routines also reflect the 'operational' theories in the heads of media professionals.

The gatekeeping concept

The term 'gatekeeping' has been widely used to describe the process by which selections are made in media work, especially decisions whether or not to admit a particular news story to pass through the 'gates' of a news medium into the news channels. The concept originated in the research of the social psychologist Kurt Lewin (1947) into decisions about family food purchases. He noted that information has to flow along certain channels which contain 'gate areas', where decisions are made, under the influence of various favourable or unfavourable forces. This idea was taken up by White (1950) in research on the selection decisions of the telegraph-wire editor of a local newspaper (the controller of these particular gates).

Initially most interest was focused on the large number of items which failed to gain entry and on the reasons for rejection. In the nature of the early research, there was a tendency to emphasize the subjective character of news selection decisions. Subsequently, more attention has been given to systematic influences on selection which can be considered as either 'organizational' or 'ideological'. The former refers primarily to bureaucratic routines, the second to values and cultural influences which are not purely individual and personal but which stem also from the social (and national) setting of news activity. The fact that news is strongly influenced by routine was recognized long ago by Walter Lippman (1922), when he wrote: 'without standardization, without stereotypes, without routine judgements, without a fairly ruthless disregard of subtlety, the editor would soon die of excitement' (p. 123).

Ideological versus organizational factors in news selection

The first studies of 'gatekeeping' (White, 1950; Gieber, 1956) were restricted in scope to the activity within newsrooms of choosing from among a large number of incoming wire telegrams and pictures from news agencies for the content which makes up or governs the bulk of news in a typical paper. The early findings emphasized the influence of subjective (and arbitrary) personal judgement, but the patterns of selection which were observed, on the basis of content analysis, were too consistent to be explained in this way. It became clear that the content of news media tends consistently to follow the same general pattern and that different organizations behave in a similar way when confronted by the same events and under equivalent conditions (Glasgow Media Group, 1976; McQuail, 1977; Shoemaker and Reese, 1991). There appears to be a stable perception on the part of news decision-makers about what is likely to interest an audience and a good deal of consensus within the same social-cultural settings (Hetherington, 1985).

An alternative explanation to that of subjective individual judgement is to be found in the concept of 'news values', which refers to widely held and stable views about what is likely to interest the news public on grounds of relevance and intrinsic interest. While the general idea of news values was already familiar, a study of foreign news in the Norwegian press by Galtung and Ruge (1965) led to the first clear statement of the news values (or 'news factors) which would be most influential in deciding whether or not a potential news 'event' would be noticed by the news media and brought into the distribution channels.

Galtung and Ruge hypothesized that events would become news the more they fitted certain organizational and also some cultural or 'ideological' criteria. This idea surfaces widely in research on media organizations, though with different notions of what counts as ideological. Hall (1973), for instance, used it in a political sense to refer to the substance of news photos, which were also chosen because of their technical quality and dramatic or sensational effect. The notion of a 'media logic' (see page 230) also embraces the twin ideas of organizational and technical suitability plus a media-cultural component. The 'ideological' news factors described by Galtung and Ruge refer mainly to values which are embedded in Western society — especially those which stem from an individualist and materialist philosophy.

Aside from their intrinsic content, some events are more likely to become news than others, because they lend themselves to the formal procedures of gathering and processing by news organizations, which often work on a 24-hour (or more frequent) publication time scale. For this reason, news organizations prefer events that fit the following criteria: having a short time span (being sudden); having great scale and intensity; being clear and unambiguous; being unexpected; being culturally close to the intended public; and having continuity — being already in the news and consistent with past images and expectations. In addition to suitability for routine processing, it is obvious that the presence or absence of the *facilities* for recording and transmitting events plays a major part in selection. There is a self-fulfilling effect from the location of reporters and equipment in particular places.

Alternative approaches to the study of news selection

The gatekeeping concept, despite its usefulness and its potential for dealing with many different media situations, has a built-in limitation in its implication that news arrives in ready-made and unproblematic event-story form at the 'gates' of the media, where it is either admitted or excluded. The gatekeeping framework is largely based on the assumption (which is widespread in much news content analysis) that there is a given, finite, knowable reality of events in the 'real world', from which it is the task of the media to select according to appropriate criteria of representativeness or relevance. As Fishman (1980, p. 13), writes, 'most researchers assumed that news either reflects or distorts reality and that reality consists of facts and events out there which exist independently of how newsworkers think of them and treat them in the news production process'. For Fishman, the central concern should be the 'creation of news', and in this he has been followed by a number of other influential theorists.

It is clear that the eventual news content of the media arrives by several different routes and in different forms. It may have to be sought out or ordered in advance, or its 'discovery' may have to be systematically planned. At times it also has to be internally manufactured or constructed. Such a process of construction, like the selection of news, is not random and subjective. It takes place largely according to schemes of interpretation and of relevance which are those of the bureaucratic institutions that either are sources of news or process events (police departments, courts, welfare agencies, government committees, etc.). According to Fishman (1982), 'what is known and knowable by the media depends on the information-gathering and information-processing resources' of these agencies. The main factors which influence eventual choice can be considered under the headings of 'people', 'place' and 'time', usually in one combination or another.

People and selection

The fact that some people and institutions get more attention and privileged access as sources has already been mentioned. News people have their own preferred sources and are also linked to prominent figures by institutional means — press conferences, publicity agents, etc. Studies of news reporters (for example, Tuchman, 1978; Fishman, 1980) make clear that one thing which they do not share with their colleagues is their sources and contacts. News is often reports of what prominent people say about events rather than reports of the events themselves.

Probably the best-known example of person as event is that of the US President — a power figure supported by a large and effective publicity machine. As one study (Grossman and Kumar, 1981) noted, in all the variety of possibilities for reporting the President there is one constant imperative — closeness to senior officials and, if possible, the President in person on as exclusive a basis as possible. This underlies the fact that a great deal of news gathering revolves around people, especially since people are more permanently available than events, and (unlike institutions) they can speak. It is often from prominent individuals that exclusives and scoops can be obtained by well-connected journalists.

The significance of personal contacts (and 'inside dopesters') in any kind of media work involving attention to current social reality has been underlined by research as well as by informal accounts of news producers. What we see of the world through media eyes is often the result of chance encounters or informal communication networks developed by people in the media. The power to make news which attaches to certain offices also helps to account for the differential influence of certain sources and the potential for 'pseudo-events' to be assembled around the activities of prominent people. The relative status of people in the news is one of the elements of 'media logic', discussed below (page 230).

Elliott's (1972) study of the making of a documentary about racial prejudice showed the large extent to which the eventual content on screen was determined by ideas and preconceptions held initially within the production team and by the personal contacts they happened to have which could help to realize their ideas. This restores some faith in the relevance of communicator and personal values (see page 201), although documentary is not the same as news, where subjectivity is very limited. In fact, as Tunstall (1993) shows, British television producers do often exercise their personal preferences, although the scope varies according to 'market' conditions.

Location and selection

Spatial relationships have some obvious effects on the flow and selection of news in that these will be governed by physical proximity. The nearer the location of news events is to the city, region or nation of the intended audience, the more likely it is to be noticed. Nearness may, however, be overridden as a factor by other considerations, such as power or the intrinsic character of events (for instance, scale and negativity) (Galtung and Ruge, 1965). The fact that recognition of events as news has to involve a specific location helps to explain the success with which authorities (especially in war situations) can manage news, by virtue of their power over physical access. Aside from the simple need to be able to observe, the conventions of objective news require evidence of location, and what has no verifiable location is a 'non-event'.

The importance of location was emphasized by Walter Lippman (1922) in his account of the routinization of news gathering. He wrote that news consists of events which 'obtrude', above what is normal, and which can be anticipated by observation at those places where past newsworthy events have happened or been made public — such as courts, police stations, parliaments, airports and hospitals. News media are normally linked to a 'net' which covers the globe, its nodal points marked by the presence of an agency or a correspondent.

The news net The idea of a 'news net' was developed by Tuchman (1978) as an image of a device designed to 'catch' news, like fish. Its capacity depends on the fineness of the mesh and the strength of its fibre. The finest strands of the net (for small fish) are provided by 'stringers', with stronger elements from reporters and the wire services. There is a hierarchy involved, with status in the news net determining whose information is more likely to be identified as news (preference goes to seniority and to own reporters rather than news agencies):

> The spatial anchoring of the news net at centralized institutions is one element of the frame delineating strips of everyday reality as news. . . . The news net imposes a frame upon occurrences through the cooperation of the complex bureaucracy

associated with the dispersion of reporters. . . . [Finally,] the news net incorporates three assumptions about readers' interests: readers are interested in occurrences at specific localities; they are concerned with the activities of specific organizations; they are interested in specific topics. (Tuchman, 1978, pp. 23, 25)

The news net has a very tight weave at places where power is concentrated, like the Washington–New York corridor or the Paris–Bonn–London triangle. The pre-planning of news coverage in spatial terms thus involves a set of presuppositions about where news is likely to happen, which will have a certain self-fulfilling tendency. This tendency is witnessed by the great continuity of flow of news from regions like the Middle East and Southern Africa in recent years, once these have been established as sites for events and as foci of political concern. The corollary of this is that news flow can usually be less easily generated from locations where sudden and unexpected events take place.

Routinely, the influence of location on events takes place through the assignment of reporters to places where news 'events', as constructed in beliefs about what will interest the audience (an aspect of typification), are likely to occur. Most news organizations have a structure of desks or departments which is partly based on location — such as city news, crime news (courts and police) and politics. Traditionally, on local media at least, this was expressed in terms of a series of 'beats'.

The news beat, as explained by Fishman (1980), is not only *territorial* and *topical* (subject-defined), it is also a social setting — a network of social relations involving reporters and sources who frequent particular places. The news beat is established in order to facilitate the uncovering of 'news events', but it inevitably leads to the construction of events. What happens in a certain place (on the news beat) is much more likely to be defined as news just because it is observed (compared to a 'non-event', which is another event which is not observed).

Pre-definitions of news and planned events   There are various accounts of how the planning of future event coverage strongly influences the content of coverage. Following an idea of Lang and Lang (1953), Halloran et al. (1970) studied the sequence of events preceding a planned demonstration and protest march in London in 1968, directed against US war policy in Vietnam. They showed how media stories in the weeks before the event pre-defined it as both significant and violent, fomented by foreigners and with potential threats to property and even the social order (it was supposedly a 'year of revolution').

One result of this 'pre-structuring' of the meaning and course of the event was to shape the organizational and physical arrangements for event coverage as well as the ideas about its nature. In fact, the planned event was relatively peaceful, but the news apparatus was committed to an alternative version and found it difficult to reconcile the reality with the advance picture established. The result was distortion and unbalanced reporting. Similar phenomena have been noticed in relation to planned military events, like the 1982 British expedition to the Falklands, the Gulf War of 1991 and the initially peaceful US 'invasion' of Somalia in 1992. More commonly, the problem for the media organization is a reverse one — to catch up organizationally with unplanned events in unexpected locations.

Time and selection

Not surprisingly, since it is built into the definition of news, time has enormous influence as a consideration on selection. Timeliness is an essential ingredient of both novelty and relevance, both of which are highly prized in news, and it also reinforces one of the most significant properties of communication technology — its capacity to overcome barriers of time (as well as space). The importance of a 'first' or scoop with a newspaper is often greater than that of any other factor in deciding on selection and prominence.

Typification of news by time   As well as a net to capture space, there is also a frame for dealing with time. Tuchman (1978) has illuminated the nature of this particular aspect of the 'news net', since time underlies the typification of events as news. The net she describes, distributed in space and time, is designed to maximize the chance of capturing news events when and where they are likely to occur and the efficiency of dealing with them. Typifying events according to their time scale — especially in relation to the news production cycle — increases the chance of actually reporting as news those events that fit the conventional definitions of news. News people implicitly operate with a time-based typology of news which helps in planning their work (see Figure 8.1).

The main types are 'hard news', dealing with immediate events, and 'soft news', mainly background or time-free news. In addition there are three other categories: 'spot' (very new, immediate, just breaking) news, 'developing' news, and 'continuing' news. There is also a time dimension, according to which news can be classified as 'pre-scheduled', 'unscheduled' or 'non-scheduled'. The first refers to 'diary' events that are known about in advance and for which coverage can be planned; the second to news of events that happen unexpectedly and need to be immediately disseminated — the most difficult for routine handling, but not the largest category of news; the third relates to news (usually soft) that is not tied to any particular time and can be stored and released at the convenience of the news organization. The typification of events in this way narrows the range of uncertainty, but also encourages the tendency to rely on 'continuing' news and on pre-scheduled or non-scheduled event news, thus telling against uniqueness and novelty.

The extraordinary influence of time in the news operation has been especially noticed in broadcasting, and Schlesinger (1978) refers to a 'stop-watch culture', which goes beyond what is needed for practical purposes: 'It is a form of fetishism in which to be obsessed about time is to be professional

Time dimension

News type		Pre-scheduled	Unexpected	Non-scheduled
	Hard	●	●	
	Soft			●
	Spot		●	
	Developing		●	
	Continuing	●	●	

Figure 8.1 *Time and types of news (Tuchman, 1978)*

in a way which newsmen have made peculiarly their own' (p. 105). Its consequence, in his view, is to do some violence to history and reduce the meaningfulness of news. Molotch and Lester (1974) suggest a fourfold typology of events of which the largest category is that of 'routine events', the three others being 'accidents', 'scandals' and 'serendipity' (chance). Routine events, however, are divided into those where 'event promoters have habitual access to the news assemblers', those where 'event promoters seek to disrupt the routine access of others in order to make events of their own', and those where 'the access is afforded by the fact that the promoter and news assemblers are identical'. The last category includes normal reporting and the 'pseudo-event' (the non-event staged for the media). This typology has implications for the exercise of source power.

News selection factors

- Powerful people have more access
- Personal contacts influence attention
- Places where events happen
- Places where the media are located
- Places where power is exercised
- Predictability and routine
- Proximity
- Timeliness of events
- Timing in relation to news cycle

The question of selection 'bias'

This account of media selection has avoided reference to the concept of 'bias', or consistent deviation in a particular direction, in part because this concept implies that there is an objective reality which news is supposed to reflect. Even so, it does look as if the factors which play a part in 'gatekeeping' also have some consistent and predictable outcomes for the picture of the world conveyed by the media. To that extent, organizational and bureaucratic factors can be said to have some potentially ideological consequences. At the very least, there is likely to be an accentuation of the content characteristics which go with ease of collection. These characteristics include ready availability and low cost, conformity to expectation and stereotype, closeness to power and authority, and being interesting without disturbance. Conformity to the pre-definition of the news product is a form of bias when this pre-definition is a somewhat artificial construct of an enclosed and self-supporting professional group.

This discussion of selection has been concerned primarily with the question of news, on which we have most evidence and where selection is a critical factor (often because of what is *not* chosen). The factors which operate in relation to other kinds of content and also have a bearing on the representation of social reality are, however, likely to take a similar overall pattern (see pages 255–6).

Access to the media for society

The question of access to the media (and thus to society itself as audience) by any one institutional element of the society has already been raised at several points. The initial frame of reference in Chapter 3 represents the media as creating (or occupying) channels between the institutions of society and its members. One of the main kinds of pressure on media organizations shown in Figure 7.2 is that for access by social and political interests. Much of the normative theory discussed in Chapter 5 turns in the end on the question of who in society should have access and on what terms.

Even in modern states, claiming to offer a high degree of freedom to their media, there are clear expectations, sometimes backed by considerable pressure, that mass media will make channels available for society-wide communication, especially 'downwards' from leaders or elites to the base of society. Whether this takes place by government command, by purchase of time/space in a free market or by the media playing the rules of the game (for instance, whatever the leader says is news) may not matter much to the eventual outcome, although it matters a good deal to the media, since the freedom to withhold access is an important right.

A continuum of media autonomy

The situation may be conceptualized in terms of a continuum, at one extreme of which the media are totally 'penetrated' by, or assimilated to, outside interests, whether state or not, and at the other end of which the media are totally in control and free to exclude or allow in as they will. Pluralistic theory assumes that the diversity of organizations and possibilities for access will ensure an adequate mix of opportunity for 'official' voices of society and for critical, alternative views.

'Access for society' means more, however, than giving a platform for opinions, information, etc. It also relates to the *manner* in which media portray what passes for the reality of society. They may do this in ways which alter, distort or challenge it. In the end, the question of societal access involves a very complex set of conventions over the terms according to which media freedoms and societal claims can be exercised and reconciled. In this matter, much depends on the standardized characteristics of formats and genres and on the manner in which they are intended to portray social reality or are understood to do so by their audiences.

This question has been illuminated for the case of television production in one country (Britain) by Elliott (1972), but his ideas could be developed to apply to press media and to other national media systems. His typology (Figure 8.2) shows the variability of competence of the media organization over the giving or withholding of access to other would-be communicators. It portrays an inverse relationship between the degree of freedom of access available to society and the degree of extensiveness of control and action by media personnel. The more extensive the scope of control by the media themselves (scope of production), the more limited the direct access by the society. The reference is to a varying degree of intervention or mediation by the media as between the 'voice of society' or social reality on the one hand and the society as audience on the other. This formulation underlines the basic conflict between media autonomy and social control. Access is bound to be a site of struggle.

Actuality content as a contested zone

This schema shows the variable degree to which social 'reality' is filtered by the media, with news and documentary falling at a midpoint on the scale, so that the scope for producers to select and shape is more or less balanced against the scope for society to claim direct access to the audience. Editorial freedom is also in balance with the scope for the audience to achieve a view of reality. In such 'actuality' material, there is an audience expectation of having a view of reality, but also a recognition of the right of the media to set criteria of selection and presentation. Apart from its other merits, this typology reminds us that news, on which so much study of media selection has been concentrated, is only one of several kinds of message about reality that have to pass through the 'gates' of the media.

In practice, it is at the intermediate stages of the continuum (the sphere of actuality) where most potential for conflict arises and where media organizations have to defend their choices and priorities in relation to both society and public. This area extends beyond news and documentaries to

Scope of production	Production function	Directness of access by society	Type of access	Television example
Limited ↑	1 Technical facilitation	Total ↑	1 Direct	Party broadcast
	2 Facilitation and selection		2 Modified direct	Education
	3 Selection and presentation		3 Filtered	News
	4 Selection and compilation		4 Remade	Documentary
	5 Realization and creation	↓	5 Advisory	Realistic social drama
↓ Extensive	6 Imaginative creation	Zero	6 No control by society	Original television drama

Figure 8.2 *A typology of production scope and directness of access by society (Elliott, 1972): access by society is inversely related to communicator (editorial) autonomy*

encompass 'docu-dramas', historical dramas and many 'realistic' serials which portray police, medicine, the military, etc. The more sensitive and powerful the external representatives of these domains of reality happen to be, the more careful the media have to be and the more obliged they are to avoid sensitive areas or to employ irony, allegory, fantasy and other long-known devices for evading direct accountability. It is not only self-interested authority which exerts constraints, but also the possibility of unintended and unwanted effects on reality itself (such as causing panic, crime, suicide or terrorism).

Relations with sources

Media of all kinds depend on having a readily available supply of source material, whether this is book manuscripts to publish, scripts to film or reports of events to fill newspapers and television. The third of these has received most attention in the study of media organizations, since it gives rise to fundamental issues concerning independence and the mediation of social reality. Relations with news sources are essential to news media and they often constitute a very active two-way process. The news media are always looking for suitable content, and content (not always suitable) is always looking for an outlet in the news.

The Westley–MacLean model described above (page 50) shows communication organizations as brokers between would-be 'advocates' trying to convey their view of social reality and a public interested in reliable information about this reality. For their own purposes, news media establish regular contacts with informed insiders and experts, in order to secure timely, authoritative or otherwise inaccessible information, especially in advance of competitors. Correspondingly, regular contacts are initiated and maintained by would-be sources themselves, in order to secure favourable access. This applies especially to political actors, large firms, public institutions, show-business personalities, etc.

Ericson et al. (1987) even designate a special category of 'source media' whose main activity is to supply journalists with what they are looking for on behalf of source organizations of the kind mentioned. Source media consist of press conferences, press releases, public relations, etc. In addition, the media are continually collecting their own material by direct observation, information-gathering and reporting on a day-to-day and event-guided basis. They also routinely use the services of information suppliers, especially national or international news agencies, news film agencies, television exchange arrangements, etc.

Even this does not exhaust the possibilities, especially by leaving out of account the degree to which media serve as sources for each other in unchartable combinations and permutations. Aside from the continuous feeding on each other by press and television, both as sources and as objects of information and comment, there are important relations of content provision from the film industry to television and from music to radio. This is one aspect of the 'intertextuality' of media (see page 238). Research on mass communication has signalled three main aspects that result in an inevitable symbiosis between media and their sources, as follows.

The planning of supply

First, there is the matter of the high degree of planning and predictability which goes with any large-scale continuous media production operation. The media have to have an assured supply for their own needs and thus have to 'order' content in advance, whether of news, fiction or other entertainment. This need is reflected in the growth of secondary organizations (such as news agencies) which provide content regularly. It also implies some inconsistency with the notion of media as neutral carriers or mirrors of the ongoing culture and news of the society. It conflicts with the ideals of novelty, spontaneity and creativity which are often part of the media self-image. If supply has to be planned well in advance according to advance specifications, the reality is very far from this ideal.

Asymmetrical relationships and assimilation

Secondly, there is the question of imbalance between information suppliers and media takers of information or other content. Some sources are more powerful than others or have more bargaining power because of their status, market dominance or intrinsic market value. Gandy (1982) has referred to the 'information subsidies' which are given selectively by powerful interest groups in order to advance their causes. This situation is reflected, for instance, in the privileged access of the more politically and economically powerful and the favoured position of richer media and media systems in the world. Media organizations are far from equal in their degree of access to sources which can further enhance their position.

Thirdly, there is the question of assimilation which arises when there exists a mutual interest on the part of the media and would-be external communicators (advocates or sources). There are obvious examples when political leaders want to reach large publics, but less obvious collusion arises in routine news coverage where reporters depend on sources likely to have both inside information and an interest in the way it is published. This applies to sources such as politicians, officials and the police.

Assimilation has been said to occur (by Gieber and Johnson, 1961) if the degree of collaboration which exists for mutual benefit between reporter and source reaches a point where it conflicts with the 'distributive' role normally expected from those who claim to inform the public. Although this type of relationship may be justified by its success in meeting the needs of the public as well as those of the media organization, it also conflicts with expectations of critical independence and professional norms, and can lend itself to the suppression or manipulation of information in the interest of certain actors or institutions (Chibnall, 1977; Murphy, 1976; Fishman, 1980).

Molotch and Lester (1974) showed how news could be controlled by those in a position to manage publicity about events, if not the events themselves. They call these 'event promoters' and argue that with reference to 'routine events' the event promoters have several opportunities for gaining access on their own terms. They can claim habitual access to the 'news assemblers' (that is, journalists), or they can use their power to disrupt the routine access of others and create 'pseudo-events' of their own which gain media attention. There is often a more or less institutionalized collusive relationship between politicians or officials and press which may serve a range of purposes without necessarily being manipulative in its effect (Whale, 1969; Tunstall, 1970; Sigal, 1973).

This is especially evident in election campaigns, which lend themselves to the staging of 'pseudo-events' ranging from press conferences to major policy statements or demonstrations. In some spheres assimilation between news media and sources is virtually complete. Politics, government and law enforcement are three prime examples, but major sports provides another and big business is not far behind in being able to claim media attention more or less at will and in having a good deal of control over the flow of information.

Public relations and news

Assimilation in the sense used above is also promoted by the activities of professional public relations agencies. There is considerable evidence to suggest that well-organized suppliers of information can be effective and that a good deal of what is supplied by public relations agencies to the news media does get used (Turow, 1989; Shoemaker and Reese, 1991). A study by Baerns (1987), for instance, found that political reporting in one German *Land* was predominantly based on official press releases and news conferences. This is probably not exceptional, but it reflects the fact that journalists tend differentially to rely on official or bureaucratic sources for certain kinds of news (see Fishman, 1980), and the same pattern would not apply to all kinds of news. Journalists would normally be suspicious of self-serving public relations handouts. In the end, however, it does seem that rather little of the news we receive is the outcome of enterprise and investigation on the part of journalists (Sigal, 1973), though it may still be both reliable and relevant.

According to Gans (1979), the sources who are most successful in gaining access to (elite) news media are likely to be powerful, well resourced and well organized for supplying journalists with the kind of 'news' they want at the right moment in time. Such sources are both 'authoritative' and 'efficient' and they often enjoy 'habitual access' to the news media, in the sense meant by Molotch and Lester (1974). There is a potential limit to the independence and diversity of news media from the difficulty they have in turning away such source material.

Source access to news

- Efficient supply of suitable material
- Power and influence of source
- Good public relations
- Dependency of media on limited source
- Mutual self-interest in news coverage

Media-organizational activity: processing and presentation

The processing of the 'raw material' of news, which usually consists of data about a supposed reality, begins at the first moment of selection and can be considered in terms of a series of decisions and choices directed towards the achievement of a product which fits the goals of the media organization. As we have seen, many media have mixed goals, so this process is a very complex one, involving a good deal of bargaining and substitution of one goal for another. The general aim, nevertheless, is to produce something which meets professional or craft standards of quality and has a good chance of success with the audience. The organizational processes involved are typically very hierarchical rather than democratic or collegial, although *within* particular production units the latter may apply.

Most accounts of the structure of formal media organizations, especially relating to news (for example, Tunstall, 1971, 1993; Hetherington, 1985; Ericson et al., 1987, Shoemaker and Reese, 1991), report a fairly similar hierarchical form of control. In large commercial media corporations, the board of directors, representing shareholders, has initial and final power, while executive management is subdivided according to different operations. Shoemaker and Reese (1991), for instance, show an organizational chart for the *Wall Street Journal*, headed by the board of the controlling company (Dow Jones Inc.). Top management supervises the work of two levels of editorships, classified by a topic (such as foreign, investment, media and entertainment, and law) or by function (such as page-one editor, spot news desk editor and enterprise editor). These different editorial desks are served by reporters. Such formal charts primarily reflect and serve the need to allocate and control the use of resources and plan the division of labour.

Internal processing of information

It takes a different kind of chart to see how the media product is actually processed. Ericson et al. (1987) have shown how news organizations arrange the sequence of inputs and decisions. There are two main lines of activity, which start with 'ideas' for news (originating in other media, routine observations, agencies, etc.). Ideas lead to one line which is that of story development, and ideas are also fed by a second 'sources' line. Sources can be reactive (routine) or proactive (enterprise). The two lines are closely connected since particular stories lead to the development of and search for sources. The two lines correspond more or less to the two stages of the 'double action' model of news flow described by Bass (1969) — essentially news gathering and news processing. The processing line follows from story assignments made by the assignment editor and goes through a sequence of news conference, play decisions (prominence and timing), layout or line-up, final news editing, content page make-up or television anchor script, and final line-up. This sequence can be fed up to the penultimate stage by source input. A schematic version of this is given in Figure 8.3.

In general, the sequence extends from a phase where a universe of substantive ideas is considered, through a narrowing down, according to news judgements and to what is fed from the source channel, to a third phase, where format, design and presentation decisions are taken, until the last phase, where technical decisions are likely to be paramount.

This model for news processing is compatible with what seems to occur in other situations, where reality content is also processed, although over a longer time scale and with more scope for production to influence content (see Figure 8.2 above). For instance, Elliott (1972), in his study of the making of a television documentary series, distinguishes three 'chains': a *subject*

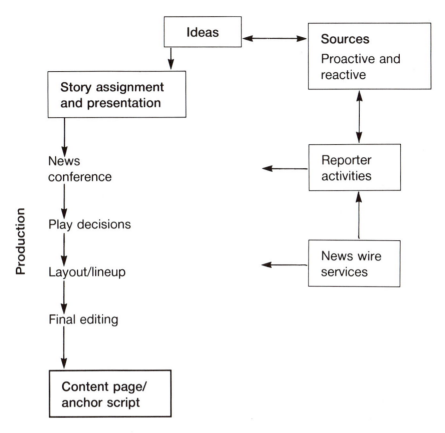

Figure 8.3 *Intra-organizational processing, from ideas to the news (based on Ericson et al., 1987): news as published has internal as well as external origins, and both types are processed jointly*

chain concerned with assembling programme ideas for the series; a *contact* chain connecting producer, director and researcher with their contacts and sources; and a *presentation* chain in which realities of time-slot and budget were related to customary ideas for effective presentation (such as having plenty of illustrative film and having a well-known television personality to act as presenter). The first two correspond to the 'Ideas' and the 'Sources' routes in Figure 8.3, while presentation matters arise at the later stages of the 'production' line.

An alternative model of organizational selection

These examples apply to cases where media processing takes place within the boundaries of the same organization. The music industry offers a different model, although there is still a sequence from ideas to transmission.

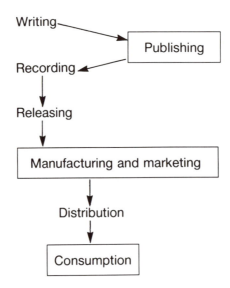

Figure 8.4 *Decision sequence in the music industry (Ryan and Peterson, 1982): the elements in the sequence are often organizationally separate*

Ryan and Peterson (1982) have drawn a model of the 'decision chain' in the popular music industry, which consists of six separate links: (1) from song writing to publishing; (2) from demo tape to recording (where producer and artist are selected); (3) and (4) from recording to manufacturing and marketing; (5) and (6) from there to consumption via radio, juke-box, live performance or direct sales (see Figure 8.4). In this case, the original ideas of song-writers are filtered through music publishers' ideas concerning presentation (especially artist and style), which then play a part in promoting the product in several different markets. Different from the previous examples is the linkage between several organizationally separate agencies and tasks. Processing takes place on the basis of a prediction about what the next 'gatekeeper' in the chain will think, the key being the overall 'product image'.

The question of bias again

When content is subjected to organizational routines there is often an accentuation of the characteristics of any initial selection bias. This seems to happen not only to news but to other kinds of content as well, since a high proportion of content acquired or started as projects never reaches distribution (this is especially true of the film industry, which is profligate with creative talent). This accentuation can mainly be accounted for by the wish to maximize output according to a tried and trusted product image. Some media products live on for years and are resold, remade or recycled indefinitely.

Media organizations tend to reproduce selectively according to criteria which suit their own goals and interests. These may sometimes be professional and craft criteria, but more weight is usually given to what sells most or gets highest ratings. Among commercially relevant criteria, cheap and easy production according to a proven formula of success carries most weight. The more that the same criteria are applied at successive stages of decision-making, the more pre-existing biases of form and content are likely to endure while variety, uniqueness and unpredictability will take second place. Bias in this sense may mean no more than favouring products which are both easy to reproduce and popular with audiences, but it also differentially reinforces certain elements of the media culture and increases conformity with organizational policy.

Standardization and organizational logics

Although mass communication is a form of mass production, the standardization implied in this term relates in the first instance to multiple reproduction and distribution. The individual items of media content do not have to share all the characteristics of mass-produced products. They can easily be original, unique and highly differentiated (for instance, the one-off performance of a sports event, a television talk-show or a news programme, which will never be repeated identically). In practice, however, the technology and organization of mass media production are not neutral and do exert a standardizing influence. Initial diverse and unique content items or ideas are fitted to forms which are both familiar to media producers and thought to be familiar to audiences. These forms are those most suitable for efficient production according to specifications laid down by the organization.

These specifications are of an economic, a technological and a cultural kind. We can speak of an economic logic, a technological logic and a media cultural logic, each of which leaves a distinctive mark on the cultural product through its influence on production decisions. Pressures for **economic** efficiency stem from the need to minimize cost, reduce conflict and ensure continuity and sufficiency of supply. Cost reduction exerts pressure according to different time schemes — in the long run it may lead to the introduction of new technology, in the short run to maximizing output from existing staff resources and equipment and avoiding expensive or loss-making activities. The main pressures on media processors — to save time, use technology efficiently, save money and meet deadlines — are so interrelated that it is easier to see them in their combined consequences than in their separate operation.

The **technological** logic is quite obvious in its effects, which keep changing as a succession of major new inventions has affected different media industries. Film was changed by the coming of sound and colour; the newspaper industry by continuous advances in printing and information transmission; and television by the portable video camera, satellites and general miniaturization of equipment. We can expect high-definition television to make its mark steadily on production standards, to take an example from the near future.

The pressure of technology is experienced mainly as a result of inventions which set higher technical standards for lower prices and which progressive media organizations have to keep up with (whether audiences know or care or not) in order to compete. The investment in technical facilities leads to pressure for their maximum use, and prestige as well as utility becomes a factor. New technology often means more speed, flexibility and capacity, but it establishes norms which put pressure on all media organizations to conform and eventually influences audience expectations about what is most professional or acceptable.

The logic of media culture

Media organizations apply a form of cultural standardization during the processing of media raw material. It has already been suggested that media are constrained by their 'definitions' and associated expectations as to what they are 'good for' in general and what sort of content they can best offer and in what form. Within the media, the main types of content — news, sports, drama, entertainment, advertising — also follow standardized formats which are rooted in traditions (media-made or culturally inherited), ways of work, ideas about audience taste and interest, pressures of time or space. Altheide and Snow (1979) were the first to use the term 'media logic' to capture the systematic nature of pre-existing definitions of what a given type of content should be like.

The concept has been especially useful for identifying the predilection of media producers for factors which they believe will increase audience attention and satisfaction. In relation to informational content, media logic places a premium on immediacy, such as dramatic illustrative film or photos, on fast tempo and short 'sound bytes', and on personally attractive presenters and relaxed formats (such as the so-called 'happy news' format). Media logic also operates on the level of content — for instance, in political campaigns it leads to a preference for personalization, for controversiality and for attention to the 'horse race' (for example, as measured by opinion polls) rather than the issues (Graber, 1976b; Hallin and Mancini, 1984; Mazzoleni, 1987). The 'bias' of media logic is predictable and systematic, embedded in media-organizational working arrangements and forward planning. Hallin (1992) demonstrated that there was a clear correlation in US news coverage of elections between 'horse-race coverage' and sound-byte news — the more of the former, the less of the latter.

Altheide (1985) advanced the concept of 'media format' to refer to 'the internal organization or logic of any shared symbolic activity' (p. 14). The idea is of a *dominant form*, to which mass communicators are more or less constrained to conform. Formats refer not only to broad categories of content but also to unit ideas and representations of reality — akin to stereotypes. They are useful not only to producers but also to audiences, who learn to differentiate within the mosaic of what is offered according to formats which they have learned. According to Altheide (1985), formats are not only a key to understanding much media production but also relevant to questions of effect on society, since they shape the perception of reality acquired from media.

Alternative models of decision-making

In a review of the mechanisms according to which culture is produced in the commercial-industrial world of mass media, Ryan and Peterson (1982) describe five main frameworks for explaining how decisions are made in the media arts. Their first model is that of the **assembly line**, which compares the media production process to the factory, with all skills and decisions built into the machinery and with clear procedural rules. Because media-cultural products, unlike material goods, have to be marginally different from each other, the answer is overproduction at each stage.

The second model is that of **craft and entrepreneurship**, in which powerful figures, with established reputations for judging talent, raising finance and putting things together, manage all the creative inputs of artists, musicians, engineers, etc., in innovative ways. This model applies especially to the film business but could also hold for publications in which editors may play the role of personally charismatic and powerful figures with a supposed flair for picking winners.

The third model is that of **convention and formula**, in which members of a relevant 'art world' agree on a 'recipe', a set of widely held principles which tell workers how to combine elements to produce works in the particular genre. Fourthly, there is the model of **audience image and conflict**, which sees the creative production process as a matter of fitting production to an image of what the audience will like. Here decisions about the latter are central, and powerful competing entrepreneurs come into conflict over them.

The final model is that of the **product image**. Its essence is summarized as follows:

> Having a product image is to shape a piece of work so that it is most likely to be accepted by decision makers at the next link in the chain. The most common way of doing this is to produce works that are much like the products that have most recently passed through all the links in the decision chain to become . . . successful. (Ryan and Peterson, 1982, p. 25)

This model does not assume there to be a consensus among all involved, or an entrepreneur, or an agreed audience image. It is a model which seems closest to the notion of 'professionalism', defined as the special knowledge of what is a good piece of media work, in contrast to the prediction of what will succeed commercially.

Most studies of media production seem to confirm the strong feeling held by established professionals that they know how best to combine all the available factors of production within the inevitable constraints. This may be achieved at the cost of not actually communicating with the audience, but it does secure the integrity of the product.

Five models of media decision-making

- The assembly line
- Craft and entrepreneurship
- Convention and formula
- Audience image
- Product image

Ryan and Peterson's typology is especially useful in stressing the *diversity* of frameworks within which a degree of regularity and predictability can be achieved in the production of cultural goods (including news). There are different ways of handling uncertainty, responding to outside pressures and reconciling the need for continuous production with artistic originality or journalistic freedom. The concepts of manufacturing or routine bureaucracy, often invoked to apply to media production, should be used with caution.

Conclusion: the attention-gaining imperative

We need to recall the dominant influence of the 'publicity' model, compared to the 'transmission' or 'ritual' models of communication (as described in Chapter 2). The transmission model captures one image of the media organization — as a system for efficiently turning events into comprehensible information or ideas into familiar cultural packages. The ritual model implies a private world in which routines are followed largely for the benefit of the participants and their clients. Both capture some element of the reality (which is itself very heterogeneous). The publicity model helps to remind us that mass communication is often primarily a business, and show business at that. Its roots are as much in the theatre and the showground as in politics, art or education. Appearance, artifice and surprise (the fundamentals of 'media logic') often count for more than substance, reality, truth or relevance. At the core of many media organizations, there are contrary tendencies which are often in tension, if not at open war, with each other, making illusory the search for any comprehensive theory of the media organization.

PART IV
CONTENT

9

ISSUES, CONCEPTS AND VARIETIES OF DISCOURSE

Why study media content?

The most visible and accessible evidence of how mass communication works is the vast and enormously varied body of 'messages' and 'meanings' which are continuously being transmitted and received from all kinds of different media. The distinction between message and meaning is a significant one, since the physical text of the message in print, sound or pictorial image is what we can directly observe and is in a sense 'fixed', while the meanings which are embedded in the texts or perceived to be present by their producers or eventual audiences are largely unobservable and not fixed. Such meanings are both diverse and often ambiguous.

Theory and research concerning mass media content are both fissured by this distinction and by the choice which is offered between attending to the message or to the meaning, which largely parallels the choice between a 'transport' and a 'ritual' (or cultural) model of communication (see pages 50–1). This also exposes problems in speaking about content at all. Even so, generalizations about the content of mass media as a whole, or a particular type of content, especially with reference to 'bias' (of meaning) or probable effect, are often encountered. This tendency has been encouraged by the patterned and standardized forms which media content often takes.

The reasons for studying media content in a systematic way stemmed initially either from an interest in the potential effects of mass communication, whether intended or unintended, or from a wish to understand the appeal of content for the audience. Both approaches have a practical basis, from the point of view of mass communicators, but they have gradually widened to embrace a larger range of theoretical issues. Early studies of content reflect concern about the informational content of news, the portrayal of crime, violence and sex in popular entertainment, the use of media as propaganda and the performance of media in respect of racial or other kinds of prejudice.

Most early research tended to assume that content reflected the purposes and values of its originators, more or less directly, that 'meaning' could relatively directly be discovered or inferred from messages and that receivers would understand messages more or less as intended by producers. It was even thought that 'effects' could be discovered from the seeming 'message' built into content. More broadly, the content of mass media has often been regarded by social commentators as more or less reliable evidence about the culture and society in which it is produced. This assumption, for instance, underlies the school of 'cultural indicators' — treating media content as an expression of the dominant message about society (Signorielli and Morgan, 1990; and see Chapter 14).

This serves to identify one of the most prominent and recurrent issues — that of the relation between media messages and 'reality'. There are several alternative ways in which this relationship can be interpreted (as noted below, pages 255–7), but most basic is the question of whether media content does, or should, reflect the social reality, and if so, which or whose reality? A good deal of theory has developed around the question itself as well as around possible answers which have been put forward. The issue is complicated not only by the uncertainty over what constitutes meaning (both of messages and of 'reality') but also by the great range of types of content, with their widely varying 'reality claims' — ranging from hard information to musical fantasy (see Elliott, 1972; and see page 241).

Critical questions and alternative discourses

As we have already seen (Chapter 5), a broad set of normative questions about media content have been posed from the perspective of society. These questions range from the matter of the portrayal of violence, ethnicity or gender to aspects of media independence, information quality or diversity. The main drift of media performance analysis (Krippendorf, 1980) is towards being able to pose and answer questions more or less objectively about how well or not the media attain certain normatively approved ends. A separate tradition of critical enquiry has led to more fundamental questions being asked about the way the mass media manipulate or dominate on behalf of established power. In respect of content, this has led to questions about ideology in media content, especially ideology with a class, racial or gender bias. Critical enquiry into content necessarily starts out with a clearly articulated social-theoretical position — for instance, that of feminism, or Marxism or anti-racism — and its practitioners are themselves committed to a chosen goal.

These and related issues of media content have surfaced in theoretical discussions in a confusing variety of forms and terminologies. There are fragments of theory about media in which a clear role is attributed to content, but there is no coherent theory of content as such. Nor is there any consensus on the appropriate method of research, and issues of how best to analyse media 'texts' have themselves been an object of much theoretical discussion. The question of the variety and defining characteristics of different media genres has also arisen in this context. The concept of *genre* appears to be an essential tool in the analysis of media content, since it provides an organizing framework to cope with the enormous volume of what the media offer and a path to understanding how meaning may be constructed out of the experience of reading, watching and viewing.

The aim of the following sections will be to provide a brief guide to ideas and terms organized according to the issues introduced above, with broad questions of genre and of research strategies reserved for Chapter 10. The sections are somewhat uneven in their level and range of reference. Each heading serves to describe a topic in this terrain and to indicate a particular 'discourse' or framework of discussion in which a set of terms are used in a certain way about a given topic. The word 'discourse' itself is one term which has acquired a wider currency in some accounts of media content. Fiske (1987, p. 14), for instance, describes it as 'a language or system of representation that has developed socially in order to make and circulate a coherent set of meanings about a topic area'. The sections which follow deal with discourse around: the media *text* itself; the *semiological* approach to media content; *information science*; *performance analysis*; and *critical perspectives* on content. The main purpose is to illustrate and introduce the main themes and to define key concepts.

The cultural text and its meanings

One form of discourse has grown up around the discussion and analysis of media texts, especially with the rise of cultural studies and its convergence on an existing tradition of mass communication research. The origins of cultural studies are somewhat mixed, including traditional literary and linguistic analysis of texts, semiology and Marxist theory. A convincing effort to bring much disparate theory together has been made by Fiske (1987), especially for the purpose of analysing and understanding popular (television) culture. New definitions of the media text have been developed along with ways of identifying some key features.

The concept of text

The term 'text' has been used in two basic senses, one of them to refer very generally to the message itself — the printed document, film, television programme or musical score, as noted above. An alternative usage, recommended by Fiske (1987), is to reserve the term 'text' for the meaningful outcome of the encounter between content and reader. For instance, a television programme 'becomes a text at the moment of reading, that is, when its interaction with one of its many audiences activates some of the meanings/pleasures that it is capable of provoking' (p. 14). It follows from this definition that the same television programme can produce many different texts in the sense of accomplished meanings. Summing up this point, Fiske tells us that 'a programme is produced by the industry, a text by its readers' (p. 14). It is important, from this perspective, to see that the word 'production' applies to the activities of both the 'mass communicators' and the audiences.

This is a central point in what is essentially a theory of media content viewed from the point of view of its reception rather than its production or intrinsic meaning. Other essential elements in this approach are to emphasize that the media text (in the first or 'programme' sense) has many potential alternative meanings which can result in different readings. Mass media content is thus in principle **polysemic**, having multiple potential meanings for its 'readers' (in the generic sense of audience members). Fiske argues that polysemy is a necessary feature of truly popular media culture, since the more potential meanings there are, the greater the chance of appeal to different audiences and to different social categories within the total audience.

Multiplicity of textual meaning has an additional dimension, as Newcomb (1991) reminds us. Texts are constituted out of many different **languages** and systems of meaning. These include the codes of dress, physical appearance, class and occupation, religion, ethnicity, region, social circles and many more. Any words in a spoken language or interactions in a drama can have different meanings in relation to any or several of these other languages.

Differential encoding

Despite this polysemic character, the discourses of particular examples of media content are often designed or inclined to control, confine or direct the taking of meaning, which may in turn be resisted by the reader. This discussion relates to Hall's (1973a/1980) model of **encoding/decoding** (discussed in Chapter 2), according to which there is usually a 'preferred reading' encoded in a text — the meaning which the message producer would like the receiver to take. On the whole, it is the 'preferred readings' which are identified by analysis of overt content — the literal or surface meaning plus the ideology. As Fiske (1987) also reminds us, the text as produced by the reader is not confined in its meaning by the boundaries which are set on the production side between programmes or between content categories. A 'reader' of media texts can easily combine, for instance, the experience of a programme with that of advertisements inserted in it, or with adjoining programmes.

This is one aspect of the **intertextuality** of media, and it applies also to crossing boundaries between media (such as film, books and radio). Intertextuality is not only an accomplishment of the reader but also a feature of media themselves, which are continually cross-referencing from one medium to another, and the same 'message', story or type of narrative can be found in very different media forms and genres. Television, according to Fiske (1987), gives rise to a 'third level of intertextuality' — referring to the texts that viewers make themselves and reproduce in conversation or in writing about the media experience. Ethnographic researchers into media audiences draw on such 'third-level' texts when they listen in on conversations or organize group discussions to hear about how the media are experienced (for example, Radway, 1984; Ang, 1985; Liebes and Katz, 1986).

Codes are systems of meaning whose rules and conventions are shared by members of a culture or by what has been called an 'interpretative community' (for instance, a set of fans of the same media genre, author or performer). Codes help to provide the links between media producers and media audiences by laying the foundation for interpretation. We make sense of the world by drawing on our understanding of communicative codes and conventions. Particular gestures, expressions, forms of dress and images, for example, carry more or less unambigous meanings within particular cultures which have been established by usage and familiarity. An example of a film code (Monaco, 1981) is an image combining a weeping woman, a pillow and money, to symbolize shame.

Open versus closed texts

In the particular discourse about media content under discussion, the content may be considered to be more or less 'open' or 'closed' in its meanings. According to Eco (1979), an open text is one whose discourse does not try to constrain the reader to one particular meaning or interpretation. Different kinds and actual examples of media text can be differentiated according to their degree of openness. For instance, in general, news reports are intended not to be open but to lead to a uniform informational end, while serials and soap operas are often loosely articulated and lend themselves to varied 'readings'. This differentiation is not always consistent as between genres, and there can be large variations within genres in the degree of textual openness. In the case of commercial advertisements, while they are intended to achieve a long-term goal benefiting the product advertised, the form of advertisement can range from the playful and ambiguous to the one-dimensional 'hard sell' or simple announcement. It has also been argued that television in general has a more open and ambiguous text than cinema film (Ellis, 1982).

The distinction between open and closed texts has a potential ideological significance. In their discussion of the television portrayal of terrorism, for instance, Schlesinger et al. (1983) argued that a more open portrayal also leads to alternative viewpoints, while a closed portrayal tends to reinforce the dominant or consensual view. They make another distinction between a 'tight' or 'loose' storyline, reinforcing the tendency of the closed versus open choice. They conclude that television news is in general both closed and tight, while documentary and fiction are more variable. They observe that, in the case of fiction, the larger the (expected) audience, the more closed and tight the representation of terrorism, thus converging on the 'official' picture of reality as portrayed on the news. This suggests some form of ideological control (probably self-censorship), with risks not being taken with a mass audience.

Narrative

The text as narrative has for long been an object of study, and the narrative concept has proved useful in understanding a variety of media contents, since basic narrative forms span a wide range of types, including advertisements and news 'stories' as well as the more obvious candidates of drama and fiction. In one way or another, most media content tells stories, which take rather patterned and predictable forms. The main function of narrative is to help make sense of reports of experience. It does this in two main ways: by linking actions and events in a logical sequential or causal way; and by providing the elements of people and places which have a fixed and recognizable (realistic) character. Narrative helps to provide the logic of human motive which makes sense of fragmentary observations, whether fictional or realistic.

Darnton (1975) argues that our conception of news results from 'ancient ways of telling stories'. News accounts are typically cast in narrative form, with principal and minor actors, connected sequences, heroes and villains, beginning, middle and end, signalling of dramatic turns and a reliance on familiar plots. The analysis of news narrative structure has been formalized in the 'discourse analysis' tradition, especially by van Dijk (1983, 1985), who has developed an empirically based framework for the analysis of news based on the concept of 'news schemata', which provide a syntax of news stories.

The general categories are followed implicitly by news producers (part of their 'working theory'). Bell has extended and applied van Dijk's framework, which he summarizes as follows:

> A news text will normally consist of an abstract, attribution and the story proper. . . . A story consists of one or more episodes, which in turn consist of one or more events. Events must contain actors and action, usually express setting, and may have explicit attribution. . . . As well as those elements which present the central action, we recognize three additional categories that can contribute to an event: follow-up; commentary and background. (1991, p. 169)

Bell remarks that 'the most striking character of news discourse comes from the non-chronological order of its elements', which he attributes to the need to obey news values rather than ordinary narrative norms. Fragments of information are selected by a journalist and reassembled in newsworthy order (see Chapter 10 on news genre).

Seriality

There has been a revival of interest in narrative theory (Oltean, 1993), especially as a result of the great attention given to television drama, serials and series in media studies (for example, Seiter et al., 1989). Narrative theory owes much to the work of Propp (1968), who uncovered the basic similarity of narrative structure of Russian folk tales. Modern popular media fiction also testifies to the high degree of constancy and similarity of a basic plot. For instance, Radway (1984) described the basic narrative logic of mass-produced romance stories for women in terms of a series of stages, starting with a disturbance for the heroine, through an antagonistic encounter with an aristocratic male, by way of a separation, to a reconciliation and a sexual union, concluding with a restoration of identity for the heroine.

While basic plots can be found in many different genres, with a range of established but familiar variations, there are other narrative differences to note. Television series can, for instance, be clearly differentiated from serials, using narrative theory. The series consists of a set of discrete stories which are terminated in each episode. In the cases of serials, the story continues without end from one episode to the next. In both cases there is continuity, primarily achieved by retaining the same principal characters. However, there is a difference: in series, the heroes and heroines (subjects) remain constant, while the villains (objects) differ from one episode to another. The same characters go through different narrative sequences in the same settings. In between episodes, as Oltean (1993) remarks, 'the marionettes stay put in a cabin placed outside the fictional reality'.

By contrast, with serials (such as normal soap operas, which in their original form were broadcast daily) the same cast of characters appears each time, and an illusion is fostered that they continue their life actively between episodes. They 'remain fictively active' (Oltean). Another aspect of narrative underlined by Oltean is the difference between 'linear' and 'parallel' processing. In serials there is a transition from one storyline to the next, while in series there is a 'meta-story' (concerning the permanent characters), with several different storylines as they encounter their new adventures week by week. The series organizes stories according to a principle of linearity, while serials (such as soap operas) prefer parallel processing — with a network of concurrent storylines involving different sub-groups of the permanent cast of characters interacting and interweaving on varying time scales.

Realism

Narrative often depends on assumptions about realism and helps to reinforce a sense of reality, by invoking the logic, normality and predictability of human behaviour. The conventions of realistic fiction were established by the early forms of the novel, although they were preceded by realism in other arts. On the one hand, realism of media depends on a certain attitude that what is portrayed is 'true to life', if not literally true in the sense of having actually occurred. Realistic fiction depends on the belief that it *could* occur or might have done so. Even fantastic stories can be made realistic if they use actual settings and social backgrounds and gain verisimilitude from applying plausible logics of action.

There are also techniques of writing and filming which emphasize realism. In the former case, accurate documentary-like descriptions and concrete, logical and sequential storytelling achieve the result. In filming, aside from representing real places, a continuous flow of action serves to create a realistic illusion. There are also classic realistic stylistic devices (Monaco, 1981). One of these is the 'shot–reverse–shot', which moves the camera from one speaker to a partner in a dialogue to create the illusion for the spectator of involvement in the ongoing conversation (Fiske, 1987).

Film and television can also employ in fiction the 'documentary' mode or style, which is established on the basis of learned conventions. In general, documentary style relies on real places and social settings to create the illusion of actuality. According to Fiske (1987), media realism leads in a 'reactionary' (rather than a radical) direction because it 'naturalizes' the status quo — makes it seem normal and therefore inevitable. In the terms used above, realism goes in the direction of 'closure', since the more real-seeming the portrayal, the more difficult for the reader, who is likely to take the reality of the world for granted, to establish any alternative meanings. This relates back to the Schlesinger et al.'s (1983) evidence about differing degrees of openness and closure in news and fiction.

Differential 'reading' of texts

Although the broad approach to media content under review does assume that meaning is variable, according to an interpretation by the reader, there is also a recognition of the 'bias of encoding' in the form of 'preferred meanings'. One aspect of this relates to the notion of the 'inscribed reader' (Sparks and Campbell, 1987). Particular media contents can be said, in line with the theory of Bourdieu (1986), to 'construct' a reader, a construction which can to some extent be 'read back' by an analyst on the basis of the set of concerns in the text as written. The 'inscribed reader' is also the kind of reader who is primarily *addressed* by a message. A similar concept is that of the 'implied audience' (Deming, 1991).

The process by which this works has also been called **interpellation** or appellation and usually refers back to the ideology theories of Althusser (1971). According to Fiske (1987, p. 53), 'interpellation refers to the way any use of discourse "hails" the addressee. In responding . . . we implicitly accept the discourse's definition of "us", or . . . we adopt the subject position proposed for us by the discourse.' This feature of discourse is widely exploited in advertising (Williamson, 1978), where advertisements commonly construct and project their image of a model consumer of the product in question. They then invite 'readers' to recognize themselves in these images. Such images normally associate certain desirable qualities (such as chicness, cleverness, youth or beauty) with using the product, and generally this is flattering to the consumer as well as to the product.

Gendered media texts

The concept of an inscribed (written-into) or interpellated reader can be used to analyse the audience image sought by particular media, in terms of class, cultural taste, age or lifestyle (Sparks and Campbell, 1987). It is widely argued that many kinds of media content, following the same line of argument, are differentially gendered — they have built in some bias towards the supposed characteristics of one or other gender — presumably for reasons of appealing to a chosen audience, or simply because many language codes are innately gendered.

Fiske (1987) gives an example based on the television police series *Cagney and Lacey*, which features two women as the chief protagonists. In the series, 'the discourse of gender . . . underwrites a number of codes to discourage us from adopting the masculine point of view that is normal in patriarchal television'. The female active role is 'represented as a controlling, active person upon whom the camera dwells not in order to display her sexual attractiveness, but to explore and convey the manner in which she is controlling the scene' (p. 53).

A number of writers (for example, Geraghty, 1991) have argued that the soap opera as a genre is intrinsically 'gendered' as female narrative, by way of its characterization, settings and dialogue and the positioning of male and female roles. Modleski (1982) suggested that the loose structure of the typical soap opera matches the fragmented pattern of the housewife's daily work. By contrast, television action serials can often be said to be gendered in a masculine way. Some of the differences (as with advertising) are certainly caused by simply planning to appeal to different audience groups, following conventional and often stereotyped ideas about male–female differences. Mass-produced romances of the kind described by Radway (1984) are clearly 'gendered' from the start and mostly written by women as well as openly for women. However, this is not likely to be the whole explanation, and 'gendering' can take subtle and not always intended forms, which makes the pursuit of the topic worthwhile.

For example, a study of female and male film directors by Patsy Winsor, reported by Real (1989), showed a number of significant differences in the content of popular films made by men and women. Female film directors were noticeably less inclined to include acts of physical aggression or to associate them so strongly with men. They showed women in more active roles and in several different and less predictable ways produced distinctive texts. The study concluded that, notwithstanding the constraints of popular film-making, there was some evidence of the emergence of a 'women's aesthetic'.

Studying the popular

The approach to content which has been reviewed has seemed especially suited to the study of popular mass entertainment — especially fictional and dramatic forms, which seek to involve the reader in a fantasy, but usually in realistic settings. The aim of such media content is to convey not any specific meaning but simply 'entertainment' — taking people out of themselves and into other worlds of the imagination, caught up in dramatic actions and emotions. The texts employed for this purpose tend to be relatively 'open' and do not have to work hard at the cognitive level.

Outside the sphere of popular fiction, there is likely to be a greater tension between the postulate of polysemy and the view that texts are structured in certain ways to achieve their audience and their effect. The inscribed texts of media news, for instance, are much more closed and determinate in their informational purpose, even if they also can be differentially or even aberrantly 'decoded' (Eco, 1979).

The cultural text approach

- Media texts are jointly produced with their readers
- Texts may be differentially encoded
- Texts are 'polysemic' — many potential meanings
- Media texts are related to other texts (intertextual)
- Media texts employ different narrative forms
- Media texts are variably open or closed
- Texts are realistic or fabulative

Structuralism and semiology

Another influential universe of thinking about media content which formed a significant precursor to the 'discourse of cultural texts', as just outlined, has origins in the general study of language. Basically, structuralism refers to the way meaning is constructed in texts, the term applying to certain 'structures of language', consisting of signs, narrative or myths. In general, languages have been said to work because of in-built structures, and theorists have been drawn to try to uncover these underlying structures in order to reveal hidden meanings. The term 'structure' implies a constant and ordered relation of elements, although this may not be apparent on the surface and requires decoding. In general, it has been assumed that such structures are located in and governed by particular cultures — much wider systems of meaning, reference and signification. Semiology is a more specific version of the general structuralist approach. There are several classic explications of the structuralist or semiological approach to media content (for example, Barthes, 1967, 1977; Eco, 1977) and now several useful introductions and commentaries (such as Burgelin, 1972; Hawkes, 1977; Fiske, 1982).

Structuralism is a development of the linguistics of de Saussure (1915) and combines with it some principles from structural anthropology. Structuralism differs from linguistics in two main ways: it is concerned not only with conventional verbal languages but also with any sign-system which has language-like properties; and it directs its attention less to the sign-system itself than to chosen texts and the meaning of texts in the light of the 'host' culture. It is thus concerned with the elucidation of cultural as well as linguistic meaning, an activity for which a knowledge of the sign-system is instrumental but insufficient on its own.

Towards a science of signs

North American (C.S. Peirce, 1931–5) and British (C.K. Ogden and I.A. Richards, 1923) scholars subsequently worked towards the goal of establishing a 'general science of signs' (semiology or semiotics). This field was to encompass structuralism and other things besides, thus all things to do with **signification** (the giving of meaning by means of language), however loosely structured, diverse and fragmentary. The concepts of 'sign-system' and 'signification' common to linguistics, structuralism and semiology derive mainly from de Saussure. The same basic concepts were used in somewhat different ways by the three theorists mentioned, but the following are the essentials.

A **sign** is the basic physical vehicle of meaning in a language — any 'sound-image' that we can hear or see and which usually **refers** to some object or aspect of reality, about which we wish to communicate, which is known as the **referent**. In human communication, we use signs to convey meanings about objects in the world of experience to others, who interpret the signs we use, on the basis of sharing the same language or knowledge of the sign-system we are using (for instance, non-verbal communication). According to de Saussure, the process of signification is accomplished by two elements of the sign. He called the physical element (word, image, sound) the **signifier** and used the term **signified** to refer to the mental concept invoked by a physical sign in a given language code (Figure 9.1).

Normally in language systems, the connection between a physical signifier (such as a word) and a particular referent is arbitrary, but the relation between signifier and signified (meaning or concept conveyed) is governed

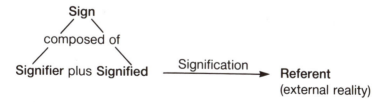

Figure 9.1 *Elements of semiology: signs in meaning systems have two elements — physical plus associated meanings in the culture and in use*

by the rules of culture and has to be learned by the particular 'interpretative community'. In principle, anything which can make a sense-impression can act as a sign, and this sense-impression has no necessary correspondence with the sense-impression made by the thing signified (for instance, the word 'tree' does not look at all like a representation of an actual tree). What matters is the sign-system or 'referent-system' which governs and interrelates the whole process of signification.

Generally, the separate signs gain their meaning from the systematic differences, contrasts and choices which are regulated in the linguistic or sign-system code and from the values (positive or negative valence) which are given by the rules of the culture and the sign-system. Semiology has sought to explore the nature of sign-systems which go beyond the rules of grammar and syntax and regulate complex, latent and culturally dependent meanings of texts.

Connotation and denotation

This has led to a concern with connotative as well as denotative meaning — the associations and images invoked and expressed by certain usages and combinations of signs. **Denotation** has been described as the 'first order of signification' (Barthes, 1967), because it describes the relationship within a sign between the signifier (physical aspect) and signified (mental concept). The obvious straightforward meaning of a sign is its denotation. Williamson (1978) gives an example of an advertisement in which a photo of the film star Catherine Deneuve is used to advertise a French brand of perfume. The photo denotes Catherine Deneuve.

Connotation relates to a second order of signification, referring to the associated meaning which may be conjured up by the object signified. In the example of the advertisement, Catherine Deneuve is generally associated by members of the relevant language (and cultural) community with French 'chicness'. The relevance of this to advertisers is that the connotation of the chosen model (here a film star) is transferred by association to a perfume which she uses or recommends.

Perhaps the first demonstration of this approach to text analysis was provided by Barthes (1977) in his analysis of a magazine advertisement for Panzani foods. This showed an image of a shopping bag containing groceries (the physical signifier), but these in turn were expected to invoke positive images of freshness and domesticity (the level of connotation). In addition, the red and green colours also signified 'Italianness' and could invoke a myth of culinary tradition and excellence. Thus signification commonly works at two levels (or orders) of meaning — the surface level of literal meaning, and the second level of associated or connotated meaning. The activation of the second level requires some deeper knowledge or familiarity with the culture on the part of the reader.

Barthes extended this basic idea by introducing the concept of a **myth**.

Often the thing signified by a sign will have a place in a larger discrete system of meaning, which is also available to the member of a particular culture. Myths are pre-existing and value-laden sets of ideas derived from the culture and transmitted by communication. For instance, there are likely to be myths about national character or national greatness, or concerning science or nature (its purity and goodness), which can be invoked for communicative purposes (as they often are in advertising).

Denotative meaning has the characteristics of universality (same fixed meaning for all) and objectivity (references are true and do not imply evaluation), while connotation involves both variable meaning according to the culture of the recipient and elements of evaluation (positive or negative direction). The relevance of all this for the study of mass communication should be evident. Media content consists of a large number of 'texts' (in the physical sense), often of a standardized and repetitive kind, which are composed on the basis of certain stylized conventions and codes, often drawing on familiar or latent myths and images present in the culture of the makers and receivers of texts (Barthes, 1972).

Uses of semiology

The application of semiological analysis opens the possibility of revealing more of the underlying meaning of a text, taken as a whole, than would be possible by simply following the grammatical rules of the language or consulting the dictionary meaning of separate words. It has the special advantage of being applicable to 'texts' which involve more than one sign-system and signs (such as visual images and sounds) for which there is no established 'grammar' and no available dictionary. Without semiology, for instance, it would hardly have been possible for Williamson (1978) to have carried out her seminal study of advertisements.

Much media content is of a similar kind. However, semiological analysis presupposes a thorough knowledge of the originating culture and of the particular genre. According to Burgelin (1972, p. 317), 'the mass media clearly do not form a complete culture on their own . . . but simply a fraction of such a system which is, of necessity, the culture to which they belong'. Moreover, it follows from the theory summarized above that a text has its own immanent, intrinsic, more or less given and thus objective meaning, apart from the overt intention of sender or the selective interpretation of the receiver. As Burgelin also comments (p. 316), 'there is nobody, and nothing, outside the message which can supply us with the meaning of one of its elements'.

This body of theory supplies us with an approach, if not exactly a method, for helping to establish the 'cultural meaning' of media content. It certainly offers a way of describing content: it can shed light on those who produce and transmit a set of messages; it has a special application in opening up layers of meaning which lie beneath the surface of texts and deny simple description at the 'first level' of signification. It is also useful in certain kinds of evaluative research, especially as directed at uncovering the latent ideology and 'bias' of media content.

Structuralism/semiology

- Texts have meanings built in by way of language
- Meanings depend on a wider cultural and linguistic frame of reference
- Texts represent processes of signification
- Sign-systems can be 'decoded' on the basis of knowledge of culture and sign-system
- Meanings of texts are connotative, denotative or mythical

Media content as information

A different discourse around media content originates in the information theory approaches popularized by the work of Shannon and Weaver (1949). The roots are intermingled with the basic transmission model (see pages 49–50), which conceives communication as essentially the intentional transfer of information from sender to receiver, by way of (physical) channels, which are subject to noise and interference. According to this model, communication is judged by the efficiency (volume and cost) and effectiveness in achieving the planned 'transfer'. The concept of information has proved difficult to define, because it can be viewed in different ways, but the central element is probably the capacity to 'reduce uncertainty'. Information is thus defined by its opposite (randomness or chaos).

Information theory

According to Frick (1959), the insight which led to the development of information theory was the realization that 'all the processes which might be said to convey information are basically selection processes'. The mathematical theory of communication provided an objective approach to the analysis of communication texts. The basis for objectivity (quantification) is the binary (yes/no) coding system, which forms the basis for digital computing. All problems of uncertainty can ultimately be reduced to a series of either/or questions and the number of questions required to solve a problem of meaning equals the number of items of information and is a measure of information quantity.

This line of thinking provides a tool for the analysis of the informative content of texts and opens up several lines of research. There is an in-built bias to a view of communication content as embodying rational purposes of the producers and to an instrumental view of media messages. The approach is also fundamentally *behaviourist* in its assumptions. For obvious reasons, most application of this kind of theory has been to 'informative' kinds of content (such as news). Nevertheless, all media texts that are systematically encoded in known 'languages' are open in principle to analysis in terms of information and uncertainty reduction. Photographs, for instance, at the level of denotation, often present a series of 'iconic' items of information, signs which can be read as references to objects in the 'real world'.

Up to a point, iconic images are as informative as words, sometimes more so, and can also indicate certain kinds of relations between objects (such as relative distance) and give detailed information about colour, size, texture, etc. Fictional narratives can also be treated as informational texts, by assuming what they represent to be informative. For purposes of quantifying the amount of information which is sent or received and for measuring some aspects of the quality of messages, it need not matter which type of media content is at issue.

Applications in the study of content

Four examples of how the assumptions of information theory can be used in the analysis of media content can be found in certain measures of informativeness, readability, diversity and information flow. There are a number of different ways of measuring the 'information value' (in the sense of capacity to reduce uncertainty) of media texts. The simplest approach is to count the number of 'facts' in a text, with alternative possibilities for defining what constitutes a fact (often it is conceived as a basic verifiable unit of objective information). Research by Asp (1981) involved a measure of 'information value' (or informativity) of news on certain controversial issues, based on three different indicators of news content, having first established a universe of relevant factual points in all news reports.

One measure was of **density**: the proportion of all relevant points in a given report; secondly, **breadth**: the number of different points as a proportion of the total possible; thirdly, **depth**: the number of facts and reported motives helping to explain the basic points (some subjective judgement may be involved here). An **information value index** was calculated by multiplying the density score by the breadth score. While factualness can be formally measured in this and similar ways, it cannot be assumed that information density or richness will make communication any more effective, although it may represent (good) intentions on the part of the reporters and a potential for being informative.

An alternative is to measure **readability** — another valued quality of journalistic texts. Approaches to measurement have mainly followed the idea that news is more readable when there is more **redundancy** (the reverse of information density). The simple idea is that an 'information-rich' text packed full of factual information which has a high potential for reducing uncertainty is also likely to be very challenging to a (not very highly motivated) reader. This is also related to the variable of being closed or open — information-rich texts are generally closed, not leaving much room for interpretation.

There is experimental support for the view that the less information in a text, the easier it generally is to read and understand. The main (experimental) tool for measuring readability is called the **cloze procedure** (Taylor, 1953) and involves a process whereby a reader has to substitute words for systematically omitted words. The ease of substitution is the measure of ease of reading, since texts with many redundant words give rise to fewer problems. This is not the only measure of readability, since measures of **sensationalism** achieve much the same result, though without the same basis in information theory (Tannenbaum and Lynch, 1960).

If we can measure the information in media content, and if we can categorize items of information in a relevant way, it follows that we can also measure the (internal) **diversity** of texts. A typical diversity question (see below) might be the degree to which news gave equal or proportionate attention to the views of several different political parties or candidates. Chaffee (1981), for instance, suggested using Schramm's (1955) measure of **entropy**, which involved calculating the number of categories and the evenness of distribution of media space/time between categories (of information or opinion). There is more diversity where we find more categories (a wide range of opinion) and less diversity where there is very unequal attention to different categories (one opinion tends to dominate news coverage).

As noted, the informational approach can be used for measuring the volume of **flow of information**. This arises in theory and research concerning the 'information society'. For instance, Ito (1981) describes the methods by which communication flow (through all channels) in Japan and some other countries has been continuously measured. This comparative 'census' of information requires a common unit measure for information volume, and this is achieved by measuring 'words' and finding equivalents for words for other kinds of media content (such as television picture or music). Certain assumptions were made to convert all media forms to the word unit, based on the normal flow of speech (so many words per minute). In this way, the time taken by music can be given a word equivalent score, while still and moving pictures are converted to words by noting the number of visible words that could be written on a picture. This is obviously a very crude measure of information volume, but it is practical for purposes of comparison between media forms, between countries and over time. It also illustrates another aspect of the 'informational discourse'.

The evaluative dimension of information

From the examples given of the informational approach it looks as if it is very one-dimensional and hard to apply to non-factual aspects of content. It seems insensitive to the different levels of meaning which have already been mentioned and offers no place for alternative interpretations of a message. From the informational perspective, ambiguous or open texts are simply more redundant or chaotic. It is also unclear how this kind of objective analysis can cope with the *evaluative* dimension of information (which is always present in news).

While this critique is valid, there are possibilities for the objective analysis of the value direction of texts. These depend on the assumption (which can be empirically supported) that signs often carry positive or negative loadings in their own natural languages or code systems, certainly for those who are members of the relevant 'interpretative community'. It follows that references to people, objects or events can objectively convey values.

The work of Osgood et al. (1957) on the evaluative structure of meaning in a language laid the basis for developing objective measures of value direction in texts. The essence of the approach (see van Cuilenburg et al., 1986) is to identify frequently recurring words according to their 'common meaning' (their relative positive or negative weight in everyday use) and to record the extent to which words of different value direction are (semantically) connected with relevant attitude objects in the news (such as political leaders, policies, countries and events). In principle, by such procedures, it is possible to quantify the 'inscribed' evaluative direction of attitude in media content. Moreover it is possible to uncover **networks** of semantically associated 'attitude objects', and this sheds further light on value patterns (implied by association) in texts. This method does have the potential to allocate an evaluative meaning to whole texts, as well as to 'facts' or items of information, within a particular culture and society. Contextual knowledge is, however, a necessary condition, and the method departs from the purity of information theory.

Communication as information

- Communication is to be defined as transfer of information from sender to individual receiver
- Media texts are bodies of information
- Information is essentially the reduction of uncertainty
- Information quality and the informativeness of texts are measurable
- The evaluative direction of information is measurable

Media performance discourse

The evaluation of mass media content according to a number of normative criteria has resulted in an extensive body of research into media content which needs to be treated here separately (and very briefly). The tradition of research is usually characterized by a reference to some public interest (or good of society) as the source and point of reference for content criteria (McQuail, 1992). Although a given set of values provide the starting point for analysis of media, the **procedures** adopted are those of a neutral scientific observer, and the aim is find independent evidence which will be relevant to public debate about the role of media in society (Stone, 1987; Lemert, 1989). The evidence sought for should relate to particular media but needs also to have a general character.

It could be said that this particular discourse is about the politics of media content. It adjoins and occasionally overlaps with the critical tradition, which is discussed below, but differs in that it stays within the boundaries of the system itself, accepting the goals of the media in society more or less on their own terms (or at least the more idealistic goals). The normative background and the general nature of the principles have already been sketched (Chapter 5). What follows are some examples of the testable expectations about the quality of media provision which are implied in the various performance principles.

Freedom and independence

Perhaps the foremost expectation about media content is that it should reflect or embody the spirit of free expression, despite the many institutional and organizational pressures which have already been described. It is not easy to see how the quality of freedom (and here the reference is primarily to news, information and opinion functions of media) can be recognized in content. Several general aspects of content can, even so, be identified as indicating more or less freedom (from commercial, political or social pressure). For example, there is the general question of editorial vigour or activity, which should be a sign of using freedom and shows itself in a number of ways. These include: actually expressing opinions, especially on controversial issues; willingness to report conflict and controversy; following a 'pro-active' policy in relation to sources (thus not relying on press handouts and public relations, or being too cosy with the powerful); and giving background and interpretation as well as facts.

The concept of 'editorial vigor' was coined by Thrift (1977) to refer to several related aspects of content, especially dealing with *relevant* and significant local matters, adopting an argumentative form and providing 'mobilizing information' — the latter referring to information which helps people to *act* on their opinions (Lemert, 1989). Some critics and commentators also look for a measure of advocacy and of support for 'underdogs' as evidence of free media (Entman, 1989). Investigative reporting may also be regarded as a sign of news media using their freedom, although (as Paletz and Entman, 1981, note) it may also support rather than challenge the status quo, pursuing targets which are socially or politically marginalized such as criminals, political extremists, the 'politically incorrect', foreigners or minority groups who are sometimes stigmatized (like gypsies and homosexuals).

In one way or another, most mass media content could be assessed in terms of the 'degree of freedom' exhibited. Outside the sphere of news, one would look for innovation and unexpectedness, nonconformity and experimentation in cultural matters. The most free media are also likely to deviate from conformity in matters of taste and be willing to be unpopular with audiences as well as with authorities. However, if so, they are not likely to remain *mass* media.

Content diversity

After freedom, probably the most frequently encountered term in the 'performance discourse' is diversity. The range of meanings of the term is itself very wide, as we have seen, although it essentially refers to the presence of a wide range of choice for audiences, on all conceivable dimensions of interest and preference, many and different opportunities for access for voices and sources in society, and a true or sufficient reflection in media of the varied reality of experience in society. The expectation of diversity in these terms applies especially to news and information, but also and in much the same way to fiction and even entertainment. In this context we can really only speak of content diversity if we apply some external standard to media texts — whether of audience preference, social reality or (would-be) sources in society. Lack of diversity can be established only by identifying sources, references, events, types of content, etc., which are missing or underrepresented. In themselves, media texts cannot be said to be more or less diverse in any absolute sense.

Objectivity in news

The standard of news objectivity has given rise to much discussion of journalistic media content, under various headings, especially in relation to some form of **bias**, which is the reverse of objectivity. As indicated already, the ruling norms of most Western media call for a certain practice of neutral, informative reporting of events, and it is against this positive expectation that much news has been found deficient. However, objectivity is a relatively complex notion when one goes beyond the simple idea that news should reliably (therefore honestly) report what is really going on in the world (Hackett, 1984). On the one hand, there are several sub-components of the idea that news tells us about reality. On the other hand, the expectation of **neutral** reporting is also open to various interpretations.

The simplest version of the idea that news tells us about the real world can be referred to as **factuality** (see Chapter 5). This refers to texts made up of distinct units of information which are necessary for understanding or acting upon a news 'event'. In journalistic terms it means at least providing dependable (correct) answers to the questions Who?, What?, Where?, When? and maybe Why?, and going on from there. A systematic approach to the assessment of factuality in the sense of 'information value' has already been discussed. News can be more or less 'information rich' in terms of the number of facts offered.

For analysing news quality, however, one needs more refined criteria. In particular, one asks if the facts given are **accurate** and whether they are sufficient to constitute an adequate account — the criterion of **completeness**. Accuracy itself can mean several things, since it cannot be directly 'read' or 'measured' from inspection of texts alone. One meaning of accuracy is conformity to independent records of events, whether in documents, other media or eyewitness accounts. Another meaning is more subjective — accuracy is conformity of reports to the perception of the source of news or the subject of the news (object of reporting). Accuracy may also be a matter of internal consistency within news texts.

Completeness is equally difficult to pin down or measure, since complete accounts of even simple events are not possible or necessary. Although one can always make assessments and comparisons of news in terms of more or less information, the question really turns on how much information is needed or can reasonably be expected, which is a subjective matter. We are quickly into another dimension of factuality — that of the **relevance** of the facts offered. Again it is a simple notion that news information is relevant only if it is interesting and useful (and vice versa), but there are competing notions and criteria of what counts as relevant. One source of criteria is what *theory* says news ought to be like. Another is what professional *journalists* decide is most relevant, and a third is what an *audience* actually finds interesting and useful. These three perspectives are unlikely to coincide on the same criteria or on the assessment of content.

Theory tends to equate relevance with what is *really* significant in the longer perspective of history and what contributes to the working of society (for instance, informed democracy). From this point of view, a good deal of news, such as about personalities, 'human interest', sport or entertainment, is not regarded as relevant. Journalists tend to apply professional criteria and a feel for news values which balance the longer-term significance with what they think their public is interested in.

One study of US journalists (Burgoon, quoted in McQuail, 1992, p. 218) showed a decided split between perceptions of 'significance' and 'interest' as factors in news judgement. Relevance was seen as having to do first of all with things 'which affect people's lives', secondly with things which are interesting or unusual, thirdly with facts which are timely or relate to nearby or large-scale happenings. In the end, it is the audience which decides what is relevant, and there are too many different audiences for a generalization to be useful. Even so, it is clear that much of what theory says is relevant is not perceived as such by much of the audience much of the time.

The issue of what counts as **impartiality** in news seems relatively simple but can also be complex in practice, not least because there is little chance of achieving a value-free assessment of value freedom. Impartiality is appreciated mainly because many events involve conflict and are open to alternative interpretations and evaluations (this is most obviously true of political news, but much the same could be said of sports). Most generally, the normal standard of impartiality calls for balance in the choice and use of sources, so as to reflect different points of view, and also neutrality in the presentation of news — separating facts from opinion, avoiding value judgements or emotive language or pictures. The term 'sensationalism' has been used to refer to forms of presentation which depart from the objectivity ideal, and measures of news text sensationalism have been developed (for example, Tannenbaum and Lynch, 1960).

There have also been attempts to show how the choice of words can reflect and imply value judgements in reporting on sensitive matters, for instance relating to patriotism (Glasgow Media Group, 1985) or race (Hartman and Husband, 1974; van Dijk, 1991). There are also indications that particular uses of visuals and camera shots can lead the viewer in certain evaluative directions (Tuchman, 1978; Kepplinger, 1983). Impartiality often comes down in the end simply to the absence of intentional or avoidable 'bias' and 'sensationalism'.

Reality reflection or distortion?

Bias in news content can refer, especially, to distorting reality, giving a negative picture of minority groups of many kinds, neglecting or misconstruing the role of women in society, or differentially favouring a particular political party or philosophy (see Shoemaker and Reese, 1991). There are many such kinds of news bias which stop short of lies, propaganda or ideology but often overlap with and reinforce similar tendencies in fictional content. While the territory of media bias is now almost boundless and still extending, we can summarize the most significant and best-documented generalizations in the following statements, first about news, then about fiction. In the case of news:

- Media news overrepresents the social 'top' and official voices in its sources.
- News attention is differentially bestowed on members of political and social elites.
- The social values which are most underlined are consensual and supportive of the status quo.
- Foreign news concentrates on nearer, richer and more powerful nations.
- News has a nationalistic (patriotic) and ethnocentric bias in the choice of topics and opinions expressed and in the view of the world assumed or portrayed.
- News reflects the values and power distribution of a male-dominated society.

- Minorities are differentially marginalized, ignored or stigmatized.
- News about crime overrepresents violent and personal crime and neglects many of the realities of risk in society.
- Politically relevant news tends to be neutral or support parties to the right of the spectrum.

The fictional content of mass media which has been analysed from a similar perspective of trueness to reality or implicit (unwitting) bias leads to the following generalizations:

- Occupational distribution of characters is highly skewed to the higher-status occupations, especially in law enforcement, medicine, the military, show business, etc.
- Ethnic minorities have tended to be in lower-status or dubious social roles, although this may be modified, without necessarily becoming more realistic.
- Women have tended to appear in stereotyped occupational and domestic roles and generally more passive and in the background.
- Fictional violence, just as crime in the news, is portrayed in a wildly unrealistic light, on almost all conceivable dimensions.
- Fiction which deals with social or political conflict tends either to support consensual values or to avoid the issues.
- Homosexuality tends to be either ignored or treated stereotypically (rarely positively).

A critique of the reality-reflection norm

It is striking how much of the discussion of media content in terms of performance comes down to the question of relation to reality — as if media ought obviously to reflect more or less proportionately and accurately the distributions which can be empirically measured 'out there', or ought to be 'fair' as between the advantaged and the disadvantaged. This assumption provides an essential basis for much criticism of media performance and has often been a key ingredient in research on media effects (for instance, in cultivation analysis) but is itself open to· question. According to Schulz (1988), it derives from an antiquated 'mechanistic' view of the relationship between media and society, more or less akin to the 'transportation model' of communication effects. It fails to recognize the essential specificity, arbitrariness and, sometimes, autonomy of media texts and neglects the active participation of the audience in the making of meaning.

Truth is accountable not only in statistical terms, and few can really believe it to be so. The critique of media 'distortion' of reality often gives too much authority to quantitative criteria and largely fails to recognize the 'decoding' skills of experienced audience members, who are capable of distinguishing between fiction and reality and can learn about social reality from the most unlikely content.

Apart from this fundamental doubt about the expectation of proportional reality-reflection, there are several reasons why media content should *not* normally be expected to 'reflect' reality in any literal (statistically representative) way. Functionalist theory of media as agents of social control, for instance, would lead us to expect that media content would overrepresent the dominant social and economic values of the society by symbolically rewarding those who conform and 'punishing' deviance. We would also expect social elites and authorities to have more visibility and access. Indeed, the media do reflect the social reality of inequality when they tip the scales of attention towards the powerful in society and towards powerful nations in the world (Gerbner and Marvanyi, 1977).

Critical theory offers a consistent mirror image of this view, positing much the same effects on content (a bias to the ruling class and established order) but stemming from a different perspective. We have also seen that organizational pressures towards routine and standardization are likely to lead to a very selective and 'skewed' representation of the society outside the media. The need for authoritative news sources and the requirements of 'news values' are an obvious source of statistical 'distortion'. In addition, fictional media often deliberately seek to attract an audience by overpopulating their stories with characters who lead more exciting lives and are richer, younger, more fashionable and more beautiful than the typical audience member (Martel and McCall, 1964).

Above all, perhaps, the simple fact that mass media are generally oriented to the interests of their audiences as 'consumers' of information and entertainment can easily account for most of the evidence of reality distortion summarized above. It is clear that audiences like many things which are inconsistent with reality-reflection — especially fiction, fantasy, the unusual and bizarre, myths, nostalgia and amusement. The media are often sought out precisely as an alternative to and an escape from reality. When people look for models to follow or for objects of identification, they are as likely to seek an idealized as a realistic object or model. Viewed from this point of view, the patterns observed in content are not difficult to account for.

In summary

This does not exhaust the range of media performance discourse but is sufficient to indicate the approach to media content which is typically involved. Other questions which have been taken up have been introduced in Chapter 5 and include issues of crime and violence in media, the representation of local and national issues and culture, and the 'cultural quality' of the mass media in many different aspects. The essentials of the approach are a definition of some aspect of media performance as 'problematic' according to wider social or cultural principle, a definition of content indicators designed to reflect the normative concept at issue (diversity, objectivity, etc.), and the application of empirical measurement to produce evidence about the level of performance of a given body of content.

Media performance approach to content

- Mass media content can be assessed according to social norms
- The most relevant criteria are independence, diversity, objectivity and reality-reflection
- These qualities can be measured in media content

Critical perspectives on content

While performance assessment as described involves taking a critical view of the media, what is at issue here is not just criticism of the media for failing in their (often self-chosen) tasks but fundamental criticism of the established media. There are several sources for such approaches, but critiques based on social class, gender and ethnicity have probably been the most significant. Equally relevant is the perspective from, or on behalf of, the Third World, with reference to established Western media. Each of these perspectives has been well represented in the media theory and research literature, sometimes under the aegis of 'cultural studies' (especially the gender-based critique).

Marxist approaches

The most central tradition of criticism has been based on Marxist theory and has focused especially on the relation of media content to class differences and class conflict. The Marxist critical paradigm has shown some capacity for transfer to other topics, but not without inconsistencies and gaps. Grossberg (1991) has pointed to several variations of Marxist cultural interpretation which relate in particular to the issue of the 'politics of textuality'. He identifies three 'classical' Marxist approaches, of which the most relevant derive from the Frankfurt School and ideas concerning 'false consciousness'.

The original Marxist critique presumed that an image of the world favourable to the ruling class or the capitalist system would be embedded in media texts and be more or less taken over uncritically by their subordinated audiences. As a result audiences would fail to develop the will to resist. Later approaches distinguished by Grossberg are 'hermeneutic' (interpretative) or 'discursive' in character, and again there are several variants. Compared to classical approaches, however, the main differences are, first, that 'decoding' is recognized as problematic and, secondly, that texts are seen as not just 'mediating' reality but actually constructing experience and acquiring identity.

It is possible to cite only fragmentary examples of critical content approaches. Most attention has probably been given to news, because of its ideological significance in defining the social world and the world of events. Drawing on various sources, including Barthes and Althusser, Stuart Hall (1977) argued that the practice of signification through language establishes maps of cultural meaning which promote the dominance of a ruling-class ideology, especially by establishing a hegemony. This involves containing subordinate classes within superstructures of meaning which frame all competing definitions of reality within the range of a single hegemonic view of things.

News contributes to this task in several ways. One is by 'masking' aspects of reality — especially by ignoring the exploitative nature of class society or by taking it for granted as 'natural'. Secondly, news produces a 'fragmentation' of interests, which undermines the solidarity of subordinate classes. Thirdly, news imposes an 'imaginary unity or coherence' — for instance, by invoking concepts of community, nation, public opinion and consensus. There is a good deal of news analysis (for example, Glasgow Media Group, 1976, 1980, 1985) which lends support to this critical interpretation of how (and why) news is the way it is.

Commercialism

Another example of the critical approach relates to advertising (more or less following the classical Marxist approach as identified above). Williamson (1978) in her study of advertising applies the familiar concept of 'ideology', which is defined (Althusser, 1971) as representing 'the imaginary relationship of individuals to their real conditions of existence'. Althusser also says that 'All ideology has the function (which defines it) of "constituting" individuals as subjects.' For Williamson, the ideological work of advertising is accomplished (with the active co-operation of the 'reader' of the advertisement) by transferring significant meanings and ideas (sometimes myths) from experience (such as beauty, success, happiness, nature and science) to commercial products and by that route to ourselves.

The commercial product becomes a way to achieve the social or cultural state and to be the kind of person we would like to be. We are 'reconstituted' by advertising but end up with an imaginary (and thus false) sense of real selves and of our relation to the real conditions of our life. This has the same ideological tendency attributed to news in critical theory — masking real exploitation and fragmenting solidarity. A very similar process is described by Williamson (1978) in terms of 'commodification', referring to the way advertising converts the 'use value' of products into an 'exchange value', allowing us (in our aspiration) to acquire (buy) happiness or other ideal states.

The ideological work of advertising is essentially achieved by constituting our environment for us and telling us who we are and what we really want. In the critical perspective, all this is illusory and diversionary. What the effect of advertising might actually be is beyond the scope of any analysis of content, but it is possible to work back from content to intention, and the critical terminology of 'manipulation' and 'exploitation' is easier to justify than is the case with ideology in news. In general, 'commodification' in relation to culture implies that something is taken away from people by the commercial 'consciousness industry' and then sold back to them. It is one expression of the process of 'alienation' whereby we lose touch with our own nature (and culture).

The original members of the Frankfurt School viewed most forms of mass culture (see page 97) as both alienating and exploitative — encouraging false consciousness and concealing the reality of social division, and at the same time keeping the working class when not working in a soporific state of escapism: the new 'opium of the people' to replace religion. This version of a critique of mass culture largely replaced the original more elitist or moralistic critique of industrialized popular culture. It seems now to be both out of fashion and fundamentally delegitimated. There are several reasons for this, apart from the sheer sterility of the argument between critics and defenders of the 'masses' and the ultimate impossibility of proving the intrinsic superiority of any particular taste preferences.

On the question of cultural quality

First, a hierarchical concept of culture has to be rejected as a basis for the critique of culture (since hierarchy is itself a part of culture). The older critique tended also to be ethnocentric — privileging the cultural achievements of the 'home' cultural tradition. Secondly, the new school of popular cultural studies has, if nothing else, demonstrated that popular culture is both rich and varied in meanings and cannot be encapsulated in some formula. Cultural populism undermines aesthetic or moral discrimination, for good or ill, and both the practice of cultural criticism and the standards to be applied have to be re-examined. Thirdly, the culture of postmodernity (see page 104) supports many different value perspectives on the popular arts and entertainments and suggests alternative criteria of quality.

These developments represent a potential advance in understanding of culture, although they do not in themselves falsify or replace the older critique of mass culture nor establish the 'equality' of all cultural forms. They add another dimension to the analysis, but it remains true that cultural forms can be differentiated according to some 'objectifiable' criteria and that there are significant cultural belief systems which hold on to the notion of hierarchy of value (often independently of actual personal preference).

Culture inherently lends itself to discrimination in some value terms between one practice and another and is also inclined, by definition, to be ethnocentric.

Amongst the many criteria still available for distinguishing between symbolic cultural artefacts according to 'cultural quality' the following can be found: degree and type of craft skill involved; originality; cultural authenticity; values expressed; integrity of purpose; numerical popularity; attribution of 'quality'; social relevance; class-cultural features; degree of commodification; and durability of appeal. There are many possible candidates for assessing what is essentially the 'diversity' of culture, which are not ruled out by the advent of 'cultural populism' (McGuigan, 1992).

It has been suggested (by Schrøder, 1992) that there are essentially three kinds of cultural standards to be applied: the aesthetic (there are many dimensions), the ethical (questions of values, integrity, intended meaning, etc.) and the 'ecstatic' (measured by popularity, pleasure and performative value — essentially aspects of consumption). In brief, one can say that developments of cultural theory have significantly extended the scope of critical cultural study, even for those who remain convinced of more or less universal and absolute standards of quality.

Gender-based critique

There are several varieties of critical *feminist* perspective on media content (Rakow, 1986; van Zoonen, 1991); but approaches which are either radical or simply more up to date go well beyond the critique of media stereotyping, neglect and marginalization of women that was common in the 1970s (see, for example, Tuchman et al., 1978). As Rakow points out, media content can never be a true account of reality, and it is less important to change media representations (such as having more female characters) than to challenge the underlying sexist ideology of much media content. An example of a new basis for critique (Long, 1991) is the very fact that theory and research have tended to 'overvalorize' the public sphere as distinct from the private or domestic sphere. This shows up, for instance, in differential attention (given by researchers) to politics, war, business and sports, in which men are more likely than women to be active and prominent (Brown, 1990). Forms of media content which are most popular with women have been relatively neglected (gendered texts are also rank-ordered texts). Such media forms as romances (Radway, 1984), magazines (Hermes, 1994) and soap operas (Hobson, 1982) have had to be deliberately rescued from obscurity and assumed irrelevance (Modleski, 1982).

Most central to critical feminist analysis is probably the broad question (going beyond stereotypes) of how texts 'position' the female subject in narratives and textual interactions and in so doing contribute to a definition of femininity in collaboration with the 'reader'. Essentially the same applies to masculinity, and both fall under the heading of 'gender construction'. For the feminist critique, a dual question necessarily arises: first, the extent to which commercial media texts intended for the entertainment of women (like soap operas or romances) can ever be liberating when they embody the realities of patriarchal society and family institutions (Radway, 1984; Ang, 1985); and secondly the degree to which new kinds of mass media texts which challenge gender stereotyping and try to introduce positive role models can have any 'empowering' effect for women (while remaining within the dominant commercial media system).

Ultimately the answers to these questions depend on how the texts are received by their audiences. Radway's (1984) study of romantic fiction argued that there is some element of liberation, if not empowerment, through what is essentially a woman's (own) genre, but she also acknowledges the patriarchal ideology of the form: 'the romance also provides a symbolic portrait of the womanly sensibility that is created and required by patriarchal marriage and its sexual division of labour. . . . [It] underscores and shores up the very psychological structure that guarantees women's commitment to marriage and motherhood' (p. 149).

Critical perspectives on content

- Typical mass media content embodies the inequalities of society, especially in respect of *class*, *gender*, *dominant ideologies*, *commercialism* and other forms of exploitation
- The main task of content analysis should be to uncover these tendencies and show how they work

---

A variety of literary, discourse and psychoanalytic methods have been used in the critical feminist study of content. There seems to be no dominant theory or method, rather a unity of research concerns and a methodological eclecticism, placing a strong emphasis on interpretation rather than quantification. In general, also, the 'false consciousness' model, implying a more or less automatic 'transfer' of gender positioning, has been discarded, and even content study has to look back to encoding and forward to alternative possibilities for 'decoding'.

Critical attention to the topic of media representation of ethnic minorities and 'race' has in general followed a similar line (Hartman and Husband, 1974; van Dijk, 1991).

Conclusion

These various frameworks and perspectives for theorizing about media content often imply sharp divergences of methods of research as well as differences of purpose. The full range of alternative methods cannot be discussed here, but the main options will be set out in Chapter 10.

10

GENRES AND METHODS OF ANALYSIS

Media genres and formats

In general use, the term *genre* simply means a kind or type and it is often loosely applied to any distinctive category of cultural product. In film theory, where it originates, the term has been controversial, because of the tension between individual creative authorship and location in a genre. An emphasis on the genre tends to credit the value of a work to a cultural tradition rather than to an individual artist, who simply follows the rules laid down by the particular school of production. In relation to most mass media content, however, the concept of genre is useful and not especially controversial, since the question of artistic authorship does not usually arise.

Defining genre

For our purpose, genre can refer to any category of content which has the following characteristics:

- It has an identity recognized more or less equally by its producers (the media) and its consumers (media audiences).
- This identity (or definition) relates to its purposes (such as information, entertainment or sub-variants), its form (length, pace, structure, language, etc.) and its meaning (reality reference).
- It has been established over time and observes familiar conventions; it tends to preserve cultural forms, although these can also change and develop within the framework of the original genre.
- A particular genre, as already implied, will follow an expected structure of narrative or sequence of action, draw on a predictable stock of images and have a repertoire of variants of basic themes.

The genre may be considered as a practical device for helping any mass medium to produce consistently and efficiently and to relate its production to the expectations of its customers. Since it helps individual media users to plan their choices, it can also be considered as a mechanism for ordering the relations between the two main parties to mass communication. According to Andrew, genres (of film) are specific networks of formulas which deliver a certified product to a waiting customer. They ensure the production of meaning by regulating the viewers' relation to the image and narrative construction for him or her. In fact, genres construct the proper spectators for their own consumption. They build the desires and then represent the satisfaction of what they have triggered. (1984, p. 110)

This view implies a high degree of media determinism which needs to be qualified, but it is at least consistent with the aspirations of media organizations to control the environments in which they operate.

Two genre examples: western movies and television soap operas

A relatively early example of the application of the genre idea was suggested by Hall (1980) in respect of the once standard 'B-movie western'. In his analysis, genre depends on the use of a particular 'code' or meaning system, which can draw on some consensus about meaning among users of the code (whether encoders or decoders) in a given culture. According to Hall, we can speak of a genre where coding and decoding are very close and where meaning is consequently relatively unambiguous, in the sense of being received much as it is sent. The classic western movie is then said to derive from a particular myth concerning the conquest of the US west and involving such elements as displays of masculine prowess and womanly courage, the working out of destiny in the wide open spaces and the struggle of good versus evil. The particular strength of the western genre is that it can generate many variant forms which can also be readily understood in relation to the original basic form. For instance, we have seen the psychological western, the parody western, the 'spaghetti' western, the comedy western and the soap opera western. The meaning of the variant forms often depends on the reversal of elements in the original code.

More recent developments of media-cultural studies have given prominence to several familiar television genres and provided the boundaries for particular fields of enquiry. A noteworthy example is the attention paid to soap operas, partly on account of their identification as a *gendered* form of television (Modleski, 1982; Allen, 1987, 1989; Hobson, 1989; Geraghty, 1991). The feminine characteristics of the soap opera genre were said to reside in its form of narrative, preference for dialogue over action and attention to values of extended families and the role of mothers and housewives.

The soap opera is also a very typical example of a serial form of narrative. The great interest in the serial *Dallas* during the 1980s (Ang, 1985; Liebes and Katz, 1990), for somewhat different reasons, also drew attention to the soap opera as a genre, but also stretches the meaning of the term to include a media product which was very different from the early North American radio or television daytime serial. Even so, the wide and long currency of the term 'soap opera' applied to different kinds of drama confirms, in some measure, the validity and utility of the concepts of genre and soap opera.

While genre is a useful concept for finding one's way in the luxuriant abundance of media output and for helping to describe and categorize content, it is not a very powerful tool of analysis, since there are simply too many possibilities for applying it. The distinction between one genre and another is not easy to ascertain objectively, and the correspondence of recognition and understanding by producers and audience, named above as a characteristic of a genre, is not easy to demonstrate. It may be a more useful term in relation to films and books, where individual acts of choice are made and paid for, guided by experience, taste and publicity, and lead to established preference (such as for detective fiction, science fiction, romance or spy stories). In the case of television, one genre shades into another for producers and for unselective viewers alike. Even so, it has been shown that inter-genre differences can be used to differentiate between types of television producer (Tunstall, 1993).

Media format and logic

The genre concept has also been useful in a somewhat adapted form for analysing media formats. Altheide and Snow (1979), for instance, developed a mode of analysis of media content, employing the terms 'media logic' and 'media format'. The first refers essentially to a set of implicit rules and norms which govern how content should be processed and presented to take most advantage of the characteristics of a given medium and to fit the needs of the media organization (including the media's perception of the needs of the audience). The operation of a media logic, according to Altheide (1985), implies the existence of a 'media grammar' which governs how time should be used, how items of content should be sequenced and what devices of verbal and non-verbal communication (codes) should be used. Altheide sees content as tailored to fit media formats and formats as tailored to fit listener/viewer preferences and assumed capacities.

The formats are essentially subroutines for dealing with specific themes within a genre. For instance, Altheide (1985) describes a 'format for crisis' in television news, which transcends the particularities of events and gives a common shape to the handling of different news stories. The main conditions necessary for the news handling of a crisis on a continuing basis are accessibility (to information or to the site of the crisis), visual quality (of film or tape), drama and action, relevance to the audience and thematic unity.

Following the same line of thought, Mazzoleni (1987) has suggested that, in the field of political communication, a 'media logic' has tended to encroach on a 'political logic' in the selection and presentation of politics, during campaigns especially, showing itself in a concentration on personalities and details of campaign events rather than on abstract political ideas.

He has applied the hypothesis to the case of a traditionally very politicized television system, that of Italy (see also Hallin and Mancini, 1984). Without using the same terminology, a very similar hypothesis had already been applied to the study of election campaigns in the United States (Graber, 1976b) and in Denmark (Siune, 1981).

Media content frames

Graber (for example, 1981) has made notable contributions to the study of political languages in general and its television versions in particular. She confirms the points made by Altheide in her comment that 'television journalists have developed repertoires — another possible term for frames, logics or sub-genre formats of highly stereotyped cues for many specific situations in politics'. She argues convincingly that the encoding and decoding of audiovisual languages is essentially *different* from that of verbal languages in being more associational, connotative and unstructured and less logical, clearly defined and delimited. The systematic analysis of audiovisual languages is, nevertheless, still at an early stage.

Visual language

An exploration of this fertile terrain lies outside the scope of this book, but a few more remarks are in order on the distinctive features of audiovisual 'languages', if the term is allowable (see Adams and Schreibman, 1978; Geis, 1987). A comparison between print media and film/television media suggests the following contrasts, which derive from language rather than social factors. Television (and film) is, in general, less regulated by agreed (linguistic) codes, more ambiguous in meaning, lacking in clear authorship (or indication of source), more open, more concrete, more universal and more information rich.

It does not appear that the distinctive features of television have yet been harnessed to achieve more communicative effectiveness. Both print and audiovisual media have their own in-built inefficiencies and both are severely limited by human information-processing capacity. It may be the case that the full potential of audiovisual languages (and the same applies to alphanumeric-pictorial forms) has simply not yet been realized in a period of rapid change of technology and experimentation with new forms and purposes of communication media.

Before leaving the subject of genres, formats and related concepts, it is worth emphasizing that they can, in principle, cut across the conventional content categories of media output, including the divide between fiction and non-fiction. Fiske (1987) underlines the essential *intertextuality* of genres. This is not too surprising, given the long tradition which allows fiction to draw on real-life situations or historical events for its subject matter, although it may undermine the reality claims of media news and information.

Schlesinger et al. (1983) provide a demonstration by analysing the portrayal of terrorism on British television both in news and current affairs and in dramatic fiction.

Mass media genres

- Genres are defined equally by producers and readers of media content
- Genres are identified by function, form and content
- Genres both preserve and help to develop textual forms
- Genres are aids to production and to reading of texts
- Genres are characterized by their own logics, formats and language

---

The news genre

The newspaper is, arguably, the archetype as well as the prototype of all modern mass media (Tunstall, 1977, p. 23), and 'news' is the central ingredient of the newspaper (though far from the only one). To some extent, radio and television were modelled on the newspaper, with regular news as their chief anchor point. News merits special attention in a discussion of media content just because it is one of the few original contributions of the mass media to the range of cultural forms of expression. It is also the core activity according to which a large part of the journalistic (and thus media) occupation defines itself.

Further, news provides the component which elevates or distinguishes something called a newspaper from other kinds of print media and often earns it a special status or protection in society, allowing it to express opinion in the name of the public. Media institutions could barely exist without news, and news could not exist without media institutions. Unlike almost all other forms of authorship or cultural creation, news-making cannot be done privately or even individually. The institution provides both the machinery for distribution and the guarantee of credibility and authority.

What is news?

Despite the central position of news in the media, the question 'What is news?' is one which journalists themselves seem to find distinctly metaphysical and difficult to answer except in terms of their intuition, 'feel' and innate judgement. Attempts to answer it by analysis of media content have not been very revealing. It happens that the two 'founding fathers' of the sociology of news were both former or practising journalists and drew on their own experience in tackling the question of the nature of the news.

Walter Lippman (1922, p. 216) focused on the process of news gathering, which he saw as a search for the 'objective clear signal which signifies an event'. Hence, 'news is not a mirror of social conditions, but the report of an aspect that has obtruded itself'. Our attention is thus directed to what is noticeable (and worthy of notice) in a form suitable for planned and routine inclusion as a news report. For this reason newspapers routinely survey such places as police stations, law courts, hospitals and legislatures, where events are likely to be first signalled.

The second early commentator on news, Robert Park (1940), paid much more attention to the essential properties of the news report. His starting point was to compare it with another 'form of knowledge', history, which is also a record of past events, and to place news on a continuum that ranges from 'acquaintance with' to 'knowledge about'. News is located somewhere in the middle of this continuum. The result of Park's comparison of news with history can be distilled into a few main points:

- News is timely — about very recent or recurrent events.
- News is unsystematic — it deals with discrete events and happenings, and the world seen through news alone consists of unrelated happenings, which it is not the primary task of news itself to interpret.
- News is perishable — it lives only when the events themselves are current, and for purposes of record and later reference other forms of knowledge will replace news.
- Events reported as news should be unusual or at least unexpected, qualities which are more important than their 'real significance'.
- Apart from unexpectedness, news events are characterized by other 'news values' which are always relative and involve subjective judgements about likely audience interest.
- News is mainly for orientation and attention-direction and not a substitute for knowledge.
- News is predictable.

The last paradoxical and provocative point was explained by Park as follows:

> if it is the unexpected that happens it is not the wholly unexpected which gets into the news. The events that have made news in the past, as in the present, are actually the expected things . . . it is on the whole the accidents and incidents that the public is prepared for . . . the things that one fears and that one hopes for that make news. (1940, p. 45)

A similar point was put more succinctly by Galtung and Ruge (1965) in the remark that 'news' are actually 'olds'. Another characterization of news was offered by Warren Breed (1956), who listed the following terms as descriptive of news: 'saleable', 'superficial', 'simple', 'objective', 'action-centred', 'interesting' (as distinct from significant), 'stylized' and 'prudent'. He also suggested dimensions along which an item of news might be placed:

news versus truth; difficult versus routine (in terms of news gathering); and information versus human interest.

Much depends on whether the events which make news are 'visible' or not to the public or to news producers. According to Hall (1973), there are three basic 'rules of news visibility': (1) its link to an event or occurrence (the component of action); (2) its recency; and (3) its newsworthiness or link to some important thing or person. Noteworthy, in Hall's view, is that news is itself responsible for creating over time the 'consensus' knowledge by which newsworthiness is recognized by newspeople and accepted as such by the public. He writes: 'the ideological concepts embodied in photos and texts in a newspaper do not produce new knowledge about the world. They produce recognition of the world as we have already learnt to appropriate it.' This essentially coincides with Park's claim that news is predictable.

The news genre

- Timeliness and recency
- Unexpectedness
- Predictability of type
- Fragmentary nature
- Perishability
- Signalling
- Shaped by values
- Interesting
- Factualness

News and human interest

In Breed's characterization of news it is at one point contrasted with 'human interest', implying that the former has to do with serious information, the latter with something else — perhaps entertaining, personalized or sensational. In practice it seems hard to separate the two, and both have been elements in the newspaper since its earliest appearances. A classic study by a pupil of Park, Helen McGill Hughes (1940), examined the relationship between the two forms of content and concluded that the (US) newspaper had been 'transformed from a more or less sober record into a form of popular literature'.

In her view, a human interest story is not intrinsically different from other news stories but takes its character from the particular attitude which the writer adopts towards the reader — it is a story which is intended to divert, but also one which is told, as it were, from the reader's point of view. It can, in consequence, be told only by a reporter who is 'able to see the world as his/her readers do'. Hence it is more akin to gossip or the folk tale. The characteristics of news are derived in part from much older traditions of storytelling (Darnton, 1975). Certainly readers are often more attracted to 'human interest' than to 'news' about politics, economics and society (Curran et al., 1981; Dahlgren and Sparks, 1992).

As with other genres, there are variants which depend on the central code of the news. One example is that of gossip, especially concerning media stars or other celebrities, which purports to offer objective information but usually has no deep significance or any material relevance. The conventions and codes of the news genre can also be used in advertising or in satirical media performances, which outwardly observe the news form, but are totally inverted. So-called 'tabloid television' — sensational, gossipy, weird information — is another example of the stretching of a genre. The news genre is also capable of adaptation and extension to new circumstances. News had to be in some degree reinvented for radio, television and pictorial possibilities. The 'happy news' format of television news which was introduced in the 1970s for greater audience appeal has been widely adopted (Dominick et al., 1975).

News values and the structure of news

One general conclusion from the many content studies is that news exhibits a rather stable and predictable overall pattern when measured according to conventional categories of subject matter. There are variations from one country to another and one medium type to another, and the pattern is naturally responsive to major events, such as war and world crisis. Nevertheless, the stability of news content is often remarkable. The most influential explanation of news values is probably that offered by Galtung and Ruge (1965), who identified and interrelated the main factors influencing the selection of (foreign) news in Norwegian newspapers. In essence they found three types of factor: organizational, genre-related and socio-cultural.

The organizational factors are the most universal and least escapable and they also have some 'ideological' consequences. Among genre-related factors are: a preference for events which fit advance audience expectations (consonance with past news); a bias towards what is unexpected and novel within the limits of what is familiar; a wish to continue with events already established as newsworthy; and a wish for balance among types of news events.

Galtung and Ruge identified socio-cultural influences that derive from 'Northern European' culture. From this perspective, news values tend to favour events which are about elite people, elite nations and negative happenings. Events big on all these values are believed to produce most audience interest, and these values are consistent with several of the organizational and genre-related selection requirements. Thus 'bigness' goes with eliteness; personal actions fit the short time scale and are least ambiguous and most 'bounded'; negative events often fit the production time schedule, are unambiguous and can be personalized (such as disasters, killings and crimes).

Primary news values in Western media

- Scale of events
- Closeness
- Clarity
- Short time scale
- Relevance
- Consonance
- Personification
- Negativity
- Significance
- Drama and action

News bias

This interpretative framework has been found to apply fairly widely and not only to foreign news. It tells us a certain amount about the kind of event that will tend to be reported and, by implication, about what will be neglected. Thus it is predictive of a pattern of one general kind of news 'bias'. News will tend not to deal with distant and politically unimportant nations, non-elites, ideas, institutions and structures, long-term undramatic processes (such as social change itself) or many kinds of 'good news'. The theory does not offer a complete explanation of all regularities of news composition, however, and an alternative, less psychological and more structural approach to explanation has been recommended by Rosengren (1974), who argues that several features of news flows can be accounted for by political and economic factors. He demonstrates that flows of trade between countries are good predictors of mutual news attention. The same has been found to be true of international treaty relationships (Ito and Koshevar, 1983). With respect to domestic news, it is plausible that the giving or withholding of news attention has as much to do with political and economic factors as with the news values of individual news selectors or the news value attached to events.

The question of news structure has often been discussed in terms of bias, although we should not assume any deliberate tendency to mislead. Organizational explanations or the influence of hidden cultural elements are to be preferred. In addition, since judgements of news value are often relative and based on a journalistic 'feel for the news' at the particular moment, there will usually be strong elements of subjectivity. The standards of objectivity which are built into the news code are more likely to be expressed in the manner of handling and reporting events than in the selection or the neutrality of presentation.

The form of the news report

The strength of the news genre is attested by the extent to which certain basic features are found across the different media of print, radio and television, despite the very different possibilities and limitations of each. The shared elements of form can be summarized as having to do with recurrence, neutrality and facticity. Newspapers and news bulletins show great constancy over time in appearance, in length or duration and in the balance of types of content, such as foreign, political, sports, economic, or human interest news (McQuail, 1977).

Much the same is true of television news, so that the number of items does not vary much from one bulletin to another with the same news service. There is even a steady relationship between type of content and average length (Glasgow Media Group, 1976). Some of these features of regularity are found to be much the same in different countries (Rositi, 1976; Heinderyckx, 1993). What is striking is the extent to which a presumably unpredictable universe of events seems open to incorporation, day after day, into much the same temporal, spatial and topic frame. It is true that deviations occur, at times of crisis or exceptional events, but the news form is posited on the normality and predictability of the world of events.

Another main aspect of news form has to do with indications of relative significance of events and of types of content and with ways of structuring the whole. Indicating significance is mainly achieved by the sequencing of content and the relative amount of space or time allocated. According to what the Glasgow Media Group (1980) calls 'viewers' maxims', it will be understood that first-appearing items in television news are most 'important' and that, generally, items receiving more time are also more important. However, it has not been easy to turn daily observation into systematic theory or general statement. Television news bulletins are generally constructed with a view to arousing initial interest, by highlighting some event, maintaining interest through diversity and human interest and holding back some vital information to the end (sports results and weather forecast), then sending the viewer away at the close with a light touch.

The Glasgow Media Group argued that the hidden purpose or effect of this is to reinforce a 'primary framework' of normality and control and a view of the world which is essentially ideological. The world is 'naturalized' (see also Tuchman, 1978). Rositi's (1976) search for the latent organization in the television news of four European countries led to rather modest but interesting results: 'perhaps the only latent organization to be found at the level of the entire news program is that described as the movement from a fragmented image of society to its recomposition through the homogeneity of interests and political representation'.

The regularities described characterize the dominant Western news form, and it is possible that media operating under different 'press theories' will exert different kinds of regularity. There are almost certainly significant and systematic differences between television news-giving in different societies, although these are more likely to follow cultural and institutional lines of demarcation which are different from national and language frontiers. A comparison of US and Italian television news, for instance, led to the conclusion that each system's news gives a significantly different conception of what politics is about (Hallin and Mancini, 1984). The main differences were attributed to the much larger space occupied by a public sphere, other than the state, in the case of Italy, with the result that in the USA journalists have a much larger role as representatives of the public than they adopt, or are credited with, in Italy. A comparison of the basic news formats of seventeen main evening television news bulletins in Western Europe found relatively minor deviations of practice (Heinderyckx, 1993).

Storytelling versus factual reporting

Many aspects of news form are clearly related to the pursuit of objectivity in the sense of facticity or factualness (Tuchman, 1978). The language of news is 'linear', elaborating an event report along a single dimension with added information, illustration, quotation and discussion (see also Bell, 1991). According to the Glasgow Media Group (1980, p. 160) 'the language of news seems to be in a form which would allow of a fairly simple test of its truth or falsity. It has the appearance of being entirely *constative* (propositional and capable of being shown to be true or false) and not *performative*.'

Both terms are taken from J.L. Austin and were used by Morin (1976) in an attempt to describe the basic ambiguity of the news discourse. According to her (structuralist) analysis of the news form, an event has to be rendered into a 'story about an event' and in the process of doing so involves a negotiation between two opposed modes — that of the 'performative', which is also the interpretative and the 'fabulative' (storytelling) mode, and that of the 'constative', which is also the 'demonstrative' and factual mode. Thus 'pure facts' have no meaning, and 'pure performance' stands far removed from the irreversible, rationally known fact of history, which news is generally supposed to purvey. In Morin's view, different kinds of story involve different combinations of both and can be plotted against the two 'axes' of the television discourse.

There is little doubt of the vital nature of facticity to the news genre. As Smith puts it, 'The whole idea of news is that it is beyond a plurality of viewpoints' (1973, p. 174). In his view, without an attribution of credibility by the audience news could not be distinguished from entertainment or propaganda. This may point to one reason why Gans's (1979) seemingly reasonable plea for 'multi-perspective news' is unlikely to receive universal acclaim and why the secular trend in news development has been away from ideology and towards neutrality. Despite this, there is little reason to modify Gerbner's (1964) conclusion from a study of the French press that 'there is no fundamentally non-ideological, apolitical, non-partisan news-gathering and reporting system'.

Two versions of the news sequence

Despite the progress of media research and theory there remains a gap between two different conceptions of the news-making process — a gap which separates the 'common-sense' journalistic view from media theory. Four elements are related in a different sequence in the two views: events, criteria of news selection (news values), news interests of the public and news report. The 'view from the media' emphasizes the reality-responsive quality of news, and the theoretical viewpoint the structured and autistic nature of the news selection process. According to the former (journalistic) view, the normal news sequence is as follows:

events → news criteria → news report → news interest.

This sequence begins with the world of unpredictable happenings which 'obtrude' and break the normality and to which news media respond by applying criteria concerning relative significance for their public. They compile objective news reports of the chosen events, and the public responds with attention and interest or not, a datum which feeds into subsequent selection behaviour.

The alternative (theoretical) model of the sequence is:

news interest → news criteria → events → news report.

Here the starting point is experience of what gains the attention of the public, which contributes to a rather stable and enduring set of news criteria, including the organizational and genre requirements. News events are only recognized as newsworthy if they conform to these selection criteria. News reports are then written, guided more by the news organization's own requirements and routine practices than by reference to the 'real world' of events or what audiences 'really' want or need.

It is not necessary to make an absolute choice between the models, but they cannot both be true to what happens. The second version is a further illustration of the influence of the 'publicity' (attention-gaining) model described in Chapter 2.

Questions of research method

The various frameworks and perspectives for theorizing about media content often imply sharp divergences of methods of research. The full range of alternatives cannot be discussed here, since there are many different methods for different purposes (several have already been introduced). Methods range from simple and extensive classifications of types of content for organizational or descriptive purposes to deeply inter-pretative enquiries into specific examples of content, designed to uncover subtle and hidden potential meanings. Following the line of theoretical demarcation introduced in Chapter 2, we can broadly distinguish between quantitative and descriptive enquiry into overt meaning, on the one hand, and more qualitative, deeper and more interpretative enquiry, on the other. There are also enquiries directed to understanding the very nature of the various 'media languages' and how they work, especially in relation to visual imagery and sounds.

Where is meaning?

Theory has been perennially preoccupied with the question of the 'location' of meaning. Does meaning coincide with the intention of the sender, or is it embedded in the language, or is it primarily a matter of the receivers' interpretation (Jensen, 1991)? As we have seen from the previous chapters, mass-communicated information and culture are produced by complex organizations, whose purposes are usually not very specific and yet also often predominate over the aims of individual communicators within them. This makes it hard to know what the 'sender's' intention really is — who can say, for instance, what the purpose of news is, or whose purpose it is? The option of concentrating on the message itself as the source of meaning has been the most attractive one, partly for reasons of practicality. The physical texts themselves are always available for direct analysis, and they have the advantage (compared to human respondents) of being 'non-reactive' to the investigator. They do not decay with time, although their context does decay and with it the possibility of really knowing what they originally meant to senders or to receivers.

It is impossible to 'extract meaning' from media content texts without also making assumptions which themselves shape the meaning extracted — for instance, the assumption that the amount or frequency of attention to something is a reliable guide to message meaning, intention and effect. The findings of content analysis can never 'speak for themselves'. In addition, the 'languages' of media are far from simple and still only partially understood, especially where they involve music and visual images (both still and moving) in many combinations, drawing on numerous and varied codes and conventions.

Dominant versus alternative paradigms again

The choices of research method generally follow the division between a dominant empirically oriented paradigm and a more qualitative (and often critical) variant (see Chapter 2). The former is mainly represented by traditional 'content analysis', which was defined by Berelson (1952, p. 18) as 'a research technique for the objective, systematic and quantitative description of the manifest content of communication'. This assumes that the surface meaning of a text is fairly unambiguous and can be read by the investigator and expressed in quantitative terms. In fact, it is assumed that the numerical balance of elements in the text (such as the number of words or space/time allocated to a set of topics) is a reliable guide to the overall meaning. Several relatively sophisticated forms of quantitative content analysis have been developed which go well beyond the simple counting and classifying of units of content that were characteristic of early research. There remains, even so, a fundamental assumption that media content is encoded according to the same language as the reality to which it refers.

The alternative approach is based on precisely the reverse assumption — that the concealed or latent meanings are the most significant, and these cannot be directly read from the numerical data. In particular, we have to take account not just of relative frequency but of links and relationships between elements in the text, and also to take note of what is missing or taken for granted. We need to identify and understand the particular discourse in which a text is encoded. There are alternative ideas about how to go about the task of qualitative research into content (see Jensen and Jankowski, 1992), but in general we need to be aware of the conventions and codes of any genre that we study, since these indicate at a higher level what is going on in the text. In contrast, content analysis may permit the conflation of several different kinds of media text, ignoring discursive variety.

Both varieties of analysis can claim some measure of scientific reliability. They deploy methods which can, in principle, be replicated by different people, and the 'findings' should be open to challenge according to some (not always the same) canons of scientific procedure. Secondly, they are both designed to deal with regularity and recurrence in cultural artefacts rather than with the unique and non-reproducible. They are thus more appropriate for application to the symbolic products of the culture industries than to those of the 'cultural elite' (such as 'works of art'). Thirdly, they avoid judgements of moral or aesthetic value (another sense of being objective). Fourthly, all such methods are, in principle, instrumental — means to other ends. They can be used to answer questions about the links between content, creators, social context and receivers.

Traditional content analysis

Basics

'Traditional' content analysis, following Berelson's (1952) definition (see above), is the earliest, most central and still most widely practised method of research. Its use goes back to the early decades of the century (cf. Kingsbury and Hart, 1937). The basic sequence in applying the technique is: (1) to choose a universe or sample of content; (2) to establish a category frame of external referents relevant to the purpose of the enquiry (such as a set of political parties or countries which may be referred to in content); (3) to choose a 'unit of analysis' from the content (this could be a word, a sentence, an item, a whole news story, a picture, a sequence, etc); (4) to seek to match the content to the category frame by counting the frequency of the references to relevant items in the category frame, per chosen unit of content; and (5) to express the results as an overall distribution of the complete universe or chosen content sample in terms of the frequency of occurrence of the sought-for referents.

The procedure is based on two main assumptions: that the link between the external object of reference and the reference to it in the text will be reasonably clear and unambiguous; and that the frequency of occurrence of chosen references will validly express the predominant 'meaning' of the text in an objective way. The approach is, in principle, no different from that adopted in surveys of people when one chooses a population (here a media type or subset), draws a sample within it for respondents representative of the whole (the units of analysis), collects data about individuals according to variables and assigns values to these variables. As with the survey, content analysis is held to be reliable (reproducible) and not unique to the investigator. The method produces a statistical summary of a much larger media reality. It has been used for many purposes but especially for comparing media content with a known frequency distribution in 'social reality'.

Limits to content analysis

The traditional approach has many limitations and pitfalls, which are of some theoretical interest as well as practical relevance. The usual practice of constructing a category system before applying it involves the risk of an investigator imposing his or her meaning-system rather than 'taking' it from the content. Even when care is taken to avoid this, any such category system must be selective and potentially distorting. The outcome of content analysis is itself a new text, the meaning of which may, or even must, diverge from the original source material. This result is also based on a form of 'reading' of content which no actual 'reader' would ever, under natural circumstances, undertake. The new 'meaning' is neither that of the original sender, nor that of the text itself, nor that of the audience, but a fourth construct, one particular interpretation. Account cannot easily be taken of the context of a reference within a text or of the text as a whole. Internal relationships between references in texts may also be neglected in the process of abstraction. There is an assumption that 'coders' can be trained to make reliable judgements about categories and meanings.

The boundaries of the kind of content analysis described are, in fact, rather elastic, and many variants can be accommodated within the same basic framework. The more one relaxes requirements of reliability, the easier it is to introduce categories and variables that will be useful for interpretation but 'low' in 'objectivity' and somewhat ambiguous. This is especially true of attempts to capture references to values, themes, settings, style and interpretative frameworks. Content analyses often display a wide range of reliability, because of attempts to include some more subjective indicators of meaning.

Quantitative and qualitative analysis compared

The contrast between traditional content analysis and interpretative approaches can now be summarized. Some differences are self-evident. First, structuralism and semiology (the main interpretative approaches; see pages 244–7) do not involve quantification, and there is even an antipathy to counting as a way of arriving at significance, since meaning derives from textual relationships, oppositions and context rather than from number and balance of references. Secondly, attention is directed to latent rather than to manifest content, and latent (thus deeper) meaning is regarded as actually more essential. Thirdly, structuralism is systematic in a different way from content analysis — giving no weight to procedures of sampling and rejecting the notion that all 'units' of content should be treated equally.

Fourthly, structuralism does not allow the assumption that the world of social and cultural 'reality', the message and the receiver all involve the same basic system of meanings. Social reality consists of numerous more or less discrete universes of meaning, each requiring separate elucidation. The 'audience' also divides up into 'interpretative communities', each possessing some unique possibilities for attributing meaning. Media content, as we have seen, is also composed on the basis of more than one code, language or sign-system. All this makes it impossible, even absurd, to assume that any category system of references can be constructed in which a given element is likely to mean precisely the same in the 'reality', in the content, to the audience member and to the media analyst. It follows from structuralist theory that it is very difficult to carry out research which relates findings in one of these 'spheres' to findings in another.

Mixed methods are possible

This comparison does not indicate the superiority of one approach over the other, since, despite the claim at the outset that these methods have something in common, they are essentially good for different purposes. Structuralism does not offer a systematic method and is not accountable in its results according to normal standards of reliability, nor is it easy to generalize from the results to other texts, except perhaps in relation to form (for instance, comparing one genre with another). It is certainly not a way of summarizing content, as content analysis often can be.

For some purposes, it may be permissible and necessary to depart from the pure form of either 'Berelsonian' or 'Barthian' analysis, and a number of studies have used combinations of both approaches, despite their divergent assumptions. An example of such a hybrid approach is the work on British television news of the Glasgow Media Group (1976, 1980, 1985), which combined rigorous and detailed quantitative analysis of industrial news with an attempt to 'unpack' the deeper cultural meaning of specific news stories. The school of 'cultural indicators', as represented by Gerbner and colleagues (see pages 364–6), has also sought to arrive at the 'meaning structure' of dominant forms of television output by way of systematic quantitative analysis of overt elements of television representation.

There are methods which do not easily belong to either of the main approaches described. One is the psychoanalytic approach favoured at an early stage of content study, which focuses on the motivation of 'characters' and the underlying meaning of dominant themes in the popular (or less so) culture of a given society or period (for example, Wolfenstein and Leites, 1947; McGranahan and Wayne, 1948; Kracauer, 1949). Other variants have already been noted — for instance, the analysis of narrative structure (Radway 1984) or the study of content functions. Thus Graber (1976a) named the following set of functions of political communication: to gain attention; to establish linkages and define situations; to make commitments; to create policy-relevant moods; to stimulate action (mobilize); to act directly (words as actions); and to use words as symbolic rewards for actual or potential supporters.

Such possibilities are a reminder of the *relative* character of most analysis of content, in that there has always to be some outside point of reference or purpose according to which one chooses one form of classification rather than another. Even semiology can supply meaning only in terms of a much larger system of cultural meanings and sense-making practices.

Types of media content analysis compared

Message content analysis	Structural analysis of texts
• Quantitative	• Qualitative
• Fragmentary	• Holistic
• Systematic	• Selective
• Generalizing, extensive	• Illustrative, specific
• Manifest meaning	• Latent meaning
• Objective	• Relative to reader

One recurrent problem with all methods and approaches is the gap that often exists between the outcome of content analysis and the perceptions of the creators or the audience. The creators tend to think of what is unique and distinctive in what they do, while the audience is inclined to think of content in terms of a mixture of conventional genre or type labels and a set of satisfactions which have been experienced or are expected. The version extracted by the content analyst is thus not very recognizable to the two main sets of participants in the mass communication enterprise (producers and receivers) and often remains a scientific or literary abstraction.

Conclusion

The future of content analysis, one way or another, has to lie in relating 'content' as sent to the wider structures of meaning in a society. This path can probably best be followed by way of discourse analysis which takes account of other meaning systems in the originating culture or by way of audience reception analysis which takes seriously the notion that readers also make meanings. Both are necessary in some degree for an adequate study of content.

PART V
AUDIENCES

11

THEORY AND RESEARCH TRADITIONS

The origin and diversity of audiences

The 'audience' has been a familiar term in communication research since its earliest days — it is the collective word to denote the 'receivers' in the simple sequential model of the mass communication process (source, channel, message, receiver, effect) deployed by pioneers in the field. There is an established discourse in which 'audience' simply refers to readers, viewers or listeners of one or another media channel or of this or that type of content or performance. There seems to be nothing conceptually difficult about the word, and it is one of the few terms which can be shared without difficulty by media practitioners and theorists alike. It has also entered into everyday usage, seemingly recognized by the media public as an unambiguous description of themselves.

The audience has been an object of enquiry for diverse reasons. Most obviously, perhaps, knowledge about the audience is an essential tool for communicators and media organizations. Certainly the latter collect and use information about the audience for purposes of management, accounting and planning. Equally obviously, the study of the audience is necessary for the very different purpose of studying media effects. Information about the audience is also a form of feedback and evaluation. For students of society and behaviour, media use calls for study because it is such a large component in everyday life and has many other interrelations. The reasons for popular attachment to media are not always obvious and attract curious attention. Finally, we cannot get very far with questions of the meaning of what is communicated without enlisting the help of audiences.

Not surprisingly, in the light of this variety of motive, there is a potential for differences of meaning about audiences and for conflicts of view. One reason for difficulty is that the audience for most mass media is not strictly knowable at all (it cannot be directly observed), so that the term 'audience' has an abstract and debatable character; it becomes a counter in a media or business game but is no longer an identifiable social collectivity (if it ever was). According to Allor (1988), 'The audience exists nowhere; it inhabits no real space, only positions within analytic discourses.' It seems that the audience is now little more than a metaphor drawn from another context — that of the theatre and live performance — which bears little relation to the diverse realities of modern communications media.

Past, present and future of the media audience

The origins of the present-day audience for mass media are presumably to be found in the public theatrical and musical performances as well as games and spectacles of ancient times. Greek and Roman cities of any size would have a theatre or arena for such purposes. No doubt these were preceded by various kinds of more informal gatherings for similar purposes. The significance of the Greco-Roman invention lies in heralding numerous features of present-day media audiences, especially:

- the planning and organization of viewing and listening;
- the public character of the events;
- the secular content of performance and display — the main purpose was enjoyment, entertainment and education;
- the voluntary and individual acts of choice involved in attending.

According to this view, the audience, as a set of spectators for public events of a secular kind, was already institutionalized more than two thousand years ago, with its own customs, expectations and rules about the time, place and content of performances, conditions for entry, etc. It was a typically urban phenomenon, often with a commercial basis and with a differentiation of content based on differences of class and status. The audience was one element in a larger institution, which included professional writers, performers, producers and entrepreneurs. The phenomenon of public entertainment and display attracted sponsorship, could serve political ends and was an object of public surveillance.

Several features, nevertheless, distinguish the early form of audience from the modern media equivalent. Most important is the fact that the original audience was *localized* in one place and time — they were the occupants of the 'auditorium', the space in which they could hear and see what was going on. Their interlocutors spoke directly to them, and performances were always 'live' and open to view. This means that the audience was always relatively small (though it could be many thousands) and also potentially active within itself and interactive with performers. The original audience had a potential collective life of its own. These same conditions still prevail in many circumstances of public display and spectatorship — in theatres, stadiums, race-tracks, etc. What has happened is not really a continuous development from an early form to that of the media audience, but the social invention of a new variant, which overlaps with the earlier 'audience' and borrows its name, sometimes with misleading results.

The rise of a reading public

The line of development of the media audience was based on a new invention — the printed book — and along with it the phenomenon of a reading public. The printing of books, starting in the mid-fifteenth century, gradually led to an organized arrangement for the supply of non-religious written texts which could be bought by individuals and were used for practical purposes as well as for instruction, entertainment and enlightenment. Only by the late sixteenth century does it make much sense to speak of a reading public in the sense of a set of individuals keen and able to buy, read and collect books for their private purposes. Such publics were localized in cities and states, limited by social class and language (although served by translations), and supplied by a growing number of printer-publishers and authors, sometimes supported by sponsors and patrons (Febvre and Martin, 1984).

Within a larger literary cultural institution, the reading public became identifiable as those who could and did read books and followed the work of particular authors or on particular subjects. Its emergence was a very gradual and slow process, extending from the sixteenth to the nineteenth centuries. The book was not the only print form involved, since from at least the early eighteenth century many periodical magazines and newspapers were also likely to have a regular following. The print media industry was large and ramifying and also in many places the object of censorship or control. In advance of the nineteenth-century inventions which made printed media products cheap and plentiful, the reading public or audience for printed matter was already subject to a variety of divisions and social definitions, especially with reference to content (genres) and social categories of reader.

The use of the term 'audience' to refer to these different sets of readers, with its implication of shared social and mental space, is not so inappropriate, even if the boundaries of physical space were largely broken. It was possible to belong to an 'audience' (a circle of listeners) for a certain author or for a particular topic or set of ideas without belonging physically to a particular social group or being in a particular place (the city, for instance).

This view of the early audience was soon made obsolete by a series of changes of technology and society, especially by the great increase in urban population, improved land communications and increasing literacy, together with other social and economic changes which had, by the end of the nineteenth century, transformed the rather small world of book and periodical production into large-scale industries serving millions. These media industries sought to recruit and shape audiences according to their own plans and interests. In turn this helped to establish the concept of the audience as an aggregate defined by its preferences and social-economic standing and also as a paying public — a new consumer market.

Early conceptualization of the audience as a mass

The invention of film and the cinema form of distribution added a crucial extra element. The moving picture shown in halls reproduced the original 'locatedness' of 'reception', and the cinema created the first genuine mass audience. It probably helped in the transfer of the term from the live theatre to the mass media and demoted the term 'public'. The film audience constituted an 'active crowd', although it could not really *interact* with its object of attention, except very indirectly. The main difference from the theatre was that there was no live performance (aside from the musical accompaniment), and the show was always and everywhere the same. There was also much greater possibility for very many people to share much the same experience as a spectator, across boundaries of time and space.

The first theoretical formulation of the media audience concept stemmed from a wider consideration of the changing nature of collective life in modern society. The sociologist Robert Park, influenced by continental European studies of crowd behaviour and also interested in the forces which promote social integration or disintegration, laid the groundwork. His pupil Herbert Blumer (1939) provided an explicit framework in which the audience could be located as an example of a new form of collectivity made possible by the conditions of modern societies. The term he used for the audience was 'mass', which he differentiated from older social forms — especially the group, the crowd and the public (see Chapter 2).

The new type of audience was large and widely dispersed; its members could not know each other; its composition was always shifting; it lacked any sense of self-identity, as a consequence of its size and heterogeneity; it was governed by no rules; it appeared not to act for itself but to be acted on from outside; and just as its own internal relations were impersonal, so were the relations between any source and the mass audience also necessarily impersonal. For reasons of its great scale, the mass media audience cannot 'talk back' to its sources, and the technology of mass media distribution is not usually arranged to make this technically possible. The communicative relationship involved is typically calculative as well as being impersonal. There is also often a large social distance between the mass media audience and a more powerful, expert or prestigious source and thus an asymmetric relationship.

This concept of the mass audience is an 'ideal type' rather than a description of any reality, an accentuation of features which might be found under the conditions of mass production and distribution of news and entertainment. It had (and may still have) a pejorative connotation, as a result of the strong positive value often attached to association, belonging and identity and of a critique of modern mass society, in which individuals are seen to be either lost or manipulated.

There was a significant turning point in the history of mass communication theory, during the 1940s and 1950s (Delia, 1987), when the atomistic conception of the mass audience was challenged by researchers (see especially Friedson, 1953; Katz and Lazarsfeld, 1955). Research hailed the 'rediscovery of the group', finding evidence to show that it had never disappeared in reality, even in the seemingly unfavourable conditions of the industrial city. There was a reminder that actual audiences consisted of many overlapping networks of social relations based on locality and other interests, and that the media themselves were incorporated into these. The notions of 'personal influence' and 'opinion leader' presumed a situation in which contact with the media was mediated by a variety of social contacts who served to guide, filter and interpret contact with the media. The communal and social group character of audiences was seemingly restored (for example, Merton, 1949; Janowitz, 1952).

Despite this, the set of ideas equating media audiences with a faceless and manipulable mass (whether real or just perceived as such) has continued to exert some influence. Gitlin (1978) set out to demolish much of the supposed 'rediscovery of the group' as an ideological device to conceal or obscure the dominance and power of monopoly media. Another effort to redeem the autonomy of the audience, by way of discovering the 'active' or 'obstinate' audience, has been criticized for much the same reasons. Nevertheless, recent developments both in the media themselves and in thinking about them tend in the same direction. First, the development of new and interactive media promises a technological antidote to the mass phenomenon. Secondly, those working within the cultural studies tradition have reasserted the autonomy of the 'real' audience at the point of reception of media and demonstrated that the issue does depend very much on what (or whose) perspective one adopts (Ang, 1991). Both these positions are assessed later.

From mass to market

It appears from the above discussion that there has never been a single really appropriate collective word for the receivers of mass communication. Each general term carries implications or connotations which are either too wide, too narrow or too value laden in some respect. This certainly applies to the term 'media market', which is widely current to designate a set of media 'consumers' or the target group of media advertisers. The term 'media market' is applied to regions served by media, to social-demographic categories or to the actual or potential consumers of a given media service or product. While the concept is simply pragmatic for commercial media industries, its use implies a number of properties of audiences which are theoretically problematic and open to criticism. In general, this criticism reflects the critique of the mass, which has been mentioned, since the media market has many of the characteristics of the mass.

It specifies the link between sender and receiver as a 'calculative' act of buying or consumption, rather than a normative or social one, narrowing down the range of possibilities for much public communication. Secondly, it ignores the internal relations of the set of consumers, since these are of little interest to service providers. Thirdly, it privileges social-economic criteria in characterizing audiences. Fourthly, the concept tends to limit attention to the act of consumption, with a consequent bias in research on the audience. Effective communication and the quality of audience experience are of minor importance in 'audience-as-market' thinking. Fifthly, the view of the audience as market is inevitably the view 'from the media' and within the terms of the media-industrial discourse. Market membership is not normally a basis for social or cultural self-identification, and the discourse of market thinking is manipulative in tendency.

The audience as market can be defined as an *aggregate of actual or potential consumers of media services and products, with a known social-economic profile*. There are, as noted, similarities with the concept of mass, although a media market may also be conceived of as geographically located, socially differentiated and with a known pattern of interests and preferences. Under modern conditions, the 'mass market' is only one of many possible market forms.

The audience as market

- Members are an aggregate of individual consumers
- Boundaries based primarily on economic criteria
- No necessary internal relationships between members of a given market
- No social or normative relations with the source of communication
- No consciousness of membership or identity as an audience
- No basis for continuity
- Research is interested only in size and individual behaviours

---

The duality of the audience

An alternative starting point for discussing types of mass media audience can be found in the observation that audiences originate either in *people* and society or in *media* and their contents. Media provision may respond to demands from community and society — for instance, the needs of a local community or a political party — or to the assumed individual content preferences of particular sectors of the audience — for instance, demand for sports, comedy, financial news or education. Both represent communication needs which arise out of pre-existing social experience. The difference between 'social' and 'individual' is also a macro–micro distinction, relating on the one hand to complete groups or social categories (a class, a community, a political public, etc.) and on the other to overlapping subsets of individuals within the total media audience which express this or that requirement from mass communication.

On the 'media side', there is also a division according to the source of an audience. Audiences can be created by the media, brought into being by some innovation of technology or some completely new channel or title. In this sense we can speak of the 'television audience' or the audience for music videos. The term 'audience' also refers to those who choose some particular kind of content, some performance or compelling presentation (possibly of limited duration). The media are continuously seeking to develop and hold new audiences for particular types of content, publications or 'shows'. In doing so they may anticipate what might otherwise be a spontaneous demand or identify needs which as yet have not been expressed.

A typology

In the continual flux of media audience formation and change the distinction made here between people-originated and media-originated audiences cannot be very strictly and empirically applied, since, over time, media-created needs become indistinguishable from 'spontaneous' needs, or both fuse inextricably, with few potential social or personal communication needs which are not already met in some way or another. Nevertheless, the theoretical distinction between receiver- and sender-created demand is a useful one for mapping out the different versions of audience that we may encounter. The distinction is set out in Figure 11.1.

The four types of audience can be characterized as follows, with indications of further subdivisions within each main category. These categories are not, of course, mutually exclusive, and the primary character of a given audience is not easy to determine empirically. The assessment has to be made on the basis of wider knowledge of a media system and a

	Society as source		Media as source	
	Macro	Micro	Micro	Macro
	I	II	III	IV
	Pre-existing social group (public)	Personal need (gratification set)	Content (fans or taste culture)	Channel or medium audience

Figure 11.1 *A typology of mass media audience formation: different origins give rise to different concepts of audience*

society. The following remarks explain more fully why and how the four types are to be differentiated.

The social group   Basically this will correspond with an existing social grouping (such as a community or membership of a political, religious or ethnic minority) and with shared social characteristics of place, social class, politics, culture, etc. It also exemplifies the concept of audience as a public in the sense of an active, interactive and relatively autonomous social group, formed on the basis of some common interest, purpose or experience. Publics in this sense are often formed on the basis of politics, local community, ethnicity or commitment to some cause or issue. Publics are often marked by a consciousness of identity and some potential for mobilization for chosen ends. There are likely to be some normative ties between audience and media source and between members of the audience mutually. Such audiences are likely to be more stable over time than others, with continuity of membership, and are likely to respond actively to what their chosen media provide.

The gratification set   This forms on the basis of some individual purpose or need existing independently of the media, relating, for instance, to a political or social issue or a general need for information or for some emotional, affectual satisfaction. It is also likely to be fairly homogeneous in terms of its composition, active in expressing demands which shape supply and also selective. Such audiences are, however, not social groups but aggregates of individuals engaged in essentially the same consumer behaviour.

A term which can apply to this version of the audience as well as to a media-created audience is **taste culture**. This has been defined by Gans (see Lewis, 1981) as an 'aggregate of similar content chosen by the same people'. The differentiating factor lies in the **origin** of the formation — some taste cultures derive from similarities between people; others are media creations.

Fan group or taste culture   This kind of audience will be formed on the basis of an interest in a particular author, director or type of content (or genre), or through attraction to a particular personality (or a particular cultural or intellectual taste). Otherwise, it lacks any clear social definition or categorization. Its composition will change over time, although some such audiences may also be stable. Its existence is owed entirely to the content offered, and when this changes (as, for instance, at the end of a long-running show or the death or decline of a star), the audience has to disperse or re-form in other ways.

Occasionally such kinds of audience are encouraged by the media to form into social groups (as with fan clubs) or they spontaneously transform themselves into social groups, with characteristic patterns of dress, behaviour and speech. Fiske (1992) suggests that 'fandom' demonstrates the productive power of audiences, creating new and deeper meaning from the materials made available, rather than successful manipulation. There is, consequently, an element of normative attachment, especially where a high degree of identification or involvement arises. This type of audience is normatively ambiguous. Attempts at exploitation are common and often associated with merchandising of products linked to media images, characters, themes, etc.

Channel or medium audience   Recruited to and held by habit or loyalty to a particular media source — for example, a newspaper, magazine or radio or television channel — such audiences are numerous and changing. Often they are encouraged to form by the media for commercial reasons. Whether formed spontaneously, gradually over time or by deliberate attempts at market management, such loyalty can give to this kind of audience some of the characteristics of the public or social group — stability over time, boundaries and awareness of identity. For most commercial media, however, audiences of this kind are more like aggregates or markets, and relationships between audience and source are likely to be non-moral and calculative (as with the 'mass'). Members are typically consumers of the media product in question and customers for other products to be advertised or merchandised.

Comparisons and contrasts

There is a degree of tension as well as of simple differentiation involved in the contrast between society-origination and media-origination, which underlies the typology described. The former goes with strong social and normative ties and mutuality of benefit, while the latter is mainly characterized by (would-be) manipulation from above and (individual) self-interested calculation from 'below'. One reflects the view 'from society', the other the view 'from the media'. It might also be argued, however, that the former is associated with stronger social control and the latter with more individual choice in a free market for information and culture. It would not be appropriate to make a simple value judgement, even if much of the normative social theory which is applied to media seems to favour the values associated with 'society-origination'. These values can be rationally argued for but are sometimes based on nostalgia for a lost community and solidarity.

The contrast also has implications for research into audiences, since socially originated audiences are likely to require more qualitative and intensive methods and more study of social and political contexts. The research needs in respect of the media-originated audience are easier to satisfy by extensive quantitative survey research in which precise behavioural measures of attention-giving play an important part. The audiences of fans drawn to particular genres have, however, also increasingly attracted their share of intensive research, as the motives for such attachments seem to call for interpretation (for example, Levy, 1977; Radway, 1984; Ang, 1985; Liebes and Katz, 1986; Seiter et al., 1989; Lewis, 1992).

Implications of new media for the audience concept

Much of this framework of ideas continues to provide the backdrop against which discussion of new media developments has taken place. Four main changes have occurred with a potential for affecting the nature of the audience (and ideas about it). First there has been a revolution in the possibilities for delivering television (and radio) broadcasting as a result of cable and satellite (or both). Supply was previously limited by the range of terrestrial transmitters carrying a very few channels. The result has been a so-called **abundance** of supply and a greatly increased choice at any one moment for most individuals. This has also changed the situation in which choice is made. Adding to this fact of increased supply (at lower cost) is the gradual increase in reception possibilities as apparatus becomes cheaper (more sets per household).

A second change has been the rapid development of new ways of recording, storage and retrieval of sound and pictures, beginning to approach the flexibility of print storage. The innovation with the single greatest impact is probably the video recorder, which shifts control of reception time from sender to 'receiver', thus increasing the abundance and choice noted above. A consequence of greater choice is also a potential decline in the homogeneity of audience experience as a result of **individualization** in behaviour and personalization of choice. However, this is balanced by an increased potential for very large worldwide audiences to be recruited for events or spectacles of great interest.

The third innovation is the possibility of **interactive use** of various media, as a result of computer-based systems. One-way systems become two-way or even multiple networks. The media user acquires control of the information environment. Interactive media networks have been welcomed by some as the basis for local-community-based or wider-interest-based types of association. In principle, this would seem to run counter to the whole trend of media history, restoring a human scale and individuality to mediated social communication, reasserting the equality of power of the receiver at the periphery with the dominant centralized sender. However, it is not just interactivity which is significant in recent change; also significant is the **interconnectedness** of new technologies which underlies the 'logic' of electronic media growth (Neuman, 1991, p. 48).

Fourthly, there is the increased **internationalization** of transmission and reception. This means that audiences are no longer confined to one place or within one set of national, language or cultural boundaries.

End of the audience?

In any event, the concept of audience in its original sense does seem to be abolished or to become a misnomer (for reasons other than those cited above), replaced by a very differentiated set of more or less active customers for information services of unlimited variety. As pointed out in Chapter 2, the pattern of flow and use of informational and cultural services is in the process of shifting from 'allocutory' to 'consultative' and 'conversational' types. These indicate new types of audiences which are simply not accounted for in the typology represented in Figure 11.1. We have to think of other kinds of social formations: sets of information seekers or sharers which call for novel kinds of identification. This will open up new frontiers with other communication activities — for instance, those based on the telephone (Frissen, 1992; Martin, 1991).

The very concept of mass medium is threatened, since no one will be obliged to accept the same package of information at the same time as anyone else. Arguably, without a mass medium there is no audience, only chance similarities of patterns of media use. While this is a theoretical possibility it is not yet close to realization, and the most far-reaching technical possibilities have extended rather than replaced older patterns of 'audience behaviour'. This serves as a reminder that audiences are a product not only, or mainly, of technology and media-industrial development but of social life (just as they are not just a product of market managers). There are continuing social and behavioural forces which generate the formation of diverse audiences.

If those forces were to fail, we would be more likely to find ourselves in the atomized and alienated state which the early mass media were accused of generating than in an interactive Utopia. The new media would be unlikely to offer salvation. Each of the types and associated concepts of audience described is dependent in some way on a given set of media-technological possibilities and on social-historical circumstances and is liable to change. Neuman's (1991) review and assessment of the consequences of new technology for audience homogeneity or diversity lead to the conclusion that forces working in one direction more or less balance the forces in the opposite direction, indicating a non-determined and open-ended future.

Or escape of the audience?

It is simply more difficult than in the early days of the media to 'account' for the audience experience and to answer the question, 'Who receives what?' The growth of 'interactive' and 'interconnected' media, although still at a very early stage, is likely to promote further the fragmentation and specialization of media use but also to give the audience member a potentially more active role. Under pressure of current media changes, the whole concept of the audience as a group or set receiving much the same content at the same time and place is increasingly anachronistic. Under conditions of great diversity of supply and flexibility of use by individuals, the early concept of audience as mass seems even less appropriate than was once the case. There are fewer opportunities for an audience to form as a heterogeneous mass, although when it does happen, it is on a scale greater than ever before — as with world audiences for sporting events.

The challenge to the audience as public or social group has other sources and arises from two main tendencies: one within media themselves, which, as they professionalize, have tended to weaken their direct links with political and social movements; the other, the trend to 'secularization' (decline in ideology) and growth in consumer-mindedness in many Western societies in the last decade or two.

Change but not revolution

Nevertheless, it is likely that the 'public' is changing only its manifestation, becoming more localized, issue- and interest-specific, less identified with either a single informed elite public or the following of a major political party. If anything, the market concept is likely to become even more widely current under the conditions described, since the application of yet more media innovations, the greater production of media content of all kinds and the increase of available time and money to spend on media require yet more detailed specifications of target groups and the cultivation of more and more specialized 'markets'.

New technologies — consequences for audiences

- Multiplication, fragmentation, segmentation of audiences
- Greater differentiation by source, medium, content, time and place
- Greater choice, more autonomy for media consumers
- Audience behaviour more selective, interactive, consultative
- Internationalization of reception
- More interconnectedness between uses and content received
- Audiences even more invisible to and unaccountable by research

---

Three traditions of research into audiences

In keeping with the theoretical diversity which characterizes the study of the audience we can distinguish several varieties of approach (Schrøder, 1987; Jensen and Rosengren, 1990). These reflect differences of purpose and also the basic division, outlined in Chapter 2, between structural, behavioural and cultural approaches. While there are different ways of explaining the alternatives, and finer distinctions to be made, this threefold division serves well enough for present purposes.

Jensen and Rosengren (1990) distinguish five traditions in their review of audience research: effects; uses and gratifications; literary criticism; cultural studies and reception analysis. They place little emphasis on one of the main purposes and traditions of audience research, which is simply that of counting and classifying audiences for better media-organizational control. This should certainly count as a research tradition, although it has been practised largely within the walls of media organizations and has low visibility in theoretical discussions. For present purposes of introducing key theoretical issues concerning the audience, we can confine ourselves to describing three main variant approaches under the headings 'structural', 'behavioural' and 'social-cultural'.

The structural tradition of audience measurement

The needs of media industries gave rise to the earliest and simplest kinds of research, which were designed to obtain some reliable estimates of what were otherwise unknown quantities — especially the size of radio audiences and the 'reach' of print publications (the number of potential readers as opposed to the circulation or print-run), data which were essential to management, especially for gaining paid advertising. In addition to size it was important to know about the social composition of audiences in basic terms — the who and where of the audience. These elementary needs gave rise to an immense industry interconnected with that of advertising and market research but also serving the management needs of particular media.

The term 'structural' is used because the goal of such research is essentially descriptive of the audience in terms of its composition and its relation to the social structure of the population as a whole. It is also the main kind of research that is carried out on behalf of media organizations. The audience could be measured in terms not only of demographics but also of content preferences, opinions and responses to programmes. This research essentially provides a form of feedback in a relatively fast and comprehensible form. The main method is the sample survey, but this can be supplemented and even supplanted in some cases by other forms of data collection — audience diaries and (for television) meters installed in receivers to record channel use and viewer activity and response.

The structural approach, with its typical methodologies, can do much more than provide management feedback data. It can be used in research into communication effects, as when opinion, attitude or reported behaviour data (such as on voting) are interrelated with media 'exposure', especially when a time dimension or a panel design is introduced (as by Lazarsfeld et al., 1944, to cite an early example). It can be used to study the 'flow' of an audience over time between different channels and content types (for example, Emmett, 1972; Barwise and Ehrenberg, 1988). It can be used to establish typologies of viewers, listeners and readers (for example, Espe and Seiwert, 1986; McCain, 1986; Weimann et al., 1992). It can shed light on the relation between media use and social conditions. It may serve as an important tool in the accountability of (for instance, public service) media to the society or sponsor.

The structural approach has also been adapted to explore group relations within the audience, patterns of influence (Katz and Lazarsfeld, 1955) and, later, studies of diffusion of innovation (Rogers and Kincaid, 1981; Rogers, 1986). A range of different theoretical issues have been tackled by methods which belong to this tradition — for instance, the relation between mass culture and social structure (Wilensky, 1964; Neuman, 1982), and the comparative merits of television and the press as sources of information (Robinson and Levy, 1986).

The behaviourist tradition

Almost as old as the structural approach (perhaps older) were the many research variants, originating primarily in the field of social psychology, which sought to establish the effects of media messages on individual behaviour, opinions, attitudes and values. Much early effects research adopted the experimental or quasi-experimental approach, in which communication conditions (of message, channel and reception) were manipulated in the search for general lessons about how better to communicate or about the unintended consequences of messages (Klapper, 1960). Two early examples were the Payne Fund studies into the effects of film on youth (for example, Blumer and Hauser, 1933) and the wartime studies into film as a motivational tool (Hovland et al., 1949). The appeal of and response to portrayals of violence and related phenomena in the media have mainly been investigated within this tradition.

There was also research into the motives and selection patterns of audiences for the new mass media, also conducted in a social-psychological mode (for example, Cantril and Allport, 1935, on the radio audience; Waples et al., 1940, on reading; Lazarsfeld and Stanton, 1949, on different media genres). The line of development of this tradition proceeded by way of many studies into mass media violence (see Comstock et al., 1978, for an overview) and into the uses (positive as well as harmful) of mass media by children (Schramm et al., 1961). A distinctive sub-tradition (with links to sociology) later crystallized out in the form of research into the motives for media choice and the perceived uses and gratifications of media behaviour (Blumler and Katz, 1974; Rosengren et al., 1985).

There is obviously much diversity of purpose, theory and method in this broad and enduring band of work, but it has some distinctive differences from (and also correspondences with) the structural tradition. Among the similarities are the attachment to measurement, quantification and statistical method and the tendency to serve either the media industry, its clients, or the official guardians of society and public morality. Distinctively different from the structural approach is the acceptance of the experimental method, the more theoretical orientation (seeking some kind of behavioural laws), its psychologism and attraction to mental measurement (of attitudes, emotions, states of mind).

In general, we can find in this tradition (especially in its 'uses and gratifications' variant) a much stronger inclination (strengthening over time) to treat the audience as the active participant in what is always an interaction between media sender and receiver. Not surprisingly, given the overlap noted, some audience research projects have combined both structural and behavioural approaches. A good example is the long-term Swedish panel study of television and children's development (Rosengren and Windahl, 1989).

The social-cultural tradition and reception analysis

The most recent addition to the range of audience research approaches derives mainly from literary criticism and cultural studies and from the criticial research tradition outlined in Chapter 2. An important step was the rejection of the 'power of the text' and along with it the notion of the inevitable submission of the subordinate classes to the power of the capitalist or state-controlled media. The body of theory discussed above (pages 52–3) concerning the possibility of 'differential decoding' according to social or subcultural position turned out to be a great liberator in audience research. At first attempts were made (for example, Morley, 1980) to show that messages could be read differently than intended, by differently constituted social and cultural groups. Soon, as critical-theory-guided decoding research merged into the general rise of media-cultural studies research, it became simply axiomatic to expect and not too hard to prove that most media messages were essentially 'polysemic' and open to several possible interpretations.

The other main strand of the culturalist approach involved a view of media use as such as a significant element in 'everyday life', a set of practices which could be understood only in relation to the particular social context and to other practices. Media reception research emphasized the study of audiences as sets of people with unique, though often shared, experiences and as 'in charge' of their own lives. This aspect of the tradition pointed to the need for detailed ethnographic descriptions of particular audiences and particular kinds of content.

The main features of the culturalist (reception) tradition of audience research can be summarized as follows (though not all are exclusive to this approach):

- The media text has to be 'read' through the perceptions of its audience, which constructs meanings and pleasures from the media texts offered (and these are never fixed or predictable).
- The very process of media use as a set of practices and the way in which it unfolds are the central object of interest.
- Audiences for particular genres often comprise 'interpretative communities' which share much the same experience, forms of discourse and frameworks for making sense of media.

- Audiences are never passive, nor are their members all equal, since some will be more experienced or more active fans than others.
- Methods have to be 'qualitative' and deep, often ethnographic, taking account of content, act of reception and context together.

It is clear that this tradition has little in common with either the structuralist or the behaviourist approach. The former has been roundly denounced from a culturalist and ethnographic position. Ang (1991) criticized the mainstream audience research tradition for adopting an 'institutional' view which aims to produce commercial and institutional knowledge of an abstraction of the audience for purposes of control and manipulation. The media institutions have no real interest in **knowing** their audiences, only in being able to prove there is one of a certain size and composition, by way of systems and techniques of measurement (such as 'people meters') which convince their clients but can never begin to capture the true essence of 'audiencehood'. Behaviourist and psychological approaches may get nearer to the goal of describing the nature of audience experience, but the outcomes of research remain abstract, individualized and desiccated renderings which also lend themselves to manipulative purposes.

Three audience research traditions compared

	Structural	Behavioural	Cultural
Main aims	Describe composition; enumerate; relate to society	Explain and predict choices, reactions, effects	Understand meaning of content received and use in context
Main data	Social-demographic; media and time use	Motives; acts of choice; reactions	Perceptions of meaning; social and cultural context
Main methods	Survey and statistical analysis	Survey; experiment; mental measurement	Ethnography; qualitative

Questions of audience structure

The institutional needs of the media have generated a very large amount of data which closely describe the size and composition of audiences for all media on a continuous basis. The patterns which emerge are generally found to be very stable over time, but they do change and are especially liable to disruption when the media change — most recently, for instance, with the arrival of cable and satellite television. From a theoretical point of view, what is most relevant is to understand the factors which shape the structure of audiences. In line with the basic 'duality' of audiences, the question of structure can also be approached from two sides — that of people and that of the media themselves. For present purposes, this implies the need for two kinds of description — first of media audiences in terms of their social composition, and secondly of people in terms of their media use (sometimes known as media behaviour). Not surprisingly, most of the research discussed in this section derives from the structural tradition of audience research.

Types of audience

Starting on the 'media side', we should first take note of the different realities to which the term 'media audience' refers. To some extent these are the result of different media types and distribution systems, but some distinctions apply across different media. The main alternative terms are:

- The **potential audience** — meaning all those who are able to be reached, depending on several factors, especially: having the receiving or play-back equipment; location (residing in the zone of distribution, or market); and some social-demographic factors such as income, level of education, age and gender, depending on how the medium is defined.
- The **paying audience** — this takes several different forms, but especially the purchasers of copies of newspapers, books, records, video recordings, etc.; those who pay admission to the cinema; and subscribers to particular media services like cable or satellite channels.
- The **audience reached** — this varies from medium to medium, but for print media it means the numbers who actually read each newspaper, magazine, etc., while for television or radio it measures the number tuned in to a particular channel or programme: usually expressed as the 'ratings'.

There are many variants of each and an increasing complexity of possibilities. But in general these three basic types identify various populations (aggregates) which form the audiences from the point of view of media suppliers. There are a number of other relevant concepts of audience to note. One is that of **density of circulation or reach**. This refers to the proportion of a given population of people or households in an area (market) who are reached by a particular channel or publication. It is also a spatial measure of media impact.

Another concept is that of **cumulative audience** over time, referring to the number or proportion of a given potential audience who are reached over a given period. For instance, a given newspaper or magazine (title) is likely to have a higher cumulative audience (the number seeing any copy) over a month than the circulation or readership of a particular issue in its circulation period. It is one important measure of the audience of a television series (how large is the total audience for one or more episodes?) or for a type of content (what proportion watch *some* television news in an average week?).

Aside from this, there are a variety of **internal** audiences to be measured — for instance, for a particular programme or type of content on television or, in the case of a newspaper, the degree of reader attention to particular sections or types of content. There is almost no limit to the variety of possibilities for identifying audience populations (aggregates of people or households), which can be expressed in terms of absolute numbers or proportions of some base (usually a potential or target audience). These aggregates are usually described in terms of factors which are of interest to media planners and advertisers, especially social-demographic factors such as income, education, place of residence, age and gender. Increasingly, new kinds of variable have been introduced to classify audiences — especially matters to do with lifestyle, tastes or psychological variables. Essentially these are marketing devices designed to classify media consumers in ways of interest to circulation managers or advertisers.

Data about people and their media use behaviour provide additional and complementary information about the structure of audiences. Instead of describing 'audiences' in terms of their composition, we describe populations in terms of media use. A common approach is by way of 'time budgets', which enables relevant social-demographic groups to be described in terms of the way they allocate their time as between different media or variations in the amount of use of a particular medium over time. Such data commonly show systematic differences between, for instance, social-economic and age groups and also differences between countries in the disposition of time available for media (for example, Espé and Seiwert, 1986; McCain, 1986). Questions of audience diversity can be settled by looking at data concerning relative homogeneity in terms of relevant indicators. For some purposes (such as cultural indicators research), it may be relevant to discriminate between degrees of media use (such as light versus heavy viewers).

Explanations of audience structure and composition

There is a great deal of stability over time in media use behaviour, and there are recurrent patterns in different media and different countries. Much of the stability (and variation) is accounted for by a few basic factors which influence the size and composition of media audiences. The two most common have to do with age and social class (or income and education), because both tend to determine the availability of free time and of money for media use.

Age (really, life-cycle) influences availability and content choice. Thus, as young children, we are confined more or less to the range of family-chosen media and watch more television. As we acquire freedom, we make more independent choices and go outside the home, leading to a pattern of radio listening and cinema-going (see von Feilitzen, 1976). With acquisition of our own family and work responsibilities, we return to a domestic context but with different interests, giving more time to newspaper reading and information generally. With more spare income after the growing up of our own children, media consumption diversifies and then contracts again with old age, leading to a return to more domestic media (television and books) and more 'serious' content choices (Comstock et al., 1978).

Social class position, as represented by income, governs the pattern of media use, and within this pattern higher income tends to diminish the place of television because of wider media and non-media leisure choices. Higher education and professional work responsibility may also lead to different content choices — more informational content or content favoured by dominant educational and cultural values.

Such findings and others which relate, with less consistency, to differences of gender and locality help to describe and predict the overall shape of audiences, and the underlying factors at work are not hard to recognize. However, there are also explanations on the side of media industries themselves. One explanation is simply historical, since some media tend to acquire a particular definition and audience appeal which is perpetuated and cemented over time. The daily newspaper, for instance, was developed for a predominantly male, urban middle-class readership and it still tends to appeal differentially to the same categories of people.

Aside from this, all commercial media need to maintain clear demographic profiles, for purposes of advertisers, and many of the stable elements in audience structure simply reflect the results of media market management. In so far as media operate under competitive market conditions, the structure of media provision (and thus of audiences gained) is likely to reflect the broad pattern of expressed audience demand — in terms of content requirements and the availability of audience time and money to support demand. This begs the larger question of whether audiences create demand or respond to what is offered, but it has to be accepted as a plausible explanation and a constraint on alternative possibilities.

Audience formation and flow

Related to the question of audience structure and social composition is that of how choices tend to be made on a continuous basis, thus the *dynamics*, rather than the *statics*, of media audiences. This is a very large question which can be dealt with only superficially and selectively. Most evidence relates to the broadcast television audience, although somewhat similar processes can be assumed to operate in relation to other media — for instance, to newspapers which engage in competition for readers and subscribers. In line with the treatment of audience structure, we can approach the question from two sides, that of the audience and that of the media. What influences choice of content and what factors of content and presentation help to draw and keep audience attention? These questions are answered with reference to television and with the aid of a single model (Figure 11.2 below) representing the joint working of these two sets of influences. The model is influenced by the work of Webster and Wakshlag (1983), who also sought to explain the process of viewer choice.

Audience-side factors

The most important factors are described in a sequence which goes from the more general to the more specific, from earlier (in time) to nearer the moment of media attention:

- **General social and cultural circumstances**, especially aspects of life-cycle position (age- and family-related) and cultural background (including education and social milieu).
- **Availability** for reception, in terms of place and time. Obviously patterns of work, sleep and other time uses have a strong impact on audience recruitment.
- **Habits** of media use and affinity for particular media (or channels). Individuals seem to have consistent habits and preferences for media which lead them to be more or less available, more or less selective and active in the amount and kind of their media use.
- General **content preferences, tastes and interests** in relation to media. In general, most people also seem early on to form particular patterns of likes and dislikes for broad kinds of content (for instance, as between television sport, news, comedy and soap operas). (See also the evidence on 'uses and gratifications', page 318.)
- **Awareness of alternatives**. Actual choice will be governed by the pattern of personal tastes and interests, but only in so far as the viewer is informed about alternative possibilities at the time of availability.
- **Context of viewing**. The operation of personal choice will usually depend on whether a person is watching alone or with others, has control of the decision or not, and is watching in a motivated way or not. In family viewing situations, actual choices are often compromises which do not reflect individual preference. They are often the result of inertia, simply inheriting a programme from a channel which is already on.

Medium-side variables

Obviously, audience formation has to depend on what is made available by the medium and on how it is presented. The relevant factors can be summarized as comprising the following:

- Deliberate **appeals to particular social-demographic groups** (for instance, children, youth, women or residents of a particular area).
- **Genre-based appeals** which invite audiences to attend according to the variety of possible tastes and kinds of programming (information, sporting, action adventure, domestic, etc.).
- Degree and kind of **advance publicity** and self-presentation.
- **Timing and scheduling** of programmes, planned in the light of awareness of differential audience availability, typical taste patterns and awareness of competition. Within certain limits, the size and composition of audiences are susceptible to some degree of manipulation by programme providers.

A model of the audience-formation process

The central spine of the model shown in Figure 11.2 depicts a sequence of choice from the general 'preference' set which most experienced television viewers can be assumed to possess. This orders our preferences and orients us to the expected satisfactions to be gained from viewing television. First, there is the generalized pleasure of watching television as a way of passing time which may guide channel preference. This general set is broadly influenced by the social-cultural factors noted above and also by past experience of the media and their typical content. It shades into the content preference set. Along the way, a viewer makes or accepts a specific content choice which is influenced (on the 'viewer side') more proximately by availability at a given time, by the degree of awareness of alternatives and by the context of viewing as described above. At the same time, choice is constrained (on the 'medium side') by what the media (or a particular channel) are actually offering at the moment in time (available options) and possibly by their publicity strategies.

For presentation purposes, the figure separates the two sets of influence, although it recognizes their interaction in showing general preferences as shaped both by what the media have chosen to offer (often a pattern over a long period of time and thus part of audience experience) and by what the audience member brings in the way of general needs, influenced by social-cultural experience and current circumstances. These are the more long-term and fundamental matters, which are also located furthest in time from the act of choosing or attending to media (media use). In practice, this model 'takes off' from a point where choices have already been reduced and a certain 'repertoire' of media use has already been established by habit and circumstance.

Expectancy-value theory

The model does not represent the extent to which expectations based on experience (a form of feedback) play a part in the ongoing process (although

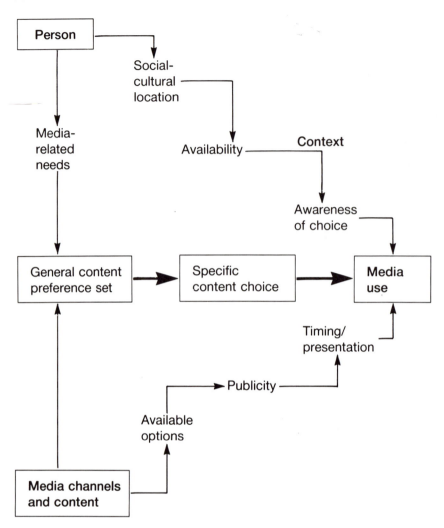

Figure 11.2 *A model of viewer and media influence on media use (audience formation): influences flow both from people and from media*

this has been mentioned). Perhaps the most useful theoretical framing has been provided by 'expectancy-value theory'. Most theory concerning personal motivations for media use acknowledges that the media offer rewards which are expected (thus predicted) by potential members of an audience on the basis of relevant past experience. These rewards can be thought of as experienced psychological effects which are valued by individuals (they are sometimes called media 'gratifications'). Such rewards can be derived from media use in general or from types or actual items of content, and they provide guidance (or feedback) for subsequent choices,

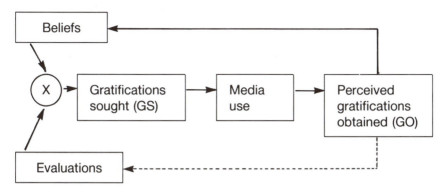

Figure 11.3 *An expectancy-value model of media gratifications sought and obtained (Palmgreen and Rayburn, 1985)*

adding to the stock of media-relevant information. A model of the process involved has been proposed by Palmgreen and Rayburn (1985), based on the principle that attitudes (here towards media) are an outcome of empirically located beliefs and of values (personal preferences). The resulting 'expectancy-value' model is depicted in Figure 11.3.

In general the model shown in Figure 11.3 expresses the proposition that media use is accounted for by a combination of perception of benefits offered by the medium and the differential value attached to these benefits. This helps to cover the fact that media use is shaped by *avoidance* as well as by varying degrees of positive choice among the potential gratifications expected from the media. The model distinguishes between expectation (gratifications sought or GS) and satisfactions (gratifications obtained or GO) and identifies an *increment* over time from media use behaviour. Thus, where GO has a noticeably higher value than GS we are likely to be dealing with situations of high audience satisfaction and high ratings of appreciation and attention. The reverse pattern can also occur, providing clues to falling circulation, sales or ratings and channel switching in the case of television.

Conclusion: multi-channel futures

Much of the theory concerning audience choice-making has related to conditions in which audience members were faced with a limited number of main choices (for instance, the three networks in the United States or the two or three channels once available in European countries). The arrival of multichannel cable has changed the situation for many and undermined the theory. Not only are there more channels, but there are special-interest channels as well as general ones and also more television sets per household. The situation is further complicated by the introduction of remote-control devices and video recorders. One attempt to model the new situation, by Heeter (1988), proposes that viewers develop their own strategy for selection, guided by programme information and personal observation, which they employ on a regular basis. The main new elements are the concepts of 'channel familiarity' and 'channel repertoire' (the set of channels watched regularly). The general sequence of selection is likely to be: informed search, with particular reference to an established personal repertoire; decision to view; re-evaluation; renewed search; and so on. In general, the new condition seems to call for higher information-processing skills (which are very unevenly distributed) than did the previous situation of channel scarcity.

12

THE SOCIAL CHARACTER OF AUDIENCE EXPERIENCE

The audience as an active social group

It is clear from Chapter 11 that even if, for some purposes of accounting or control, the media audience can be viewed as a mass or an aggregate, mass media use can also be very much a social activity, which is integrated into everyday life and thus into the life of the numerous overlapping social groups to which most people belong. This is true whether or not actual audiences can be considered to be social groups in themselves. Occasionally, there is some correspondence between a particular bounded social group and the audience for a particular mass medium. For instance, the residents of a local community, a political party, a religious faith or an ethnic minority might also constitute the readership for an associated publication or a radio or television audience. It may happen, the other way round, that being a fan of a particular medium, show, genre or performer/author gives rise to an active social group, with a more or less bounded and self-conscious membership and some degree of interaction.

Despite these possibilities, most mass media use, most of the time, does not constitute a group activity for most people, although it can still have a strongly 'social' character, according to a number of different criteria. These include: sociability of media use; normative controls or systematic social evaluation applied to media content and use; media uses in personal and social life; and the structuring of media use activity according to other dynamic principles of social and interpersonal relations — for instance, those based on class, gender, age or social power in general.

It has already been shown that audience composition (and thus choice) reflects demographic, and especially social-economic, differences, not in itself surprising since these are often built into the planning of media provision. There are also numerous 'taste cultures' (aggregates of similar content chosen by the same people) which associate preferences for particular content genres with a typical social-demographic profile. George Lewis (1992) discusses this point in relation to different musical preferences, noting, for instance, that the fans of punk rock were likely to have been young, white and male. On the other hand, rap and hip-hop musical styles have been favoured by young blacks. Lewis notes: 'the central fact is that we pretty much listen to and enjoy the same music that is listened to by other people we like or with whom we identify' (1992, p. 140).

Several diverse studies suggest that media content can itself provide a significant basis for identification or provide support for subcultural identities. This may be especially true of various youth subcultures, especially where other elements, such as class and ethnicity, are also involved. The media often provide stylistic markers for establishing group boundaries. The phenomenon is not confined to youth, since there are examples relating to social status and to national identity. The links between social factors and cultural expression and performance in media are often salient and potent.

Sociability in media use

There is also little doubt that much media use is sociable, contrary to the image in mass society theory of the audience as made up of isolated individuals, in an atomized society. While it is true that the rise of mass media increased the possibility for solitary attention to more channels of public communication (radio, newspapers, cinema, etc.) and reduced the dependency of the individual on other people for human contact, media use is in practice as sociable or as solitary as a person wants it to be. Certain media are more intrinsically solitary in use than others — for instance, books and recorded music (Brown, 1976) — but other media (especially television and film) are typically very sociable.

The sociability of 'audience behaviour' has several aspects, including: attending to media in order to maintain peer-group relationships (Riley and Riley, 1951; Rosengren and Windahl, 1989); the widespread reference to media experience as a basis for conversational exchange and lubrication of informal social contacts; and the substitution of media personalities for missing real-life models or interlocutors (Noble, 1975). There is also a large body of evidence testifying to the great importance of television viewing as a focus for, and a structuring principle of, family interaction (Morley, 1986; Lull, 1990). Television provides opportunities both for participating in the family circle and distancing oneself from it.

Social uses of media

James Lull's (1982) research into the social uses of television, based on participant observation of family media use, has confirmed, or added to, what was already established. He offers a useful framework and presents a fivefold typology of uses: structural, relational, affiliation or avoidance, social learning, and competence/dominance. The first of these categories, 'structural', refers to uses of media as background, providing companionship, regulating patterns of activity and talk. Mendelsohn (1964) earlier described radio as 'bracketing' the day and creating or controlling 'moods'. The 'relational' heading is similar to what was earlier called the 'coin of exchange' function of media use: the media provide common ground for talk, topics, illustrations — pegs on which to hang opinions.

The 'affiliation or avoidance' dimension refers to media as an aid to gaining or avoiding physical and verbal contact and also to the function of the media in increasing 'family solidarity', maintaining relationships and decreasing tension. 'Social learning' has mainly to do with various aspects of socialization. 'Competence/dominance' has to do with role enactment and reinforcement, with validation of arguments, with being an 'opinion leader' (Katz and Lazarsfeld, 1955) or 'first with the news', and so on.

In line with Lull's observation and with much everyday experience, Lindlof and Traudt (1983) have argued that television, far from undermining the family as was once supposed, probably helps to reduce tension in families and to maintain some personal space in a cramped physical environment. It is certainly becoming clear that most normal human activities habitually take place in the presence of television. Ethnographic research into the domestic setting of television use in particular has revealed the extent to which something as apparently simple as viewing television is governed by complex unspoken rules and understandings, which vary from one family to another, although there are some general principles (of the kind just mentioned). Morley (1986, 1992) has done much to explore this terrain. He quotes Anderson (1987, p. 164) as follows: 'Family viewing, for example, is no more casual and spontaneous than the family dinner. It is accomplished by competent actors with great improvisational skill' (Morley, 1992, p. 184).

Bausinger's (1984) study of domestic media consumption summarized several points which are relevant to understanding the social character of media use, especially that: the use of one medium is related to that of others; media are rarely used in a single-minded, concentrated way; their use is integrated into other everyday activities; media use is a collective activity, taking place in relation to family, friends and colleagues; and media and interpersonal communication are interconnected.

Normative framing of media use

Early critique of media 'addiction'

The preceding discussion is a reminder of the extent to which research into the media audience has taken place within a normative, even judgemental, framework. If we need proof that audience behaviour has a decidedly evaluative dimension, we need think only of the frequency with which questions concerning the audience are framed in 'problem' terms (Barwise and Ehrenberg, 1988, p. 138 ff.). Among the first such problems identified were various negative effects on family life if children (or their parents) spent too much time on supposedly 'passive' viewing, instead of interacting as a family group. 'Addiction' to television was identified as a potential danger (Himmelweit et al., 1958) or as a symptom of some personal malaise and failure to develop or connect with reality.

There was early evidence to suggest that high use of television was indeed correlated with poor social adjustment by children (for example, Maccoby, 1954; Horton and Wohl, 1956; Pearlin, 1959; McLeod, et al., 1965; Halloran et al., 1970; Noble, 1975). In respect of adults, heavy use of television and other media was associated empirically with other indicators of social marginality, especially sickness, old age, unemployment and poverty. It was never really demonstrated whether media use was a **cause** of poor social adjustment or just a correlate or even a compensation for it (Rosengren and Windahl, 1972). Media use can promote good social contacts (Hedinsson, 1981; Rosengren and Windahl, 1989), and unusually high media use does not in itself have to be viewed as pathological.

The normative framing of media use seems at first to run counter to the view that media use is a voluntary, free-time, 'out-of-role' and generally pleasurable activity, more or less unrelated to social obligation. While individual media use is relatively uncontrolled compared to many other types of social behaviour, it is institutionally regulated at several levels. A societal framework of norms and regulations has been discussed earlier (Chapter 5), and it would be surprising if we could not discern related patterns of evaluation and discrimination at other levels. Audience research continually uncovers the existence of value systems which informally regulate 'media behaviour' in several ways.

Content-based norms

First, there are values governing content and often involving fine distinctions, depending on context, between one type of content and another. For example, Alasuutari (1992) showed that Finnish television viewers deployed a sort of 'moral hierarchy', according to which news and information were highly regarded and soap operas seen as a 'low' form of content. Even so, value judgements were kept separate from personal preferences and actual behaviour. Secondly, there are often clear differences in the value attributed by audiences to different media for different purposes (for instance, newspapers versus television as a source of political information). Both these types of normative judgement may be deployed in relation to parental control of media use.

Thirdly, audiences consistently make value judgements about the performance quality of their media experiences, whether these relate to music, television programmes or newspapers. The television viewer is also often a critic of sorts (Liebes and Katz, 1989; Leggatt, 1991). Fourthly, there are normative expectations held by the audience about the obligations of media producers and distributors to provide certain services and *not* to provide others (for instance, pornography and violence). The media attract stable and firmly held opinions and attitudes among the public (Gunter and Winstone, 1993).

There is too much evidence on these matters to summarize, but it all adds up to the conclusion that media are viewed by their audiences within a complex framework of expectation and judgement. This framework may not be routinely activated, but it is ever present in the background. The values most frequently expressed about content are rather familiar and often stem from traditional judgements embedded in the culture and handed on mainly by the institutions of education, family and religion. They seem to favour the informational, educational or moral over entertainment and popularity. As Bourdieu (1986) has extensively shown, aesthetic judgements are also related in predictable ways to occupational (and therefore class) position. Media evaluation often reflects middle-class (bourgeois) values, with parents less inclined to limit the use of books and newspapers than television and popular music, regardless of content.

Guilty audiences

It is mainly in the imposition of norms for media use in family contexts that we are aware of normative control of media (Geiger and Sokol, 1959; Brown and Linné, 1976; Hedinsson, 1981; Rosengren and Windahl, 1989), but similar normative prescriptions have a much wider distribution. For instance, Steiner (1963) found a tendency long ago for viewers to show a certain amount of guilt over high levels of television use, which he attributed to a legacy from the Protestant ethic, which frowns on 'unproductive' uses of time. Among middle-class audiences, especially, a sensitivity to this value persists.

Radway (1984) found similar kinds of guilt feelings among keen female readers of romantic fiction and for similar reasons: 'guilt is the understand-able result of their socialization within a culture that continues to value work above leisure and play' (p. 105). In both examples, guilt was more evidenced in words than in behaviour, reflecting an awareness of social desirability. In her study of readers of women's magazines, Hermes (1994) found that within the interpretative repertoires of women readers there was a place both for feelings of duty to read a feminist publication and for guilt at enjoying traditional women's magazines. Barwise and Ehrenberg (1988) suggest that such guilt feelings (in relation to television) are typically quite weak (Hermes, 1994, would probably agree in respect of magazines), but their persistence and widespread occurrence are, nevertheless, striking.

Audience attitudes to the media have often been investigated, usually in the context of inter-media comparisons (cf. Comstock et al., 1978, pp. 128–40). People voice complaints about media and they also appreciate them. Positive appreciation usually outweighs criticism, but what matters is the fact that the performance of the media is so widely regarded as a proper topic for public attitudes and opinion. Audiences expect to be informed and entertained and expect conformity to some norms of good taste and morality, perhaps also to other values such as those of the local community, patriotism or democracy.

Attachment and dependence

Related to the normative status of media is the degree of attachment to media use as an activity. The more important the media are to people, the more likely they are to attract positive or negative value judgement both about content and about the practice itself. How important are media to people? Some researchers have made very strong claims for the dependence of people on their media. In an early study, for instance, Steiner (1963) reported that many would feel lost without television (but this was in the early days). Radway (1984) also makes clear that the devoted women readers of romance fiction regard reading as a very important part of their daily and personal life. No doubt this is true of many other groups of media fans, including soap opera viewers (cf. Hobson, 1982).

Although people can and do exhibit strong feelings of deprivation when denied their regular dose of familiar media (Radway, 1984, found readers comparing romances to a necessary but harmless, drug; see also Berelson, 1949), there is some uncertainty about the real strength of attachment at normal times. Himmelweit and Swift (1976), for instance, on the basis of a longitudinal study of media use and preferences, concluded that 'the media form part of the background rather than the foreground of the leisure life and interests of adolescents and young men: they are used far more than they are valued'.

The truth is probably that dependence, and hence valuation, varies a good deal according to individual circumstances and that under some conditions — for instance, confinement to home, low income or some forms of stress — the strength of attachment and level of appreciation are indeed very high, whether for television, books or radio. But this is still consistent with other evidence that media use is for many people a second choice activity when compared to going out or 'real' social interaction with friends. It may be that some media, or some genres, are intrinsically higher or lower in their involvement potential. Hermes (1994), for instance, suggests that women's magazines as a category of media are typically 'very easy to put down' and not very salient in daily life. There is also the possibility that some audience enjoyment is obtained precisely from the uninvolved playful attention to content which is not regarded seriously (Ang, 1985).

Gendered media use

One of the clearest demonstrations of the social regulation of media use has come from more qualitative and ethnographic studies of television use which take their starting point in gender differences. Audience statistics have always tended to show some patterns of difference between men and women, but these are often just superficial reflections of different time-use patterns. The real differences emerge only from the detailed study of content and reception taken together. Radway's account of women readers of romances clearly showed that there are a wide range of satisfactions derived from a genre written for women. These satisfactions relate very specifically to the self-perceived needs of the kind of audience studied. For example, women felt a need to escape from household routine and demands of family into a time-use and imaginary world which was designed for them as women and could not really be shared by men.

Media use as 'social' behaviour

- Media use (selection and time) is socially and culturally differentiated
- Media use (content and behaviour) is governed by formal and informal norms
- Media use is often structured by patterns of social relations
- Media use is often integrated into the rest of social life
- Media use is itself often sociable and a basis for other social interaction
- People are often strongly attached to chosen media use behaviours

---

The intrinsically gendered character of the soap opera genre (see page 264) has also been explored from the point of view of the audience in several studies (for example, Hobson, 1989). It has been said that the structure of the narrative matches the typically fragmented routine of the housewife as viewer. According to Morley (1986, 1992), television viewing in general is strongly gendered, especially because of the relation with social power in the family. His ethnographic research demonstrates that there are clear patterns of difference between men and women in power over choice of viewing, in amount and style of viewing and in content preferences. Some of the differences are familiar, others less obvious. For instance, women are less likely to plan viewing and more likely to do other things while viewing, to view or to give way to the choice of others for social, rather than content, reasons, to talk about television, to feel guilty about viewing alone, and to have content preferences related to their family and domestic roles. Somewhat opposite conclusions about gender differences in *cable* television viewing were drawn by Pearse (1990) (women were more inclined to plan).

Interesting also is the extent to which a whole range of communication technologies, including computers, video recorders, 'camcorders' and the telephone are gendered in use in more or less consistent ways (Silverstone, 1990; Frissen, 1992). If there is a key to the patterns it probably lies in the great degree to which societies, social roles and the minutiae of everyday life are still very much differentiated by gender and by associated and deeply rooted assumptions.

Audience–sender relationships

In speaking of social interaction within the audience, the most obvious reference is to personal contacts between people, but a certain kind of social relation can also develop between audience and sender in mass communication. This can occur either when a sender is genuinely trying to communicate or when both sender and receiver are oriented to the same communicative ends (for instance, sharing in the expression of some pleasure, or aesthetic or cultural experience). However, individuals in audiences often appear to establish (vicarious) relationships with mass communication, especially with characters, stars or personalities in fiction and entertainment.

One version of this phenomenon has been aptly called 'para-social interaction' (Horton and Wohl, 1956) and others have taken up the notion. Rosengren and Windahl (1972, 1989) identified two different dimensions of media (television) relations, one 'interaction' (when someone imagines themselves being in the action or where there is a state of 'mutual stimulation'), the other 'identification' (with a screen figure). When both occur, there is a state of 'capture', which is the highest degree of 'involvement'. Although difficult to study systematically, this phenomenon is very familiar. In the case of television, fans are often strongly affected by what happens to fictional characters and talk about them as if they were real, often expressing strong emotional identifications. Realistic and long-running soap operas with fixed characters seem to lend themselves most to dissolving the line between fiction and reality. There is also documentation of the experience of becoming vicariously involved in fiction and having fantasy relationships either with fictional characters (for example, Hobson, 1982; Radway, 1984) or with real-life performers. Many dead starsand cult television series even have their post-mortem fan clubs (L. Lewis, 1992).

Noble (1975) has suggested two concepts for dealing with this kind of involvement: 'identification' and 'recognition'. He attributes the first to Schramm et al. (1961), who defined it as 'the experience of being able to put oneself so deeply into a TV character and feel oneself to be so like the character that one can feel the same emotions and experience the same events as the character is supposed to be feeling'. This concept implies some 'identity loss', while 'recognition' does not and the subjective experience even contributes to personal identity formation. Thus recognition is being able to interact with well-known television characters as if they were similar to known people in real life. It is probably significant that much of Noble's evidence was derived from research with children deprived of normal family relationships.

Noble writes: 'these characters serve as something akin to a screen community with whom the viewer regularly talks and interacts . . . this regularly appearing screen community serves for many as an extended kin grouping, whereby the viewer comes into contact with the wider society beyond his immediate family' (1975, pp. 63–4). The emphasis here is on the positive aspect of vicarious social interaction, rather than on its common association with social withdrawal and inadequacy. There is also much evidence to support the view that identification with a media star is a way of entering into a valued community and identification with other fans (L. Lewis, 1992).

The concept of audience activity

Claims and counter-claims over the passivity or activity of the media audience have abounded during the history of mass communication theory, although the balance seems now to lie with the active audience side of the argument. A good deal of the evidence discussed already about the social character of the audience implies a fair degree of engagement and involvement in media use. However, the meaning of activity has never been crystal clear and it can certainly stand for several different things.

Attention was first directed to questions of audience selectivity (one way in which activity can be expressed) because of hopes or fears concerning the manipulative power of mass communication. Critics of mass culture thought that a large and unselective audience would be exploited and culturally harmed. There was much concern for children, since passive addiction to one medium after another (comics, films, radio, television) was seen as the enemy of education, discrimination and normal personal and social development (Himmelweit et al., 1958).

It then appeared from research that selection and avoidance by targeted audiences limited the effect of even the best-planned campaigns. The solace for culture critics and educationists was mixed, since the findings also undermined expectations that media use could lead to cultural or informational betterment. Popular entertainment media content would inevitably claim a major share of audience attention, while educational content would be avoided. In any case theory fastened on the image of the 'obstinate audience' (Bauer, 1964), one which might not always be very selective in attention but was at least selective in perception and resistant to personally unwanted influence. At least the audience need not be the passive victims once envisaged by mass society theory.

Much of the discussion has focused on television, which is probably the least selectively used medium of all, because of the family context of viewing and the generalized appeal of just 'watching television'. In an influential series of studies, Ehrenberg and colleagues (see Barwise and Ehrenberg, 1988) appeared to show that selectivity was so low that the size of audiences could largely be predicted on the basis of constant factors, regardless of specific content. Not only was selectivity low, but the significance of the viewing experience was also found to be minimal.

Five modes of activity

In a review of the different meanings and concepts of audience activity, Biocca (1988) suggested five different versions which are to found in the literature, as follows.

Selectivity. Generally this refers to the ground just covered. We can describe an audience as active the more evidence there is of choice and discrimination in relation to media and content. This is mainly likely to show up in differential attention-giving, especially where this seems to have some consistency or logic. Very heavy media use (especially television viewing) is likely to be defined as 'unselective'. It would seem eccentric, nevertheless, to follow this logic to the point of counting media avoidance as a sign of 'audience activity'. All in all, selectivity is a very weak manifestation of activity, since channel switching and 'grazing' with a remote control would appear to count as being selective. On the other hand, many other kinds of media selection behaviour, such as renting videos, buying books and records or borrowing from a library, do seem properly to count as 'active'.

Utilitarianism. Here the audience is the 'embodiment of the self-interested consumer'. Media consumption represents the satisfaction of some more or less conscious need, such as those postulated in the 'uses and gratifications' approach. Active media use here implies rational and motivated choice guided by experience and also, if appropriate, some utility experienced after the event (for instance, ability to make some informed choice). By definition it also covers 'selectivity', although there can be selectivity without utilitarianism.

Intentionality. An active audience according to this definition is one which engages in active cognitive processing of incoming information and the making of conscious choices on this basis.

Resistance to influence. Following the lines of the 'obstinate audience' idea, the activity concept here emphasizes the power which members of the audience have to set limits to unwanted influence or learning. The reader, viewer or listener remains 'in control' and unaffected, except as determined by personal choice.

Involvement. There are different versions of what this means and how it might be recognized, but in general, the more an audience member is 'caught up' or 'engrossed' in the ongoing media experience, the more he or she is involved. This can also be called 'affective arousal'. Rosengren and Windahl (1972, 1989) distinguish between a state of 'capture', which includes identification with a screen figure and a sense of being part of the action, and 'detachment, in which neither are present.

Although what is referred to is a mental state, it may be open to physiological measurement. Zillman (1980, 1985) has described how arousal, stimulation and excitement as a result of audiovisual experience can be experimentally simulated and measured. In general, the greater the arousal, the stronger the drive to continue the media use behaviour. Zillman sees this as especially relevant to explaining the appeal of 'entertainment' and uses of media for 'mood control'. Involvement may also be indicated by such behaviour as 'talking back' to the television screen.

These different versions of the audience activity concept do not all refer to the same point in time in relation to the actual media experience (Levy and Windahl, 1985). They may relate to *advance* expectations and choice, or to activity *during* the experience, or to the *post-exposure* time (for instance, the application of satisfactions gained from the media in personal and social life, such as in conversation). There are some relevant points which tend to be missed by the five variants outlined. For instance, activity can take the form of direct response by letter or telephone, sometimes encouraged by the media themselves. Local or community media, whether print or broadcast, may generally have more active audiences, or offer more opportunities to be active or even participant. Critical reflection on media experience, whether or not expressed in discussion or feedback, is another example of active audience response.

Audience research into the 'appreciation' by viewers of television programmes, for instance, can record above-average or below-average 'quality' ratings, and both would indicate the presence within an audience of a set of active and critical viewers. Recording and replaying from radio or television are also a specific piece of evidence of activity. We can also note that audiences can participate in the media experience by giving meaning to it in thought or words, thus actively helping to producing the eventual media 'text'.

A flawed concept

Active media use

- Selective
- Motivated
- Involved
- Planned
- Resistant to influence
- Sociable
- Critical
- Reactive
- Interactive

The general notion of 'audience activity' is evidently a very unsatisfactory concept on its own, open to diverse definitions of varying relevance to different media, sometimes manifested in behaviour, sometimes only a mentalistic construct (and hard to observe). According to Biocca (1988), it is almost empty of meaning in general, because it is *unfalsifiable*: 'It is, by definition, nearly impossible for the audience *not* to be active.' Despite the inadequacy of 'activity' as a single general term, there continue to be valid theoretical and practical reasons for its deployment in one or other of its forms, and for particular purposes.

Audience uses and gratifications

The tradition of audience research which was introduced earlier (page 296) as primarily behaviourist and individualist in its methodological tendencies was, nevertheless, also based firmly on the view that media use served a variety of needs stemming from the personal social situation of the individual. Forerunners of what was later called the 'uses and gratifications' approach (for example, Herzog, 1944; Berelson, 1949) sought to interpret the motives for content choice and the satisfactions looked for and derived from media in terms of everyday social circumstances and needs — for instance, the needs of housebound housewives for advice and status reassurance or those of newspaper readers for their daily ration of security.

Basic assumptions

The 'uses and gratifications' approach has been centrally concerned with the choice, reception and manner of response of the media audience. A key assumption is that the audience member makes a conscious and motivated choice among channels and content on offer. Another basic tenet (more or less shared with recent reception research) is that the meaning of media experience can be learned only from people themselves. It is essentially subjective and also interactive. McQuail et al. (1972, p. 144) wrote: 'media use is most suitably characterized as an interactive process, relating media content, individual needs, perceptions, roles and values and the social context in which a person is situated'.

There are several varieties of theory (see McQuail and Gurevitch, 1974; McQuail, 1984), although the earliest and dominant version tended to be functionalist in formulation. One much quoted statement (Katz et al., 1974, p. 20) of a functionalist version of the theory describes the approach as being concerned with '(1) the social and psychological origins of (2) needs, which generate (3) expectations of (4) the mass media or other sources which lead to (5) differential patterns of media exposure (or engagement in other activities), resulting in (6) need gratifications and (7) other consequences, perhaps mostly unintended ones'.

Social and psychological origins

Thus, the causes of media use are held to lie in social or psychological circumstances which are experienced as problems, and the media are used for problem resolution (the meeting of needs) in matters such as information seeking, social contact, diversion, social learning and development. If media use were unselective, then it could not be considered in any significant degree as an instrument for problem-solving or even very meaningful for the receiver. Much research over a period of forty years seems to show that audience members can and do describe their media experience in functional (that is, problem-solving and need-meeting) terms.

There is a recurrent pattern to the ideas which people produce about the utility of their media behaviour, the main elements having to do with learning and information, self-insight and personal identity, social contact, escape, diversion, entertainment and time-filling. The responses also vary a good deal according to the particular audience and the type of media content involved.

Revisionism

In the two decades since the statement by Katz et al. (cited above) was written, research has further specified the nature of motives, expected media gratifications and uses and led to theoretical revision. Progress made in naming specific gratifications has not greatly altered the picture we already possessed, but the basic proposition stated above does now call for reformulation (see Rosengren et al., 1985). Some of the preoccupations of early research and theory have proved to be dead ends or seem less relevant to understanding audience formation and behaviour. In particular, the emphasis on *needs* has been much reduced, since the concept has proved theoretically and methodologically slippery and, to a certain extent, redundant. Secondly, there is a much lower expectation that differentiation of the audience according to their perceived use and gratification would help in explaining differences in degree or kind of effects.

A reformulated version of the basic proposition would put more emphasis on certain key linkages: between social background and experience and expectations from media; between prior expectations and use of media; and between expected satisfactions and those obtained from media, with consequences for continued use. A new statement might now read:

(1) Personal social circumstances and psychological dispositions together influence both (2) general habits of media use and also (3) beliefs and expectations about the benefits offered by media, which shape (4) specific acts of media choice and consumption, followed by (5) assessments of the value of the experience (with consequences for further media use) and, possibly, (6) applications of benefits acquired in other areas of experience and social activity.

There is still an implied logic which looks conscious and rational, when expressed in this way, but it is much less mechanistic or dependent on functionalist assumptions than the earlier version.

The sequence is also more open to investigation, helped by certain theoretical and conceptual developments. First, the concept of expectation has been clarified in terms of an 'expectancy-value approach' (Palmgreen and Rayburn, 1985; and pages 303–5). The essence of this is to view media use behaviour as depending on a belief that a particular kind of media content has attributes which are perceived to carry a positive or negative value. This simple proposition opens the way to a clearer formulation of the research task: relevant attributes of media or content can be identified; respondents can be asked how they value each attribute and whether or not they apply to specific content (or media). The same researchers (for example, in Rayburn and Palmgreen, 1984) have also contributed to the handling of the linkage between audience expectation, media use and assessment after the event, by proposing a clear distinction between the first and the third of these — in the terms 'gratifications sought' versus 'gratifications obtained' (see page 305).

Motives for and satisfactions from media use

- Getting information and advice
- Reducing personal insecurity
- Learning about society and the world
- Finding support for one's own values
- Gaining insight into one's own life
- Experiencing empathy with problems of others
- Having a basis for social contact
- Having a substitute for social contact
- Feeling connected with others
- Escaping from problems and worries
- Gaining entry into an imaginary world
- Filling time
- Experiencing emotional release
- Acquiring a structure for daily routine

Some advance has been made on the question of relating social background to media choice and response (for example, McQuail et al., 1972), although it remains one of the most intractable problem areas. For instance, Blumler (1985) has made a distinction, based on extensive evidence, between 'social origins' and (ongoing) social experiences. The former seem, in general, to be more likely to go with predictable constraints on the range of choice and with compensatory, adjustment-oriented media expectations and uses. The second are much less predictable and variable in their sequence and direction of effect and often go with 'facilitation' of media use — with positive choice of, and application of, media use for personally chosen ends. Media use can thus be seen to be both limited and motivated by complex and interacting forces in society and in the personal biography of the individual. This is a sobering thought for those who hope to explain as well as describe patterns of audience behaviour.

The variety of individual motives, satisfactions and uses which have been ascribed to different kinds of media content is very large. McQuail et al. (1972) suggested an empirically derived typology of 'media–person interactions' distinguishing between four categories: informational, personal identity, integration and social interaction, and entertainment. McGuire (1974) generated a matrix of sixteen types of psychological motive for media use, derived from a basic division between cognitive and affective, and between active and passive, types of motive.

Audience involvement and entertainment

One of the most intractable tasks which has faced research into audience motivation has been that of explaining the often extraordinary appeal of certain kinds of media entertainment (Tannenbaum, 1981) as well as entertainment in general (Modleski, 1982). The very notion of 'entertainment', despite its wide currency, seems to escape definition, although Turow (1991) suggests 'performance . . . organized to attract audiences for personal satisfaction or financial profit'. He cites another definition which emphasizes the ideas of 'absorbing attention', 'leaving agreeable feelings' and having a 'diversionary' character. From the audience point of view, it is difficult to confine the concept of entertainment to any particular genre, since it can also be applied to news and even to political spectacles.

The phenomenon of spectator/reader involvement with the content of media has already been discussed. There has been a considerable amount of research on particular genres — for instance, the soap opera or romantic fiction (Radway, 1984). Other kinds of entertainment may take precedence or equal rank in popular appeal, especially those involving excitement and violence, but have received relatively little research attention. One investigator, Zillman (1980; Bryant and Zillman, 1986) has shown, using mainly experimental methods, that people form mood-specific preferences for media content, such that boredom leads to a choice of exciting content and stress a choice of relaxing content. Avoidance, escape and diversion can be demonstrated as operative factors, as can a general factor of 'arousal' or excitement which is attributed to certain media content.

More specifically, according to Zillman, the attraction of drama to spectators depends on three main elements: conflict between protagonists; valuation of the latter (as good or bad) by spectators; and experience of feelings of enjoyment or anger according to the success or failure of chosen protagonists. This process is clearly the object of manipulation by the media creator. These various contributions to understanding the appeal of cultural content, which have been summarily described here, have, when inter-related, considerable potential for explaining choice and involvement of audiences in relation to media. They can go some way to account for one of the familiar paradoxes indicated by Zillman, that of the great appeal of 'bad news' as well as of fictional disaster and horror.

Different models for different kinds of content?

This brief discussion of one of the important facets of the appeal of media entertainment raises the question of how far it makes sense to look for a single process of perception and reception, given the diversity of mass media. To some extent, the 'uses and gratifications' approach did set out on the path of exploring differences in use related to different kinds of content. But the result was to uncover simply too much diversity for any general conclusion to be drawn. While theory and investigation of media motivation and use should certainly pay due attention to the particular subject matter at issue, a general distinction might also usefully be made between 'cognitive' and 'cultural' types of content and media use (McQuail, 1984). This would also be in line with the fundamental distinction made by Carey (1975) between a 'transmission' model and a 'consummatory' (end-in-itself) view of communication. The first deals in rational uses, especially of information, for chosen ends, and is consistent with a functional view and a sequential logic. The second view tends to undermine the notion of the audience as engaging in rational, accountable behaviour.

The key difference is that symbolic cultural experience is characterized by an element of liberation from temporal and spatial constraint and subject to shaping by highly variable and unpredictable patterns of taste and content preferences, leading to emotional and/or aesthetic satisfactions. The cognitive model of use is based on a mixture of individual interests (also very variable) and purposes of a more rational, accountable sort. There is still a lack of definitive answers to most questions relating to the 'causes' of media use, but there seems to be more chance than in the past not only of describing and accounting for media use patterns but also of integrating audience research with 'reception' research. It may also be that criticisms made by Chaney (1972) and Elliott (1974) of 'uses and gratifications' research (especially for being too individualistic, mentalistic and psycho-logistic) are less applicable than when originally made, given the shift from a structural to a more subjective perspective and the relatively greater 'empowerment' of media audiences in media theory.

Audience response and feedback

In the light of the theoretical empowerment of the audience, it is now less relevant to pay attention to the many ways in which audiences are able to 'talk back' to the mass media — once thought essential for modifying the 'mass manipulative' tendencies of the media. Even so, it is useful to note that varied kinds of interaction between mass communicators and receivers do occur, some planned and managed, others spontaneous. There are three main kinds of 'feedback': one originated by the media themselves; another which seeks to speak for the audience; and a third which the audience itself initiates.

Media-originated feedback

There are many ways in which media industries seek to 'know' their audiences, especially with a view to control and future planning of activities in a market context. The media audience is a set of consumers, whose behaviour is constantly monitored by audience and reader research of both quantitative (such as ratings) and qualitative kinds (such as measures of programme or content appreciation). The limitations and aridity of much audience research have been criticized by Ang (1991), but it remains an essential source of information for management.

There is much evidence from studies of 'mass communicators', however (for example, Burns, 1977; Gans, 1979), that the actual communicators (programme makers and journalists) do not gain much from formal audience research. They simply do not find it meaningful and prefer their own informal ways of coping with uncertainty, especially by way of self-constructed audience 'images' and personal contacts (see page 210). According to Gans, news-makers tend to define the audience as people who are interested in the news, as they are. The remainder are pictured as uninterested, as intellectual critics or as anything that suits their own perspective.

Response on behalf of the audience

Along with the growing influence of the media, there has developed a very large number of active lobbies and pressure groups which claim to speak on behalf of the audience (or groups within it), with a view to saving it from itself or from the more unethical activities of the media. Commonly such groups are concerned with the family, children and morals generally, but they also speak up for ethnic and gender-based minorities and all who might be vulnerable (Montgomery, 1989). These developments should probably be considered as evidence of an active society if not always of an active audience. In many countries, it is not only voluntary activities which are involved but (semi-) public institutions designed to hear complaints from the public and adjudicate on disputed matters. Some bodies are industry-related, others are integral to mass media which have a public service role requiring sensitivity to a wide range of audience needs and interests.

Organizations with monitoring tasks 'in the public interest' are widely supplemented by a large volume of independent comment and criticism which the media themselves provide about each other. The media are often a topic of public, and even political, debate, and issues of audience protection and interest are widely and frequently aired in societies which have an active public sphere. Of some importance here is the growth of a branch of independent media research and assessment which often seeks to speak for or about the interests of the audience, in various manifestations (see McQuail, 1992).

Spontaneous feedback

In all this institutional development around the operation of the media, there remains some space for audience activity in the direct sense of individual complaint, praise or request, by way of letter, fax or phone. It has always been unclear how valuable or useful such response can be, since it is very open to manipulation. Most probably it will be considered important for local media and for small-scale media for special audiences and of doubtful value for large-scale commercial media. The growth of audience-participatory programming by way of phone-ins and studio audiences is evidence of the favour in which the *appearance* of audience contact and interaction is held. There has long been talk of even greater possibilities of audience feedback, based on interactive telecommunications. Whether or not this really empowers audiences remains doubtful.

Conclusion

It may well be that we have reached the end of the age of the mass media audience and that it is no longer a useful term for purposes of theory. There are simply too many varieties of 'sets of receivers' for diverse kinds of communication, and too much fragmentation and individualization of media use, for a single concept to capture the diversity. On the other hand, it remains an essential term for any (media) communicator who envisages some collective human destination for their message, and there are also occasions when we, as receivers, choose to consider ourselves as an audience, with shared attitudes and expectations in relation to a media source. So far no better general term has been discovered, so it is likely to live on for a time.

PART VI
EFFECTS

13

PROCESSES OF SHORT-TERM CHANGE

The premise of media effect

The entire study of mass communication is based on the premise that the media have significant effects, yet there is little agreement on the nature and extent of these assumed effects. This uncertainty is the more surprising since everyday experience provides countless, if minor, examples of influence. We dress for the weather as forecast, buy something because of an advertisement, go to a film mentioned in a newspaper, react in countless ways to media news, to films, to music on the radio, and so on. There are many reported cases of negative media publicity concerning, for instance, food contamination or adulteration, leading to significant changes in food consumption behaviour. Our minds are full of media-derived information and impressions. We live in a world saturated by media sounds and images, where politics, government and business operate on the assumption that we know what is going on in the wider world. Few of us cannot think of some personal instance of gaining significant information or of forming an opinion because of the media. Much money and effort is also spent on directing the media to achieve such effects.

And yet considerable doubt remains. The paradox can partly be explained in terms of the difference between the general and the particular. We can be sure that particular effects are occurring all the time without being able to see or predict the aggregate outcome or to know after the event how much is attributable to the media. There can be many effects, without any overall pattern or direction. The media are rarely likely to be the only necessary or sufficient cause of effect, and the relative contribution is extremely hard to assess. Despite these uncertainties, there seems to be sufficient pragmatic knowledge, based on experience, to enable the media and their clients to continue to behave as if they knew how to achieve effects.

There are many good theoretical reasons for this uncertainty, and even common sense and 'practical knowledge' waver when faced with questions of media effect in the contested areas of morals, opinion and deviant behaviour which have attracted most public notice. On many such matters there can be no question of the media being a primary cause, and we have no real 'explanation' of patterns of thought, culture and behaviour which have deep social and historical roots. Furthermore, it makes little sense to speak of 'the media' as if they were one thing rather than the carriers of an enormously diverse set of messages, images and ideas, most of which do not originate with the media themselves but 'come from society' and are 'sent back' to society by way of the media. Despite the obstacles and the inevitable inconclusiveness, the quest for media effects has proved as fascinating for social scientists as it has for the media themselves and the general public. A belief in deep and long-term consequences from the media will not easily be extinguished.

The natural history of media effect research and theory: four phases

The development of thinking about media effects may be said to have a 'natural history', in the sense of its being strongly shaped by the circumstances of time and place and influenced in an interactive way by several 'environmental' factors, including the interests of governments and law-makers, changing technology, the events of history, the activities of pressure groups and propagandists, the ongoing concerns of public opinion and even the findings and the fashions of social science. It is not surprising that no straight path of cumulative development of knowledge can be discerned. Even so, we can distinguish a number of stages in the history of the field which indicate some degree of ordered progression and reflect the accumulation of knowledge.

Phase 1: all-powerful media

In the first phase, which extends from the turn of the century until the late 1930s, the media, where they were well developed, were credited with considerable power to shape opinion and belief, to change habits of life and to mould behaviour actively more or less according to the will of those who could control the media and their contents (Bauer and Bauer, 1960). Such views were based not on scientific investigation but on observation of the enormous popularity of the press and of the new media of film and radio which intruded into many aspects of everyday life as well as public affairs.

In Europe, the use of media by advertisers, by war propagandists and by dictatorial states in the inter-war years and by the new revolutionary regime in Russia all appeared to confirm what people were already inclined to believe — that the media could be immensely powerful. Against the background of such beliefs, systematic research using survey and experimental methods, and drawing heavily on social psychology, was begun during the 1920s and 1930s. Often the motives were of a reformist or progressive kind, aiming at improving the media or harnessing them to some desirable 'pro-social' goal, such as education, combating prejudice or increasing public information.

Phase 2: theory of powerful media put to the test

This transition to empirical enquiry led to a second phase of thinking about media effect. Its beginning is well exemplified in the research literature by the series of Payne Fund studies in the United States in the early 1930s (Blumer, 1933; Blumer and Hauser, 1933; Peterson and Thurstone, 1933). This era of research into media effects continued until the early 1960s. Many separate studies were carried out into the effects of different types of content and media, of particular films or programmes and of entire campaigns. Attention was mainly concentrated on the possibilities of using film and other media for planned persuasion or information (for example, Hovland et al., 1949; Star and Hughes, 1950), on political campaigns (for example, Lazarsfeld et al., 1944; Berelson et al., 1954) or on assessing (with a view to measures of control) the possible harmful effects of media in respect of delinquency, prejudice and aggression.

Over the course of time the nature of research changed, as methods developed and evidence and theory suggested new kinds of variable which should be taken into account. Initially, researchers began to differentiate possible effects according to social and psychological characteristics; subsequently they introduced variables relating to intervening effects from personal contacts and social environment, and latterly according to types of motive for attending to media.

What now seems like the end of an era was marked by expressions of disillusion with the outcome of this kind of media effect research (for example, Berelson, 1959) and by a new statement of conventional wisdom which assigned a much more modest role to media in causing any planned or unintended effects. The still influential and useful summary of early research by Joseph Klapper, published in 1960 (though dating from 1949), appeared to set the seal on this research phase by concluding that 'mass communication does not ordinarily serve as a necessary or sufficient cause of audience effects, but rather functions through a nexus of mediating factors' (p. 8).

It was not that the media had been found to be without effects; rather, they were shown to operate within a pre-existing structure of social relationships and a particular social and cultural context. These factors took primacy in shaping the opinions, attitudes and behaviour under study and also in shaping media choice, attention and response on the part of audiences. It was also clear that information acquisition could occur without related attitude change, and attitude change without changes in behaviour (for example, Hovland et al., 1949; Trenaman and McQuail, 1961).

The new sobriety of assessment was slow to modify opinion outside the social scientific community. It was particularly hard to accept for those who made a living from advertising and propaganda and for those in the media who valued the myth of their great potency (see Key, 1961). Those with political or commercial motives for using or controlling the media did not feel they could risk accepting the message of relative media impotence which research produced. There was still room for varying asssessments, since the message of limited effect was heavily qualified and was itself a reaction against unrealistic claims.

Phase 3: powerful media rediscovered

Hardly had the 'no (or minimal) effect' been written into the textbooks when it was being challenged by those who doubted that the whole story had been written and were reluctant to dismiss the possibility that media might indeed have important social effects and be an instrument for exercising social and political power. There was plenty of contemporary evidence of the continued search for significant media effects, and some well-informed retrospective accounts of the period (for example, Lang and Lang, 1981; McLeod et al., 1991) shed considerable doubt on whether there ever was a watershed at this time between a belief in media power and one in media impotence.

In relation to public opinion effects, Lang and Lang (1981) argue that the 'minimal effect' conclusion is only one particular interpretation which has gained undue currency (see also Chaffee and Hochheimer, 1982). Lang and Lang write: 'The evidence available by the end of the 1950s, even when balanced against some of the negative findings, gives no justification for an overall verdict of "media impotence" ' (1981, p. 659). In their view, the 'no effect' myth was due to a combination of factors, most notably: undue concentration on a limited range of effects, especially short-term effects on individuals (for instance, during elections), instead of on broader social and institutional effects, and undue weight given to two publications — Katz and Lazarsfeld's *Personal Influence* (1955) and Klapper's *The Effects of Mass Communication* (1960). Nevertheless, they concede that the myth was influential enough to close off certain avenues of research temporarily.

One reason for the reluctance to accept a 'minimal effect' conclusion was the arrival of television in the 1950s and 1960s as a new medium with even more power of attraction (if not necessarily of effect) than its predecessors and with seemingly major implications for social life. The third phase of theory and research was one in which potential effects were still being sought, but according to revised conceptions of the social and media processes likely to be involved. Early investigation had relied very heavily on a model (borrowed from psychology) in which correlations were sought between degree of 'exposure' to media stimuli and measured changes of, or variations in, attitude, opinion, information or behaviour, taking account of numerous intervening variables. Again, there is little evidence for another myth — that early research into media was characterized by a simple belief in direct effects from media (the 'hypodermic needle' model) or attachment to a crude stimulus–response model of behaviour.

The renewal of effect research was marked by a shift of attention towards long-term change, cognitions rather than attitude and affect, intervening variables of context, disposition and motivation, and collective phenomena such as climates of opinion, structures of belief, ideologies, cultural patterns and institutional forms of media provision. In addition, effect research benefited from growing interest in how media organizations processed and shaped 'content' before it was delivered to audiences (for example, in Halloran et al., 1970; Elliott, 1972).

Much of what follows is taken up with a review of these newer theories of effect and of modifications of early direct-effect models. While there are many contributors to, and causes of, the revival of interest, it was Noelle-Neumann (1973) who coined the slogan 'return to the concept of powerful mass media' which serves to identify this research phase. The upsurge of left-wing political thinking in the 1960s (the New Left) also made an important contribution by crediting the media with powerful legitimating and controlling effects in the interests of capitalist or bureaucratic states.

Phase 4: negotiated media influence

Work on media texts (especially news) and audiences, and also on media organizations, beginning in the late 1970s, brought about a new approach to media effects which can best be termed 'social constructivist' (Gamson and Modigliani, 1989). In essence, this has been the development of a view of media as having their most significant effects by constructing meanings and offering these constructs in a systematic way to audiences, where they are incorporated (or not), on the basis of some form of negotiation, into personal meaning structures, often shaped by prior collective identifications. This mediating process often involves some engagement by interested social institutions and strong influence from the immediate social context of the receiver. The break with 'all-powerful media' is also marked by a methodological shift, especially away from quantitative survey methods. An early practitioner of effect research has even referred to the 'bankruptcy of behaviourism' as an explanation of media effects (Mendelsohn, 1989).

The origins of the new research phase are diverse and lie quite deep in the past. The new thinking also retains some points of similarity with early 'powerful media' theory, including, for example, theory of ideology and false consciousness, Gerbner's cultivation theory (Signorielli and Morgan, 1990) and the ideas elaborated by Noelle-Neumann (1974) in her 'spiral of silence' theory. This emerging paradigm of effects has two main thrusts: first, that media 'construct' social formations and history itself by framing images of reality (in fiction as well as news) in a predictable and patterned way; and secondly, that people in audiences construct for themselves their own view of social reality and their place in it, in interaction with the symbolic constructions offered by the media. The approach allows both for the power of media and for the power of people to choose, with a terrain of continuous negotation in between, as it were. In general, it is a formulation of the effect process which accords well with the mediation perspective outlined in Chapter 3.

There are by now a good many research studies which operate within this framework, with attention often directed at how media interact with significant social movements which are active in society (for instance, in relation to the environment, peace and the advance of women and minorities). One example is offered by Gitlin's (1980) account of the US students' movement in the late 1960s. Another is Gamson and Modigliani's (1989) account of opinion formation concerning nuclear power. A recent study by van Zoonen (1992) of the rise of the women's movement in the Netherlands has adopted a constructivist approach to assessing the contribution of the media to the events. She explains the 'social constructivist' perspective essentially as follows: the media are more than plain transmitters of movement messages and activities, but they do this selectively; it is not the transmission which counts so much as 'a particular *construction* of the movement's ideas and activities', influenced by many negotations and conflicts within the news organization. She comments: 'The media image of the movement is the result of an intricate *interaction* between movement and media', leading to a certain **public identity** and **definition**.

The constructivist approach does not replace all earlier formulations of the effect process — for instance, in matters of attention-gaining, direct stimulus to individual behaviour or emotional response. It is also not inconsistent with a good deal of earlier theory, although it departs radically in terms of method and research design by calling for much deeper, broader and more qualitative kinds of evidence, especially about the context of 'critical events' during which constructions are forged. It clearly owes more to the cultural than to the structural and behavioural traditions outlined earlier (Chapter 2), but it does not stand entirely apart from the latter, since investigation has to be located in a societal context and it assumes that eventual constructions are the outcome of numerous behaviours and cognitions by many participants in complex social events. The approach can be applied to a good many situations of presumed media influence, especially in relation to public opinion, social attitudes, political choice, ideology and many cognitions. The various formulations of frame and schema theory (Graber, 1984) can usefully be located under the same general heading.

Media power can vary with the times

Before leaving the historical aspect of research into media effects, it is worth reflecting on a suggestion by Carey (1988) that variations in **belief** in the power of mass communications may have a historical explanation: 'it can be argued that the basic reason behind the shift in the argument about the effects from a powerful to a limited to a more powerful model is that the social world was being transformed over this period'.

Powerful effects were indeed signalled in a time of world upheaval around the two world wars, while the quieter 1950s and 1960s seemed more stable, until peace was again upset by social upheaval. It does seem that whenever the stability of society is disturbed, by crime, war, economic malaise or some 'moral panic', the mass media are given some of the responsibility.

We can only speculate about the reasons for such associations in time, but we cannot rule out the possibility that media *are* actually more influential in certain ways at times of crisis or heightened awareness — as, for instance, at the time of the fall of communism in Europe or the Gulf War, or when there is a national sense of crisis. There are several reasons for this possibility. People often know about the more significant historical events only through the media and may associate the message with the medium; in times of change and uncertainty it is also highly probable that people are more dependent on media as a source of information and guidance (Ball-Rokeach and DeFleur, 1976; Ball-Rokeach, 1985); and media have been shown to be more influential on matters outside immediate personal experience. Under conditions of tension and uncertainty, government, business and other elites and interests often try to use media to influence and control opinion.

All these are arguments for the view that the power (potential effect) of media may indeed vary according to historical conditions. In a somewhat different context (that of the socializing effects of television on children), Rosengren and Windahl (1989) suggest that variations in evidence about the influence of television itself may reflect the fact that television was actually different in content and as a social experience in the 1980s compared with the 1950s when the first research was undertaken. The important if obvious point that the media are not constant as a potential influence, over time and between places, is often overlooked in the search for generalization.

Levels and kinds of effect

Media 'effects' are simply the consequences of what the mass media do, whether intended or not. The expression 'media power', on the other hand, refers to a general potential on the part of the media to have effects, especially of a planned kind. 'Media effectiveness' is a statement about the **efficiency** of media in achieving a given aim and always implies intention or some planned communication goal. Such distinctions are important for precision, although it is hard to keep to a consistent usage. Even more essential for research and theory is to observe the distinction between 'levels' of occurrence, especially the levels of individual, group or organization, social institution, whole society, and culture. Each or all can be affected by mass communication, and effects at any one level (especially a 'higher' level) often imply some effects at other levels. Most media effect research has been carried out, methodologically, at the individual level, though often with the aim of drawing conclusions relating to collective or higher levels.

Perhaps the most confusing aspect of research on effects is the multiplicity and complexity of the phenomena involved. Broad distinctions are normally made between effects which are cognitive (to do with knowledge and opinion), those which are affectual (relating to attitude and feelings) and effects on behaviour. This threefold distinction was treated in early research as following a logical order, from the first to the third and with an implied increase in significance (behaviour counting more than knowledge). In fact, it is no longer easy to sustain the distinction between the three concepts or to accept the unique logic of that particular order of occurrence (see page 340). Nor is behaviour (such as acts of voting or purchasing) necessarily more significant than other kinds of effect. To add to the complexity, much of our evidence comes from replies to questionnaires which are themselves individual acts of verbal behaviour from which we hope to reconstruct collective phenomena, often with an inextricable mixture of cognitive and affectual elements.

There are several ways of differentiating between the types of media effect. Klapper (1960) distinguished between **conversion, minor change** and **reinforcement** — respectively: change of opinion or belief according to the intention of the communicator; change in form or intensity of cognition, belief or behaviour; and confirmation by the receiver of an existing belief, opinion or behaviour pattern. This threefold distinction needs to be widened to include other possibilities, especially at levels above that of the individual (see Chapter 1).

The media can:

- cause intended change (conversion);
- cause unintended change;
- cause minor change (form or intensity);
- facilitate change (intended or not);
- reinforce what exists (no change);
- prevent change.

Any of these changes may take effect at the level of the individual, society, institution or culture.

The categories of effect are mainly self-explanatory, but the facilitation of change refers to the mediating role of media in the construction of meanings and in wider processes of change in society, in line with the most recent paradigm of media effect (phase 4, page 331). The two effect types that imply absence of any effect involve different conceptions of media processes. In the case of an individual, reinforcement is a probable consequence of selective and persistent attention on the part of the receiver to content which is congruent with existing views.

'Preventing change', on the other hand, implies the deliberate supply of one-sided or ideologically shaped content in order to inhibit change in a conforming public. Often this just refers to the repetition of consensual views and absence of any challenge. The 'no change' effect from the media, of which we have so much evidence, requires very close attention because of its long-term consequences. It is a somewhat misleading expression, since anything that alters the probability of opinion or belief distribution in the future is an intervention into social process and thus an effect.

These distinctions are not exhaustive, and new distinctions may have to be made for purposes of studying particular problems. Windahl et al. (1992) describe a proposal by Kent Asp to classify types of effect according to three variables: level, time frame and source. The level may be individual or the system; time can be short or long; the source, most generally, can be the mass medium, its message and content, or the original source of the message (such as a political party).

Lang and Lang (1981) point to yet other types of effect which have been observed, including 'reciprocal', 'boomerang' and 'third-party' effects. The first refers to the consequences for a person or even an institution of becoming the object of media coverage. A planned event, for instance, is often changed by the very fact of being televised. There is often an interaction between media and the objects of reporting. Gitlin (1980) showed, for example how the US student movement in the 1960s was influenced by its own publicity. A 'boomerang' effect, causing change in the opposite direction to that intended, is a very familiar phenomenon (or risk) in campaigning. A 'third-party' effect refers to the belief, often encountered, that other people are likely to be influenced but not oneself.

In their discussion of dimensions of effects, McLeod et al. (1991) also point to the difference between effects which are diffuse or general (such as the supposed effects of television as a medium) and those which are content specific. In the latter case, a certain in-built structure or tendency (for instance, a political bias) is singled out as the potential cause of change.

Processes of media effect: a typology

In order to provide an outline of developments in theory and research, we begin by interrelating two of the distinctions already mentioned: between the intended and the unintended, and between the short-term and the long-term. This device was suggested by Golding (1981) to help distinguish different concepts of news and its effects. He argued that, in the case of news, intended short-term effects may be considered as 'bias'; unintended short-term effects fall under the heading of 'unwitting bias'; intended long-term effects indicate 'policy' (of the medium concerned); while unintended long-term effects of news are 'ideology'. Something of the same way of thinking helps us to map out, in terms of these two co-ordinates, the main kinds of media effect process which have been dealt with in the research literature. The result is given in Figure 13.1.

The main entries in the figure can be briefly described, although their meaning will be made more explicit in the discussion of theory which follows:

Individual response: the process by which individuals change, or resist change, following exposure to messages designed to influence attitude, knowledge or behaviour.

Media campaign: the situation in which a number of media are used in an

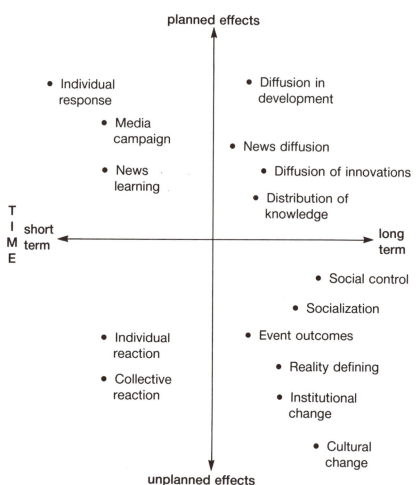

Figure 13.1 *A typology of media effects: effects can be located on two dimensions, that of time span and that of intentionality*

organized way, to achieve a persuasive or informational purpose with a chosen population. The most common examples are found in politics, advertising, fund-raising, and public information for health and safety. Campaigns tend to have the following additional characteristics: they have specific and overt aims and a limited time span and are thus open to assessment as to effectiveness; they have authoritative (legitimate) sponsorship, and their purposes tend to be in line with consensual values and with the aims of established institutions; and the population targeted for influence is usually large and dispersed.

News learning: the short-term cognitive effect of exposure to mass media news, as measured by tests of audience recall, recognition or comprehension.

Individual reaction: unplanned or unpredicted consequences of individual exposure to a media stimulus. This has mainly been noticed in the form of imitation and learning, especially of aggressive or deviant acts (including suicide), but also of 'pro-social' ideas and behaviour. The term 'triggering' has also been used. Other related types of effect include strong emotional responses, the displacement of other activities, the imitation of styles and fashions, the identification with heroes or stars, sexual arousal, and reactions of fear or anxiety.

Collective reaction: here some of the same individual effects are experienced simultaneously by many people in a shared situation or context, leading to joint action, usually of an unregulated and non-institutional kind. Fear, anxiety and anger are the most potent reactions, which can lead to panic or civil disturbance.

Diffusion in development: the planned diffusion of innovations for purposes of long-term development (often in Third World countries), using a series of campaigns and other means of influence, especially the interpersonal network and authority structure of the community or society.

News diffusion: the spread of knowledge of particular (news) events through a given population over time, with particular reference to the extent of penetration (proportion ultimately knowing) and the means by which information is received (personal versus media sources).

Diffusion of innovations: the most common reference is to the process of take-up of technological innovations within a given population, often on the basis of advertising or general publicity. It can be an unintended as well as an intended effect. The process often follows a characteristic S-curve pattern with predictable features relating to sources of influence and types of motive. Early and late innovators also tend to show different characteristics.

Distribution of knowledge: the consequences of media news and information for the distribution of knowledge as between social groups, with particular reference to different kinds of media source and to the social origins of variation.

Socialization: the informal contribution of media to the learning and adoption of norms, values and expectations of behaviour in particular social roles and situations.

Social control: refers here to systematic tendencies to promote conformity to an established order or a pattern of behaviour. The main effect is to support the legitimacy of existing authority, by way of ideology and the 'consciousness industry'. Depending on one's social theory, this can be considered either as a deliberate or as an unintended extension of socialization. Because of this ambiguity, it is 'located' in Figure 13.1 near the midpoint of the vertical co-ordinate.

Event outcomes: referring to the part played by media in conjunction with institutional forces in the course and resolution of major 'critical' events (see

Lang and Lang, 1981). Examples could include revolution, major domestic political upheavals and matters of war and peace. Less significant events, such as elections, could also figure here.

Reality defining and construction of meaning: a similar process to social control, but different in having more to do with broad structures of cognitions and frames of interpretation than with behaviour. This (very extensive) kind of effect is also different in requiring the more or less active participation of receivers in the process of constructing their own meaning.

Institutional change: the unplanned adaptation by existing institutions to developments in the media, especially those affecting their own communication functions (cf. the notion of 'reciprocal effects', page 335).

Cultural change: shifts in the overall pattern of values, behaviours and symbolic forms characterizing a sector of society (such as youth), a whole society or a set of societies. The alternative tendencies, referred to as 'centrifugal' or 'centripetal' (see pages 71–2), are relevant to this point. The possible strengthening or weakening of cultural identity may also be an example of effect (see page 114).

The entries in Figure 13.1 are intended to stand for processes of effect differentiated according to level, time span, complexity and several other conditions which have been briefly indicated. In some cases, the same basic model may apply to more than one of the processes.

Individual response and individual reaction

The stimulus–response model

Individual response and *individual reaction*, two of the entries in Figure 13.1, can be dealt with together, since they share the same underlying behavioural model, that of stimulus–response or conditioning. The model's main features can be simply represented as follows:

single message → individual receiver → reaction.

It applies more or less equally to intended and to unintended effects, although there is a significant difference between a **response** (implying some interaction with the receiver and also a learning process) and a **reaction** (which implies no choice or interaction on the part of the receiver). A more extended version of the basic response and learning process as it occurs in persuasion and opinion formation is indicated by McGuire (1973) in the form of six stages in sequence: presentation — attention — comprehension — yielding — retention — overt behaviour.

This elaboration is sufficient to show why stimulus–response theory has had to be modified to take account of selective attention, interpretation, response and recall. The model, in whatever form, is highly pragmatic, predicting, other things being equal, the occurrence of a response (verbal or behavioural act) according to the presence or absence of an appropriate stimulus (message). It presumes a more or less direct behavioural effect in line with the intention of the initiator and consistent with some overt stimulus to act in a certain way which is built into the message. In discussions of media effect, this has sometimes been referred to as the 'bullet' or 'hypodermic' theory, terms which far exaggerate the probability of effect and the vulnerability of the receiver to influence.

Much has been written of the inadequacy of such a theory, and DeFleur (1970) showed how this model was modified in the light of growing experience and research. First, account had to be taken of individual differences, since, even where expected reactions have been observed, their incidence varies according to difference of personality, attitude, intelligence, interest, etc. As DeFleur wrote: 'media messages contain particular stimulus attributes that have differential interaction with personality characteristics of audience members' (1970, p. 122). This is especially relevant, given the complexity of most media messages compared with the kind of stimulus used in most psychological experiments. Secondly, it became clear that response varies systematically according to social categories within which the receiver can be placed, thus according to age, occupation, lifestyle, gender, religion, etc. DeFleur notes that 'members of a particular category will select more or less the same communication content and will respond to it in roughly equal ways' (p. 123).

Mediating conditions

The revision of the stimulus–response model involved the identification of the conditions which mediated effects. McGuire (1973) indicated the main kinds of variable as having to do with source, content, channel, receivers and destination. There is reason to believe that messages stemming from an authoritative and credible source will be relatively more effective, as will those from sources that are attractive or close (similar) to the receiver. As to content, effectiveness is associated with repetition, consistency and lack of alternatives (monopoly situation). It is also more likely where the subject matter is unambiguous and concrete (Trenaman, 1967).

In general, effect as intended is also likely to be greater on topics which are distant from, or less important for, the receiver (lower degree of ego-involvement or prior commitment). Variables of style (such as personaliza-tion), types of appeal (such as emotional versus rational) and order and balance of argument have been found to play a part, but too variably to sustain any generalization. Channel (medium) factors have often been investigated, with mixed results, mainly because content and receiver factors dominate learning outcomes. It is also hard to discriminate between intrinsic channel differences and the differences between media in which channels are embedded (such as press versus television).

Generally, research has failed to establish clearly the relative value of different modes (audio, visual, etc.) in any consistent way, although the written or spoken verbal message seems to take primacy over pictorial images, according to measures of recall or comprehension (for example, Katz et al., 1977). As we have seen, a number of obvious receiver variables can be relevant to effect, but special notice should perhaps be given to variables of motivation, interest and level of prior knowledge. The degree of motivation or involvement has often been singled out as of particular importance in the influence process and in determining the sequence in which different kinds of effect occur (Krugman, 1965).

According to Ray (1973), the normal 'effect hierarchy' — as found, for instance, in the work of Hovland et al. (1949) — is a process leading from cognitive learning (the most common effect) to affective response (like or dislike, opinion, attitude) to 'conative' effect (behaviour or action). Ray argues, with some supporting evidence, that this model is normal only under conditions of high involvement (high interest and attention). With low involvement (common in many television viewing situations and especially with advertising) the sequence may go from cognition directly to behaviour, with affective adjustment occurring later to bring attitude into line with behaviour (reduction of dissonance — Festinger, 1957).

In itself, this formulation casts doubt on the logic and design of many persuasive communication campaigns which assume attitude to be an unambiguous correlate and predictor of behaviour. There is also a question mark against campaign evaluations based on measures of attitude change alone. The question of consistency between the three elements is also at issue. According to Chaffee and Roser (1986), high involvement is also likely to be a necessary condition for consistency of effects, and thus for a stable and enduring influence. Their preferred model of media effect involves a repetitive sequence from low involvement, through perception of dissonance and then to learning, with cumulative results. In this view, shallow and easily forgotten information can develop into a reasoned set of ideas and into action, especially under conditions of repeated exposure (as in a systematic campaign).

In any natural (non-laboratory) media situation, individual receivers will choose which stimulus to attend to or to avoid, will interpret its meaning variably and will react or not behaviourally, according to choice (Bauer, 1964). This seriously undermines the validity of the conditioning model, since the factors influencing selectivity are bound to be strongly related to the nature of the stimulus, working for or against the occurrence of an effect. Our attention should consequently be drawn away from the simple fact of experiencing a stimulus and towards the mediating conditions described above, especially in their totality and mutual interaction. This approach to the effect problem is more or less what Klapper (1960, p. 5) recommended and described as a 'phenomenistic' approach — one which sees 'media as influences working amid other influences in a total situation'.

Source–receiver relations and effect

As has been noted, trust in and respect for the source can be conducive to influence. There have been several attempts to develop theories of influence taking account of relationships between sender (or message sent) and receiver. Most of these theories refer to interpersonal relations. One framework has been suggested by French and Raven (1953), indicating five alternative forms of communication relationship in which social power may be exercised by a sender and influence accepted by a receiver. The underlying proposition is that influence through communication is a form of exercise of power which depends on certain assets or properties of the agent of influence (the communicator).

The first two types of power asset are classified as 'reward' and 'coercion' respectively. The former depends on there being gratification for the recipient from a message (enjoyment, for instance, or useful advice); the latter depends on some negative consequence of non-compliance (uncommon in mass communication). A third type is described as 'referent' power and refers to the attraction or prestige of the sender, such that the receiver identifies with the person and is willingly influenced, for affective reasons.

Fourthly, there is 'legitimate' power, according to which influence is accepted on the assumption that a sender has a strong claim to expect to be followed or respected. This is not very common in mass communication but may occur where authoritative messages are transmitted from political sources or other relevant institutional leaders. This type of power presumes an established relationship between source and receiver which predates and survives any particular instance of mass communication. Finally, there is 'expert power', which operates where superior knowledge is attributed to the source or sender by the receiver. This situation is not uncommon in the spheres of media news and advertising, where experts are often brought in for explanation, comment or endorsement. Examples of exploitation of all five types of media power can be found in advertising and informational campaigns, and more than one of these power sources is likely to be operative on any one given occasion.

A rather similar attempt to account for effects (especially on individual opinion) was made by Kelman (1961). He named three processes oi influence. One of these, 'compliance', refers to the acceptance of influence in expectation of some reward or to avoid punishment. Another, 'identification', occurs when an individual wishes to be more like the source and imitates or adopts behaviour accordingly (similar to 'referent' power). A third, 'internalization', describes influence which is guided by the receiver's own pre-existing needs and values. This last-named process may also be described as a 'functional' explanation of influence (or effect), since change is mainly explicable in terms of the receiver's own motives, needs and wishes.

Katz (1960) recommended this approach to explaining the influence of mass communication in preference to what he considered to have been dominant modes of explanation in the past. One of these he described as an 'irrational model' of humanity, which represents people as a prey to any form of powerful suggestion. An alternative view depends on a 'rational model', according to which people use their critical and reasoning faculty to arrive at opinions and acquire information. This would be consistent with a view of the individual as sovereign against propaganda and deception. Katz found both views mistaken and less likely than a 'functional' approach to account for communicative effect, thus giving most weight to the needs of receivers and to their motives for attending to communication. He argued that communication use helps individuals to achieve their objectives, maintain a consistent outlook and their self-esteem.

A model of behavioural effect

These developments of theory take one a good way from the simple conditioning model and help to account for some of the complexities encountered in research. It is obvious that in situations of unintended effect, some individuals will be more prone than others to react or respond to stimuli, 'more at risk' when harmful effects are involved. An elaboration of the basic stimulus–response model for the case of television viewing has been developed by Comstock et al. (1978) to help organize the results of research in this field, especially relating to violence. It rests on the presupposition that media experience is no different in essence from any other experience, act or observation which might have consequences for learning or behaviour.

The process depicted by the model, and shown in Figure 13.2, takes the form of a sequence following the initial act of 'exposure' to a form of behaviour on television ('TV act'). This is the first and main 'input' to learning or imitating the behaviour concerned. Other relevant inputs (enclosed within the box in Figure 13.2) are the degree of excitement and arousal ('TV arousal') and the degree to which alternative behaviours ('TV alternatives') are depicted: the more arousal and the fewer behaviours (or more repetition), the more likely learning is to take place. Two other conditions (inputs) have to do with the portrayal of consequences ('TV perceived consequences') and the degree of reality ('TV perceived reality'): the more that positive consequences seem to exceed negative ones and the more true to life the television behaviour, the more likely is learning ('P TV act') to take place. Where the conditions for effect are not met ($P=0$) the individual returns to the start of the process; where some probability of effect exists ($P>0$), the question of opportunity to act arises.

All the inputs mentioned affect the probability of learning the action (the effect), but ultimately any resulting behaviour is conditional on there being an opportunity to put the act into practice. Apart from opportunity, the most important condition is 'arousal', since without arousal (connoting also interest and attention) there will be no learning. While full confirmation of

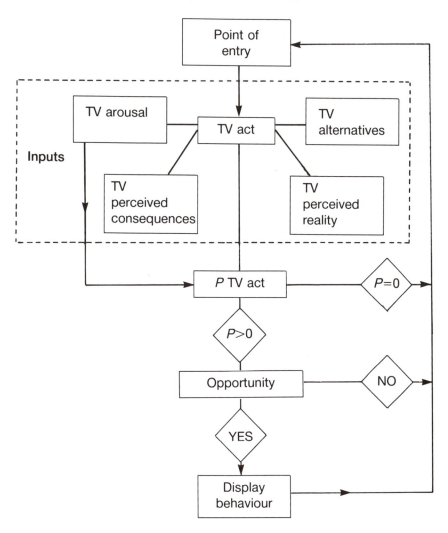

Figure 13.2 *A simplified version of Comstock et al.'s (1978) model of television effects on individual behaviour (from McQuail and Windahl, 1993): the effect process is a continuous sequence of repeated exposure to representations of behaviour ('TV acts'); effects depend on the way the behaviour is perceived, on inputs from the situation and on opportunities to act out and display the behaviour concerned*

this model from research is not yet available, it is an advance on the simple conditioning model and useful for directing attention to key aspects of any given case.

There is no need to summarize the field of study of media and violence, which underlies the process depicted, since it is periodically well reviewed (for example, Bryant and Zillman, 1986; Comstock, 1986). It is sufficient to note the following at this point: the balance of evidence supports the view that media *can* lead to violent behaviour and probably have done so; these effects occur mainly as a result of 'triggering' of aggressive acts, imitation, identification with aggressive heroes and 'desensitization', leading to a higher tolerance for real violence.

There are also substantial areas of dispute: about the extent to which media provide release from aggressive feelings rather than provoke aggressive acts; about the applicability of laboratory findings to natural settings; about the relative importance of fictional versus 'real-life' portrayal of violence; about whether media can work on their own; and about the overall significance of whatever contribution mass media actually make to the level of violence in society. It should be kept in mind that media can have 'pro-social' as well as anti-social effects and the basic processes of influence are likely to be the same.

Collective reaction effects

Three main kinds of effect are here in question: widespread panic in response to alarming, incomplete or misleading information; the amplification or spreading of crowd or mob activity; and the possible encouragement and aid given unintentionally to terrorists. The 'contagion effect' describes one important aspect of both. The first kind of effect is instanced by the much-cited reaction to the Orson Welles radio broadcast of *The War of the Worlds* in 1938, when simulated news bulletins reported a Martian invasion (Cantril et al., 1940). The second is exemplified by the hypothesized effect of the media in stimulating civil disorder in some US cities in the late 1960s. Thirdly, it is often said that media coverage is more useful to terrorists than to authorities and may also help to spread the incidence of terrorism.

Panic and rumour

In the case of the *War of the Worlds* broadcast there remains uncertainty about the real scale and character of the 'panic', but there is little doubt that in some circumstances conditions for a panic reaction to news do arise, given the increase in recent decades of civil terrorism and of the risk of a nuclear accident (Rosengren 1976; Nimmo and Combs, 1985). We are dealing here with a special case of rumour (see Shibutani, 1966), but the media contribute the element of reaching large numbers of separate people at the same moment with the same item of news (which may not be open to independent verification). The other related conditions for a panic response are anxiety, fear and uncertainty. Beyond this, precipitating features of panic seem to be incompleteness or inaccuracy of information, leading to the urgent search for information, usually through personal channels, thus giving further currency to the original message.

Civil disorder

Because of the potential threat to the established order, non-institutionalized and violent collective behaviour has been extensively studied, and the media have been implicated in the search for causes of such behaviour. It has been suggested that the media, variously, can provoke a riot, create a culture of rioting, provide lessons on 'how to riot' and spread a disturbance from place to place. The evidence for or against these propositions is thin and fragmentary, although it seems to be acknowledged that personal contact plays a larger part than media in any riot situation. There is some evidence, even so, that the media can contribute by simply signalling the occurrence and location of a riot event (Singer, 1970), by publicizing incidents which are themselves causes of riot behaviour or by giving advance publicity to the likely occurrence of rioting. In general, it seems likely that the media do have a capacity to define the nature of events, and even if they are ultimately 'on the side' of established order they can unintentionally increase the degree of polarization in particular cases.

While the media have not been shown to be a primary or main cause of rioting (see, for example, Kerner et al., 1968; Tumber, 1982), they may influence the timing or form of riot behaviour. Spilerman (1976) lends some support to this and other hypotheses, on the basis of rather negative evidence. After failing, through extensive research, to find a satisfactory structural explanation of many urban riots in the United States (that is, explanations in terms of community conditions), he concluded that television and its network news structure were primarily responsible, especially by creating a 'black solidarity that would transcend the boundaries of community'.

In treating together the topic of panic and rioting, it is worth noting that the most canvassed solution to the dangers just signalled, the control or silencing of news (Paletz and Dunn, 1969), might itself entail a local panic through lack of any explanation for observable neighbourhood disturbances.

Media and terrorism

Much terrorist violence is either planned, threatened or carried out for political objectives by people seeking, however indirectly, to use the media, and giving rise to a complex interaction between the two. The main potential benefit for terrorists is either to gain attention for a cause or to arouse public fear and alarm, which will in turn bring pressure to bear on a government. Terrorism has been said to be stimulated by the 'oxygen of publicity'. Schmid and de Graaf (1982) have also argued that violence is often a means of access to mass communication and even a message in itself. The media are inevitably implicated in this process, communicating the 'message of terrorism' because of the weight they attach to reporting violence. There are numerous interacting possibilities for effects of media coverage on terrorism, including effects on terrorists themselves, on governments, on the public and on victims of terrorists. These potential effects can be portrayed as helping either terrorists or the authorities (Alali and Eke, 1991; Paletz and Schmidt, 1992).

Despite the salience of the issue, there is little research evidence of any effect beyond what is obvious. Schmid and de Graaf find evidence of strong beliefs by police and a moderate belief by media personnel that live coverage of terrorist acts does encourage terrorism. However, Picard (1991) has dismissed the seeming evidence for contagion as both pseudo-scientific and threatening to media freedom. At most, the arguments seem about evenly divided (Paletz and Schmid, 1992). More difficult to assess are the consequences of refusing such coverage.

Contagion and imitation

An example of possible contagion effects is the sequence of aircraft hijacking crimes in 1971–2, which showed clear signs of being modelled on news reports. Holden (1986) reported correlational evidence of a similar kind which seems to point to an influence from media publicity. There has been other empirical support for the theory that press reports can 'trigger' individual but widespread actions of a pathological kind. Phillips (1980) showed that suicides, motor vehicle fatalities and commercial and non-commercial plane fatalities had a tendency to increase following press publicity for suicides or murder-suicides. He was also (1982) able to link the portrayal of suicide in television fiction (statistically) to the real-life occurrence of suicide, although the findings have been challenged on methodological grounds (Hessler and Stipp, 1985). There seems, at least, some evidence to make a plausible case for an imitation or 'contagion' effect.

The campaign

Basic features

The defining characteristics of a campaign have already been indicated, but we should pay special attention to the fact that campaigns have typically dealt with well-institutionalized behaviour that is likely to be in line with established norms and values. The model in Figure 13.3 draws attention to key features of the process. First, the originator of the campaign is almost always a collectivity and not an individual — a political party, government,

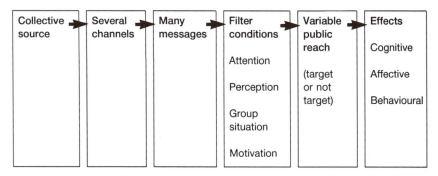

Figure 13.3 *The campaign influence process: effects (of different kinds) depend on a set of filter conditions and on the degree to which a (relevant) public is reached*

church, charity, pressure group, business firm, etc. The known position in society of the source will strongly affect its chances of success in a campaign.

Campaigns are also often concerned with directing, reinforcing and activating existing tendencies towards socially approved objectives like voting, buying goods, raising money for good causes or achieving better health and safety. The scope for novelty of effect or major change is thus often intrinsically limited, and the media are employed to assist other institutional forces. We know relatively little about such campaigns that exist to promote objectives that are controversial or ill defined (but experience is growing as a result of AIDS-related publicity).

A second point to bear in mind is that campaigns have to work ultimately through the individuals who receive and respond to messages, and thus many of the conditions of effect on individuals which have been described also apply to campaigns. However, the organized and large-scale character of campaigns makes it desirable to sketch a distinctive model of campaign influence, as in Figure 13.3. This embodies the normal condition that a campaign usually consists of many messages distributed through several media, with the chances of reach and effect varying according to the established nature of the channels and the message content. A third feature of many campaigns is that they aim to **redistribute** a limited amount of public attention, action or money (thus a zero-sum condition). This applies especially to advertising, but it is also true of politics and, in practice, to most fund-raising for charitable purposes (see Benthall, 1993).

Filter conditions

There is a set of 'filter conditions' or potential barriers which facilitate or hinder the flow of messages to the whole or chosen public. Several of these have already been discussed and they are to some extent predictable in their operation, although only in very broad terms. **Attention** is important because without it there can be no effect, and it will depend on the interest and relevance of content for the receivers, on their motives and predispositions and on channel-related factors. **Perception** matters because messages are open to alternative interpretations, and the success of a campaign depends to some extent on its message being interpreted in the same way as intended by the campaign source. Research has indicated the occurrence of 'boomerang' effects — for instance, in attempts to modify prejudice (for example, Cooper and Jahoda, 1947; Vidmar and Rokeach, 1974) — and it is a constant preoccupation of commercial and political campaigners to try to avoid counter-effects which will aid the 'opposition'. Unwanted side-effects also occur in campaigns to raise money for good causes. For instance, appeals on behalf of the Third World may also create an image of incompetence and inferiority of the region or peoples involved (Benthall, 1993).

Much has been written of the part played by the **group** in mediating the effects of campaigns (see page 350), and here we need note only that campaigns usually come from 'outside' the many groups to which people belong, according to age, life circumstances, work, neighbourhood, interest, religion, etc. Thus much of the history of media campaign research has been a struggle to come to terms with the fact that societies are not so conveniently 'atomized' and individuated as the first media campaigners expected. Group allegiance, or its absence, has consequences for whether messages are noticed and then accepted or rejected.

'Motivation' in the model (Figure 13.3) refers to the variable of type and degree of expected satisfaction on the part of the audience member which can influence either learning or attitude change. The revival of an interest in audience motives and in the 'uses and gratifications' approach more generally was influenced by the search for better prediction and explanation of effect processes (Blumler and McQuail, 1968). These 'filter conditions' together determine the composition of the public reached, and the success of a campaign is ultimately dependent on a reasonable 'fit' between composition of the planned 'target' public and the actual public reached.

Diversity of campaign effects

Finally, the entry in the model for 'effects' reminds us of the enormous diversity of possible effects, some of which will be intended and others not, some short-term and others long-term. Again, a successful or 'effective' campaign will depend on the match between planned effects and those achieved. The criteria for effectiveness have thus to be set by the sender, but evaluation should also take account of side-effects which have to be weighed in the overall balance. The model is a reminder of the complexity of campaigns and the ease with which they can go wrong. There is a very large literature on political campaigns (well reviewed in Kraus and Davis, 1976) and on other kinds of campaign (Rice and Paisley, 1981; Rice and Atkin, 1989).

There is no easy way of summarizing the results of campaign research, beyond remarking that some campaigns do seem to succeed (Mendelsohn, 1973) and others to fail (Hyman and Sheatsley, 1947), with partial failures and partial successes accounting for most cases in the research literature and probably in reality (Windahl et al., 1992). Rogers and Storey (1987, p. 831) conclude in relation to campaigns that the 'shifting conceptualization of communication effects and communication process has led to recognition that communication operates within a complex social, political and economic matrix and that communication could not be expected to generate effects all by itself'.

Reflections on the campaign

While success or failure can usually be accounted for in terms of the various conditions which have been named, a few extra remarks are in order. First, in many areas of social life, especially in politics and commerce, the campaign has become deeply institutionalized and has acquired something of a ritual character. The question that then arises is not whether campaigns produce this or that marginal advantage but whether it would be possible *not* to campaign (or to advertise) without disastrous results. Secondly, campaigners do not usually control the reality of a situation or reports about it, and circumstances may intervene to destroy or invalidate the message of a campaign. However, the greater the power to manipulate the reality (such as held by governments through policy-making or information giving), the more control there is over the outcome of a campaign.

Thirdly, most campaigns that have been studied take place under conditions of competition (counter-campaigning or with alternative courses argued). Rather too much of the theory that we have has been influenced by these circumstances, and we know relatively little about campaigning for objectives that are not contested, under conditions which make it difficult to avoid otherwise trusted media sources. These cases are more likely to occur outside 'the Western industrialized context and in closed regimes, and evidence about them could modify existing theory.

Ultimately, campaigns depend rather heavily on the relationship between sender and receiver, and there are several ways in which relations favourable to successful campaigning are forged. Several aspects have been discussed in the context of individual-level effects, but attention should be paid to the attractiveness, authority and credibility of media and sources. Especially important are moral or affective ties between audiences and media and audience belief in the objectivity and disinterest of sources.

Another dimension which should also be kept in mind is that campaigns can differ according to what Rogers and Storey (1987) call the 'locus of benefit', reminding us that some campaigns purport to be in the interests of the recipient (such as health and public information campaigns), while others are clearly on behalf of the sender (most commercial advertising). This does not necessarily give the former a decisive advantage, if they fail to meet other basic conditions of success (like reaching the intended target audience or choosing the right message), though it may endow them with advantages of receiver trust and goodwill.

There is a good deal more public knowledge available about public information campaigns than there is about advertising campaigns, although the latter are far more numerous. There is still not enough representative evidence to refute claims that the persuasive power of advertising is greatly overrated. The evidence of effectiveness is often indirect, coming mainly from the persistent behaviour of campaigners themselves.

Personal influence in campaign situations

In the study of mass media effects the concept of 'personal influence' has acquired such a high status that it has been referred to as an essential part of the 'dominant paradigm' (Gitlin, 1978). While the concept is relevant to any effect, it originated in the study of campaigns, and the circumstances of medium-term and deliberate attempts to persuade and inform are most conducive to the intervention of personal contacts as sources of influence. The underlying idea of personal influence is a simple one; its originators expressed it, in the course of their research into the 1940 US presidential election campaign (Lazarsfeld et al., 1944, p. 151), as follows: 'ideas often flow from radio and print to the opinion leaders and from them to the less active sections of the population'.

Thus two elements are involved: the notion of a population stratified according to interest and activity in relation to media and to the topics dealt with by mass media (in brief, 'opinion leaders' and 'others'); and the notion of a 'two-step flow' of influence rather than direct contact between 'stimulus' and 'respondent'. These ideas were further developed and elaborated by Katz and Lazarsfeld (1955). Since that time many students of campaigns have tried to incorporate the role of personal influence as a 'variable' in their research, and more sophisticated campaign managers have tried to apply the ideas for the more successful management of the commercial, political or social campaign purpose.

Not only has the 'personal influence' hypothesis had a strong effect on research and on campaigning itself, it has also played an important part in mass communication theory and even in media ideology. It has been invoked to explain the paucity of evidence of direct media effect and to counter the view, advanced first by mass society theorists and later by proponents of ideological determinism, that the media are powerful and rather inescapable shapers of knowledge, opinion and belief in modern societies. The 'ideological component' of personal influence theory lies in the supposition that individuals are 'protected' from manipulation by the strength of personal ties and by the group structure within which they acquire knowledge and form judgements. Much research and thought devoted to the question has gradually led to a lower degree of emphasis on the simple proposition as expressed above (for example, Okada, 1986).

While confirming the importance of conversation and personal contact as accompaniment to and perhaps modifier of media influence, research has not yet clearly shown that personal influence always acts as a strong independent or *counteractive* source of influence on the matters normally affected by mass media. Some of the evidence originally advanced by the proponents of the concept has also been re-examined, with differing conclusions (Gitlin, 1978). Secondly, it has become clear that the division between 'leaders' and 'followers' is variable from topic to topic; the roles are interchangeable, and there are many who cannot be classified as either one or the other (and may thus be outside the scope of group influence) (Robinson, 1976). Thirdly, it seems probable that what occurs is as likely to be a multi-step as a two-step flow.

It is clear that direct effects from the media can and do occur without 'intervention' from opinion leaders, and it is highly probable that personal influence is as likely to reinforce the effects of media as to counteract them. Despite these qualifications and comments on the personal influence thesis, there are circumstances where interpersonal influence can be stronger than the media: the overthrow of the Shah of Iran seems to provide a well-documented case in point (Teheranian, 1979).

Conclusion

If one goes back to the premise of media effects in the light of the theory and evidence discussed, the main message is that a simple assumption of effect from mass media is a sound one, but that the direction, degree, durability and predictability of effect are all uncertain and have to be established case by case, with only limited possibilities for generalization.

14

LONGER-TERM AND INDIRECT CHANGE

Diffusion in a development context

This chapter begins with a consideration of longer-term effects of mass media which are deliberately planned. In fact, relevant examples are hard to come by. The main case is that of communication in the field of (mainly Third World) economic and social development, where the media are consciously applied to promote long-term change. Most evidence relates to the many attempts since the Second World War to harness mass media to campaigns for technical advance or for health and educational purposes in developing countries, often following models developed in the rural United States (Katz et al., 1963). Although early theory of media and development (for example, Lerner, 1958) portrayed the influence of media as 'modernizing' simply by virtue of promoting Western ideas and appetites, the mainstream view of media effect has been as a mass educator in alliance with officials, experts and local leaders, applied to specific objectives of change.

A principal chronicler of this tradition has been Everett Rogers (1962; Rogers and Shoemaker, 1973), whose model of information diffusion envisaged four stages: information, persuasion, decision or adoption, and confirmation. This sequence is close to McGuire's (1973) stages of persuasion (see page 338). However, the role of the media is concentrated on the first (information and awareness) stage, after which personal contacts, organized expertise and advice, and actual experience take over in the adoption process. The early diffusionist school tended to emphasize organization and planning, linearity of effect, hierarchy (of status and expertise), social structure (thus also personal experience), reinforcement and feedback. Rogers (1976) has himself signalled the 'passing' of this 'dominant paradigm', its weakness lying in these same characteristics and its over-reliance on 'manipulation' from above.

Rogers and Kincaid (1981) have put forward an alternative 'convergence model' of communication which emphasizes the need for a continual process of interpretation and response, leading to an increased degree of mutual understanding between sender and receiver (see also Rogers, 1986). Newer theories of development allot to mass media a more limited role, with success depending on their remaining close to the base of the society and to its native culture. It is worth noting that mass communication is itself an innovation which has to be diffused before it can play a part in diffusion processes of the kind familiar in modern or developed societies (DeFleur, 1970; Rogers, 1986). For media to be effective, other conditions of modernity may also have to be present — such as individuation, trust in bureaucracies and in technology, and understanding of the basis of media authority, legitimacy and objectivity.

The distribution of knowledge

As we enter a new area of our media effect typology (see Figure 13.1) we have to deal with a set of topics and concepts which are difficult to locate in terms of the two main variables of time scale of effect and intentionality, especially the second. The topics are, however, united by a concern with **cognition**: each has to do with information or knowledge in the conventional sense. One has to do with a major media activity, news provision. Another deals with differential attention to issues and objects in the world: 'agenda-setting'. A third covers the general distribution of opinion and information in society, potentially leading to the variable distribution of knowledge.

These different kinds of media effect are included under the rather neutral label 'distribution of knowledge', since the media do actually distribute information and the result can be expressed as a distribution in the statistical sense. The kinds of effect dealt with here cannot be accommodated within any of the models so far presented, but various models have been developed to explain the processes at work (see McQuail and Windahl, 1993).

News diffusion and learning from news

The diffusion of news in the sense of its take-up and incorporation into what people 'know' is mainly a short- or medium-term matter but with long-term and often systematic consequences. It is also open to alternative formulations as to purpose: the media do intend in general that their audiences will learn about events, but they do not normally try to *teach* people what is in the news. The question of how much people understand and remember from the news has only slowly come to receive much systematic attention. Most research has so far concentrated on 'diffusion' — the spread of news as measured by the capacity to recall certain named events.

Four main variables have been at the centre of attention here: the extent to which people (in a given population) know about a given event; the relative importance or salience of the event concerned; the volume of information about it which is transmitted; and the extent to which knowledge of an event comes first from news media (and sometimes which particular medium) or from personal contact. The possible interactions between these four are complex, but one model of the interaction is expressed by the J-curved relationship between the proportion who are aware of an event and the proportion who heard of the same event from an interpersonal source (Greenberg, 1964).

Patterns of diffusion

The J-shape expresses the following findings: when an event is known about by virtually everyone (such as the assassination of J.F. Kennedy in 1963), a very high proportion (over 50 per cent) will have been told by a personal contact (associated conditions here being high event salience and rapid diffusion). When events are known by decreasing proportions of the population, the *percentage* of personal contact origination falls and that of media source rises (associated conditions are lower salience and slower diffusion rates). However, there is a category of events which is known about ultimately by rather small proportions of a whole population. These comprise minorities for whom the event or topic is highly salient, and the proportion of knowledge from personal contact rises again in relation to media sources, because personal contact networks are activated in these circumstances.

The pattern of news information diffusion has been shown to take a variety of forms which deviate from the 'normal' S-curve of diffusion (a slow start, then an acceleration, then a flattening as the upper limit is reached). The J-curve, just described, is one important variant type. Chaffee (1977) has suggested three alternative patterns which are sometimes found: cases of incomplete diffusion, of very rapid early acceleration and of unduly slow acceleration. We should look for different explanations in terms of either 'content-specific' factors or source variables or receiver variables, often working in combination.

Theory about news diffusion is still held back by the bias of research towards a certain class of events, especially towards 'hard news', which has a high measure of unexpectedness (Rosengren, 1973, 1987). In order to have a fuller picture of processes of news diffusion we would need more evidence about 'soft news' and more about routine or anticipated events. We are also limited by the difficulty of estimating event importance independently of the amount of attention given by the media, bearing in mind the varying interests of different sectors of the society.

Learning and comprehension

News learning research (both advanced and reviewed by Robinson and Levy, 1986) has been increasing, especially in respect of television and with particular reference to possible lessons for the improvement of the information capacity of news (for example, Findahl and Hoijer, 1981, 1985; Robinson and Levy, 1986; Woodall, 1986; Gunter, 1987; Davis and Robinson, 1989; Robinson and Davis, 1990; Newhagen and Reeves, 1992). The results so far have tended to confirm the outcome of much basic communication research of decades past (Trenaman, 1967), that story interest, relevance and concreteness aid comprehension and that both prior knowledge and the habit of discussion of news topics with others are still important, in addition to favourable educational background. Robinson and Levy consider television to be overrated as a source of knowledge of public affairs, and also that several common news production and presentation practices often work against adequate comprehension of news by audiences (see also Gunter, 1987; Davis and Robinson, 1989; Newhagen and Reeves, 1992).

A promising approach to the study of news comprehension and learning has been built on other media research into content and audiences. News content research has shown that much news is presented within frameworks of meaning which derive from the way news is gathered and processed. News is topically and thematically 'framed' for easier understanding, and it is reasonable to suppose that audiences employ some of the same frames in *their* processing of incoming news. Gurevitch and Levy (1986, p. 132) described the frames of interpretation brought by viewers to television news as 'metamessages', 'latent meanings that are embedded in audience decodings', which help to link individual sense-making to larger stories. They assume that audiences, much as journalists, have 'tacit theories' to frame their understanding of events in the world and to help in their processing of information.

Graber (1984) has developed this line of thinking to explore news processing. The **interpretative frames** or **schemas** (the idea derives from Irving Goffman) provide guides to selection, relevance and cognition and are collectively constructed and often widely shared. Graber (1984, p. 23) defines a schema as a 'cognitive structure consisting of organized knowledge about situations and individuals that has been abstracted from prior experiences. It is used for processing new information and retrieving stored information.' Schemas help in evaluating information and filling gaps when information is missing or ambiguous.

The broadest and most enduring frames may have an international currency (for instance, 'the Cold War', 'international terrorism' or 'threat to world environment'), but others may be local and specific. Graber found the actual 'schemata in people's minds' were very diverse, fragmentary and poorly organized. The ways in which schemas were used in responding to news information were also varied, with several different strategies being observed. Despite the provisional evidence and the plausibility of this approach, Woodall (1986) has warned against relying too much on it. What happens between the 'framing' of content by journalists and the appearance of similarly 'framed' information in audiences still remains something of a mystery.

Agenda-setting

The term 'agenda-setting' was coined by McCombs and Shaw (1972, 1993) to describe in more general terms a phenomenon that had long been noticed and studied in the context of election campaigns.

Lazarsfeld et al. (1944) referred to it as the power to 'structure issues'. An example would be a situation in which politicians seek to convince voters as to what, from their party standpoint, are the most important issues. This is an essential part of advocacy and attempts at influencing public opinion. As a hypothesis, it seems to have escaped the general conclusion that persuasive campaigns have small or no effects. As Trenaman and McQuail pointed out, 'The evidence strongly suggests that people *think about* what they are told . . . but at no level do they think *what* they are told' (1961, p. 178; emphasis added). The evidence collected at that time and since consists of data showing a correspondence between the order of importance given in the media to 'issues' and the order of significance attached to the same issues by the public and politicians.

This is the essence of the agenda-setting hypothesis, but such evidence is insufficient to show a causal connection between the various issue 'agendas'. For that we need a combination of content analysis of party programmes, evidence of opinion change over time in a given section of the public (preferably with panel data), content analysis showing media attention to different issues in the relevant period, and some indication of relevant media use by the public concerned. Such data have rarely, if ever, been produced at the same time in support of the hypothesis of agenda-setting, and the further one moves from the general notion that media direct attention and shape cognitions and towards examining actual cases, the more uncertain it becomes whether such an effect actually occurs.

Davis and Robinson (1986) have also criticized past agenda-setting research for neglecting possible effects on what people think concerning: *who* is important, *where* important things happen, and *why* things are important. According to Rogers and Dearing (1987), we need to distinguish clearly between three different agendas: the priorities of the media, those of the public and those of policy. These interact in complex ways and in different directions. The same authors note also that media vary in their credibility, that personal experience and the media picture may diverge, and that the public may not share the same values about news events as the media. In addition, 'real world events' may intervene in unexpected ways to upset previous agendas (Iyengar and Kinder, 1987). Reese (1991) has pointed out that much depends on the relative balance of power between media and sources, a factor which varies considerably from case to case. Each of these comments introduces new sources of variation.

Most evidence (for example, Behr and Iyengar, 1985) is inconclusive, and assessments (among them by Kraus and Davis, 1976; Becker, 1982; Reese, 1991; Rogers et al., 1993) tend to leave agenda-setting with the status of a plausible but unproven idea. The doubts stem not only from the strict methodological demands, but also from theoretical ambiguities. The hypothesis presupposes a process of influence, from the priorities of political or other interest groups to the news priorities of media, in which news values and audience interests play a strong part, and from there to the opinions of the public. There are certainly alternative models of this relationship, of which the main one would reverse the flow and state that underlying concerns of the public will shape both issue definition by political elites and that by the media, a process which is fundamental to political theory and to the logic of free media. It is likely that the media do contribute to a *convergence of the three 'agendas'*, but that is a different matter from setting any particular one of them.

The agenda-setting hypothesis

- Public debate is represented by salient issues (an agenda for action)
- The agenda derives from a combination of public opinion and political choice
- Mass media news and information reflect the content and order of priority of issues
- This representation of issues in the mass media exerts an independent effect on issue content and on relative salience in public opinion

---

Knowledge gaps

It has long been assumed that the press and broadcasting have added so greatly to the flow of public information that they will have helped to modify differences of knowledge resulting from inequalities of education and social position (Gaziano, 1983). There is some evidence from political campaign studies to show that such 'information gap-closing' between social groups can occur in the short term (for example, Blumler and McQuail, 1968). However, there has also been evidence of the reverse effect, showing that an attentive minority gains much more information than the rest, thus widening the gap between certain sectors of the public.

Tichenor et al. (1970) wrote of the 'knowledge gap hypothesis' that it 'does not hold that lower status population segments remain completely uninformed (or that the poorer in knowledge get poorer in an absolute sense). Instead the proposition is that growth of knowledge is relatively greater among the higher status segments.' There is certainly a class bias in attention to 'information-rich' sources, and strong correlations are persistently found between social class, attention to these sources and being able to answer information questions on political, social or economic matters.

There are two main aspects to the knowledge gap hypothesis, one concerning the general distribution of aggregate information in society between social classes, the other relating to specific subjects or topics on which some are better informed than others. As to the first 'gap', it is likely to have roots in fundamental social inequalities which the media alone cannot modify. As to the second, there are many possibilities for opening and closing gaps and it is likely that the media do close some and open others. A number of factors can be named as relevant to the direction of media effect. Donohue et al. (1975) put special emphasis on the fact that media operate to close gaps on issues which are of wide concern to small communities, especially under conditions of conflict, which promote attention and learning.

Nowak (1977) paid particular attention to the links between information gaps and divisions of social and economic power, focusing on practical solutions which would be helpful to specific groups with identifiable 'information needs'. He developed the concept of 'communication potential' to refer to the various resources which help people to achieve goals through communication activity. Useful in Nowak's contribution is the emphasis not only on form, presentation and manner of distribution in the 'gap-closing' enterprise but also on the kind of information involved, since not all information is equally useful to all groups.

In general, motivation and perceived utility influence information seeking and learning, and these factors come more from the social context than from the media. It has, however, been argued that different media may work in different ways and that print media are more likely to lead to a widening of gaps than is television (Robinson, 1972), because these are the favoured sources for the favoured classes. The suggestion that television can have a reverse effect (benefiting the less privileged) is based on the fact that it tends to reach a higher proportion of a given population with much the same news and information and is widely regarded as trustworthy. However, much depends on the institutional forms adopted in a given society.

Public broadcasting arrangements in Western Europe and, to a lesser extent, the national network system in the USA used to ensure (in part due to their *de facto* oligopoly) that television would provide a popular and homogeneous source of shared information about national and international concerns. Under more recent trends towards channel multiplication, a greater competition and audience fragmentation, the homogeneous audience for information is disappearing. Television is becoming a more differentiated source of information more akin to print media. The differential diffusion of new computer-based information technology also works towards increasing the division between the information-rich and the information-poor. Knowledge gap theory would indicate a widening of the gaps as a result, since people who are already information-rich, with higher information skills and more resources, would move even further ahead of informationally poorer strata. Robinson and Levy's (1986) evidence concerning news learning does not increase confidence in the capacity of television to close knowledge gaps.

Long-term unplanned change: a model

We enter an area where there is much theory and speculation but little firm evidence of confirmed relationships between the mass media and matters of values, beliefs, opinions and social attitudes. The reasons for this uncertainty are familiar: the phenomena at issue are too wide-ranging and complex to investigate reliably or fully; they call for broad historical and ideological judgements; and the flow of influence between media and social events is often reciprocal. Where evidence exists, it does little more than to illustrate and add to the plausibility of a given theory, and it may be unrealistic ever to expect more. Nevertheless, we are dealing with one of the most interesting and important aspects of the working of mass communication and can at least try to develop an intelligent way of talking about what might happen.

Each of the effect processes to be discussed can occur without planning or organization. Yet these same processes are central to social change, to normative and ideological control and to the construction and maintenance of public belief systems, climates of opinion, value patterns and forms of collective awareness as posited by many social theorists. It is hard to conceive of a society without such processes, however difficult they are to specify and quantify. More important than the question of intention (which cannot be resolved) is that of direction. Do particular processes favour conservation or change and, in either eventuality, in whose interest? Without some consideration of this question, however provisional and beyond the scope of 'media theory' alone to answer, the examination of media effects would be incomplete.

The model shown in Figure 14.1 indicates some key aspects of various types of unplanned and long-term effects which have been attributed to mass media, irrespective of purpose or direction. First, the processes at issue all presume some pattern and consistency over time in media output. Secondly, they presuppose some initial learning effects of the kind already discussed. Thus the media provide materials for recognizing and interpreting reality beyond what is available from personal experience. What is termed in

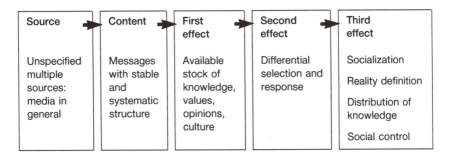

Figure 14.1   *The process of long-term unplanned media influence*

the model the 'second effect' refers to the encounter between media content and people in audiences. Here the set of 'filter conditions' signalled in the case of the campaign (Figure 13.3) operate in much the same way, but especially those which have to do with social group and cultural environment. Beyond this, the processes listed as 'third effect' need to be discussed separately. The question of 'distribution of knowledge' has already been dealt with. The main processes of long-term change relate to: socialization, the formation of opinion climates, the structuring of perceptions of reality, cultivation and acculturation, and social control and consciousness forming.

Socialization

That the media play a part in the early socialization of children and the long-term socialization of adults is widely believed, although in the nature of the case it is difficult to prove. This is partly just because it is such a long-term process and partly because any effect from media interacts with other social background influences and variable modes of socialization within families (Hedinsson, 1981). Rare longitudinal studies of development have sometimes produced strong prima facie evidence of socialization from media (for example, Rosengren and Windahl, 1989). Nevertheless, certain basic assumptions about the potential socialization effects from media are often built into policies for control of the media, decisions by media themselves and the norms and expectations which parents apply or hold in relation to the media use of their own children. The thesis of media socialization has, in fact, two sides to it: on the one hand, the media can reinforce and support other agencies of socialization; on the other, they are also viewed as a potential threat to the values set by parents, educators and other agents of social control.

The main logic underlying the socialization thesis is that the media can teach norms and values by way of symbolic reward and punishment for different kinds of behaviour as represented in the media. An alternative view is that it is a learning process whereby we all learn how to behave in certain situations and learn the expectations which go with a given role or status in society. Thus the media are continually offering pictures of life and models of behaviour in advance of actual experience.

Studies of children's use of media (for example, Wolfe and Fiske, 1949; Himmelweit et al., 1958; Noble, 1975; Brown, 1976) confirm a tendency for children to find lessons about life and to connect these with their own experience. Studies of content also draw attention to the systematic presentation of images of social life which could strongly shape children's expectations and aspirations (for example, DeFleur, 1964; Tuchman et al., 1978). These studies focus especially on occupation and gender roles, but there is also an extensive literature on political socialization (for example, Dawson and Prewitt, 1969; Dennis, 1973).

McCron (1976) pointed to a basic divergence of theory, one strand emphasizing the consensual nature of social norms and values and another viewing media along with other agencies of social control as tending to impose on subordinate groups the values of dominant classes. The latter perspective emphasizes the central conflicts of society and the possibility of change through resistance and renegotiation of meanings. In this view, the media are neither 'pro-social' nor 'antisocial' but tend to favour the values of an established order. In whichever formulation, the general proposition that media have a socialization effect is clear, but it is only indirectly founded on empirical evidence.

Reality defining and constructing

That media offer many representations of the reality of society has already been argued, and some aspects of the nature of this 'reality' have been discussed. The process of 'agenda-setting' is one way in which a frame of reference for viewing the world is constructed. If the media can convey an impression about priorities and direct attention selectively among issues and problems they can do much more. The step from such a ranking process to wider opinion-forming is not a large one, and the theory of media socialization assumes that lessons about reality are taught and learned. The basic process at work may be described by the general term 'defining the situation', and its importance rests on the familiar sociological dictum of W.I. Thomas that 'if men define situations as real they are real in their consequences'. Another general term for the same process is the 'creation of a symbolic environment' (Lang and Lang, 1981).

The spiral of silence: the formation of climates of opinion

The concept of the 'spiral of silence' derives from a larger body of theory of public opinion which was developed and tested by Noelle-Neumann over a number of years (Noelle-Neumann, 1974, 1984, 1991). The relevant theory concerns the interplay between four elements: mass media; interpersonal communication and social relations; individual expressions of opinion; and the perceptions which individuals have of the surrounding 'climate of opinion' in their own social environment. The main assumptions of the theory (Noelle-Neumann, 1991) are as follows:

- Society threatens deviant individuals with isolation.
- Individuals experience fear of isolation continuously.
- This fear of isolation causes individuals to try to assess the climate of opinion at all times.
- The results of this estimate affect their behaviour in public, especially their willingness or not to express opinions openly.

In brief, the theory proposes that, in order to avoid isolation on important public issues (like political party support), many people are guided by what they think to be the dominant or declining opinions in their environment. People tend to conceal their views if they feel they are in a minority and are more willing to express them if they think they are dominant. The result is that those views which are perceived to be dominant gain even more ground and alternatives retreat still further. This is the *spiralling* effect referred to.

In the present context, the main point is that the mass media are the most readily accessible source for assessing the prevailing climate, and if a certain view predominates in the media it will tend to be magnified in the subsequent stages of personal opinion formation and expression. The theory was first formulated and tested to explain puzzling findings in German politics where opinion poll findings were inconsistent with other data concerning expectations of who would win an election and signally failed to predict the result. The explanation offered was that the media were offering a misleading view of the opinion consensus. They were said to be leaning in a leftist direction, against the underlying opinion of the (silent) majority.

A somewhat similar view of opinion shaping by the US media in the 1970s, although with a politically different tendency, is offered by Paletz and Entman (1981), who reported the propagation by the mass media of a 'conservative myth' — the conventional journalistic wisdom that the USA had turned sharply away from the radicalism of the 1960s. As they showed, however, there was no support for this interpretation from opinion polls taken over the period in question, thus failing to uphold the 'spiral of silence' thesis.

Two Swedish studies reported in Rosengren (1981a) compared trends both in newspaper editorial opinion and in public opinion. One of these, by Rikardsson (1981), showed a very close relationship between Swedish public opinion on the Middle East issue and that of the Swedish press, both of them deviating from 'world opinion' as measured by opinion polls in several other nations. There was no time lag, however, on which to base a conclusion about the direction of effect. Another study, by Carlsson et al. (1981), on the relationship over time between party support, economic conditions and editorial direction of the press, concluded that political opinions are probably moulded first by economic conditions and second by media content. However, their data tended to support the standpoint of Noelle-Neumann and other proponents of 'powerful mass media'. A more recent and different test of the theory concerned the issue of nuclear energy. Noelle-Neumann (1991) found evidence of increasing press attention to the issue, accompanied by a steady increase in negative reporting. Over time, public support for nuclear energy also declined markedly, and the timing and sequence of changes suggested an interactive spiralling effect as predicted in the theory.

The spiral of silence theory is a close neighbour to mass society theory and involves a similar, somewhat pessimistic, view of the quality of social relations (Taylor, 1982). According to Katz (1983), its validity will depend on the extent to which alternative reference groups are still alive and well in social life. The more that is the case, the less scope there is for the process described to operate, since there will be support for minority or deviant views. Moscovici (1991) also suggests that, in general, we should pay less attention in public opinion formation to silent majorities and more to 'loud minorities', which often play a larger part in opinion change.

Structuring reality and unwitting bias

Common to much theory in this area is the view that long-term media effects occur unintentionally, as a result of organizational tendencies, occupational practices, technical limitations and the systematic application of certain news values, frames and formats. Thus, as noted above, Paletz and Entman (1981) attributed the propagation of a 'conservative myth' by US media during the 1970s mainly to 'pack journalism', the tendency of journalists to work together, arrive at a consensus, cover the same stories and use the same news sources. It is probable that during the Gulf Crisis of 1990–1 the tendency of most Western media to frame the news in a way which was both consensual and supportive of the United Nations coalition (see *Nordicom Review*, 1992) was in some degree the result of successful news management which capitalized on the news media's own routine needs and practices.

The notion that media 'structure reality' in a way which is often guided by their own needs and interests has been demonstrated. An early example was the study by Lang and Lang (1953) of the television coverage of the return of General McArthur from Korea after his recall, which showed how a relatively small-scale and muted occasion was turned (in its reporting) into something approaching a mass demonstration of welcome and support by the selective attention of cameras and commentary to points of most activity and interest. The reportage was seeking to reproduce from rather unsatisfactory materials a suitable version of what had been predicted as a major occasion.

The media coverage of a large demonstration in London against the Vietnam War in 1968 followed much the same pattern (Halloran et al., 1970). The coverage was planned for an event pre-defined (largely by the media themselves) as potentially violent and dramatic, and the actual coverage strained to match this pre-definition, despite the scarcity of suitable reality material. The same research supported the conclusion that audiences perceived the event more in line with its framing on television than as it actually transpired.

Evidence of an actual effect on how people define reality is not easy to find. However, in their study of how children came to define the 'problem' of race and immigration Hartman and Husband (1974) showed that dominant media definitions were picked up, especially where personal experience was lacking. A different kind of effect was documented by Gitlin (1980) in relation to media coverage of the US radical student movement in the late 1960s. Here the media played a major part in shaping the image of this movement for the North American public, partly according to their own needs (such as needs for dramatic action, celebrities, personalities and conflict), and caused the student movement itself to respond to this image and adapt and develop accordingly. A more recent study of the definition by the media of the women's movement in the Netherlands in its early days (van Zoonen, 1992) provides another example of a similar process at work. These cases show a hidden dimension of media bias which stems from real-life adaptation to the logic of the media (Altheide and Snow, 1991).

Most of the effects referred to here derive from 'unwitting bias' in the media, but the potential to define reality is often exploited knowingly. The term 'pseudo-events' has been used to refer to a category of event more or less manufactured to gain attention or create a particular impression (Boorstin, 1961; McGinnis, 1969). The staging of pseudo-events is now a familiar tactic in many election (and other) campaigns, but more significant is the possibility that a high percentage of media coverage of 'actuality' really consists of planned events which are intended to shape impressions in favour of one interest or another. Those most able to manipulate actuality coverage are those with most power; so the bias, if it exists, may be unwitting on the part of the media but is certainly not so for those trying to shape their own 'image'.

Cultivation

Among theories of long-term media effect, the cultivation hypothesis of Gerbner (1973) remains probably the best documented and most investigated (see Signorielli and Morgan, 1990). It holds that television, among modern media, has acquired such a central place in daily life that it dominates our 'symbolic environment', substituting its (distorted) message about reality for personal experience and other means of knowing about the world. Television is also described as the 'cultural arm of the established industrial order [which] serves primarily to maintain, stabilize and reinforce rather than to alter, threaten or weaken conventional beliefs and behaviours' (Gross, 1977, p. 180). This statement brings the cultivation effect very close to that posited by the critical theorists of the Frankfurt School and not far from later Marxist analysis. According to Signorielli and Morgan (1990), 'Cultivation analysis is the third component of a research paradigm called 'Cultural Indicators' that investigates (1) the institutional processes underlying the production of media content, (2) images in media content, and (3) relationships between exposure to television's message and audience beliefs and behaviors' (p. 15).

The theory

The central hypothesis of the research was that viewing television gradually leads to the adoption of beliefs about the nature of the social world which conform to the stereotyped, distorted and very selective view of reality as portrayed in a systematic way in television fiction and news. Cultivation is said to differ from a direct stimulus–response effect process mainly because of its gradual and cumulative character. It involves, first, learning and, secondly, the construction of a view of social reality dependent on personal circumstances and experience (such as of poverty, race or gender) and also on reference-group membership. It is also seen as an interactive process between messages and audiences.

In this theory of media effect, television provides many people with a consistent and near-total symbolic environment which supplies norms for conduct and beliefs about a wide range of real-life situations. It is not a window on or a reflection of the world but a world in itself. The resulting research has two main thrusts — one directed to testing the assumption about the consistency (and distortion) of the television 'message system', the other designed to test, by way of survey analysis, a variety of public beliefs about social reality, especially ones which can be tested against empirical indicators. The core of the ensuing analysis is the comparison between beliefs about reality and actual reality, taking account of varying degrees of habitual exposure to television. There is some basic similarity to the ideas underlying the 'agenda-setting' hypothesis (see page 356).

Testing the theory

Those who watch increasing amounts of television are predicted to show increasing divergence of perceptions of reality away from the known picture of the social world and towards the 'television' picture of the world. A major focus of the research has always been on questions concerning violence and crime, with cultivation research paying attention to its television portrayal, its actual incidence and differential risks, on the one hand, and to public awareness of and attitudes towards crime, on the other. Other topics of political and social concern have also been studied.

In an extensive review of numerous studies of the television construction of reality, Hawkins and Pingree (1983) found many scattered indications of the expected relationships, but no conclusive proof of the *direction* of the relationship between television viewing and ideas about social reality. They say that 'television *can* teach about social reality and that the relationship between viewing and social reality may be reciprocal: Television viewing causes a social reality to be constructed in a certain way, but this construction of social reality may also direct viewing behavior.'

Doubts and questions

Research into the cultivation process has been somewhat limited by its assumptions about the contents of television and the nature of television viewing. The television experience is probably more differentiated and noncumulative than allowed for in the theory and may be becoming less so as production and supply increase (both in the USA and elsewhere). Developments of thinking concerning the active construction of meaning by individuals and the diminished power of the text (see Chapter 12) also undermine the assumption of the long-term cumulative effect of powerful 'message systems'.

Several authors have raised doubts about the interpretation of the television message (for example, Newcomb, 1978) and about the causal relationship posited between television use data and survey data concerning values and opinions (Hirsch, 1980, 1981; Hughes, 1980). There is also some reason to doubt whether the 'cultivation' effect would occur elsewhere than in the United States, partly because television content and use (as well as the 'real world') are often different. The limited evidence from other countries is not yet very confirmatory. In relation to images of a violent society, Wober (1978) found no support from British data, and Doob and McDonald (1979) reported similarly from Canada. A longitudinal study of Swedish children (Hedinsson, 1981, p. 188) concluded, however, that evidence amounted to, 'if not a direct support, at least a non-refutation of Gerbner's theory'.

However plausible the theory, it is almost impossible to deal convincingly with the complexity of posited relationships between symbolic structures, audience behaviour and audience views, given the many intervening variables. Despite all this, it appears that the line of enquiry represented by cultural indicators and cultivation research is not a spent force and can lend itself to more specified and nuanced enquiries on particular topics (Signorielli and Morgan, 1990).

Social control and consciousness formation

A number of media effects have already been discussed which might belong under this heading, since the idea of socialization includes an element of social control, and some, at least, of the reality-defining tendencies that have been discussed seem to work in favour of an established social order. However, it is difficult to determine when 'social control' is to be accounted as intended or unintended. Generally the answer depends on the theory of society which one chooses to adopt. If control effects are long-term but unintended, they are accounted as 'ideology' in the terms used by Golding (1981) (as discussed in Chapter 13). If they are planned effects they are what Golding calls 'policy', but they could also be called propaganda (on behalf of some third party or agent of influence outside the media).

There is a continuum of theoretical positions. One commonly held view is that the media act non-purposively to support the values dominant in a community or nation, through a mixture of personal and institutional choice, external pressure and anticipation of what a large and heterogeneous audience expects and wants. A stronger and more critical version of this position sees the media as essentially conservative because of a combination of market forces, operational requirements and established work practices. An extreme version of this position holds that the media are actively engaged on behalf of a ruling (and often media-owning) class or bourgeois state in suppressing or diverting opposition and constraining political and social deviance. This is essentially the Marxist view of media as an instrument for the legitimation of capitalism (Miliband, 1969; Westergaard, 1977).

These alternative theories vary in their precision, in their specification of the mechanisms by which control is exercised and in the attribution of conscious purpose and power to the media. However, they tend to draw on much the same kind of evidence, most of it relating to systematic tendencies in content with very little directly about effects. A hybrid critical theory of systematic long-term effect has been developed by Herman and Chomsky (1988) in the form of a 'propaganda model'. This says that news in capitalist countries has to be 'strained' through several 'filters', especially the financial integration of the media with the rest of the economy, advertising, news management campaigns, the dominant (anti-communist) ideology of the society and reliance on official sources of information. Herman and Chomsky found a good deal of circumstantial evidence of the last-named filter at work, as have other researchers.

Herman and Chomsky take the title of their book, *Manufacturing of Consent*, from Walter Lippman (1922), who wrote (p. 158) that the 'manufacture of consent is capable of great refinements . . . and the opportunities for manipulation open to anyone who understands the process are plain enough'. Lippman's views exemplify what was referred to above as the first phase (that of 'all-powerful media') in the evolution of thinking about the power of the media, and the weakness of the Herman and Chomsky position is that they take so little account of later thinking.

Consensus maintenance: selective attention and omission

A good deal of the content-based evidence for long-term social control effects has already been discussed. The content of media with the largest audiences does appear broadly supportive of reigning social norms and conventions (an aspect of socialization and of 'cultivation'). Fundamental challenges to the national state or its established institutions are hard to find in the mass media. The argument that mass media tend towards the confirmation of the status quo is thus based on evidence both about what is present and about what is missing in media content. The former includes the rewarding (in fiction) of 'conformist' or patriotic behaviour, the high degree of attention and privileged (often direct) access given to established elites and points of view, the often negative or unequal treatment of non-institutional or deviant behaviour, the devotion of media to a national or community consensus, and the tendency to show problems as soluble within the established 'rules' of society and culture. One outcome of 'cultivation' research is evidence of a link between dependence on television and the adoption of consensual or middle-of-the-road political views (Gerbner et al., 1984).

The evidence of media omission is, in the nature of things, harder to assemble. An early effort to explore selective inattention was made by Warren Breed (1958). On the basis of what he called a 'reverse content analysis' (comparing press content with sociological community studies), Breed concluded that US newspapers consistently omitted news which would offend the values of religion, family, community, business and patriotism. He concluded that 'power' and 'class' are protected by media performance. Comparative content analyses of news in several countries have added evidence of systematic omission in the attention given to certain issues and parts of the world.

Detailed studies of news content such as those by the Glasgow Media Group (1976, 1980, 1985) or by Golding and Elliott (1979) have documented some significant patterns of omission. More importantly, perhaps, they have shown a pattern of selection which is so consistent and predictable that a corresponding pattern of news rejection can be inferred. The view that media are systematically used for purposes of legitimation of the state in capitalist society has relied heavily on evidence of what is missing in the media. Stuart Hall (1977, p. 366), drawing on the work of both Poulantzas and Althusser, named those ideological processes in the media as 'masking and displacing', 'fragmentation' and 'imposition of imaginary unity or coherence'. The first is the failure to admit or report the facts of class exploitation and conflict. The second refers to the tendency to deny or ignore common working-class interests and to emphasize the plurality, disconnection and individuality of social life. The third refers to the taking-for-granted of a national consensus, common to all classes and people of goodwill and common sense.

The construction of conformity

An additional element in the theory of conservative ideological formation by the media lies in the observation that the media define certain kinds of behaviours and groups as both deviant from, and dangerous to, society. Apart from the obviously criminal, these include groups such as teenage gangs, drug-takers, 'football hooligans' and some sexual deviants. It has been argued that the media often demonstrably exaggerate the real danger and significance of such groups and their activities (Cohen and Young, 1973) and tend to create 'moral panics' (Cohen, 1972). The effect is to provide society with scapegoats and objects of indignation, to divert attention from real evils with causes lying in the institutions of society and to rally support for the agencies of law and order.

It has also been suggested that the media tend to widen the scope of their disapproval by associating together very different kinds of behaviour threatening to society. In the pattern of coverage of terrorism, rioting or political violence they help to provide a symbolic bridge between the clearly delinquent and those engaged in non-institutionalized forms of political behaviour like demonstrations or the spreading of strikes for political reasons. In some kinds of popular press treatment, according to Hall et al. (1978), it is hard to distinguish the criminal outsider from the political 'extremist'. Within the category of antisocial elements those who rely on state benefit payments may also come to be included under the label of 'welfare scroungers' (Golding and Middleton, 1982), and the same can happen to immigrants, refugees or travelling people. The process has been called 'blaming the victim' and is a familiar feature of collective opinion forming to which the media can make an important contribution.

Media power: who benefits?

It is almost impossible to give any useful assessment of the degree to which the effects posited by this body of theory and research actually occur. First, the evidence of content is incomplete, relating only to some media in some places and times. Secondly, it has not really been demonstrated that the media in any Western country offer a coherent ideology, even if there are significant elements of consistency in selection and omission. Thirdly, many of the processes, especially those of selective use and perception, by which people resist or ignore propaganda apply here as well as in campaign situations.

Nevertheless, it would be difficult to argue that the media are, on balance, a force for major change in society, or to deny that a large part of popular content is generally conformist in tendency. It is also difficult to avoid the conclusion that, in so far as media capture attention, occupy time and disseminate images of reality and of potential alternatives, they fail to provide favourable conditions for the formation of a consciousness and identity among the less advantaged sectors of society and for the organization of opposition, both of which have been found necessary in the past for radical social reform.

The media are mainly owned and controlled either by (often large) business interests or (however indirectly) by the state — thus by the interests which also have most political and economic power. Media concentration is probably still increasing as well as extending internationally, and it remains entirely plausible that owners will pursue their long-term interests, which includes the stability of the world market system, through their own media, even if in an indirect way. As one small example, Dreier (1982) concluded that the two main elite newspapers in the USA were also the most integrated into the capitalist system and most inclined to adopt a 'corporate-liberal' perspective — an attitude of 'responsible capitalism'. He regarded this level of control to be more significant for power than any tendency to bias selection at newsroom level.

There is a good deal of prima-facie evidence that such controlling power over the media is valued (by its possessors) beyond its immediate economic yield, especially for political and social influence and status. In any case, it is no secret that most media most of the time do not see it as their task to promote fundamental change in the social system. They work within the arrangements that exist, often sharing the consensual goal of gradual social improvement. Gans's judgement (1979, p. 68) that 'news is not so much conservative or liberal as it is reformist' probably applies very widely. The media are committed by their own self-defined task and their ideology to serve as a carrier for messages (for instance, about scandals, crises and social ills) which can be an impulse to change. They probably do stimulate much activity, agitation and anxiety which disturb the existing order, within the limits of systems which have some capacity for generating change. Ultimately, the questions involved turn on how dynamic societies are and on the division of social power within them, and these take us well beyond the scope of media-centred theory.

Effects on other social institutions

As the media have developed, they have, without doubt, achieved two things: diverted time and attention from other activities; and become a channel for reaching more people with more information than was available under 'pre-mass-media' conditions. These facts have implications for any social institution which needs to gain public attention and to communicate to the society at large. Other institutions are under pressure to adapt or respond in some way to the mass media, or to make their own use of mass media channels. In doing so, they are likely to change their own practices, especially by adapting to what has been called a 'media logic' (see page 265). According to Altheide and Snow (1991, p. ix), 'today all social institutions are media institutions'. Because the transition is usually gradual, occurring along with other kinds of change, the specific contribution of the mass media to institutional change cannot be accounted for with any certainty.

The case of politics provides fairly clear evidence of adaptation to the rise of mass media, especially to the fact that the media have become a (if not *the*) main source of information and opinion for the public (see Blumler, 1970; Seymour-Ure, 1974; Graber, 1976b; Paletz and Entman, 1981; Robinson and Levy, 1986). The challenge to politics from mass media institutions has taken several forms. The diversion of time from political activity to watching television may be one of these. More important is the diversion of attention away from politically committed and partisan sources of information and ideology and towards media sources, which are more neutral, less differentiated in political terms, more commercial and more entertainment-oriented. The mass media seem increasingly to 'set the agenda' and to define political problems on a continuous day-to-day basis but guided by a more objective and informational logic. Political parties and politicians increasingly have to react to this flow of information and also come to terms with a more consensual form of public opinion.

Ideas about the influence of 'media logic' on political institutions (see Mazzoleni, 1987) include the following: that personalities (leaders) have become relatively more important; that attention has been diverted from the local and regional to the national stage; that face-to-face political campaigning has declined; that opinion polls have gained in influence; that electorates have become more volatile (more inclined to change allegiance); that general news values have influenced the attention-gaining activities of political parties as they seek to gain media access; that internal party channels of communication have been attenuated; that media tend more to determine terms of access for politicians to the public; and that 'trial by media' is a fact of public life.

The triumph of media logic over political logic finds expression in the greater interest in personalities and elections as 'horse-races' than as occasions for learning about issues and policies (Graber, 1976b). There is little doubt that election campaigns have been widely transformed into skilfully and professionally managed events more akin to advertising, public relations and marketing than traditional politics. As always, it is hard to separate out the effects of media change from broad changes in society working both on the media and on political institutions, and there is much room for dispute about the real cause of any given institutional effect.

Event outcomes

The case for studying the role of the media in the outcome of significant societal events has been persuasively put by Lang and Lang (1981), and they applied their own advice by studying the Watergate affair and the downfall of President Nixon (Lang and Lang, 1983). Other researchers (Kraus et al., 1975) have also recommended the study of what they term 'critical events', mainly elections but also other occasions of significance for society. The mass media may rarely initiate change independently, but they do provide the channels, the means and an arena for the playing-out of events in which many actors and interests are involved, often in competition with each other. The primary object of influence may not be the general media public itself but other specific organized interest groups, elites, influential minorities, etc.

The media provide horizontal channels (especially between elites) as well as vertical channels for communicating in either direction. Influence flows from the top down, but politicians often treat the media as a source of intelligence about the mood of the country. Lang and Lang (1983) noted that the media 'present political actors with a "looking-glass image" of how they appear to outsiders'. What they call the 'bystander public' (referring to the general media public) provides a significant reference group for political actors, and it is often for the benefit of a bystander public that they frame many of their actions. This is a part of a process of 'coalition-building'.

The kind of event in which the media play an active and significant part, as it unfolds, is likely to be characterized by having a public and collective character, a historic significance and a long time scale in which media and key actors interact with each other. Major international crises often meet these criteria, and there is steady growth in interest in the part played by the media in such events as the fall of the Berlin Wall, the crises in the Gulf and former Yugoslavia and the many aid missions to Third World countries.

Many other events with a shorter time scale or more local relevance might benefit from a similar research perspective. Ideally, one needs to be able to identify the main actors and agents in the affair (as distinct from media and the general public), examine their motives and the means at their disposal, record their interactions and the sequence of events in which they take part, and assess how actors and events are reported in public. No conclusion is likely to be possible until an outcome is arrived at and has entered history. No unambiguous assessment of the precise contribution of mass media can be expected, but the task cannot be avoided if the effects of media in society are to be understood.

Media and cultural change

The theories discussed in Chapter 4 set out a number of possibilities for significant effects of mass media on long-term cultural change, and the same ground need not be covered again. Despite the plausibility of many of the ideas developed about the influence of mass media on culture, there is little firm evidence of the effects posited. It is almost tautological to pose the problem, since the media (in their definitions, their contents and the practices which surround them) are by now an integral part of the cultures of 'modern' societies. It might seem easier to investigate the cultural impact of Western media on developing countries, and it makes more sense to try, but this too poses almost insurmountable problems of conceptualization and research design. The problem presented for investigation is a very large example of a recurring situation in which meanings are constructed amid continuous interaction between the receiving culture and the transmitted messages of global media. We can try to speak of processes such as 'globalization', 'cultural synchronization' and 'homogenization', but what is really there and what causes what have first to be an object of good conceptualization and theorizing before sense can be made of data (Tomlinson, 1991).

Conclusion

The influence of mass media on long-term change can never be measured, because the processes at work are interactive and often open-ended. But much can be learned about the way the media become involved in social and cultural events and changes. The spread of media influence through a range of institutional processes, such as those of international politics, development and emergency aid, environmental control, business and markets, makes the work of enquiry, however inconclusive, of continued relevance. It also calls for a continual refocusing and updating of theory.

15
ENDPIECE: LINES OF DEVELOPMENT

Mass communication endures

There has been speculation for several years about the imminent demise of the mass media (for example, Maisel, 1973), mainly on the grounds that abundant new, 'narrowcast', small-scale, interactive media are likely to render them, by comparison, increasingly limited and inflexible. The genuinely new media have begun to develop quite strongly but have made little impact as yet on the *imperium* of the old media. It is early to be certain, but it seems at least likely that several of the characteristics of the mass media (some mentioned on page 37 of this book) are simply not substitutable. The technologies and forms may change, but only mass communication can meet the requirements of political, economic and social arrangements which are themselves relatively stable. National and international politics still requires the existence of effective publicity machines and disseminators of 'mass' information. Global economics still depends on the large-scale manipulation of demand and on large units of production, of both hardware and software. Social-cultural convergence on a global scale is not simply a consequence of the media, but it is a self-sustaining tendency which, in turn, supports mass media as a multinational industry.

To draw these conclusions is to presume that mass media as we know them are driven less by technology than by their organized users and ultimate masters. In any case, it states a strong claim for the continued relevance of the category 'mass communication' as an object of theorizing, without denying that there are new growth areas which are much more clearly the result of a genuine communications revolution. In these areas, other bodies of communication theory have to be developed, which may not directly relate to the field of mass communication as outlined in this book.

The future of theory

This is not a suitable place for a critical evaluation of what passes for theory in relation to mass communication. The corpus of work described in a summary way in this book is still very fragmentary and variable in quality. At best, it barely amounts to more than a posing of many questions plus some empirical generalization based on a set of fragmentary observations which are not fully representative. Included in our assemblage of theory is much that is speculative and also essentially normative — promoting value judgements rather than providing explanations or a basis for prediction. In this respect, even so, it is neither better nor worse than most of the behavioural sciences or sociology, except in terms of its relative youth and the sparcity of the research effort which has been made relative to the very large range of mass media activities.

The reasons for slow theoretical development are much the same as in other fields – especially the essentially intersubjective character of the practices and activities involved in mass communication, their multiplicity and variety and the constant changing of the social environment in which they take place. One of the features of mass communication theory — its normative character — may from a 'scientific' point of view seem a drawback, but it cannot be eliminated or bypassed, since it is an intrinsic feature of the media phenomenon.

Having conceded this much, there does also appear to have been some genuine cumulation of knowledge and progression of thinking about a phenomenon which has remained essentially the same over a long period. Theorizing as practised in the mainstream tradition of the social sciences remains the most practical path towards setting priorities for enquiry, directing research and helping to make some overall sense of many fragmentary and diverse findings. One of the signs of progress has been the increased degree of co-operation and mutual tolerance between adherents of different paradigms, especially that based on quantification and systematic measurement and that based on hermeneutic methods, interpretation, deep description and critical perspectives.

There can be no full reconciliation on this last point, since fundamental values are at stake, but there can be agreement to differ within a common framework. Where researchers can speak to and understand each other, there can also be complementary lines of enquiry on topics of agreed interest. The dispute between 'culturalists' and 'scientific-empiricists' has generated light as well as heat, and the same is true of the disagreements between radical-critical researchers and conservative functionalists. As Rosengren comments, in a phrase which compares the search for reconciliation between theoretical opposites to the pursuit of the mythical 'tulip rose':

> much as our hearts may ache for it, we shall never see the tulip rose. But roses and tulips may grow and blossom together, just as the individual researcher may alternate between phases of, say, particular observation and more stringent methods, and just as members of different schools and traditions may draw upon each other's work. (1989, p. 28)

In the nature of these things, however, the cessation of hostilities on one front may be a sign only of the sidelining of the conflict or the outbreak of hostilities elsewhere. In this particular case, the broader climate of social thought does seem to have changed in a way which has essentially damped the fires of radical-critical thought, and a new agenda is in the making. The references made to postmodern thinking give some clue to the way things are going. Most briefly, we seem to be entering an age of pronounced disbelief in which the certainties and the equivalent of moral imperatives of progressive rationalism are themselves being undermined or abandoned. This development is very relevant for a body of theory (about mass communication) which has generally had normative sub-themes, even when at its seemingly most empirical (such as in the study of media effects). In keeping with the spirit of postmodernism, the new theoretical battle lines are not clearly drawn, and friends and enemies have not yet found a consistent way to identify each other.

The multiple logics of mass communication

One of the achievements of theory is the identification of several different 'logics' according to which the process of mass communication is actually conducted and can be analysed by the detached observer. We have escaped, at least, from the assumption that there must be one dominant perspective or standpoint from which mass communication can be analysed (for instance, according to the 'power of the mass media' or the social integration/disintegration dimension). A logic here refers to a framework of meaning in which elements of a phenomenon are coherently related to each other and a consistent pattern of action and thinking can be identified. A logic in this sense indicates priorities and draws attention to what is significant. For the observer it is a guide to selective attention and also to interpretation. The main relevant 'logics' can be named and described as follows.

There is an **industrial logic** which places media phenomena within the broader framework of a larger media industry and institution. Production processes, content selections, audience formation and technological innovations can be made sense of in economic or broader institutional terms. The key to the logic is what makes sense in the given media market circumstances and in the wider political-economic context.

An **organizational logic** operates on some of the same questions of production and selection, but within much more circumscribed limits and according to different goals. The key to this particular logic is the smooth running of the media organization, according to traditional or laid-down conventions and familiar routines of a co-operative work process which is either satisfying to those engaged in it or seen as the best way to achieve the immediate work goals.

A **technological logic** refers to the perceived capacities and qualities of a particular technology for collecting, processing, producing or transmitting media content. The key is to be found in what communication technologies are supposed to be 'good for', in respect of any of the things which mass media normally do: reporting reality, conveying information, telling stories, capturing attention, etc. The technological logic may be embedded within the organizational logic, but it has a wider currency: among would-be media communicators and audiences. The wider theoretical significance of this logic is a related tendency to media-determinism and media-centricity.

The notion of **cultural logic** is more complex and difficult to pin down. It can refer broadly to the culture of the mass media, in which case it accords with (or underlies and explains) recurring features of media practice — for instance, certain forms of storytelling or the appeal to senses of hearing and sight (sensationalism). In this sense, media-cultural logic is also exemplified by the star system, the production and recycling of celebrities of all kinds, and by the world of advertising, with its rather limited set of aims and techniques, but with changing modes and styles. Personalization, immediacy and novelty reflect the application of media-cultural logic. There is another sense of cultural logic, which derives from the culture of the society or the recipients of media. Socially defined audiences, taste cultures and sub-cultures supply the key to consistency and to an alternative path of analysis.

Some of these points overlap with the idea of a **political logic** which refers especially to the demands made on the media by powerful and organized interests in society, both inside and outside the formal political institution. The political logic is directed towards harnessing the media to the chosen ends of contenders for office and holders of power. This may sometimes mean trying to impose democratic control (for instance, in matters of culture or service to the political system), sometimes bending the media to strategic economic goals of a national society. In general the political logic works against the autonomy of mass media, however much freedom of media is proclaimed as a high principle.

Finally, there is an **informational logic** which applies to the media in some of their activities (not so much the 'news' as more basic informational functions, such as stock-market reports, sports results, weather, listings, public notices and job advertisements). This view of the media is linked to a definition of communication as 'transfer of information' and implies criteria of effectiveness and efficiency which can be applied. Many specialized media operate largely according to this model, and it plays a part in public perceptions of mass media, even when they fail to live up to expectations.

While these logics can be analytically separated, they really operate concurrently and in combination with each other. What has been referred to earlier in this book as 'media logic', for instance, describes a combination of elements drawn from the technological, organizational and cultural categories. The idea of a guiding logic is primarily a tool of analysis, but it helps to clarify the multiplicity of purposes and practices involved in this complex phenomenon. It also offers alternative and new paths for theoretical exploration.

Media as a (defective) meaning machine

One of the least ambiguous results of revised or alternative paradigms is the conclusion that mass communication is centrally about the giving and taking of meaning, although the outcomes are enormously varied and unpredictable. In part this inefficiency stems from the multiplicity of purposes served by mass media, but it also derives from the lack of fixed or unitary meanings in any media 'text' or 'message', whatever the intention of a sender might be, or the shaping by rules of language and discourse. Attempts can be made for some purposes to 'decode' the probable direction of intention or effect of media content, but there is no 'scientific' route towards an objective result of such decoding. We cannot draw sure conclusions about producers, audiences or possible effects from such research. Most fundamentally, this uncertainty derives from the essentially creative, interactive and open-ended nature of communication, in which meaningful outcomes are always negotiated and unpredictable.

Despite the undeniable personal 'power of the reader', there is also plenty of evidence that audience 'readings' do often follow conventional and predictable lines of interpretation and that familiar media genres such as news and television series are probably read, as often as not, more or less as intended. The meanings of media content and of the acts of media use are multiple — alternative interpretative communities do exist — but many media genres are understood by most of their receivers most of the time in predictable ways and much meaning is denotational and unambiguous. There is a power of the text which it is foolish to ignore.

Domains of meaning

There is clearly no general answer to questions of meaning construction, but media research and theory have indicated several elements in a more general framework of social and personal meanings, within which media play an important part. These elements can be described in terms of several recurrent dimensions or oppositions which help to answer the questions, 'What meanings?' and 'Meanings for what?' The following headings provide a tentative guide to matters on which there is both a supply of and a search for meanings. They identify, at a very general level, the topics and domains of meaning in which mass media operate for individuals and wider collectivities.

Significance   The media provide clues to what is more or less important, salient or relevant in many different contexts, from personal sex lives to global politics. Everyday life is problematic without having some kinds of answer to questions of this kind.

Reality and real-life contexts   The dimension at issue is that of reality versus fantasy, fact versus fiction, truth versus falsehood. The underlying question often lies at the heart of media genres and languages and helps initially to frame much response. This is not to assume the possibility of any absolute answer about the 'reality' of texts or interpretations.

Public versus private space   To say that media operate in the public sphere is already to privilege a domain of meaning in which the mass media carry much weight. We are likely to look to media for a guide to public meanings and definitions — those most widely shared or accepted. However, it is also arguable that media increasingly break down the conventional distinctions between private and public spaces in social life. The general notion persists that there is some boundary separating what is personal, domestic and private from what is open to view and accountable in the public sphere. This is a key matter of definition, in which mass communication plays a role.

Identity   The very large matter of social and cultural identity — who and what we are and how we are different from others — lies at the heart of many questions concerning meaning construction by the media. The media reflect and reinforce many conventional markers and boundary systems in relation to gender, class, ethnicity, religion, nationality, subculture, etc. Equally, the media do much to undermine boundaries maintained by circumstances or by other institutions. The messages of the media can also be mined for alternatives and for support for self-chosen definitions of identity.

Space and location   Related to identity but also independent is the question of location. Media meanings are structured by many clues to place. Both news and fiction can usually be understood only when they are furnished with an answer to the question, 'Where?' The media themselves are usually located at a specific point of origin and are intended for an audience which is territorially located in a nation, region or city (though perhaps decreasingly so). Much content provides implicit answers to what 'here' is like as opposed to 'there', what is near compared to what is distant. The internationalization of media may confuse the message and undermine the locatedness of meanings, but it also leads to an enriched supply of place-related meanings (Gould et al., 1984).

Time   A rather similar set of remarks relates to the question of time, with media content often accountable in terms of the present and the past, actuality and history, what is recalled compared to what is going on now or projected into the future. The media have been said to provide a collective memory, especially of the relevant past of a people, culture or society. The whole rhythm of mass media production and dissemination is guided by time in terms of the daily, weekly, seasonal and historical cycle of events, in itself an influential contribution to the taking of meaning.

All the terms mentioned here have featured at some point in the theories discussed in the book, and they are repeated now to suggest a wealth of theoretical lines of development in respect of meaning construction which have hardly been followed in any systematic way. These paths will be easier to follow if the notion of fixed, objective, encoded meaning is rejected, but they still require respect for the text and the context of production.

Power, influence and effect

Do the media have any?

For reasons which have been made clear, most direct questions about the 'power of the media' either make no sense or cannot be answered. This does not make the issue less important, but it has to be approached indirectly. It is fairly clear that the media are everywhere dependent on the rest of society, reactive to more fundamental impulses and subordinate to sources of real economic and political power. The media are nowhere expected to exercise direct power in their own interest, outside the sphere of gaining attention, communicating, informing, entertaining, making money, etc. The principle of free expression does legitimate the voicing of opposition, criticism and advocacy of alternatives, but this can better be accounted under the heading of 'influence'. Any consequences are the result of other circumstances outside the control of media themselves. Similarly, the 'power' to influence consumer behaviour by way of advertising is ultimately dependent on consumers themselves.

Whose side are the media on?

The concept of media power is open to a variety of definitions. Often it is used to refer to the question of effectiveness for achieving a given power objective, such as persuasion, mobilization or information. Media theory, in the behaviourist tradition, has quite a lot to say about the conditions of effective performance in such matters. Both evidence and theory support the view that media often can and do achieve delimited objectives and can be effective according to a chosen purpose, although within strict limits. Another formulation of power, more at home in the social-structuralist tradition, concerns the question of *whose* power the media might exercise or facilitate. Is it that of society as a whole, or a particular class or interest group? Most theory (and evidence) seems again to support the view that media, more often than not, by commission or omission, do tend to serve the interests of those who already have more political and economic power in society, especially where these are in a position to use the media for their objectives.

This is not simply to say that the power of the media is that of a dominant class, but it is consistent with the view that the media are not an independent source of power of their own and that political and economic influence which flows through the media has origins in the power centres of society. The established media, in liberal societies, often do support forces of progressive social change and express popular demands for change, but their normal operating requirements do not lead them to be in the vanguard of fundamental change. The very stance of neutrality which most media adopt makes them more vulnerable to assimilation by existing power-holders.

The mass media are so integrated into the life of most societies that it makes little sense to view them as an independent source of power or influence. Their activities are geared to the needs, interests and purposes of innumerable other actors in society. The proposition that the media are ultimately dependent on other institutional arrangements in society is not inconsistent with the fact that other institutions may also be dependent on the media, certainly in the short term. The media are often the only practical means available for transmitting information quickly and efficiently to many and for purveying 'propaganda'.

Fame and celebrity

More to the point is that the media have a virtual monopoly over a commodity which is often a necessary condition for the effective exercise of power — that of attention, fame and celebrity in the wider society. While the media are not entirely free agents in delivering this — it is their audiences which really supply the vital commodity — they have the means and generally the skill to deliver and signal public esteem for most practical purposes, at least in the short term. Fame is, however, a zero-sum commodity (there is only so much to go around before it becomes diluted — see the 'publicity model', pages 51–2) and subject to intense competition between media as well as between the would-be famous. One way in which the supply can be expanded is by turning fame into infamy, as when a prominent or popular figure falls into disgrace. The limits are still set by the amount of public attention (in terms of time), which is not in elastic supply.

Dealing in celebrity is generally a matter of mutual self-interest, since the media themselves need to provide their audiences with images of celebrity. Fame and celebrity usually depend on a wider system of meaning which has developed over time and which the mass media did not create nor completely control. It also depends on social networks and hierarchies in the society and on interpersonal processes of discourse, rumour and gossip. In some circles, media recognition is not a necessary condition of celebrity. But the range of media control is extending and leading to a collapsing of different categories of fame for specific achievements and to the rise of the notion of 'the fame of being famous'. While the famous may increasingly need the media, the media constantly need the famous in order to attract attention and certify their own importance. Without famous or celebrated performers there are unlikely to be devoted fans. There is a good deal of scope for developing theory in relation to these matters.

Questions of culture

Since culture is everything, this comment has either to be kept very short or go on indefinitely. Mass communication theory has shown a healthy capacity to extend its scope to cover many aspects of culture, especially in relation to the links with everyday life and by opening up the endlessly complex subject of the nature of 'media culture'. Media theory has on the whole benefited from the work of cultural theorists who have colonized the once rather limited territory founded mainly upon psychology, sociology and politics. Even so, there are many actively contested frontier zones, among them the question of intrinsic **cultural quality**, a notion once strongly upheld by humanistic traditions but now called into question by adherents of new populism, subculturalists, relativists of many shades and followers of postmodern cultural theory. The core issues will continue to be debated, not least because of their relevance to decisions in the field of media-cultural politics. The question of **cultural identity** and the relevance of media to its many manifestations will be one of the central issues for some time and has not yet received the analysis it deserves.

In relation to the theory of an **information society**, itself in a very uneasy state, there are several largely unexplored cultural questions which are relevant to media theory. The information society has been largely defined up to now in technological, economic and sociological terms. The *cultural* dimension of information societies seems to have been largely neglected, although postmodernistic thinking is one of the main forms in which exploration is taking place. If there is a recognizable 'information culture' corresponding to the information society (a plausible supposition), then the mass media are bound to be an important element and also an influence.

If we think of a culture as comprising a certain symbolic content, then it is media which fill much of the cultural space with images and sounds. Where the notion of culture refers to social practices, then media and communication technology are clearly influential. Where culture refers to an attitude of mind, the mass media seem to encourage attitudes both of 'modernity' and of 'postmodernity'. They also encourage confidence in science and technique and a belief (even if illusory) in the power to control reality through symbolic manipulation. If not control, they offer escape or symbolic substitutes (cf. 'virtual reality'). Many of the foundations of the information society (including trust in expert systems — Giddens, 1991) are dependent on the media for sustaining confidence. The terrain which opens up is very extensive, and its exploration will probably require much better instruments for mapping and for analysis than have been brought by the cultural theorists who were the first colonists.

Last words

If mass communication as a process is set to endure, so obviously are the institutions that carry it on. These are undergoing continual and profound changes for reasons which have been described — especially because of changing technology, which alters what is both possible and profitable. Theory of media institutions is still relatively primitive, and there is much scope for development on the basis of existing concepts and modes of analysis, largely corresponding to the different logics described above. Mass communication is alive and well, whether we like it or not, and there is plenty of work in the theory workshop.

REFERENCES

Adams, W.C. and Schreibman, F. (eds) (1978) *Television Networks: Issues in Content Research.* Washington, DC: George Washington University.

Adorno, T. and Horkheimer, M. (1972) 'The Culture Industry: Enlightenment as Mass Deception', in *The Dialectic of Enlightenment.* New York: Herder and Herder.

Alali, A.O. and Eke, K.K. (eds) (1991) *Media Coverage of Television.* Newbury Park, CA, and London: Sage Publications.

Alasuutari, P. (1992) ' "I'm ashamed to admit it but I have watched *Dallas*": The Moral Hierarchy of Television Programmes', *Media, Culture and Society,* 14, 1: 561–82.

Allen, I.L (1977) 'Social Integration as an Organizing Principle', in G. Gerbner (ed), *Mass Media Policies in Changing Cultures,* pp. 235–50. New York: Wiley.

Allen, R.C. (ed) (1987) *Channels of Discourse.* London: Allen and Unwin.

Allen, R.C. (1989) ' "Soap Opera", Audiences and the Limits of Genre', in F. Seiter et al. (eds), *Remote Control,* pp. 4-55. London: Routledge.

Allor, M. (1988) 'Relocating the Site of the Audience', *Critical Studies in Mass Communication,* 5, 3: 217–33.

Altheide, D.L. (1974) *Creating Reality.* Beverly Hills, CA, and London: Sage Publications.

Altheide, D.L. (1985) *Media Power.* Beverly Hills, CA, and London: Sage Publications.

Altheide, D.L. and Snow, R.P. (1979) *Media Logic.* Beverly Hills, CA, and London: Sage Publications.

Altheide, D.L. and Snow, R.P. (1991) *Media Worlds in the Postjournalism Era.* New York: Aldine/de Gruyter.

Althusser, L. (1971) 'Ideology and Ideological State Apparatuses', in *Lenin and Philosophy and Other Essays.* London: New Left Books.

Altschull, J.H. (1984) *Agents of Power: The Role of the News Media in Human Affairs.* New York: Longman.

Anderson, B. (1983) *Imagined Communities.* London: Verso.

Anderson, J. (1987) 'Commentary on Qualitative Research', in T. Lindlof (ed), *Natural Audiences.* Norwood, NJ: Ablex.

Andrew, D. (1984) *Concepts in Film Theory.* New York: Oxford University Press.

Ang, I. (1985) *Watching 'Dallas': Soap Opera and the Melodramatic Imagination.* London: Methuen.

Ang, I. (1991) *Desperately Seeking the Audience.* London: Routledge.

Ang, I. and Hermes, J. (1991) 'Gender and/in Media Consumption', in J. Curran and M. Gurevitch (eds), *Media and Society,* pp. 307–28. London: Edward Arnold.

Asp, K. (1981) 'Mass Media as Molders of Opinion and Suppliers of Information', in C.G. Wilhoit and H. de Bock (eds), *Mass Communication Review Yearbook,* Vol. 2, pp. 332–54. Beverly Hills, CA, and London: Sage Publications.

Baehr, H. (1980) *Women and the Media.* London: Pergamon.

Baerns, B. (1987) 'Journalism versus Public Relations in the Federal Republic of Germany', in D.L. Paletz (ed), *Political Communication Research,* pp. 88–107. Norwood, NJ: Ablex.

Bagdikian, B. (1988) *The Media Monopoly.* Boston, MA: Beacon Press.

Ball-Rokeach, S.J. (1985) 'The Origins of Individual Media-System Dependency', *Communication Research,* 12, 4: 485–510.

Ball-Rokeach, S.J. and DeFleur, M.L. (1976) 'A Dependency Model of Mass Media Effects', *Communication Research*, 3: 3–21.

Barthes, R. (1967) *Elements of Semiology*. London: Jonathan Cape.

Barthes, R. (1972) *Mythologies*. London: Jonathan Cape.

Barthes, R. (1977) *Image, Music, Text: Essays*, selected and translated by Stephen Heath. London: Fontana.

Barwise, T.P. and Ehrenberg, A.S.C. (1988) *Television and its Audience*. Newbury Park, CA, and London: Sage Publications.

Bass, A.Z. (1969) 'Refining the Gatekeeper Concept', *Journalism Quarterly*, 46: 69–72.

Bauer, R.A. (1958) 'The Communicator and the Audience', *Journal of Conflict Resolution*, 2, 1: 67–77. Also in L.A. Dexter and D.M. White (eds), *People, Society and Mass Communication*, pp. 125–39. New York: Free Press.

Bauer, R.A. (1964) 'The Obstinate Audience', *American Psychologist*, 19: 319–28.

Bauer, R.A. and Bauer, A. (1960) 'America, Mass Society and Mass Media', *Journal of Social Issues*, 10, 3: 3–66.

Bauman, Z. (1972) 'A Note on Mass Culture: On Infrastructure', in D. McQuail (ed), *Sociology of Mass Communication*, pp. 61–74. Harmondsworth: Penguin.

Bausinger, H. (1984) 'Media, Technology and Daily Life', *Media, Culture and Society*, 6, 4: 343–51.

Becker, L (1982) 'The Mass Media and Citizen Assessment of Issue Importance', in D.C. Whitney et al. (eds), *Mass Communication Review Yearbook*, Vol. 3, pp. 521–36. Beverly Hills, CA, and London: Sage Publications.

Behr, R.L. and Iyengar, S. (1985) 'TV News, Real World Cues and Changes in the Public Agenda', *Public Opinion Quarterly*, 49, I: 38–57.

Bell, A. (1991) *The Language of News Media*. Oxford: Blackwell.

Bell, D. (1961) *The End of Ideology*. New York: Collier Books.

Bell, D. (1973) *The Coming of Post-Industrial Society*. New York: Basic Books.

Beniger, J.R. (1986) *The Control Revolution*. Cambridge, MA: Harvard University Press.

Benjamin, W. (1977) 'The Work of Art in an Age of Mechanical Reproduction', in J. Curran et al. (eds), *Mass Communication and Society*, pp. 384–408. London: Edward Arnold.

Benthall, J. (1993) *Disasters, Relief and the Media*. London: I.B. Taurus.

Berelson, B. (1949) 'What Missing the Newspaper Means', in P.F. Lazarsfeld and F.M. Stanton (eds), *Communication Research 1948–9*, pp. 111–29. New York: Duell, Sloan and Pearce.

Berelson, B. (1952) *Content Analysis in Communication Research*. Glencoe, IL: Free Press.

Berelson, B. (1959) 'The State of Communication Research', *Public Opinion Quarterly*, 23, 1: 1–6.

Berelson, B. and Salter, P.J. (1946) 'Majority and Minority Americans: An Analysis of Magazine Fiction', *Public Opinion Quarterly*, 10: 168–90.

Berelson, B., Lazarsfeld, P.J. and McPhee, W.N. (1954) *Voting: A Study of Opinion Formation in a Presidential Campaign*. Chicago: Chicago University Press.

Berger, C.R. and Chaffee, S.H. (1987) 'The Study of Communication as a Science', in C.R. Berger and S.H. Chaffee (eds), *Handbook of Communication Science*, pp. 15–19. Beverly Hills, CA, and London: Sage Publications.

Biltereyst, D. (1991) 'Resisting American Hegemony: A Comparative Analysis of the Reception of Domestic and US Fiction', *European Journal of Communication*, 6, 4: 469–97.

Biltereyst, D. (1992) 'Language and Culture as Ultimate Barriers?', *European Journal of Communication*, 7, 4: 517–40.

Biocca, F.A. (1988) 'Opposing Conceptions of the Audience', in J. Anderson (ed), *Communication Yearbook 11*, pp. 51–80. Newbury Park, CA, and London: Sage Publications.

Blanchard, M.A. (1977) 'The Hutchins Commission, the Press and the Responsibility Concept', *Journalism Monographs*, 49.

Blau, P. and Scott, W. (1963) *Formal Organizations*. London: Routledge and Kegan Paul.

Blumer, H. (1933) *Movies and Conduct*. New York: Macmillan.

Blumer, H. (1939) 'The Mass, the Public and Public Opinion', in A.M. Lee (ed), *New Outlines of the Principles of Sociology*. New York: Barnes and Noble.

Blumer, H. and Hauser, P.M. (1933) *Movies, Delinquency and Crime*. New York: Macmillan.

Blumler, J.G. (1970) 'The Political Effects of Television', in J.D. Halloran (ed), *The Effects of Television*, pp. 69–104. Leicester: Leicester University Press.

Blumler, J.G. (1985) 'The Social Character of Media Gratifications', in K.E. Rosengren et al. (eds), *Media Gratification Research: Current Perspectives*, pp. 41–59. Beverly Hills, CA, and London: Sage Publications.

Blumler, J.G. (1991) 'The New Television Marketplace', in J. Curran and M. Gurevitch (eds), *Mass Media and Society*, pp. 194–215. London: Edward Arnold.

Blumler, J.G. (ed) (1992) *Television and the Public Interest*. London: Sage Publications.

Blumler, J.G. and Katz, E. (eds) (1974) *The Uses of Mass Communications*. Beverly Hills, CA, and London: Sage Publications.

Blumler, J.G. and McQuail, D. (1968) *Television in Politics: Its Uses and Influence*. London: Faber.

Boorman, J. (1987) *Money into Light*. London: Faber.

Boorstin, D. (1961) *The Image: A Guide to Pseudo-Events in America*. New York: Atheneum.

Bordewijk, J.L and van Kaam, B. (1986) 'Towards a New Classification of Tele–Information Services', *Intermedia* 14, 1: 16–21. Originally published in *Allocutie*. Baarn: Bosch and Keuning, 1982.

Bourdieu, P. (1986) *Distinction: A Social Critique of the Judgement of Taste*. London: Routledge.

Boyd-Barrett, O. (1977) 'Media Imperialism', in J. Curran et al. (eds), *Mass Communication and Society*, pp. 116–35. London: Edward Arnold.

Boyd-Barrett, O. (1980) *The International News Agencies*. London: Constable.

Boyd-Barrett, O. (1982) 'Cultural Dependency and the Mass Media', in M. Gurevitch et al. (eds), *Culture, Society and the Media*, pp. 174–95. London: Methuen.

Bramson, L. (1961) *The Political Context of Sociology*. Princeton, NJ: Princeton University Press.

Breed, W. (1955) 'Social Control in the Newsroom: A Functional Analysis', *Social Forces*, 33: 326–55.

Breed, W. (1956) 'Analysing News: Some Questions for Research', *Journalism Quarterly*, 33: 467–77.

Breed, W. (1958) 'Mass Communication and Socio-Cultural Integration', *Social Forces*, 37: 109–16.

Brown, J.R. (ed) (1976) *Children and Television*. London: Collier-Macmillan.

Brown, J.R. and Linné, O. (1976) 'The Family as a Mediator of Television's Effects', in J.R. Brown (ed), *Children and Television*, pp. 184–98. London: Collier-Macmillan.

Brown, M.E. (ed) (1990) *Television and Women's Culture*. Newbury Park, CA, and London: Sage Publications.

Bryant, J. and Zillman, D. (eds) (1986) *Perspectives on Media Effects*. Hillsdale, NJ: Laurence Erlbaum.

Burgelin, O. (1972) 'Structural Analysis and Mass Communication', in D. McQuail (ed), *Sociology of Mass Communications*, pp. 313–28. Harmondsworth: Penguin.

Burgelman, J.-C. (1986) 'The Future of Public Service Broadcasting: A Case Study for a "New" Communications Policy', *European Journal of Communication*, 1, 2: 173–202.

Burnett, R. (1990) *Concentration and Diversity in the International Phonogram Industry*. Gothenburg: University of Gothenburg.

Burns, T. (1969) 'Public Service and Private World', in P. Halmos (ed), *The Sociology of Mass Media Communicators*, pp. 53–73. Keele: University of Keele.

Burns, T. (1977) *The BBC: Public Institution and Private World*. London: Macmillan.

Burrell, G. and Morgan, G. (1979) *Sociological Paradigms and Organizational Analysis*. London: Heinemann.

Cantor, M. (1971) *The Hollywood Television Producers*. New York: Basic Books.

Cantor, M. and Cantor, J. (1992) *Prime Time Television*, 2nd edn. Newbury Park, CA, and London: Sage Publications.

Cantril, H. and Allport, G. (1935) *The Psychology of Radio*. New York: Harper.

Cantril, H., Gaudet, H. and Hertzog, H. (1940) *The Invasion from Mars*. Princeton, NJ: Princeton University Press.

Carey, J. (1969) 'The Communication Revolution and the Professional Communicator', in P. Halmos (ed), *The Sociology of Mass Media Communicators*, pp. 23–38. Keele: University of Keele.

Carey, J. (1975) 'A Cultural Approach to Communication', *Communication*, 2: 1–22.

Carey, J. (1988) *Communication as Culture*. Boston, MA: Unwin Hyman.

Carlsson, G., Dahlberg, A. and Rosengren, K.E. (1981) 'Mass Media Content, Public Opinion and Social Change', in K. Rosengren (ed), *Advances in Content Analysis*, pp. 227–40. Beverly Hills, CA, and London: Sage Publications.

Chaffee, S.H. (1977) 'The Diffusion of Political Information', in S.H. Chaffee (ed), *Political Communication*, pp. 85–128. Beverly Hills, CA: Sage Publications.

Chaffee, S.H. (1981) 'Mass Media Effects: New Research Perspectives', in C.G. Wilhoit and H. de Bock (eds), *Mass Communication Review Yearbook*, Vol. 2, pp. 77–108. Beverly Hills, CA, and London: Sage Publications.

Chaffee, S.H. and Hochheimer, J.L. (1982) 'The Beginnings of Political Communication Research in the US: Origins of the Limited Effects Model', in E.M. Rogers and F. Balle (eds), *The Media Revolution in America and Europe*, pp. 263–83. Norwood, NJ: Ablex.

Chaffee, S.H. and Roser, C. (1986) 'Involvement and the Consistency of Knowledge, Attitudes and Behavior', *Communication Research*, 3: 373–99.

Chaney, D. (1972) *Processes of Mass Communication*. London: Macmillan.

Chibnall, S. (1977) *Law and Order News*. London: Tavistock.

Clark, T.N. (ed) (1969) *On Communication and Social Influence*. Collected essays of Gabriel Tarde. Chicago: Chicago University Press.

Cohen, B. (1963) *The Press and Foreign Policy*. Princeton, NJ: Princeton University Press.

Cohen, S. (1972) *Folk Devils and Moral Panics*. London: McGibbon and Kee.

Cohen, S. and Young, J. (eds) (1973) *The Manufacture of News*. London: Constable.

Comstock, G. (ed) (1986) *Public Communication and Behavior*. New York: Academic Press.

Comstock, G., Chaffee, S., Katzman, N., McCombs, M. and Roberts, D. (1978) *Television and Human Behaviour*. New York: Columbia University Press.

Cooper, E. and Jahoda, M. (1947) 'The Evasion of Propaganda', *Journal of Psychology*, 23: 15–25.

Cox, H. and Morgan, D. (1973) *City Politics and the Press*. Cambridge: Cambridge University Press.

Cuilenberg, J.J. van (1987) 'The Information Society: Some Trends and Implications', *European Journal of Communication*, 2, 1: 105–21.

Cuilenburg, J.J. van, de Ridder, J. and Kleinnijenhuis, J. (1986) 'A Theory of Evaluative Discourse', *European Journal of Communication*, 1, 1: 65–96.

Curran, J. (1986) 'The Impact of Advertising on the British Mass Media', in R. Collins et al. (eds), *Media, Culture and Society*, pp. 309–35. Beverly Hills, CA, and London: Sage Publications.

Curran, J. (1990) 'The New Revisionism in Mass Communication Research: A Reappraisal', *European Journal of Communication*, 5, 2/3: 135–64.

Curran, J. (1991) 'Mass Media and Democracy: A Reappraisal', in J. Curran and M. Gurevitch (eds), *Mass Media and Society*, pp. 112–17. London: Edward Arnold.

Curran, J. and M. Gurevitch (eds) (1991) *Mass Media and Society*. London: Edward Arnold.

Curran, J. and Seaton, J. (1988) *Power without Responsibility*, 3rd edn. London: Fontana.

Curran, J., Gurevitch, M. and Woollacott, J. (eds) (1977) *Mass Communication and Society*. London: Edward Arnold.

Curran, J., Douglas, A. and Whannel, G. (1981) 'The Political Economy of the Human Interest Story', in A. Smith (ed), *Newspapers and Democracy*, pp. 288–316. Cambridge, MA: MIT Press.

Dahlgren, P. and Sparks, C.S. (eds) (1992) *Journalism and Popular Culture*. London: Sage Publications.

Darnton, R. (1975) 'Writing News and Telling Stories', *Daedalus*, Spring: 175–94.

Darnton, R. (1990) *The Kiss of Lamourette*. New York: Norton.

Davis, D.K. and Robinson, J.P. (1986) 'News Story Attributes and Comprehension', in J.P. Robinson and M. Levy, *The Main Source*, pp. 179–210. Beverly Hills, CA, and London: Sage Publications.

Davis, D.K. and Robinson, J.P. (1989) 'Newsflow and Democratic Society', in G. Comstock (ed), *Public Communication and Behavior*, Vol. 2. Orlando, FA: Academic Press.

Dawson, R.E. and Prewitt, K. (1969) *Political Socialization*. Boston, MA: Little, Brown.

DeFleur, M.L. (1964) 'Occupational Roles as Portrayed on Television', *Public Opinion Quarterly*, 28: 57–74.

DeFleur, M.L. (1970) *Theories of Mass Communication*, 2nd edn. New York: David McKay.

DeFleur, M.L. and Ball-Rokeach, S. (1989) *Theories of Mass Communication*, 5th edn. New York: Longman.

Delia, J.G. (1987) 'Communication Research: A History', in S.H. Chaffee and C. Berger (eds), *Handbook of Communication Science*, pp. 20–98. Newbury Park, CA, and London: Sage Publications.

Deming, C.J. (1991) '*Hill Street Blues* as Narrative', in R. Avery and D. Eason (eds), *Critical Perspectives on Media and Society*, pp. 240–64. New York: Guilford.

Dennis, J. (ed) (1973) *Socialization to Politics*. New York: Wiley.

Dervin, B. (1987) 'The Potential Contribution of Feminist Scholarship to the Field of Communication', *Journal of Communication*, 37, 4: 107–14.

Dexter, L.A. and White, D.M. (eds) (1964) *People, Society and Mass Communication*. New York: Free Press.

Dijk, T. van (1983) 'Discourse Analysis: Its Development and Application to the Structure of News', *Journal of Communication*, 33, 3: 20–43.

Dijk, T. van (1985) *Discourse and Communication*. Berlin: de Gruyter.

Dijk, T. van (1991) *Racism and the Press*. London: Routledge.

Dimmick, J. and Coit, P. (1982) 'Levels of Analysis in Mass Media Decision-Making', *Communication Research*, 9, 1: 3–32.

Dimmick, J. and Rothebuhler, E. (1984) 'The Theory of the Niche: Quantifying Competition among Media Industries', *Journal of Communication*, 34, 3: 103–19.

Docherty, T. (ed) (1993) *Postmodernism*. New York and London: Harvester/Wheatsheaf.

Dominick, J.R., Wurtzel, A. and Lometti, G. (1975) 'TV Journalism as Show Business: A Content Analysis of Eyewitness News', *Journalism Quarterly*, 52: 213–18.

Donohue, G.A., Tichenor, P. and Olien, C.N. (1975) 'Mass Media and the Knowledge Gap', *Communication Research*, 2: 3–23.

Donsbach, W. (1983) 'Journalists' Conception of Their Role', *Gazette*, 32, 1: 19–36.

Doob, A. and McDonald, G.E. (1979) 'Television Viewing and the Fear of Victimization: Is the Relationship Causal?', *Journal of Social Psychology and Personality*, 37: 170–9. Reprinted in G.C. Wilhoit and H. de Bock (eds), *Mass Communication Review Yearbook*, Vol. 1, 1980, pp. 479–88. Beverly Hills, CA, and London: Sage Publications.

Dordick, H. and G. Wang (1993) *The Information Society*. Newbury Park, CA, and London: Sage Publications.

Downing, J. (1984) *Radical Media*. Boston, MA: South End Press.

Dreier, P. (1982) 'The Position of the Press in the US Power Structure', *Social Problems*, 29, 3: 298–310.

Drotner, K. (1992) 'Modernity and Media Panics', in M. Skovmand and K. Schrøder (eds), *Media Cultures*, pp. 42–62. London: Routledge.

Eco, U. (1977) *A Theory of Semiotics*. London: Macmillan.

Eco, U. (1979) *The Role of the Reader*. Bloomington, IN: University of Indiana Press.

Edelman, M.J. (1967) *The Symbolic Uses of Politics*. Urbana, IL: University of Illinois Press.

Eldridge, J. (1993) *Getting the Message*. London: Routledge.

Eisenstein, E. (1978) *The Printing Press as an Agent of Change*, 2 vols. New York: Cambridge University Press.

Elliott, P. (1972) *The Making of a Television Series — A Case Study in the Production of Culture*. London: Constable.

Elliott, P. (1974) 'Uses and Gratifications Research: A Critique and a Sociological Alternative', in J.G. Blumler and E. Katz (eds), *The Uses of Mass Communications*, pp. 249–68. Beverly Hills, CA, and London: Sage Publications.

Elliott, P. (1977) 'Media Organizations and Occupations — an Overview', in J. Curran et al. (eds), *Mass Communication and Society*, pp. 142–73. London: Edward Arnold.

Elliott, P. (1982) 'Intellectuals, the "Information Society" and the Disappearance of the Public Sphere', *Media, Culture and Society*, 4: 243–53.

Ellis, J. (1982) *Visible Fictions*. London: Routledge and Kegan Paul.

Emmett, B.P. (1968) 'A New Role for Research in Broadcasting', *Public Opinion Quarterly*, 32: 654–65.

Emmett, B.P. (1972) 'The TV and Radio Audience in Britain', in D. McQuail (ed), *Sociology of Mass Communications*, pp. 195–219. Harmondsworth: Penguin.

Engwall, L. (1978) *Newspapers as Organizations*. Farnborough, Hants: Saxon House.

Entman, R.M. (1989) *Democracy without Citizens: Media and the Decay of American Politics*. New York: Oxford University Press.

Entman, R.M. (1991) 'Framing US Coverage of International News', *Journal of Communication*, 41, 4: 6–27.

Enzensberger, H.M. (1970) 'Constituents of a Theory of the Media', *New Left Review*, 64: 13–36. Also in D. McQuail (ed), *Sociology of Mass Communications*, pp. 99–116. Harmondsworth: Penguin.

Ericson, R.V., Baranek, P.M. and Chan, J.B.L. (1987) *Visualizing Deviance*. Toronto: University of Toronto Press.

Ericson, R.V., Baranek, P.M. and Chan, J.B.L. (1991) *Representing Order: Crime, Law and Justice in the News Media*. Toronto: University of Toronto Press.

Espé, H. and Seiwert, M. (1986) 'European Television Viewer Types: A Six-Nation Classification by Programme Interests', *European Journal of Communication*, 1, 3: 301–25.

Ettema, J.S. and Whitney, D.C. (eds) (1982) *Individuals in Mass Media Organizations*. Beverly Hills, CA, and London: Sage Publications.

Ettema, J.S. and Whitney, D.C., with Wackman, D.B. (1987) 'Professional Mass Communicators', in C. Berger and S.H. Chaffee (eds), *Handbook of Communication Science*, pp. 747–80. Beverly Hills, CA, and London: Sage Publications.

Etzioni, A. (1961) *Complex Organizations*. Glencoe, IL: Free Press.

Febvre, L. and Martin, H.J. (1984) *The Coming of the Book*. London: Verso.

Feilitzen, C. von (1976) 'The Functions Served by the Mass Media', in J.W. Brown (ed), *Children and Television*, pp. 90–115. London: Collier-Macmillan.

Ferguson, M. (1983) *Forever Feminine: Women's Magazines and the Cult of Femininity*. London: Heinemann.

Ferguson, M. (1986a) 'The Challenge of Neo-Technological Determinism for Communication Systems of Industry and Culture', in M. Ferguson (ed), *New Communication Technologies and the Public Interest*, pp. 52–70. London and Beverly Hills, CA: Sage Publications.

Ferguson, M. (ed) (1986b) *New Communication Technologies and the Public Interest*. London and Beverly Hills, CA: Sage Publications.

Ferguson, M. (ed) (1990) *Public Communication: The New Imperatives*. London and Newbury Park, CA: Sage Publications.

Ferguson, M. (ed) (1992) 'The Mythology about Globalization', *European Journal of Communication*, 7: 69–93.

Festinger, L.A. (1957) *A Theory of Cognitive Dissonance*. New York: Row Peterson.

Findahl, O. and Hoijer, B. (1981) 'Studies of News from the Perspective of Human Comprehension', in G.C. Wilhoit and H. de Bock (eds), *Mass Communication Review Yearbook*, Vol. 2, pp. 393–403. Beverly Hills, CA, and London: Sage Publications.

Findahl, O. and Hoijer, B. (1985) 'Some Characteristics of News Memory and Comprehension', *Journal of Broadcasting and Electronic Media*, 29, 4: 379–98.

Fishman, J. (1980) *Manufacturing News*. Austin, TX: University of Texas Press.

Fishman, M. (1982) 'News and Non-Events: Making the Visible Invisible', in J.S. Ettema and D.C. Whitney (eds), *Individuals in Mass Media Organizations*, pp. 219–40. Beverly Hills, CA, and London: Sage Publications.

Fiske, J. (1982) *Introduction to Communication Studies*. London: Methuen.

Fiske, J. (1987) *Television Culture*. London: Methuen.

Fiske, J. (1989) *Reading the Popular*. Boston, MA: Unwin and Hyman.

Fiske, J. (1992) 'The Cultural Economy of Fandom', in L. Lewis (ed), *The Adoring Audience*, pp. 30–49. London: Routledge.

Fjaestad, B. and Holmlov, P.G. (1976) 'The Journalist's View', *Journal of Communication*, 2: 108–14.

Frederick, H.H. (1992) *Global Communications and International Relations*. Belmont, CA: Wadsworth.

French, J.R.P. and Raven, B.H. (1953) 'The Bases of Social Power', in D. Cartwright and A. Zander (eds), *Group Dynamics*, pp. 259–69. London: Tavistock.

Frick, F.C. (1959) 'Information Theory', in S. Koch (ed), *Psychology: A Study of a Science*, pp. 611–36. New York: McGraw-Hill.

Friedson, E. (1953) 'Communications Research and the Concept of the Mass', *American Sociological Review*, 18, 3: 313–17.

Frissen, V. (1992) 'Trapped in Electronic Cages? Gender and New Information Technology', *Media, Culture and Society*, 14: 31–50.

Frith, S. (1981) *Sound Effects*. New York: Pantheon.

Gallagher, M. (1981) *Unequal Opportunities: The Case of Women and the Media*. Paris: UNESCO.

Galtung, J. and Ruge, M. (1965) 'The Structure of Foreign News', *Journal of Peace Research*, 1: 64–90. Also in J. Tunstall (ed), *Media Sociology*, pp. 259–98. London: Constable.

Gamson, W. and Modigliani, A. (1989) 'Media Discourse and Public Opinion on Nuclear Power: A Constructivist Approach', *American Journal of Sociology*, 95: 1–37.

Gandy, O. (1982) *Beyond Agenda Setting*. Norwood, NJ: Ablex.

Gans, H.J. (1957) 'The Creator–Audience Relationship in the Mass Media', in B. Rosenberg and D.M. White (eds) *Mass Culture*, pp. 315–24. New York: Free Press.

Gans, H.J. (1979) *Deciding What's News*. New York: Vintage Books.

Garnham, N. (1979) 'Contribution to a Political Economy of Mass Communication', *Media, Culture and Society*, 1, 2: 123–46.

Garnham, N. (1986) 'The Media and the Public Sphere', in P. Golding and G. Murdock (eds), *Communicating Politics*, pp. 37–54. Leicester: Leicester University Press.

Gaziano, C. (1983) 'The "Knowledge Gap": An Analytical Review of Media Effects', *Communication Research*, 10, 4: 447–86.

Gaziano, C. (1989) 'Chain Newspaper Homogeneity and Presidential Endorsements 1971–1988', *Journalism Quarterly*, 66, 4: 836–45.

Geiger, K. and Sokol, R. (1959) 'Social Norms in Watching Television', *American Journal of Sociology*, 65, 3: 178–81.

Geis, M.L. (1987) *The Language of Politics*. Berlin: Springer.

Geraghty, C. (1991) *Women and Soap Operas*. Cambridge: Polity Press.

Gerbner, G. (1964) 'Ideological Perspectives and Political Tendencies in News Reporting', *Journalism Quarterly*, 41: 495–506.

Gerbner, G. (1967) 'Mass Media and Human Communication Theory', in F.E.X. Dance (ed), *Human Communication Theory*, pp. 40–57. New York: Holt, Rinehart and Winston.

Gerbner, G. (1969) 'Institutional Pressures on Mass Communicators', in P. Halmos (ed), *The Sociology of Mass Media Communicators*, pp. 205–48. Keele: University of Keele.

Gerbner, G. (1973) 'Cultural Indicators — the Third Voice', in G. Gerbner, L. Gross and W. Melody (eds), *Communications Technology and Social Policy*, pp. 553–73. New York: Wiley.

Gerbner, G. and Marvanyi, G. (1977) 'The Many Worlds of the World's Press', *Journal of Communication*, 27, 1: 52–66.

Gerbner, G., Gross, L., Morgan, M., Signorielli, N. and Jackson-Beek, M. (1979) 'The Demonstration of Power: Violence Profile No. 10', *Journal of Communication*, 29, 3: 177–96.

Gerbner, G., Gross, L., Morgan, M. and Signorielli, N. (1984) 'The Political Correlates of TV Viewing', *Public Opinion Quarterly*, 48: 283–300.

Giddens, A. (1991) *Modernity and Self-Identity*. Oxford: Polity Press.

Gieber, W. (1956) 'Across the Desk: A Study of 16 Telegraph Editors', *Journalism Quarterly*, 33: 423–33.

Gieber, W. and Johnson, W. (1961) 'The City Hall Beat: A Study of Reporter and Source Roles', *Journalism Quarterly*, 38: 289–97.

Giffard, C.A. (1989) *UNESCO and the Media*. White Plains, NY: Longman.

Giner, S. (1976) *Mass Society*. London: Martin Robertson.

Gitlin, T. (1978) 'Media Sociology: The Dominant Paradigm', *Theory and Society*, 6: 205–53. Reprinted in G.C. Wilhoit and H. de Bock (eds), *Mass Communication Review Yearbook*, Vol. 2, 1981, pp. 73–122. Beverly Hills, CA, and London: Sage Publications.

Gitlin, T. (1980) *The Whole World Is Watching — Mass Media in the Making and Unmaking of the New Left*. Berkeley, CA: University of California Press.

Gitlin, T. (1989) 'Postmodernism: Roots and Politics', in I. Angus and S. Jhally (eds), *Cultural Politics in Contemporary America*, pp. 347–60. New York and London: Routledge.

Glasgow Media Group (1976) *Bad News*. London: Routledge and Kegan Paul.

Glasgow Media Group (1980) *More Bad News*. London: Routledge and Kegan Paul.

Glasgow Media Group (1985) *War and Peace News*. Milton Keynes: Open University Press.

Glasser, T. (1984) 'Competition among Radio Formats', *Journal of Broadcasting*, 28, 2: 127–42.

Glasser, T. (1986) 'Press Responsibility and First Amendment Values', in D. Eliott (ed), *Responsible Journalism*, pp. 81–9. Newbury Park, CA, and London: Sage Publications.

Goffman, E. (1976) *Gender Advertisements*. London: Macmillan.

Golding, P. (1981) 'The Missing Dimensions: News Media and the Management of Change', in E. Katz and T. Szecskö (eds), *Mass Media and Social Change*. London and Beverly Hills, CA: Sage Publications.

Golding, P. (1990) 'Political Communication and Citizenship', in M. Ferguson (ed), *Public Communication: The New Imperatives*, pp. 84–100. London and Newbury Park, CA: Sage Publications.

Golding, P. and Elliott, P. (1979) *Making the News*. London: Longman.

Golding, P. and Middleton, S. (1982) *Images of Welfare — Press and Public Attitudes to Poverty*. Oxford: Blackwell and Martin Robertson.

Golding, P. and Murdock, G. (1978) 'Theories of Communication and Theories of Society', *Communication Research*, 5, 3: 390–56.

Golding, P. and Murdock, G. (1991) 'Culture, Communications and Political Economy', in J. Curran and M. Gurevitch (eds), *Mass Media and Society*, pp. 15–32. London: Edward Arnold.

Gould, P., Johnson, J. and Chapman, G. (1984) *The Structure of Television*. London: Pion.

Gouldner, A. (1976) *The Dialectic of Ideology and Technology*. London: Macmillan.

Graber, D. (1976a) 'Press and Television as Opinion Resources in Presidential Campaigns', *Public Opinion Quarterly*, 40, 3: 285–303.

Graber, D. (1976b) *Verbal Behavior and Politics*. Urbana, IL: University of Illinois Press.

Graber, D. (1981) 'Political Language', in D.D. Nimmo and D. Sanders (eds), *Handbook of Political Communication*, pp. 195–224. Beverly Hills, CA, and London: Sage Publications.

Graber, D. (1984) *Processing the News*. New York: Longman.

Gramsci, A. (1971) *Selections from the Prison Notebooks*. London: Lawrence and Wishart.

Greenberg, B.S. (1964) 'Person-to-Person Communication in the Diffusion of a News Event', *Journalism Quarterly*, 41: 489–94.

Gripsrud, J. (1989) 'High Culture Revisited', *Cultural Studies*, 3, 2: 194–7.

Gross, L.P. (1977) 'Television as a Trojan Horse', *School Media Quarterly*, Spring: 175–80.

Grossberg, L. (1989) 'MTV: Swinging on the (Postmodern) Star', in I. Angus and S. Jhally (eds), *Cultural Politics in Contemporary Politics*, pp. 254–68. New York: Routledge.

Grossberg, L. (1991) 'Strategies of Marxist Cultural Interpretation', in R.K. Avery and D. Eason (eds), *Critical Perspectives on Media and Society*, pp. 126–59. New York and London: Guilford Press.

Grossman, M.B. and Kumar, M.J. (1981) *Portraying the President*. Baltimore, MD: Johns Hopkins University Press.

Gunter, B. (1987) *Poor Reception: Misunderstanding and Forgetting Broadcast News*. Hillsdale, NJ: Laurence Erlbaum.

Gunter, B. and Winstone, P. (1993) *Public Attitudes to Television 1992*. London: John Libby.

Gurevitch, M. and Levy, M. (1986) 'Information and Meaning: Audience Explanations of Social Issues', in J.P. Robinson and M. Levy, *The Main Source*, pp. 159–75. Beverly Hills, CA, and London: Sage Publications.

Gurevitch, M., Bennet, T., Curran, J. and Woollacott, J. (1982) (eds) *Culture, Society and the Media*. London: Methuen.

Habermas, J. (1989) *The Structural Transformation of the Public Sphere*. Cambridge, MA: MIT Press

Hachten, W.A. (1981) *The World News Prism: Changing Media, Changing Ideologies*. Ames, IA: Iowa State University Press.

Hackett, R.A. (1984) 'Decline of a Paradigm? Bias and Objectivity in News Media Studies', *Critical Studies in Mass Communication*, 1: 229–59.

Hagen, E. (1962) *On the Theory of Social Change*. Homewood, IL: Dorsey Press.

Haight, T. (1983) 'The Critical Research Dilemma', *Journal of Communication*, 33, 3: 226–36.

Hall, S. (1973) 'The Determination of News Photographs', in S. Cohen and J. Young (eds), *The Manufacture of News*, pp. 176–90. London: Constable.

Hall, S. (1977) 'Culture, the Media and the Ideological Effect', in J. Curran et al. (eds), *Mass Communication and Society*, pp. 315–48. London: Edward Arnold.

Hall, S. (1980) 'Coding and Encoding in the Television Discourse', in S. Hall et al. (eds), *Culture, Media, Language*, pp. 197–208. London: Hutchinson.

Hall, S. (1982) 'The Rediscovery of Ideology: Return of the Repressed in Media Studies', in M. Gurevitch et al. (eds), *Culture, Society and the Media*, pp. 56–90. London: Methuen.

Hall, S. (1989) 'Ideology and Communication Theory' in B. Dervin et al. (eds), *Rethinking Communication*, Vol. 1, *Paradigm Issues*, pp. 40–52. Newbury Park, CA, and London: Sage Publications.

Hall, S. and Jefferson, T. (1975) *Resistance through Rituals*. London: Hutchinson.

Hall, S., Clarke, J., Critcher, C., Jefferson, T. and Roberts, B. (1978) *Policing the Crisis*. London: Macmillan.

Hall, S., Hobson, D., Lowe, A. and Willis, P. (1980) *Culture, Media, Language*. London: Hutchinson.

Hallin, D.C. (1992) 'Sound Bite News: TV Coverage of Elections 1968–1988', *Journal of Communication*, 42, 2: 5–24.

Hallin, D.C. and Mancini, P. (1984) 'Political Structure and Representational Form in US and Italian TV News', *Theory and Society*, 13, 40: 829–50.

Halloran, J.D., Elliott, P. and Murdock, G. (1970) *Communications and Demonstrations*. Harmondsworth: Penguin.

Halmos, P. (ed) (1969) *The Sociology of Mass Media Communicators*. Sociological Review Monographs 13. Keele: University of Keele.

Hamelink, C. (1983) *Cultural Autonomy in Global Communications*. Norwood, NJ: Ablex.

Hardt, H. (1979) *Social Theories of the Press: Early German and American Perspectives*. Beverly Hills, CA, and London: Sage Publications.

Hardt, H. (1991) *Critical Communication Studies*. London and New York: Routledge.

Harris, N.G.E. (1992) 'Codes of Conduct for Journalists', in A. Belsey and R. Chadwick (eds), *Ethical Issues in Journalism*, pp. 62–76. London: Routledge.

Hartley, J. (1992) *The Politics of Pictures*. London: Routledge.

Hartman, P. and Husband, C. (1974) *Racism and Mass Media*. London: Davis Poynter.

Harvey, D. (1989) *The Condition of Postmodernity*. Oxford: Blackwell.

Hawkes, T. (1977) *Structuralism and Semiology*. London: Methuen.

Hawkins, R.P. and Pingree, S. (1983) 'TV's Influence on Social Reality', in E. Wartella et al. (eds), *Mass Communication Review Year Book*, Vol. 4, pp. 53–76. Beverly Hills, CA, and London: Sage Publications.

Hedinsson, E. (1981) *Television, Family and Society — the Social Origins and Effects of Adolescent TV Use*. Stockholm: Almqvist and Wiksell.

Heeter, C. (1988) 'The Choice Process Model', in C. Heeter and B.S. Greenberg (eds), *Cable Viewing*, pp. 11–32. Norwood, NJ: Ablex.

Heinderyckx, F. (1993) 'TV News Programmes in West Europe: A Comparative Study', *European Journal of Communication*, 8, 4.

Held, V. (1970) *The Public Interest and Individual Interests*. New York: Basic Books.

Hemánus, P. (1976) 'Objectivity in News Transmission', *Journal of Communication*, 26: 102–7.

Herman, E. and Chomsky, N. (1988) *Manufacturing Consent: The Political Economy of Mass Media*. New York: Pantheon.

Hermes, J. (1994) *Easily Put Down*. Oxford: Polity Press.

Herzog, H. (1944) 'What Do We Really Know about Daytime Serial Listeners?', in P.F. Lazarsfeld (ed), *Radio Research 1942–3*, pp. 2–23. New York: Duell, Sloan and Pearce.

Hess, S. (1986) *The Ultimate Insiders: US Senators in the National Media*. Washington, DC: Brookings Institute.

Hessler, R.C. and Stipp, H. (1985) 'The Impact of Fictional Suicide Stories on US Fatalities: A Replication', *American Journal of Sociology*, 90, 1: 151–67.

Hetherington, A. (1985) *News, Newspapers and Television*. London: Macmillan.

Himmelweit, H.T and Swift, T. (1976) 'Continuities and Discontinuities in Media Taste', *Journal of Social Issues* 32, 6: 133–56.

Himmelweit, H.T., Vince, P. and Oppenheim, A.N. (1958) *Television and the Child*. London: Oxford University Press.

Hirsch, F. and Gordon, D. (1975) *Newspaper Money*. London: Hutchinson.

Hirsch, P.M. (1973) 'Processing Fads and Fashions: An Organization-Set Analysis of Culture Industry Systems', *American Journal of Sociology*, 77: 639–59.

Hirsch, P.M. (1977) 'Occupational, Organizational and Institutional Models in Mass Communication', in P.M. Hirsch et al. (eds), *Strategies for Communication Research*, pp. 13–42. Beverly Hills, CA, and London: Sage Publications.

Hirsch, P.M. (1980) 'The "Scary World" of the Non-Viewer and Other Anomalies — a Re-analysis of Gerbner et al.'s Findings in Cultivation Analysis, Part 1', *Communication Research*, 7, 4: 403–56.

Hirsch, P.M. (1981) 'On Not Learning from One's Mistakes, Part II', *Communication Research*, 8, 1: 3–38.

Hirsch, P.M., Miller, P.V. and Kline, F.G. (eds) (1977) *Strategies for Communication Research*. Beverly Hills, CA, and London: Sage Publications.

Hobson, D. (1982) *Crossroads: The Drama of Soap Opera*. London: Methuen.

Hobson, D. (1989) 'Soap Operas at Work', in F. Seiter et al. (eds), *Remote Control*, pp. 130–49. London: Routledge.

Holden, R.T. (1986) 'The Contagiousness of Aircraft Hijacking', *American Journal of Sociology*, 91, 4: 876–904.

Holub, R. (1984) *Reception Theory*. London: Methuen.

Homet, R.S. (1990) 'Communications Policy-Making in West Europe' in J.L. Martin and R.F. Hébert (eds), *Current Issues in International Communication*. New York: Longman.

Hopkins, M. (1970) *Mass Media in the Soviet Union*. New York: Pegasus.

Horton, D. and Wohl, R.R. (1956) 'Mass Communication and Para-Social Interaction', *Psychiatry*, 19: 215–29.

Hoskins, C. and Mirus, R. (1988) 'Reasons for the US Dominance of the International Trade in Television Programmes', *Media, Culture and Society*, 10: 499–515.

Hoskins, C., Mirus, R. and Rozeboom, W. (1989) 'US Television Programs in the International Market: Unfair Pricing?', *Journal of Communication*, 39, 2: 55–75.

Hovland, C.I., Lumsdaine, A.A. and Sheffield, F.D. (1949) *Experiments in Mass Communication*. Princeton, NJ: Princeton University Press.

Howitt, D. and Cumberbatch, G. (1975) *Mass Media, Violence and Society*. New York: John Wiley.

Huaco, G.A. (1963) *The Sociology of Film Art*. New York: Basic Books.

Hughes, H.M. (1940) *News and the Human Interest Story*. Chicago: University of Chicago Press.

Hughes, M. (1980) 'The Fruits of Cultivation Analysis: A Re-examination of Some Effects of TV Viewing', *Public Opinion Quarterly*, 44, 3: 287–302.

Hutchins, R. (1947) 'Commission on Freedom of the Press', *A Free and Responsible Press*. Chicago: University of Chicago Press.

Hyman H. and Sheatsley, P. (1947) 'Some Reasons Why Information Campaigns Fail', *Public Opinion Quarterly*, II: 412–23.

Innis, H. (1950) *Empire and Communication*. Oxford: Clarendon Press.

Innis, H. (1951) *The Bias of Communication*. Toronto: University of Toronto Press.

Ito, Y. (1981) 'The "Johoka Shakai" Approach to the Study of Communication in Japan', in G.C. Wilhoit and H. de Bock (eds), *Mass Communication Review Yearbook*, Vol. 2. Beverly Hills, CA, and London: Sage Publications.

Ito, Y. and Koshevar, I.J. (1983) 'Factors Accounting for the Flow of International Communications', *Keio Communication Review*, 4: 13–38.

Iyengar, S. and Kinder, D.R. (1987) *News That Matters: Television and American Opinion*. Chicago: University of Chicago Press.

Jackson, I. (1971) *The Provincial Press and the Community*. Manchester: Manchester University Press.

Jameson, F. (1984) 'Postmodernism: The Cultural Logic of Late Capitalism', *New Left Review*, 146, July–August: 53–92.

Jameson, F. (1991) *Postmodernism*. London: Verso.

Jankowski, N., Prehn, O. and Stappers, J. (eds) (1992), *The People's Voice*. London: John Libby.

Janowitz, M. (1952) *The Community Press in an Urban Setting*. Glencoe, IL: Free Press.

Janowitz, M. (1968) 'The Study of Mass Communication', in *International Encyclopedia of the Social Sciences*, Vol. 3, pp. 41–53. New York: Macmillan and Free Press.

Janowitz, M. (1975) 'Professional Models in Journalism: The Gatekeeper and Advocate', *Journalism Quarterly*, 52, 4: 618–26.

Janowitz, M. (1981) 'Mass Media: Institutional Trends and Their Consequences', in M. Janowitz and P.M. Hirsch (eds), *Reader in Public Opinion and Mass Communication*, 3rd edn. pp. 303–21. New York: Free Press.

Jansen, S.C. (1988) *Censorship*. New York: Oxford University Press.

Jay, M. (1973) *The Dialectical Imagination*. London: Heinemann.

Jensen, K.B. (1991) 'When Is Meaning? Communication Theory, Pragmatism and Mass Media Reception', in J. Anderson (ed), *Communication Yearbook 14*, pp. 3–32. Newbury Park, CA, and London: Sage Publications.

Jensen, K.B. and Jankowski, N. (eds) (1992) *A Handbook of Qualitative Methodologies*. London: Routledge.

Jensen, K.B. and Rosengren, K.E. (1990) 'Five Traditions in Search of the Audience', *European Journal of Communication*, 5, 2/3: 207–38.

Johnstone, J.W.L., Slawski, E.J. and Bowman, W.W. (1976) *The News People*. Urbana, IL: University of Illinois Press.

Jowett, G. and Linton, J.M. (1980) *Movies as Mass Communication*. Beverly Hills, CA, and London: Sage Publications.

Kaplan, E.A. (1987) *Rocking around the Clock: Music Television, Postmodernism and Consumer Culture*. London: Methuen.

Kaplan, E.A. (1992) 'Feminist Critiques and Television', in R.C. Allen (ed), *Channels of Discourse Reassembled*, pp. 247–83. London: Routledge.

Katz, D. (1960) 'The Functional Approach to the Study of Attitudes', *Public Opinion Quarterly*, 24: 163–204.

Katz, E. (1977) *Social Research and Broadcasting: Proposals for Further Development*. London: BBC.

Katz, E. (1983) 'Publicity and Pluralistic Ignorance: Notes on the Spiral of Silence', in E. Wartella et al. (eds), *Mass Communication Review Yearbook*, Vol. 4, pp. 89–99. Beverly Hills, CA, and London: Sage Publications.

Katz, E. (1988) 'Communications Research since Lazarsfeld', *Public Opinion Quarterly*, 51, 2: 525–45.

Katz, E. and Dayan, D. (1986) 'Contents, Conquests and Coronations: Media Events and Their Heroes', in C.F. Graumann and S. Moscovici (eds) *Changing Conceptions of Leadership*. Berlin: Springer Verlag.

Katz, E. and Lazarsfeld, P.F. (1955) *Personal Influence*. Glencoe, IL: Free Press.

Katz, E. and Szecskö, T. (eds) (1981) *Mass Media and Social Change*. Beverly Hills, CA, and London: Sage Publications.

Katz, E., Lewin, M.L. and Hamilton, H. (1963) 'Traditions of Research on the Diffusion of Innovations', *American Sociological Review*, 28: 237–52.

Katz, E., Gurevitch, M. and Haas, H. (1973) 'On the Use of Mass Media for Important Things', *American Sociological Review*, 38: 164–81.

Katz, E., Blumler, J.G. and Gurevitch, M. (1974) 'Utilization of Mass Communication by the Individual', in J.G. Blumler and E. Katz (eds), *The Uses of Mass Communication*, pp. 19–32. Beverly Hills, CA, and London: Sage Publications.

Katz, E., Adoni, H. and Parness, P. (1977) 'Remembering the News — What the Picture Adds to the Sound', *Journalism Quarterly*, 54: 231–9.

Keane, J. (1991) *The Media and Democracy*. Oxford: Polity Press.

Kellner, D. (1990) *Television and the Crisis of Democracy*. Boulder, CO: Westview Press.

Kelman, H. (1961) 'Processes of Opinion Change', *Public Opinion Quarterly*, 25: 57–78.

Kepplinger, H.M. (1983) 'Visual Biases in TV Campaign Coverage', in E. Wartella et al. (eds), *Mass Communication Review Yearbook*, Vol. 4, pp. 391–405. Beverly Hills, CA, and London: Sage Publications.

Kerner, O. et al. (1968) *Report of the National Advisory Committee on Civil Disorders*. Washington, DC: GPO.

Key, V.O. (1961) *Public Opinion and American Democracy*. New York: Alfred Knopf.

Kingsbury, S.M. and Hart, M. (1937) *Newspapers and the News*. New York: Putnams.

Kivikuru, A. and Varis, T. (eds) (1985) *Approaches to International Communication*. Helsinki: Finnish National UNESCO Commission.

Klapper, J. (1960) *The Effects of Mass Communication*. New York: Free Press.

Köcher, R. (1986) 'Bloodhounds or Missionaries: Role Definitions of German and British Journalists', *European Journal of Communication*, 1, 1: 43–64.

Kornhauser, W. (1959) *The Politics of Mass Society*. New York: Free Press.

Kornhauser, W. (1968) 'The Theory of Mass Society', in *International Encyclopedia of the Social Sciences*, Vol. 10, pp. 58–64. New York: Macmillan and Free Press.

Kracauer, S. (1949) 'National Types as Hollywood Represents Them', *Public Opinion Quarterly*, 13: 53–72.

Kraus, S. and Davis D.K. (1976) *The Effects of Mass Communication on Political Behavior*. University Park, PA: Pennsylvania State University Press.

Kraus, S., Davis, D.K., Lang, G.E. and Lang K. (1975) 'Critical Events Analysis', in S.H. Chaffee (ed), *Political Communication Research*, pp. 195–216. Beverly Hills, CA, and London: Sage Publications.

Krippendorf, K. (1980) *Content Analysis*. Beverly Hills, CA, and London: Sage Publications.

Krugman, D.M. and Reid, L.N. (1980) ' "The Public Interest" as Defined by FCC Policy Makers', *Journal of Broadcasting*, 24, 3: 311–25.

Krugman, H.E. (1965) 'The Impact of Television Advertising: Learning without Involvement', *Public Opinion Quarterly*, 29: 349–56.

Kumar, C. (1975) 'Holding the Middle Ground', *Sociology*, 9, 3: 67–88. Reprinted in J. Curran et al. (eds), *Mass Communication and Society*, pp. 231–48. London: Edward Arnold.

Lang, K. and Lang, G.E. (1953) 'The Unique Perspective of Television and its Effect', *American Sociological Review*, 18, 1: 103–12.

Lang, G. and Lang K. (1981) 'Mass Communication and Public Opinion: Strategies for Research', in M. Rosenberg and R.H. Turner (eds), *Social Psychology: Sociological Perspectives*, pp. 653–82. New York: Basic Books.

Lang, G. and Lang, K. (1983) *The Battle for Public Opinion*. New York: Columbia University Press.

Lasswell, H. (1948) 'The Structure and Function of Communication in Society', in L. Bryson (ed), *The Communication of Ideas*, pp. 32–51. New York: Harper.

Lazarsfeld, P.F. and Stanton, F. (1949) *Communication Research 1948–9*. New York: Harper and Row.

Lazarsfeld, P.F., Berelson, B. and Gaudet, H. (1944) *The People's Choice*. New York: Duell, Sloan and Pearce.

Lee, M.A. and Solomon, N. (1990) *Unreliable Sources: A Guide to Detecting Bias in News Media*. New York: Lyle Stewart.

Leggatt, T. (1991) 'Identifying the Undefinable', *Studies of Broadcasting*, 27: 113–32.

Leiss, W. (1989) 'The Myth of the Information Society', in I. Angus and S. Jhally (eds), *Cultural Politics in Contemporary America*, pp. 282–98. New York and London: Routledge.

Lemert, J.B. (1989) *Criticizing the Media*. Newbury Park, CA, and London: Sage Publications.

Lerner, D. (1958) *The Passing of Traditional Society*. New York: Free Press.

Levy, M. (1977) 'Experiencing Television News', *Journal of Communication*, 27: 112–17.

Levy, M. and Windahl, S. (1985) 'The Concept of Audience Activity', in K.E. Rosengren et al. (eds), *Media Gratification Research*, pp. 109–22. Beverly Hills, CA, and London: Sage Publications.

Lewin, K. (1947) 'Channels of Group Life', *Human Relations*, 1: 143–53.

Lewis, G.H. (1981) 'Taste Cultures and Their Composition: Towards a New Theoretical Perspective', in E. Katz and T. Szecskö (eds), *Mass Media and Social Change*, pp. 201–17. Newbury Park, CA, and London: Sage Publications.

Lewis, G.H. (1992) 'Who Do You Love? The Dimensions of Musical Taste', in J. Lull (ed), *Popular Music and Communication*, 2nd edn, pp. 134–51. Newbury Park, CA, and London: Sage Publications.

Lewis, L. (ed) (1992) *The Adoring Audience*. London: Routledge.

Lichtenberg, J. (ed) (1990) *Democracy and Mass Media*. Cambridge: Cambridge University Press.

Lichtenberg, J. (1991) 'In Defense of Objectivity', in J. Curran and M. Gurevitch (eds), *Mass Media and Society*, pp. 216–31. London: Edward Arnold.

Lichter, S.R. and Rothman, S. (1986) *The Media Elite: America's New Power Brokers*. Bethesda, MD: Adler and Adler.

Liebes, T. and Katz, E. (1986) 'Patterns of Involvement in Television Fiction: A Comparative Analysis', *European Journal of Communication*, 1, 2: 151–72.

Liebes, T. and Katz, E. (1989) 'Critical Abilities of TV Viewers', in F. Seiter et al. (eds), *Remote Control*, pp. 204–22. London: Routledge.

Liebes, T. and Katz, E. (1990) *The Export of Meaning: Cross-Cultural Readings of 'Dallas'*. Oxford: Oxford University Press.

Lindlof, T. and Traudt, P. (1983) 'Mediated Communication in Families', in M. Mander (ed), *Communications in Transition*. New York: Praeger.

Lippman, W. (1922) *Public Opinion*. New York: Harcourt Brace.

Livingstone, S. (1991) 'Audience Reception: The Role of the Viewer in Retelling Romantic Drama', in J. Curran and M. Gurevitch (eds), *Mass Media and Society*, pp. 285–306. London: Edward Arnold.

Long, E. (1991) 'Feminism and Cultural Studies', in R. Avery and D. Eason (eds), *Cultural Perspectives on Media and Society*, pp. 114–25. New York and London: Guilford Press.

Lull, J. (1982) 'The Social Uses of Television', in D.C. Whitney et al. (eds), *Mass Communication Review Yearbook*, Vol. 3, pp. 397–409. Beverly Hills, CA, and London: Sage Publications.

Lull, J. (1990) *Inside Family Viewing*. New York and London: Routledge.

Lull, J. (ed) (1992) *Popular Music and Communication*. Newbury Park, CA, and London: Sage Publications.

Lull, J. and Wallis, R. (1992) 'The Beat of Vietnam', in J. Lull (ed), *Popular Music and Communication*, pp. 207–36. Newbury Park, CA, and London: Sage Publications.

McBride, S. et al. (1980) *Many Voices, One World*. Report by the International Commission for the Study of Communication Problems. Paris: UNESCO; London: Kogan Page.

McCain, T. (1986) 'Patterns of Media Use in Europe: Identifying Country Clusters', *European Journal of Communication*, 1, 2: 231–50.

Maccoby, E. (1954) 'Why Do Children Watch TV?', *Public Opinion Quarterly*, 18: 239–44.

McCombs, M.E. and Shaw, D.L. (1972) 'The Agenda–Setting Function of the Press', *Public Opinion Quarterly*, 36: 176–87.

McCombs, M.E. and Shaw, D.L. (1993) 'The Evolution of Agenda-Setting Theory: 25 Years in the Marketplace of Ideas', *Journal of Communication*, 43, 2: 58–66.

McCormack, T. (1961) 'Social Theory and the Mass Media', *Canadian Journal of Economics and Political Science*, 4: 479–89.

McCron, R. (1976) 'Changing Perspectives in the Study of Mass Media and Socialization', in J. Halloran (ed), *Mass Media and Socialization*, pp. 13–44. Leicester: International Association for Mass Communication Research.

McGinnis, J. (1969) *The Selling of the President*. New York: Trident Press.

McGranahan, D.V. and Wayne, L. (1948) 'German and American Traits Reflected in Popular Drama', *Human Relations*, 1, 4: 429–55.

McGuigan, J. (1992) *Cultural Populism*. London: Routledge.

McGuire, W.J. (1973) 'Persuasion, Resistance and Attitude Change', in I. de Sola Pool et al. (eds), *Handbook of Communication*, pp. 216–52. Chicago: Rand McNally.

McGuire, W.J. (1974) 'Psychological Motives and Communication Gratifications', in J.G. Blumler and E. Katz (eds), *The Uses of Mass Communications*, pp.167–96. Beverly Hills, CA, and London: Sage Publications.

McLelland, D.W. (1961) *The Achieving Society*. Princeton, NJ: Van Nostrand.

McLeod, M.J., Ward, L.S. and Tancill, K. (1965) 'Alienation and Uses of Mass Media', *Public Opinion Quarterly*, 29: 583–94.

McLeod, J.M., Kosicki, G.M. and Pan, Z. (1991) 'On Understanding and Not Understanding Media Effects', in J. Curran and M. Gurevitch (eds), *Mass Media and Society*, pp. 235–66. London: Edward Arnold.

McLuhan, M. (1962) *The Gutenberg Galaxy*. Toronto: Toronto University Press.

McLuhan, M. (1964) *Understanding Media*. London: Routledge and Kegan Paul.

McQuail, D. (ed) (1972) *Sociology of Mass Communications*. Harmondsworth: Penguin.

McQuail, D. (1977) *Analysis of Newspaper Content*. Royal Commission on the Press, Research Series 4. London: HMSO.

McQuail, D. (1984) 'With the Benefit of Hindsight: Reflections on Uses and Gratifications Research', *Critical Studies in Mass Communication*, 1: 177–93.

McQuail, D. (1986) 'Is Media Theory Adequate to the Challenge of the New Communications Technologies?', in M. Ferguson (ed), *New Communication Technologies and the Public Interest*, pp. 1–17. Beverly Hills, CA, and London: Sage Publications.

McQuail, D. (1987) 'The Functions of Communication: A Non-Functionalist Overview', in C.R. Berger and S.H. Chaffee (eds), *Handbook of Communication Science*, pp. 327–49. Beverly Hills, CA, and London: Sage Publications.

McQuail, D. (1990) 'Caging the Beast: Constructing a Framework for the Analysis of Media Change in West Europe', *European Journal of Communication*, 5, 2/3: 313–32.

McQuail, D. (1992) *Media Performance: Mass Communication and the Public Interest*. London and Newbury Park, CA: Sage Publications.

McQuail, D. and Gurevitch, M. (1974) 'Explaining Audience Behaviour', in J.G. Blumler and

E. Katz (eds), *The Uses of Mass Communications*, pp. 287–306. Beverly Hills, CA, and London: Sage Publications.

McQuail, D. and Siune, K. (eds) (1986) *New Media Politics*. London: Sage Publications.

McQuail, D. and Windahl, S. (1993) *Communication Models*, 2nd edn. London: Longman.

McQuail, D., Blumler, J.G. and Brown, J. (1972) 'The Television Audience: A Revised Perspective', in D. McQuail (ed), *Sociology of Mass Communication*, pp. 135–65. Harmondsworth: Penguin.

Maisel, R. (1973) 'The Decline of Mass Media', *Public Opinion Quarterly*, 37: 159–70.

Marcuse, H. (1964) *One-Dimensional Man*. London: Routledge and Kegan Paul.

Martel, M.U. and McCall, G.J. (1964) 'Reality-Orientation and the Pleasure Principle', in L.A. Dexter and D.M. White (eds), *People, Society and Mass Communication*, pp. 283–333. New York: Free Press.

Martin, M. (1991) *'Hello Central'? Gender, Technology and Culture in the Formation of Telephone Systems*. Montreal: Queens University Press.

Mazzoleni, G. (1986) 'Mass Telematics: Facts and Fiction' in D.McQuail and K. Siune (eds), *New Media Politics*, pp. 100–14. London: Sage Publications.

Mazzoleni, G. (1987) 'Media Logic and Party Logic in Campaign Coverage: The Italian General Election of 1983', *European Journal of Communication*, 2, 1: 55–80.

Media Studies Journal (1993) 'The Media and Women without Apology', Special Issue Vol. 7, 1, 1/2.

Melody, W.H. (1990) 'Communications Policy in the Global Information Economy', in M.F. Ferguson (ed), *Public Communication: The New Imperatives*, pp. 16–39. London and Newbury Park, CA: Sage Publications.

Mendelsohn, H. (1964) 'Listening to Radio', in L.A. Dexter and D.M. White (eds), *People, Society and Mass Communication*, pp. 239–48. New York: Free Press.

Mendelsohn, H. (1966) *Mass Entertainment*. New Haven, CT: College and University Press.

Mendelsohn, H. (1973) 'Some Reasons Why Information Campaigns Can Succeed', *Public Opinion Quarterly*, 37: 50–61.

Mendelsohn, H. (1989) 'Phenomenistic Alternatives', *Communication Research*, 16, 4: 82–7.

Merrill, J. (1974) *The Imperatives of Freedom*. New York: Hastings House.

Merton, R.K. (1949) 'Patterns of Influence', in *Social Theory and Social Structure*, pp. 387–470. Glencoe, IL: Free Press.

Merton, R.K. (1957) *Social Theory and Social Structure*. Glencoe, IL: Free Press.

Meyer, P. (1987) *Ethical Journalism*. New York and London: Longman.

Meyrowitz, J. (1985) *No Sense of Place*. New York: Oxford University Press.

Miliband, R. (1969) *The State in Capitalist Society*. London: Weidenfeld and Nicolson.

Mills, C.W. (1951) *White Collar*. New York: Oxford University Press.

Mills, C.W. (1956) *The Power Elite*. New York: Oxford University Press.

Modleski, T. (1982) *Loving with a Vengeance: Mass-Produced Fantasies for Women*. London: Methuen.

Molotch, H.L. and Lester, M.J. (1974) 'News as Purposive Behavior', *American Sociological Review*, 39: 101–12.

Monaco, J. (1981) *How to Read a Film*. New York: Oxford University Press.

Montgomery, K.C. (1989) *Target: Prime-Time*. New York: Oxford University Press.

Morin, V. (1976) 'Televised Current Events Sequences or a Rhetoric of Ambiguity', in *News and Current Events on TV*. Rome: Edizioni RAI.

Morley, D. (1980) *The 'Nationwide' Audience: Structure and Decoding*. BFI TV Monographs No. 11. London: British Film Institute.

Morley, D. (1986) *Family Television*. London: Comedia.

Morley, D. (1992) *Television, Audiences and Cultural Studies*. London: Routledge.

Morrison, D. and Tumber, H. (1988) *Journalists at War*. London and Newbury Park, CA: Sage Publications.

Moscovici, S. (1991) 'Silent Majorities and Loud Minorities', in J. Anderson (ed), *Communication Yearbook 14*, pp. 298–308. Newbury Park, CA, and London: Sage Publications.

Mowlana, H. (1985) *International Flows of Information*. Paris: UNESCO.

Mowlana, H. (1986) *Global Information and the World Economy*. New York and London: Longman.

Murdock, G. (1990) 'Redrawing the Map of the Communication Industries', in M. Ferguson (ed), *Public Communication*, pp. 1–15. London and Newbury Park, CA: Sage Publications.

Murdock, G. and Golding, P. (1977) 'Capitalism, Communication and Class Relations', in J. Curran et al. (eds), *Mass Communication and Society*, pp. 12–43. London: Edward Arnold.

Murphy, D. (1976) *The Silent Watchdog*. London: Constable.

Negus, K (1993) *Producing Pop*. London: Edward Arnold.

Neuman, W.R. (1982) 'Television and American Culture: The Mass Media and the Pluralistic Audience', *Public Opinion Quarterly*, 46: 471–87.

Neuman, W.R. (1991) *The Future of the Mass Audience*. Cambridge: Cambridge University Press.

Newcomb, H. (1978) 'Assessing the Violence Profile on Gerbner and Gross: A Humanistic Critique and Suggestion', *Communication Research*, 5, 3: 264–82.

Newcomb, H. (1991) 'On the Dialogic Aspects of Mass Communication', in R. Avery and D. Easton (eds), *Critical Perspectives on Media and Society*, pp. 69–87. New York and London: Guilford Press.

Newhagen, J.E. and Reeves, B. (1992) 'The Evening's Bad News', *Journal of Communication*, 42, 2: 25–41.

Nimmo, D.D. and Combs, J.E. (1985) *Nightly Horrors: Crisis Coverage by Television Network News*. Knoxville, TN: University of Tennessee Press.

Noble, G. (1975) *Children in Front of the Small Screen*. London: Constable.

Noelle-Neumann, E. (1973) 'Return to the Concept of Powerful Mass Media', *Studies of Broadcasting*, 9: 66–112.

Noelle-Neumann, E. (1974) 'The Spiral of Silence: A Theory of Public Opinion', *Journal of Communication*, 24: 24–51.

Noelle-Neumann, E. (1984) *The Spiral of Silence*. Chicago: University of Chicago Press.

Noelle-Neumann, E. (1991) 'The Theory of Public Opinion: The Concept of the Spiral of Silence', in J. Anderson (ed), *Communication Yearbook 14*, pp. 256–87. Newbury Park, CA, and London: Sage Publications.

Nordenstreng, K. (1974) *Informational Mass Communication*. Helsinki: Tammi.

Nordenstreng, K. (1984) *The Mass Media Declaration of UNESCO*. Norwood, NJ: Ablex.

Nordicom Review (1992) 'The Gulf War in the Media', Special Issue No. 2.

Nowak, K. (1977) 'From Information Caps to Communication Potential', in M. Berg et al. (eds), *Current Theories in Scandinavian Mass Communication*, pp. 230–58. Grenaa, Denmark: GMT.

Ogden, C.K. and Richards, I.A. (1923) *The Meaning of Meaning*. Reprinted 1985. London: Routledge and Kegan Paul.

Okada, N. (1986) 'The Process of Mass Communication: A Review of Studies of the Two-Step Flow Hypothesis', *Studies of Broadcasting*, 22: 57–78.

Oltean, O. (1993) 'Series and Seriality in Media Culture', *European Journal of Communication*, 8, 1: 5–31.

Osgood, K., Suci, S. and Tannenbaum, P. (1957) *The Measurement of Meaning*. Urbana, IL: University of Illinois Press.

Padioleau, J. (1985) *Le Monde et le Washington Post*. Paris: PUF.

Paletz, D.L. and Dunn, R. (1969) 'Press Coverage of Civil Disorders: A Case-Study of Winston-Salem', *Public Opinion Quarterly*, 33: 328–45.

Paletz, D.L. and Entman, R. (1981) *Media, Power, Politics*. New York: Free Press.

Paletz, D. and Schmidt, A. (eds) (1992) *Terrorism and the Media*. Newbury Park, CA, and London: Sage Publications.

Palmgreen, P. and Rayburn, J.D. (1985) 'An Expectancy-Value Approach to Media Gratifications', in K.E. Rosengren et al. (eds), *Media Gratification Research*, pp. 61–72. Beverly Hills, CA, and London: Sage Publications.

Park, R. (1940) 'News as a Form of Knowledge', in R.H. Turner (ed), *On Social Control and Collective Behavior*, pp. 32–52. Chicago: Chicago University Press, 1967.

Parkin, F. (1972) *Class Inequality and Political Order*. London: Paladin.

Peacock, A. (1986) *Report of the Committee on Financing the BBC*. Cmnd 9824. London: HMSO.

Pearlin, L. (1959) 'Social and Personal Stress and Escape Television Viewing', *Public Opinion Quarterly*, 23: 255–9.

Pearse, E.M. (1990) 'Audience Selectivity and Involvement in the Newer Media Environment', *Communication Research*, 17: 675–97.

Peirce, C.S. (1931–35) *Collected Papers*, edited by C. Harteshorne and P. Weiss, Vols II and V. Cambridge, MA: Harvard University Press.

Pekurny, R. (1982) 'Coping with Television Production', in J.S. Ettema and D.C. Whitney (eds) *Individuals in Mass Media Organizations*, pp. 131–43. Beverly Hills, CA, and London: Sage Publications.

Peters, A.K. and Cantor, M.G. (1982) 'Screen Acting as Work', in J.S. Ettema and D.C. Whitney (eds), *Individuals in Mass Media Organizations*, pp. 53–68. Beverly Hills, CA, and London: Sage Publications.

Peterson, R.C. and Thurstone, L.L. (1933) *Motion Pictures and Social Attitudes*. New York: Macmillan.

Phillips, D.P. (1980) 'Airplane Accidents, Murder and the Mass Media', *Social Forces*, 58, 4: 1001–24.

Phillips, D.P. (1982) 'The Impact of Fictional TV Stories in Adult Programming on Adult Fatalities', *American Journal of Sociology*, 87: 1346–59.

Phillips, E.B. (1977) 'Approaches to Objectivity', in P.M. Hirsch et al. (eds), *Strategies for Communication Research*, pp. 63–77. Beverly Hills, CA, and London: Sage Publications.

Picard, R.G. (1985) *The Press and the Decline of Democracy*. Westport, CT: Greenwood Press.

Picard, R.G. (1989) *Media Economics*. Newbury Park, CA, and London: Sage Publications.

Picard, R.G. (1991) 'News Coverage as the Contagion of Terrorism', in A.A. Alali and K.K. Ede (eds), *Media Coverage of Terrorism*, pp. 49–62. London and Newbury Park, CA: Sage Publications.

Picard, R.G., McCombs, M., Winter, J.P. and Lacy, S. (eds) (1988) *Press Concentration and Monopoly*. Norwood, NJ: Ablex.

Pool, I. de Sola (1973) 'Newsmen and Statesmen — Adversaries or Cronies?', in W.L Rivers and N.J. Nyhan (eds), *Aspen Papers on Government and Media*. London: Allen and Unwin.

Pool, I. de Sola (1983) *Technologies of Freedom*. Cambridge, MA: Belknap Press of Harvard University Press.

Pool, I. de Sola and Shulman, I. (1959) 'Newsmen's Fantasies, Audiences and Newswriting', *Public Opinion Quarterly*, 23, 2: 145–58.

Pool, I. de Sola, Inose, H., Talaki, N. and Hurwitz, R. (1984) *Communication Flows: A Census in the US and Japan*. Amsterdam: North Holland Press.

Preston, W., Herman, E.S. and Schiller, H.I. (1989) *Hope and Folly: The US and UNESCO 1945–85*. Minneapolis, MN: University of Minnesota Press.

Propp, V. (1968) *The Morphology of Folk Tales*. Austin, TX: University of Texas Press.

Pye, L.W. (1963) *Communications and Political Development*. Princeton, NJ: Princeton University Press.

Radway, J. (1984) *Reading the Romance*. Chapel Hill, NC: University of North Carolina Press.

Rakow, L. (1986) 'Rethinking Gender Research in Communication', *Journal of Communication*, 36, 1: 11–26.

Ray, M.L. (1973) 'Marketing Communication and the Hierarchy of Effects', in P. Clarke (ed), *New Models for Communication Research*, pp. 147–76. Beverly Hills, CA, and London: Sage Publications.

Rayburn, J.D. and Palmgreen, P. (1984) 'Merging Uses and Gratifications and Expectancy-Value Theory', *Communication Research*, II: 537–62.

Real, M. (1989) *Supermedia*. Newbury Park, CA, and London: Sage Publications.

Reese, S.D. (1991) 'Setting the Media's Agenda: A Power Balance Perspective', in J. Anderson (ed) *Communication Yearbook 14*, pp. 309–40. Newbury Park, CA, and London: Sage.

Rice, R.E. and Atkin, C. (eds) (1989) *Public Communication Campaigns*, 2nd edn. Newbury Park, CA, and London: Sage Publications.

Rice, R.E. and Paisley, W.J. (eds) (1981) *Public Communication Campaigns*. Beverly Hills, CA, and London: Sage Publications.

Ridder, J. de (1984) *Persconcentratie in Nederland*. Amsterdam: VU Uitgeverij.

Rikardsson, G. (1981) 'Newspaper Opinion and Public Opinion', in K.E. Rosengren (ed), *Advances in Content Analysis*, pp. 215–26. Beverly Hills, CA, and London: Sage Publications.

Riley, M.W. and Riley, J.W. (1951) 'A Sociological Approach to Communications Research' *Public Opinion Quarterly*, 15, 3: 445–60.

Rivers, W.L., Schramm, W. and Christians, G.C. (1980) *Responsibility in Mass Communications*. New York: Harper and Row.

Robinson, J.P. (1972) 'Mass Communication and Information Diffusion', in F.G. Kline and P.J. Tichenor (eds), *Current Perspectives in Mass Communication Research*, pp. 71–93. Beverly Hills, CA, and London: Sage Publications.

Robinson, J.P. (1976) 'Interpersonal Influence in Election Campaigns: 2-Step Flow Hypotheses', *Public Opinion Quarterly*, 40: 304–19.

Robinson, J.P. and Davis, D.K. (1990) 'Television News and the Informed Public: An Information Processing Approach', *Journal of Communication*, 40, 3: 106–19.

Robinson, J.P. and Levy, M. (1986) *The Main Source*. Beverly Hills, CA, and London: Sage Publications.

Rogers, E.M. (1962) *The Diffusion of Innovations*. Glencoe, IL: Free Press.

Rogers, E.M. (1976) 'Communication and Development: The Passing of a Dominant Paradigm', *Communication Research*, 3: 213–40.

Rogers, E.M. (1986) *Communication Technology*. New York: Free Press.

Rogers, E.M. (1993) 'Looking Back, Looking Forward: A Century of Communication Research', in P. Gaunt (ed), *Beyond Agendas: New Directions in Communication Research*, pp. 19–40. Newhaven, CT: Greenwood Press.

Rogers, E.M. and Dearing, J.W. (1987) 'Agenda-Setting Research: Where Has It Been? Where Is It Going?', in J. Anderson (ed), *Communication Yearbook 11*, pp. 555–94. Newbury Park, CA, and London: Sage Publications.

Rogers, E.M. and Kincaid, D.L. (1981) *Communication Networks: Towards a New Paradigm for Research*. New York: Free Press.

Rogers, E.M. and Shoemaker, F. (1973) *Communication of Innovations*. New York: Free Press.

Rogers, E.M. and Storey, D. (1987) 'Communication Campaigns', in C.R. Berger and S.H. Chaffee (eds), *Handbook of Communication Science*, pp. 817–46. Beverly Hills, CA, and London: Sage Publications.

Rogers, E.M., Dearing, J.W. and Bregman, D. (1993) 'The Anatomy of Agenda-Setting Research', *Journal of Communication*, 43, 2: 68–84.

Rosenberg, B. and White, D.M. (eds) (1957) *Mass Culture*. New York: Free Press.

Rosengren, K.E. (1973) 'News Diffusion: An Overview', *Journalism Quarterly*, 50: 83–91.

Rosengren, K.E. (1974) 'International News: Methods, Data, Theory', *Journal of Peace Research*, II: 45–56.

Rosengren, K.E. (1976) 'The Barseback "Panic"'. Unpublished research report, Lund University.

Rosengren, K.E. (ed) (1981a) *Advances in Content Analysis*. Beverly Hills, CA, and London: Sage Publications.

Rosengren, K.E. (1981b) 'Mass Media and Social Change: Some Current Approaches', in E. Katz and T. Szecskö (eds), *Mass Media and Social Change*, pp. 247–63. Beverly Hills, CA, and London: Sage Publications.

Rosengren, K.E. (1983) 'Communication Research: One Paradigm or Four?', *Journal of Communication*, 33, 3: 185–207.

Rosengren, K.E. (1987) 'The Comparative Study of News Diffusion', *European Journal of Communication*, 2, 2: 136–57.

Rosengren, K.E. (1989) 'Paradigms Lost and Regained', in B. Dervin et al. (eds), *Rethinking Communication*, pp. 21–39. Newbury Park, CA, and London: Sage Publications.

Rosengren, K.E. and Windahl, S. (1972) 'Mass Media Consumption as a Functional Alternative', in D. McQuail (ed), *Sociology of Mass Communications*, pp. 166–94. Harmondsworth: Penguin.

Rosengren, K.E. and Windahl, S. (1989) *Media Matter*. Norwood, NJ: Ablex.

Rosengren, K.E., Palmgreen, P. and Wenner, L. (eds) (1985) *Media Gratification Research: Current Perspectives*. Beverly Hills, CA, and London: Sage Publications.

Roshco, B. (1975) *Newsmaking*. Chicago: University of Chicago Press.

Rositi, F. (1976) 'The Television News Programme: Fragmentation and Recomposition of Our Image of Society', in *News and Current Events on TV*. Rome: Edizioni RAI.

Rosten, L.C. (1937) *The Washington Correspondents*. New York: Harcourt Brace.

Rosten, L.C. (1941) *Hollywood: The Movie Colony, the Movie Makers*. New York: Harcourt Brace.

Royal Commission on the Press (1977) *Report*. Cmnd 6810. London: HMSO.

Ryan, J. and Peterson, R.A. (1982) 'The Product Image: The Fate of Creativity in Country Music Song Writing', in J.S. Ettema and D.C. Whitney (eds), *Individuals in Mass Media Organizations*, pp. 11–32. Beverly Hills, CA, and London: Sage Publications.

Salvaggio, J.L (1985) 'Information Technology and Social Problems: Four International Models', in B.D. Ruben (ed), *Information and Behavior*, Vol. I, pp. 428–54. Rutgers, NJ: Transaction Books.

Saussure, F. de (1915) *Course in General Linguistics*. English trans. London: Peter Owen, 1960.

Schement, J. and Stout, D.A. (1988) 'A Time-Line of Information Innovation', in B.D. Ruben (ed), *Information and Behavior*, Vol. III, pp. 395–423. Rutgers, NJ: Transaction Books.

Schiller, H. (1969) *Mass Communication and American Empire*. New York: Augustus M. Kelly.

Schiller, H. (1989) *Information and the Crisis Economy*. Norwood, NJ: Ablex.

Schlesinger, P. (1978) *Putting 'Reality' Together: BBC News*. London: Constable.

Schlesinger, P. (1987) 'On National Identity', *Social Science Information*, 25, 2: 219–64.

Schlesinger, P., Murdock, G. and Elliott, P. (1983) *Televising Terrorism*. London: Comedia.

Schmid, A.P. and de Graaf, J. (1982) *Violence as Communication*. Beverly Hills, CA, and London: Sage Publications.

Schramm, W. (1955) 'Information Theory and Mass Communication', *Journalism Quarterly*, 32: 131–46.

Schramm, W. (1964) *Mass Media and National Development*. Stanford, CA: Stanford University Press.

Schramm, W., Lyle, J. and Parker, E. (1961) *Television in the Lives of Our Children*. Stanford, CA: Stanford University Press.

Schrøder, K.C. (1987) 'Convergence of Antagonistic Traditions?', *European Journal of Communication*, 2, 1: 7–31.

Schrøder, K.C. (1992) 'Cultural Quality: Search for a Phantom?', in M. Skovmand and K.C. Schrøder (eds), *Media Cultures: Reappraising Transnational Media*, pp. 161–80. London: Routledge.

Schudson, M. (1978) *Discovering the News*. New York: Basic Books.

Schudson, M. (1991) 'The New Validation of Popular Culture', in R.K. Avery and D. Eason (eds), *Critical Perspectives on Media and Society*, pp. 49–68. New York and London: Guilford.

Schulz, W. (1988) 'Media and Reality'. Unpublished paper for Sommatie Conference, Veldhoven, the Netherlands.

Schwichtenberg, C. (1992) 'Music Video', in J. Lull (ed), *Popular Music and Communication*, pp. 116–33. Newbury Park, CA, and London: Sage Publications.

Seiter, F., Borchers, H. and Warth, E.-M. (eds) (1989) *Remote Control*. London: Routledge.

Sepstrup, P. (1989) 'Research into International TV Flows', *European Journal of Communication*, 4, 4: 393–408.

Sepstrup, P. (1990) *The Transnationalization of TV in West Europe*. London: John Libbey.

Seymour-Ure, C. (1974) *The Political Impact of the Mass Media*. London: Cole.

Shannon, C. and Weaver, W. (eds) (1949) *The Mathematical Theory of Communication*. Urbana, IL: University of Illinois Press.

Shibutani, T. (1966) *Improvised News*. New York: Bobbs Merrill.

Shils, E. (1957) 'Daydreams and Nightmares: Reflections on the Criticism of Mass Culture', *Sewanee Review*, 65 ,4: 586–608.

Shoemaker, P.J. (1984) 'Media Treatment of Deviant Political Groups', *Journalism Quarterly* 61, 1: 66–75, 82.

Shoemaker, P.J. and Reese, S.D. (1991) *Mediating the Message*. New York and London: Longman.

Siebert, F., Peterson, T. and Schramm, W. (1956) *Four Theories of the Press*. Urbana, IL: University of Illinois Press.

Sigal, L.V. (1973) *Reporters and Officials*. Lexington, Mass: Lexington Books.

Sigelman, L. (1973) 'Reporting the News: An Organizational Analysis', *American Journal of Sociology*, 79: 132–51.

Signorielli, N. and Morgan, M. (eds) (1990) *Cultivation Analysis*. Newbury Park, CA, and London: Sage Publications.

Silverstone, R. (1990) 'TV and Everyday Life', in M.F. Ferguson (ed), *Public Communication: The New Imperatives*, pp. 173–89. London and Newbury Park, CA: Sage Publications.

Silverstone, R. (1991) 'From Audiences to Consumers', *European Journal of Communication*, 6, 2: 135–54.

Singer, B.D. (1970) 'Mass Media and Communications Processes in the Detroit Riots of 1967', *Public Opinion Quarterly*, 34: 236–45.

Singer, B.D. (1973) *Feedback and Society*. Lexington, MA: Lexington Books.

Siune, K. (1981) 'Broadcast Election Campaigns in a Multiparty System', in K.E. Rosengren (ed), *Advances in Content Analysis*, pp. 177–96. Beverly Hills, CA, and London: Sage Publications.

Siune, K. and Truetzschler, W. (1992) *Dynamics of Media Politics*. London and Newbury Park, CA: Sage Publications.

Slack, J.D. (1984) *Communication Technology and Society*. Norwood, NJ: Ablex.

Smith, A. (1973) *The Shadow in the Cave*. London: Allen and Unwin.

Smith, A. (1989) 'The Public Interest', *Intermedia*, 17, 2: 10–24.

Smith, A.D. (1990) 'Towards a Global Culture', *Theory, Culture and Society*, 7, 2/3: 171–91.

Smythe, D.W. (1972) 'Some Observations on Communications Theory', in D. McQuail (ed), *Sociology of Mass Communications*, pp. 19–34. Harmondsworth: Penguin.

Smythe, D.W. (1977) 'Communications: Blindspot of Western Marxism', *Canadian Journal of Political and Social Theory*, I: 120–7.

Snow, R.P. (1983) *Creating Media Culture*. Beverly Hills, CA, and London: Sage Publications.

Sparks, C. and Campbell, M. (1987) 'The Inscribed Reader of the British Quality Press', *European Journal of Communication*, 2, 4: 455–72.

Spilerman, S. (1976) 'Structural Characteristics and Severity of Racial Disorders', *American Sociological Review*, 41: 771–92.

Squires, J.D. (1992) 'Plundering the Newsroom', *Washington Journalism Review*, 14, 10: 18–24.

Stamm, K.R. (1985) *Newspaper Use and Community Ties: Towards a Dynamic Theory*. Norwood, NJ: Ablex.

Star, S.A. and Hughes, H.M. (1950) 'Report on an Education Campaign: The Cincinnati Plan for the UN', *American Sociological Review*, 41: 771–92.

Steiner, G. (1963) *The People Look at Television*. New York: Alfred Knopf.

Stone, G.C. (1987) *Examining Newspapers*. Beverly Hills, CA, and London: Sage Publications.

Surgeon General's Scientific Advisory Committee (1972) *Television and Growing Up: The Impact of Televised Violence*. Washington, DC: GPO.

Tannenbaum, P.H. (ed) (1981) *The Entertainment Functions of Television*. Hillside, NJ: Laurence Erlbaum.

Tannenbaum, P.H. and Lynch, M.D. (1960) 'Sensationalism: The Concept and its Measurement', *Journalism Quarterly*, 30: 381–93.

Taylor, D.G. (1982) 'Pluralistic Ignorance and the Spiral of Silence', *Public Opinion Quarterly*, 46: 311–55.

Taylor, W.L. (1953) 'Cloze Procedure: A New Tool for Measuring Readability', *Journalism Quarterly*, 30: 415–33.

Teheranian, M. (1979) 'Iran: Communication, Alienation, Revolution', *Intermedia*, 7, 2: 6–12.

Thomsen, C.W. (ed) (1989) *Cultural Transfer or Electronic Imperialism*. Heidelberg: Carl Winter Universitätsverlag.

Thoveron, G. (1986) 'European Televised Women', *European Journal of Communication*, 1, 3: 289–300.

Thrift, R.R. (1977) 'How Chain Ownership Affects Editorial Vigor of Newspapers', *Journalism Quarterly*, 54: 327–31.

Tichenor, P.J., Donohue, G.A. and Olien, C.N. (1970) 'Mass Media and the Differential Growth in Knowledge', *Public Opinion Quarterly*, 34: 158–70.

Tomlinson, J. (1991) *Cultural Imperialism*. London: Pinter.

Traber, M. and Nordenstreng, K. (1993) *Few Voices, Many Worlds*. London: World Association for Christian Communication.

Trenaman, J.S.M. (1967) *Communication and Comprehension*. London: Longman.

Trenaman, J.S.M. and McQuail, D. (1961) *Television and the Political Image*. London: Methuen.

Tuchman, G. (1978) *Making News: A Study in the Construction of Reality*. New York: Free Press.

Tuchman, G., Daniels, A.K. and Benet, J. (eds) (1978) *Hearth and Home: Images of Women in Mass Media*. New York: Oxford University Press.

Tumber, H. (1982) *Television and the Riots*. London: British Film Institute.

Tunstall, J. (1970) *The Westminster Lobby Correspondents*. London: Routledge and Kegan Paul.

Tunstall, J. (1971) *Journalists at Work*. London: Constable.

Tunstall, J. (1977) *The Media Are American*. London: Constable.

Tunstall, J. (1983) *The Media in Britain*. London: Constable.

Tunstall, J. (1991) 'A Media Industry Perspective', in J. Anderson (ed), *Communication Yearbook 14*, pp. 163–86. Newbury Park, CA, and London: Sage Publications.

Tunstall, J. (1992) 'Europe as a World News Leader', *Journal of Communication*, 42, 3: 84–99.

Tunstall, J. (1993) *Television Producers*. London: Routledge.

Tunstall, J. and Palmer, M. (eds) (1991) *Media Moguls*. London: Routledge.

Turow, J. (1982) 'Unconventional Programs on Commercial Television: An Organizational Perspective', in J.S. Ettema and D.C. Whitney (eds), *Individuals in Mass Media Organizations*, pp. 107–29. Beverly Hills, CA, and London: Sage Publications.

Turow, J. (1989) 'PR and Newswork: A Neglected Relationship', *American Behavioral Scientist*, 33: 206–12.

Turow, J. (1991) 'A Mass Communication Perspective on Entertainment', in J. Curran and M. Gurevitch (eds), *Mass Media and Society*, pp. 160–77. London: Edward Arnold.

Varis, T. (1974) 'Television Traffic — a One-Way Street'. Paris: UNESCO.

Varis, T. (1984) 'The International Flow of Television Programs', *Journal of Communication*, 34, 1: 143–52.

Vidmar, N. and Rokeach, M. (1974) 'Archie Bunker's Bigotry: A Study of Selective Perception and Exposure', *Journal of Communication*, 24: 36–47.

Wackman, D.B., Gilmor, D.M., Gaziano, C. and Dennis, E.E. (1975) 'Chain Newspaper Autonomy as Reflected in Presidential Campaign Endorsements', *Journalism Quarterly*, 52: 511–20.

Wallis, R. and Baran, S. (1990) *The World of Broadcast News*. London: Routledge.

Waples, D., Berelson, B. and Bradshaw, F.R. (1940) *What Reading Does to People*. Chicago: University of Chicago Press.

Weaver, D. and Wilhoit, C.G. (1986) *The American Journalist*. Bloomington, IN: University of Indiana Press.

Weaver, D. and Wilhoit, C.G. (1992) 'Journalists — Who Are They Really?', *Media Studies Journal*, 6, 4: 63–80.

Weber, M. (1948) 'Politics as a Vocation', in H. Gerth and C.W. Mills (eds), *Max Weber: Essays*. London: Routledge and Kegan Paul.

Webster, J.G. and Wakshlag, J.J. (1983) 'A Theory of TV Program Choice', *Communication Research*, 10, 4: 430–46.

Weimann, G., Wober, M. and Brosius, H. (1992) 'TV Diets: Towards a Typology of TV Diets', *European Journal of Communication*, 7, 4: 491–515.

Westergaard, J. (1977) 'Power, Class and the Media', in J. Curran et al. (eds), *Mass Communication and Society*, pp. 95–215. London: Edward Arnold.

Westerståhl, J. (1983) 'Objective News Reporting', *Communication Research*, 10, 3: 403–24.

Westley, B. and MacLean, M. (1957) 'A Conceptual Model for Mass Communication Research', *Journalism Quarterly*, 34: 31–8.

Whale, J. (1969) *The Half-Shut Eye*. London: Macmillan.

White, D.M. (1950) 'The Gatekeeper: A Case-Study in the Selection of News', *Journalism Quarterly*, 27: 383–90.

Whitney, D.C., Wartella, E. and Windahl, S. (eds) (1982) *Mass Communication Review Yearbook*, Vol. 3. Beverly Hills, CA, and London: Sage Publications.

Wilensky, H.L. (1964) 'Mass Society and Mass Culture: Interdependence or Independence?', *American Sociological Review*, 29, 2: 173–97.

Wilhoit, G.C. and de Bock, H. (eds) (1980 and 1981) *Mass Communication Review Yearbook*, Vols 1 and 2. Beverly Hills, CA, and London: Sage Publications.

Williams, R. (1958) *The Long Revolution*. London: Chatto and Windus.

Williams, R. (1961) *Culture and Society*. Harmondsworth: Penguin.

Williams, R. (1975) *Television, Technology and Cultural Form*. London: Fontana.

Williamson, J. (1978) *Decoding Advertisements*. London: Marion Boyars.

Windahl, S., Signitzer, B. and Olson, J. (1992) *Using Communication Theory*. London and Newbury Park, CA: Sage Publications.

Winsor, P. (1989) 'Gender in Film Directing', in M. Real, *Supermedia*, pp. 132–64. Newbury Park, CA, and London: Sage Publications.

Winston, B. (1986) *Misunderstanding Media*. Cambridge MA: Harvard University Press.

Wintour, C. (1973) *Pressures on the Press*. London: André Deutsch.

Wober, J.M. (1978) 'Televised Violence and the Paranoid Perception: The View from Great Britain', *Public Opinion Quarterly*, 42: 315–21.

Wolfe, K.M. and Fiske, M. (1949) 'Why They Read Comics', in P.F. Lazersfeld and F.M. Stanton (eds), *Communication Research 1948–9*, pp. 3–50. New York: Harper and Brothers.

Wolfenstein, M. and Leites, N. (1947) 'An Analysis of Themes and Plots in Motion Pictures', *Annals of the American Academy of Political and Social Sciences*, 254: 41–8.

Womack, B. (1981) 'Attention Maps of Ten Major Newspapers', *Journalism Quarterly*, 58 (2): 260–5.

Woodall, G. (1986) 'Information Processing Theory and Television News', in J.P. Robinson and M. Levy, *The Main Source*, pp. 133–58. Beverly Hills, CA, and London: Sage Publications.

Wright, C.R. (1960) 'Functional Analysis and Mass Communication', *Public Opinion Quarterly*, 24: 606–20.

Wright, C.R. (1974) 'Functional Analysis and Mass Communication Revisited', in J.G. Blumler and E. Katz (eds), *The Uses of Mass Communications*, pp. 197–212. Beverly Hills, CA, and London: Sage Publications.

Zillman, D. (1980) 'The Anatomy of Suspense', in P.H. Tannenbaum (ed), *The Entertainment Functions of Television*, pp. 133–63. Hillsdale, NJ: Laurence Erlbaum.

Zillman, D. (1985) 'The Experimental Explorations of Gratifications from Media Entertainment', in D. Zillman and J. Bryant (eds), *Selective Exposure to Communication*, pp. 225–39. Hillsdale, NJ: Laurence Erlbaum.

Zoonen, L. van (1988) 'Rethinking Women and the News', *European Journal of Communication*, 3, 1: 35–52.

Zoonen, L. van (1991) 'Feminist Perspectives on the Media', in J. Curran and M. Gurevitch (eds), *Mass Media and Society*, pp. 33–51. London: Edward Arnold.

Zoonen, L. van (1992) 'The Women's Movement and the Media: Constructing a Public Identity', *European Journal of Communication*, 7, 4: 453–76.

Zuylen, J. van (1977) 'The Life Cycle of the Family Magazine'. PhD thesis, University of Amsterdam.

INDEX